CHASING CHARLEY

MIKE LAUTERBORN

authorHOUSE®

AuthorHouse™
1663 Liberty Drive
Bloomington, IN 47403
www.authorhouse.com
Phone: 1 (800) 839-8640

Published by AuthorHouse 11/06/2018

ISBN: 978-1-5462-6775-1 (sc)
ISBN: 978-1-5462-6774-4 (e)

Library of Congress Control Number: 2018913306

Print information available on the last page.

This book is printed on acid-free paper.

SYNOPSIS

In 1960, acclaimed American author John Steinbeck (*Grapes of Wrath, Of Mice and Men*) embarked on a three-month road trip around the United States with his wife's gentleman poodle, Charley, in tow. Steinbeck's aim was to rediscover the country he had last roamed as a young man. Ultimately, the journey would be as much about self-discovery. The resulting book, *Travels with Charley*, was a bestseller and is now counted among the classic American road novels.

In 2003 writer Mike Lauterborn set off by van to follow Steinbeck's path, to both learn about the author and see how America and Americans had changed in the intervening 40-plus years. Along the way, he hoped to find some of the people and places Steinbeck had encountered while taking in new sights and experiences. *Travels with Charley* aided Lauterborn during the planning stages of his own trip and prepared him for hardships Steinbeck had also faced, including vehicle troubles, adverse weather, solitude and health woes. The author's words would inspire, console and haunt the young writer.

Ultimately, the trail would lead Lauterborn to some of America's most enduring landmarks, from broad rivers, rugged coastlines and azure blue volcanic lakes to barren deserts, quaint small towns and sprawling cities. He met people from all walks of life and was struck by their common resilience, work ethic and patriotism. In the end, however, he was most impressed by the formidable scope of the journey the ailing Steinbeck had undertaken. This book is a tribute to the author's tireless pursuit of the noble quest.

DEDICATION

To my Mom for sparking my desire to travel, my Dad for his writing guidance and constant support and my sons, Evan and Phillip, for inspiring my own childlike wonder.

PART ONE

Inspiration

Inspiration can strike in the strangest of places. For me, the place was the Westport Public Library book sale in Spring 2003. As I ran my finger along rows of dusty spines, my eyes settled on a worn paperback with a faded cover and yellowed pages. Not much to look at, but the words that slept inside would have a profound effect and send me on a journey that literally followed in the author's footsteps.

John Steinbeck's *Travels with Charley: In Search of America* became a No. 1 national bestseller following its release in the summer of 1962. The book chronicles the author's three-month, 34-state, 10,000-mile journey around the U.S. with Charley, his wife's gentleman French poodle. Together, the two prowled the postcard landscapes of New England, crept along the mysterious lonely byways of the northern states and visited Steinbeck's boyhood haunts and acquaintances in California. Returning home through the South, they dined and hunted with rich Texans and witnessed firsthand the disturbing state of race relations in New Orleans. Ultimately, they beat it back to New York and the welcoming arms of Steinbeck's wife, Elaine.

The book is now counted among other classic "road trip" novels, including Jack Kerouac's *On the Road*, Charles Kuralt's *America* and William Least Heat-Moon's *Blue Highways*. At first glance, *Travels* seems somewhat of a non-sequitur for Steinbeck, better known for such classic American novels as *The Grapes of Wrath*, *East of Eden* and *Of Mice and Men*. Even he surprised himself by pursuing the genre, remarking to his agent some months before the trip that it was "such an odd book to be coming from me." Ultimately, the book would be as much about self-discovery as the journey itself.

Steinbeck was 58 when he set out in September 1960 to rediscover a country he had last rambled as a young man. He was feeling his age, and wanted to shed his self-image as a "humbling, dull, stupid, lazy oaf who must be protected, led, instructed and hospitalized." He viewed the project as "a frantic last attempt to save my life and the integrity of my creative pulse. … The antidote for the poison of the professional man."

I found Steinbeck's urgency all too familiar. As a teen, I'd longed to travel the country by car, but college, work and family intervened and the dream was sidelined. Then, in Fall 2002, I went into business for myself, which allowed me to dictate my own schedule. The time had come to satisfy my wanderlust, and *Travels with Charley* would serve as a catalyst.

I resolved to follow in Steinbeck's footsteps. My plan was to trace his route in the same spirit and manner, to learn more about the author and to see how America and Americans had changed in the intervening 40-plus years. With luck, I would find some of the very people and locales Steinbeck had visited. At the same time, I hoped to take in new sights and experiences and soak up regional culture and history. I also expected to learn more about myself.

My wife, Marlene, was at first skeptical of the project. She understood my love of writing and knew that I'd kept journals of past travels. She had even encouraged me for some 10 years to write a book — but this was not exactly the project she had in mind. I had a compatriot in Steinbeck, whose friends referred to his own planned trip as "quixotic." He responded by naming his truck *Rocínante*, after Don Quixote's horse.

Marlene's doubt turned to irritation and near disbelief, however, when she learned I wasn't planning on taking her or our two young boys. It was a difficult decision, but I knew that to bring them would have broken with Steinbeck's own approach and distracted from the research process. Nevertheless, my absence would be particularly hard on my sons, who were accustomed to having me as a constant in their lives. My eldest son, Evan, grew uncharacteristically quiet as the trip neared. I swallowed hard and pledged to check in with them as often as possible from the road.

Next we addressed Marlene's fears. Steinbeck's wife worried about John prior to his trip, as he had recently suffered a stroke. In Marlene's case, she worried for my safety, particularly because I was traveling alone and have a penchant to talk with anyone and everyone, no matter what their character. Like most men, though, I felt I could handle myself and deal with any potential hazard I encountered. After dispensing a large dose of cautionary advice, Marlene resigned herself to the project.

In time, other family members and friends also weighed in. Heading up the cheering section were my father and brother, both published authors and seasoned travelers. Like me, others fondly remembered reading *Travels with Charley*. Several people pined about their own missed opportunities. Some simply said, "Cool!"

Others sympathized with Marlene. "I would never let *my* husband go," sniped one. I imagined Steinbeck had heard similar criticism. As he did, I stayed the course.

Timing was an early consideration. Steinbeck left his Sag Harbor, New York, home in late September. The weather had already turned crisp, hurricanes posed a threat and his late start also meant he would likely encounter snow — all of which I hoped to avoid. I also wanted to avoid Labor Day weekend traffic, expected to be the thickest in eight years, with some 28 million people planning to drive 50 miles or more.

I decided to stay through my boys' first days of school, figuring that, after that point, Marlene would have an easier time managing things at home. I chose Saturday, September 6 as my departure date.

For his trip, Steinbeck chose a General Motors pickup fitted with a cabin built by the Wolverine Camper Company of Gladwin, Michigan. The cabin was equipped with a bed, stove and refrigerator. Steinbeck reasoned that in a truck, "I can get into a countryside not crossed by buses. I can see people not in movement but at home in their own places." The welcoming cabin would enable him to "invite a man to have a beer in my home, thereby forcing an invitation from him."

I began my search by trying to contact Wolverine for a modern version of *Rocínante*, but the company had all but shut its doors years ago. After several false starts and just a week before my departure, I finally found a suitable vehicle.

Tucked away at the back of a dealer's lot sat a 1995 Ford E-150 Mark III Hi-Top conversion van in a shade of green like Steinbeck's truck. Though far from the complete home *Rocínante* had been, it did offer a fold-down bed and would serve my purposes well enough. It came equipped with a TV, VCR and CD player. Though Steinbeck would likely have disapproved of these creature comforts, they would be welcome in remote areas and in those moments when I was too fatigued to write.

Stocking the van was my next priority. Steinbeck had already published several successful novels by the time he took his journey, so money wasn't an issue for him. I claimed no such advantages. So, to help offset expenses, I put my promotion experience to use and turned to Corporate America. This was an awkward decision, as I knew some would perceive it as "selling out." If not for the support, however, the project might never have gotten off the ground.

Following a barrage of phone calls, e-mails, faxes, letters and face-to-face meetings, I had secured a variety of products and services. Camping mainstay Coleman supplied a grill, cooking supplies, a heater and roadside emergency kit; Kampgrounds of America (KOA) kicked in with a discount membership; ExxonMobil helped with prepaid gas cards;

PolarMAX provided turtlenecks, pullovers and other clothing for northern climes; Gerber Legendary Blades sent a batch of handy tools; Rolling Rock supplied citronella candles so I could enjoy a beer in peace; while Frito-Lay (a former client) fixed me up with chips and salsa. Thankfully, CompUSA donated a Mac iBook with AOL service, a welcome update from Steinbeck's notebooks and manual typewriter.

Steinbeck packed hunting and fishing gear so those he encountered wouldn't suspect the true intent of his journey. I, too, included fishing gear as a conversation starter. But firearms were another matter. I didn't own a gun, nor did I think it safe or wise to bring one — particularly in the wake of the September 11, 2001, terrorist attacks and resulting intensified security. That kind of conversation piece could land me in jail.

"What about a dog?" I was asked time and again. The original Charley had been a gift from Steinbeck to his wife. Prior to his trip, John asked if he could bring the poodle with him. Elaine was happy to let the dog join him, as Charley was a good watchdog. (In truth, his bark was worse than his bite.) Charley was also a great icebreaker. "Many conversations en route began with, 'What kind of dog is that?'" Steinbeck later recalled.

For my part, I did not own a dog, and it seemed excessive to drag one along with me on the road for the sake of authenticity. And while Charley was a fine companion, he was also somewhat of a distraction to the author. Still, a dog would offer companionship. No, this was *Chasing Charley* — there would be no substitute for the original. The downside to my decision would be a degree of loneliness, but I thought the trade-off was still positive.

My final task was to name the van. As Steinbeck's understudy in spirit, I chose *El Rucío*, after the donkey ridden by Don Quixote's loyal servant, Sancho Panza. (Coincidentally, Steinbeck had adapted the *Travels with Charley* title from Robert Louis Stevenson's 1879 novel, *Travels with a Donkey*.)

I later remarked to Marlene that Sancho's wife Teresa was also good-hearted, endured his exploits and supported him with her prayers. As with the rest of my bad jokes, she endured this one with a sigh and then a smile. I would miss that smile on the road.

PART TWO

Steinbeck's Spirit

Before retracing John Steinbeck's route around the country, I wanted to visit his weekend retreat in Sag Harbor, the starting point of his own journey 40-odd Septembers before. By sitting at his table, browsing his books and strolling familiar ground, I hoped to gain insight into the author's life and a better perspective prior to my own trip.

Sadly, I had missed meeting John's wife, Elaine, in person, as she passed away that April at age 88 following a long illness. Six weeks before my departure, however, Elaine's sister, Jean Boone, invited me to the seaside residence, which lies just across Long Island Sound from my own home. Jean had inherited the place and shared its upkeep with her companion of 27 years, Ray Downey.

Packing various literature and clippings and a bottle of red wine, I set off late one morning on the interstate, headed northeast for the ferry out of New London. A little before 2pm, I drove up a ramp into the belly of the *Mary Ellen*, entered the cabin and settled on a long bench with a newspaper for the 16-mile crossing. On the first leg of his trip in 1960, Steinbeck made the reverse crossing on this same ferry route.

An hour and 40 minutes later, as the ferry neared Orient Point, I went up on deck to watch the approach. I had the romantic notion that I might spot a submarine heading out from the base in Groton, as Steinbeck had upon his crossing. Alas, no sub, just a fierce wind that forced my retreat inside.

A sign welcomed me to LONG ISLAND'S WINE COUNTRY as I rolled from the ship, headed west toward Greenport, where I would connect with the North Ferry to Shelter Island. Lining the route were vineyards attended by brown-skinned workers and market stands displaying juicy cherries, fresh-picked flowers and other fresh goods. Perhaps Steinbeck was drawn to the region for its resemblance to his native Salinas, California.

The North Ferry was a much smaller vessel than the *Mary Ellen*, and boarding was on a first-come, first-served basis. Again I set the emergency brake and paid my fare, then walked to the prow to watch the approach. A passing crewman blithely warned, "You might be getting wet in a minute — the swells get pretty big out here." Almost as he spoke, one such swell swamped the deck and flooded my boat shoes. Thwarted again, I sloshed back to wait it out in the driver's seat.

The next stretch of road meandered across Shelter Island to the South Ferry for the hop to Sag Harbor. Here, high hedgerows hid shingled homes and tennis courts, while tanned young preppy couples drifted happily about. The South Ferry was of similar size and the crossing equally brief. I didn't bother to step out this time, having learned my lesson.

The manicured properties of Sag Harbor were also tucked behind tidy hedges, mostly of the privet type, brought over by the English and grown as living fences. Steinbeck would have encountered similar scenery in his travels throughout Britain, and he probably appreciated the privacy the hedges afforded — particularly in later life as his fame spread.

A lantern-bedecked bridge led into Sag Harbor Village, a town that was likely quiet and quaint in the author's day but had become mobbed with sightseers. I stopped at a bookstore on the main for directions, and a clerk pointed me toward the Steinbeck home.

Hugging a horseshoe-shaped cover, the large backyard was shaded by the same massive oaks Charley surely "christened" years before. Jean and Ray rose from hammocks to greet me. Apologizing for her casual attire, Jean ducked inside to change while I surveyed the property.

Behind the modest main house was a smaller bunkhouse where Steinbeck's two sons once lived, a tool-filled workshop and a small in-ground pool John had built for Elaine. Down on the water was the original pier. Just prior to John's trip, Hurricane Donna laid siege to Long Island and the little cove, submerging the pier under four feet of water and casting adrift the author's 22-foot cabin cruiser, the *Fayre Eleyne.* John braved the storm to secure the ship.

Overlooking the water on tiny Bluff Point was a hexagonal writing cottage where the author would hole up to both write and read. It was a serene, inspiring setting, so quiet one could hear the oar strokes of passing kayaks, the rustle of windblown trees and the occasional soft ting of a bell John placed high in one of the oaks.

Steinbeck sought refuge here as he worked on *The Acts of King Arthur and His Noble Knights*, a modern English translation of Sir Thomas Malory's *Morte d'Arthur.* Inspired by his project, he named the cottage *Geoyous Garde*, after Sir Lancelot's castle. His books rested undisturbed on a high shelf — among them, the same edition as mine of *Travels with Charley.* Small stones set in concrete on the doorstep spelled out

AROYNT. Borrowed from Shakespeare's *Macbeth*, the Old English word means "begone" — an author's version of a welcome mat.

Jean, Ray and I sat around a small table on the brick patio, nibbling crackers and Brie in the shade of an awning. John enjoyed a nip or two, so it seemed fitting that we discuss the author between sips of vodka on the rocks. Over the next few hours, as the waning sun bathed us in its rosy glow and biting midges made themselves known, Jean searched the past for stories about her late brother-in-law.

Raising her glass, she recounted John's favorite toast: "Here's to Ava Gardner." Why Ava? Steinbeck was to have escorted the actress to a West Coast dinner party, but she fell ill, so John accompanied actress Ann Sothern and a friend instead. The friend was Elaine. With tears in her eyes, Jean spoke about her recently departed sister and how John once lovingly remarked that Elaine's faults were "precious few." (Both were cremated, and their ashes now rest side by side at a cemetery in Salinas.) Jean also spoke of John's sons, Johnny, who died prematurely at age 44 of a post-operative pulmonary aneurysm, and Thom, a lecturer and screenwriter in California.

From their Sag Harbor days, Jean recalled how John, when not writing, would make things with his hands — whittling and gluing together strange contraptions like a mobile made from bird figurines and the skeleton of an old umbrella. Jean laughed again at the memory of holes John would dig throughout the yard to bake clams he'd harvested with some of the locals.

I learned that it was not a stroke the author had suffered the winter before his trek but a TIA (transient ischemic attack) — an ailment Steinbeck referred to as "one of those carefully named difficulties which are the whispers of approaching age." His seizures would last minutes or hours, resulting in temporary loss of vision, difficulty speaking and walking, numbness and tingling. The affliction was enough to give him pause about taking his trip. In fact, it was a sign of developing arterial sclerosis, to which he succumbed at age 66 in December 1968 (ten days before my fourth birthday).

Jean was gracious enough to grant me a tour of the house. Amid seaside scenes by the likes of John Morris, collected shells and other mementos were photos of family and famous friends. Among the latter were actors John Malkovich and Gary Sinise, with whom Elaine grew acquainted.

(Sinise played Tom Joad in the 1991 TV adaptation of *The Grapes of Wrath* and directed and co-starred with Malkovich in a 1992 film version of *Of Mice and Men.*) The narrow passageway connecting the kitchen and master bedroom had been dubbed the "Hall of Fame," as photos were arranged from floor to ceiling. A snapshot of the couple's beloved poodle, Charley, was relegated to the bathroom, though perhaps as a private joke.

Our conversation migrated inside to wicker couches in the glass-enclosed porch. I told Jean of a recent visit Marlene and I made to Manhattan to catch the musical *Man of La Mancha* and how the performance made me wonder how literally John had intended his self-comparison to the show's unlikely hero, Don Quixote. In fact, an early working title of *Travels with Charley* had been *Operation Windmills.*

I later discovered that Steinbeck had a lifelong fascination with medieval romance, in particular Malory's *Morte d'Arthur.* The tales revolve around the knights' fruitless search for the Holy Grail, representing spiritual fulfillment. *Don Quixote* is actually a parody of the genre that Miguel de Cervantes based on Arthurian legend. Quixote is in search of spiritual fulfillment and, predictably, fails.

Steinbeck initiated two journeys in connection with these works: one to the La Mancha region in central Spain to retrace Don Quixote's route, and another to Britain in 1959 to track down places mentioned in *Morte d'Arthur.* He never followed up with a book about the trip to Spain, but he had begun writing *Acts of King Arthur* when he suffered his stroke. The attack shook him up and seems to have inspired his own quest for spiritual fulfillment à la *Travels with Charley.* Of course, that quest also failed, as the author didn't find the "ideal" America of his youth. In a further irony, he would never complete *Acts of King Arthur* — the unfinished work was published posthumously in 1976.

Jean reflected on John's inquisitive nature and how he retained everything he read. Indeed, he was as passionate about reading as writing. Coincidently, in recent weeks, media queen and talk show host Oprah Winfrey had named John's *East of Eden* (1952) as her latest Book Club selection. Jean said John would have been pleased with the honor, not so much for the financial boost, but because it would expose the book to readers that may not have otherwise discovered it.

Though the author became wealthy over time, Jean believes John valued money only for the learning experiences it afforded — that his quest was intellectual, not material. The humble house in which he chose to spend his final days seems to bear out that opinion.

As the evening wound down, Steinbeck's spirit filled the room, and I imagined the author in khakis and Wellingtons, reclined in his easy chair with a snifter of brandy, eager for an update about the America he so loved to roam. Night had fallen as I began the long circle home, having missed the last ferry back to New London.

PART THREE

The Chase Begins

As Steinbeck's departure date drew near, he entertained doubts about leaving home for so long. The author described his pangs in *Travels with Charley*: "My warm bed and comfortable house grew increasingly desirable and my dear wife incalculably precious. To give these up for three months for the terrors of the uncomfortable and unknown seemed crazy."

On the eve of my own departure, I understood his feelings all too well. There was little time to devote to any lingering doubts, however, as the waning hours were crammed with last-minute chores and details. After proudly ushering our sons to their first day of the school year, Marlene and I sat down to coordinate bill paying and other tasks. Next up was a photo shoot for the local newspaper, *The Minuteman*. Finally, I went shopping to stock up on food and accessories necessary for meal preparation.

Over the course of the evening, our kitchen served as a staging area. I had packed for trips before, but never for a months-long odyssey over thousands of road miles. A mound of supplies quickly overtook the counters and floor. I headed to bed that night convinced I would have to do some serious paring come morning. Exhausted from the day's pace, I slept soundly.

Day 1: Leaving home

Saturday, September 6, 2003 — the morning of my departure. I awoke surprisingly calm and somehow managed to shoehorn everything into the van. The emergency kit, grill and camping gear fit in back, food and utensils filled the midsection, and clothes, maps, books, laptop computer, cell phone and stationery went up front. For indulgences, I stashed bags of nachos beneath the bed and stocked the VCR hutch with a dozen tapes from our home library.

I dread prolonged goodbyes, so after a family breakfast of eggs, fried potatoes and most welcome coffee, followed by a round of hugs and kisses, I climbed aboard *El Rucío* and was off.

Favoring Steinbeck's Sag Harbor in setting and feel, Fairfield is a coastal community of sprawling properties and historic churches on avenues lined with flowering dogwoods. Foot traffic dominates our quaint downtown, where small shops front the famed Boston Post Road. Shaded by firs, the requisite gazebo on the green serves as a concert bandstand in summer, Santa's throne in winter and host to candlelight ceremonies year-round. Down by Long Island Sound, Colonial-era homes and clapboard Cape Cods overlook a sliver of beach. Elaine Steinbeck spent time here when she worked as a stage manager at the nearby Westport Country Playhouse.

When I first mapped out my trip, the plan was to follow I-95 along the coast to New Haven, then turn north toward Hartford. But I'd read that it was the 65th anniversary of the opening of the Merritt Parkway, a scenic route that parallels the interstate. Built when drivers cared more about the journey than making good time, it was a fitting road to open the trip. Steinbeck, who despised and became flustered in traffic, would have approved.

Back then gas was a mere 20 cents a gallon, and motorists often rode the parkway simply to take in the scenery, enjoying the leafy, winding path through sleepy little towns. While still picturesque, it suffered from rush-hour congestion and routine accidents, like most of the region's highways, including the notorious expressway on Steinbeck's Long Island. The traffic was with me, though, and I rode on beneath cloudless skies. A slight nip in the air hinted at autumn.

Between Bridgeport's commercial sprawl and Stratford's busy Sikorsky Airport, a sign for Trumbull caught my attention. In Summer 2003, this woodsy enclave offered proof of nature's resilience when a bear mauled a high school football player out searching for his dogs. Just miles away, construction work was wrapping up on a new bridge spanning the Housatonic.

Farther up the parkway, Milford was home to a regional Frito-Lay distribution center, a 40,000-square-foot warehouse stacked 40 feet high with chips, dips, cookies, crackers and meat products. The very thought made me hungry.

Off to the east, removed from the fray, lay stately New Haven, home to Yale University and an array of theaters, art galleries and international cuisine. The city had recently hosted a search for *America's Next Top Model* while also welcoming a College Championship segment of the popular TV trivia program *Jeopardy*. (*"Alex, I'll take Potpourri for $100."*)

Beside a tunnel near Woodbridge, I spotted a highway patrolman pointing a handheld radar gun. Normally, I'd have broken a sweat, but given that the top speed of my nearly 18-foot-long land yacht was only 85, I didn't even flinch. With more than 15,000 miles ahead of me, I was in no hurry.

Neither, apparently, was the pair of wild turkeys I spotted strutting along the shoulder near Wallingford. It reminded me of the morning I stepped from our house to get the paper and discovered a large Tom in our driveway. I barely registered on the feathered visitor's radar as he wobbled on down the road.

Past Meriden I crossed a wide swath of the Connecticut River, looking broad and beautiful. Originating in Quebec, the river borders Vermont and New Hampshire, bisects Massachusetts and Connecticut and flows into Long Island Sound at Old Lyme.

At Rocky Hill a sign marked the turnoff for Dinosaur State Park, built around a grouping of rocks imprinted with dinosaur tracks. I tried to imagine the great prehistoric beasts stomping across Connecticut's golf courses and laying waste to its yacht clubs.

Jolting me from my daydream was Hartford's skyline, anchored by the old United States Firearms Manufacturing Company building, whose striking onion dome flaunted gold stars on a navy field. The region had long been an industrial hub, home to firearms, textile and automobile manufacturers. Among the companies in adjacent East Hartford was Parker X-Ray, whose technicians scan aircraft and space shuttle parts for flaws, like doctors seeking out bone fractures. When the company launched in 1952, it shared warehouse space with peach baskets and jars of mayonnaise.

It was here I linked up with Steinbeck's route. The author gave the state capital a pass, describing it as "lousy with traffic." He remarked how American cities resemble each other, "like badger holes, ringed with trash ... surrounded by piles of wrecked and rusting automobiles, and almost smothered with rubbish." Not exactly a ringing endorsement. Still, the town can always boast Katharine Hepburn. A Hartford native, the actress died in late June 2003 at the formidable age of 96.

As I passed through town, a car zipped by bearing the license plate C-ROBIN, no doubt a reference to the ugly, spiny fish common along the coast. In coming weeks I would spot dozens more vanity plates, a newfound fad in Steinbeck's time. Minutes later I was overtaken by a hybrid gas/electric car, just a twinkle of an idea in 1960. I would swear its driver cast a disapproving look at my gas-slurping craft.

Steinbeck's next stop had been Deerfield, Massachusetts, where he paused at Eaglebrook School to visit his then 12-year-old son Johnny. On the way to Deerfield, I detoured to the New England Air Force Museum at Bradley International Airport in Windsor Locks, where volunteers had been working tirelessly for years to restore a B-29A Superfortress, used during WWII to attack targets deep inside Japan. A history buff and onetime war correspondent for the *New York Herald Tribune*, Steinbeck likely would have appreciated the restoration effort.

Acquired by the Museum in 1973, the B-29A was shipped from Maryland in pieces. Six years later, as a team worked to reassemble the plane, a tornado tore through, destroying two dozen aircraft and badly damaging the Superfortress. The plane sat outside for some 20 years, sheltering bees and nesting birds, until staff could rebuild the facility and launch preservation efforts. Housed in a large hangar, 120 aircraft of all shapes and sizes were showcased. Another 16 were on display outside.

The center of attention was the B-29A, a beautiful silver bird with an aluminum skin and 141-foot wingspan. A worker busy painting a star and bar on the underside of the starboard wing told me that the aircraft is actually "a Frankenstein," pieced together from two planes — the fore section of one and rear section, from the bomb bay aft, of another. Painted on the side was JACK'S HACK, the nickname given the plane by its original crew.

In the museum café I spoke with four retired flyers, all project volunteers, on a sandwich break. They explained that the plane was one of only about 25 intact B-29s in the U.S. The only one in flying condition was *Fifi*, based in Midland, Texas. I recalled seeing that craft when it visited a county airport in suburban New York in the mid-1980s. One of the men further informed me that the "B" in B-29A stands for bomber and the "A" refers to the site where the plane was built — in this case, the Boeing plant in Seattle, which I hoped to visit later in my trip.

As was often the case in recent years, our discussion shifted to terrorism, in particular the threat posed to and by aircraft. I mentioned that a Superfortress is featured in the 1975 suspense thriller *Target Manhattan*, a book I'd stumbled across a few weeks before my trip. The plot centers on two evildoing aircraft builders who try to extort $5 million from city coffers by circling the plane and threatening to crash it into Midtown if the money was not paid — the stuff of mediocre pulp fiction until September 11.

From the parking lot I made a cell phone call to Tim Von Jess, Eaglebrook's director of development and alumni relations. He confirmed a meeting we'd scheduled and remarked that my timing was perfect — the "calm before the storm" of the new school year. As our call ended, I wondered how having a cell phone might have impacted Steinbeck's travel plans. For me, it was a critical tool, allowing me to keep up on home matters, confirm appointments and plan trip details on the fly.

From Windsor Locks, it was a quick sprint up I-91 to the state border (MASSACHUSETTS WELCOMES YOU), not far from the Six Flags New England amusement park. Opened in 1940 on the site of a riverside picnic grove, the sprawling modern theme park long ago replaced its vintage carousel and classic wooden roller coaster.

Beyond it lay Springfield, offering a convention center, museums, colleges, hotels and the Naismith Memorial Basketball Hall of Fame, capped with a monstrous silver basketball. Nearby Holyoke offered the Volleyball Hall of Fame, marking the site where the sport was born in 1895.

My route into historic Deerfield passed several farms and the Yankee and New England Candle companies. Mature corn stalks taller than the van bowed in the breeze and the smell of fresh mowed grass filled the air.

Passing another farm, I drove beneath a broad archway and up a winding hill to Tim's home, Stoddard House, a former Eaglebrook dormitory.

I approached the screened-in porch and knocked. There on a table, fresh-picked tomatoes and cucumbers ripened in the sun. Tim, his wife Jodi, their toddler Mason and dog Riley welcomed me inside, and we sat around the kitchen table to chat. Through his position at the school, Tim was able to research past enrollees, including Johnny Steinbeck. While his portrait of the young man was interesting, much of it was also troubling.

John IV entered Eaglebrook in Fall 1958 and lived in Gibbs House. The well-traveled son of the famous author was fond of reading, but he was also enrolled in football, skiing and baseball. Outwardly, at least, he seemed to like being there. Perhaps because Johnny seemed so well adjusted, his father felt comfortable traveling to Somerset, England in March 1959 and living there for eight months while he researched *Acts of King Arthur.*

While abroad, Steinbeck received an evaluation about his son. Eaglebrook's instructors said the boy was bright, creative and had lots of potential, but that he was not applying himself and often seemed confused, anxious and preoccupied — not that surprising, given Steinbeck's status as an absentee father. Johnny also told counselors that his father was too demanding. Steinbeck accepted the instructors' advice and asked them to warn the boy about the consequences if his performance did not improve.

Soon after, the author began to suffer seizures, for which his doctor prescribed months of bed rest. Steinbeck paid little heed, remarking at the time, "I have neither training in nor tolerance for illness, which makes me a rebellious patient." In late September of the following year, he began his journey with Charley. His first stop was to visit Johnny, as concerns mounted about his son's well being. (The concern was warranted, as a few months later the boy failed to fall in line and was dismissed from Eaglebrook.)

In *Travels,* Steinbeck wrote that he arrived too late in the day to disturb Johnny, so he spent the night at a dairy farm up the hill. He added that his visit to campus the next morning stirred quite a bit of excitement, as "two hundred teen-age prisoners of education" herded out to greet him and crowd, fifteen at a time, into the cramped cabin. Once back on the road, he stopped to make sure there were no stowaways. A good yarn, though Steinbeck took a bit of writer's license.

What had actually transpired, the author reported in a letter to Elaine the following day. He had, in fact, arrived around noon, entertained staff inside *Rocínante* and lunched with Johnny, with whom he "talked well and easily," often in French, about the boy's studies. Soccer practice followed, then, in early evening, a fireside powwow, during which new boys were welcomed to the school. After the event, Steinbeck took Johnny out for a forgettable steak dinner at "a doleful little roadside place." Only then did he head up to the farm, where he "went to sleep and overslept so that [he] barely made church." The author's small fiction is certainly forgivable, as this stop was more of a subdued family affair.

Tim led me up to the school for a look. The former estate was perched on a hillside overlooking the Pioneer Valley, at the foot of the Berkshires. A rustic cabin on the grounds was rumored to be one of Rudyard Kipling's former retreats and where he may have written *Captains Courageous.* Tim directed me farther up the mountain to Hilltop Farm, where Steinbeck rested that fall night in 1960.

To my great surprise, Arthur Rogers, the farmer who hosted the author, still lived on the property. I pulled up the drive, introduced myself and was welcomed in by 73-year-old "Ar," his wife Jan and their mini schnauzer Ernie. Arthur scared up coffee and we sat in a sunny back room to chat. A rose-colored fishing hat covered his tuft of white hair.

A geologist for Shell Oil in his early career, Arthur was lured to rural life in 1952 after meeting his first wife, Anne Davenport, a popular English teacher at Eaglebrook. A granddaughter of the founder of nearby Hilltop Academy, Anne had, coincidentally, taught Steinbeck's son, as well as Sen. John Warner's boy and the then-king of Jordan. At the start, Arthur had "no understanding of the horrors" of farming and, while Anne worked at the school, he tried to make a go of the property. Ultimately, it became inactive and Arthur began serving as president of the Deerfield Land Trust. Local maps were tacked up around the room.

Arthur recalled it was late afternoon when Steinbeck pulled up. He recognized the author from photographs but feigned nonchalance. The camper did arouse his interest, though, and Arthur (age 30 at the time) asked to look inside. The author showed the farmer Texas longhorn horns and an old-fashioned car horn that Steinbeck sounded, saying, "That'll bring the heifers." Arthur and Anne asked him to dinner, but he politely refused and instead bought some fresh milk from them.

Before I left, Arthur gave me a tour of the house, which was built in 1900 with money made in the lumber business in Milwaukee. The main beams were shipped in from out of state, a method that would have been very costly by today's standards. I reciprocated by giving Arthur the nickel tour of my van, then bid him farewell. I hadn't planned on finding the farm, let alone meeting Arthur. Anyway, it was late afternoon, and I had dinner plans at the home of my friends, the Wolkes, in Meriden, New Hampshire.

I rejoined 91 North and soon passed through Greenfield, a stone's throw east of Shelburne Falls, the latter the highlight of a recent family trip. On the Deerfield River, the town centered on the Bridge of Flowers, an old trolley bridge wreathed with plant life tended by the local women's club. Restored trolleys carried folks back and forth along a short length of track to a museum devoted to trolley history. From the street, visitors were able to peer straight into the local glassworks as artisans created colorful handblown vases, bottles and bowls. The river cascaded down a stretch of falls past a swimming hole ringed with large boulders.

Shelburne Falls also had the distinction of being the home of Lois Cronk, who at age 90 won her first U.S. women's golf title, at the 2003 National Senior Olympics in Virginia Beach. She achieved the feat despite a run-in at one point with a turtle that grabbed her ball and tried to drag it into a pond.

From Greenfield, it was a short hop to the state line (WELCOME TO VERMONT, GREEN MOUNTAIN STATE). As I crossed, a local FM station was broadcasting calypso, a bizarre contrast to the New England scenery. As the song ended, the DJ urged listeners to enjoy the region's balmy Indian summer.

Steinbeck's path had curled in the same direction, past "roadside stands piled with golden pumpkins and russet squashes and baskets of red apples." The author stopped to buy apples and cider and browse stands of moccasins, deerskin gloves and goat-milk candy. He described Vermont's villages as "neat and white-painted and unchanged for a hundred years except for traffic and paved streets." The scenery remains as changeless and enchanting today.

A long, steady climb through Putney and Bellows Falls led to Rockingham and a stop for gas. As I manned the pump, I recalled a family overnight at Camp Plymouth State Park in nearby Okemo. On the way, we'd called in to Chester Depot, a one-horse town with a tumbledown firehouse, stately Town Hall, village hardware and market where we bought sandwiches on locally made rolls called bulkies. We stayed in a cabin at the park, sunned and swam on serene Echo Lake, cooked out and stargazed well into the night. At first light we landed a smallmouth bass, which went from lake to pan to grateful bellies in minutes.

I pulled away from the pump and, in my reverie, got turned around. Eventually, I righted my course, followed signs past miles of cornfields and farms and rejoined 91, trailing it to Ascutney. There, I left the interstate for a back road past barns and broad fields dotted with hay bales wrapped in white plastic. Splashes of red hinted at the autumn leaf spectacular to follow. I crossed the Windsor-Cornish covered bridge over the Connecticut River at the state border (WELCOME TO NEW HAMPSHIRE, THE GRANITE STATE, BIENVENUE), then followed Stage Road through tiny colonial

Plainfield, established before America declared its independence. From 120N, a dirt road marked the final stretch to the Wolkes' home in Meriden.

The sky blazed crimson as I parked for the night. Thom, his wife Evy and their young daughters, Sonja and Anna, came out to meet me. The girls pored over the van and bounced up and down on the bed while I caught up with their parents. A woodpecker rapped on a nearby tree as Anna recounted a recent family blackberry-picking excursion. Once the girls had satisfied their curiosity, we headed inside for pork roast dinner. Dessert was locally made apple pie served on clay dishware made by Evy, a potter. While we ate, the girls made crayon drawings to decorate the van.

We moved to the family room to sample regional microbrews and listen to music by folk singer Bill Morrissey (from Tamworth, New Hampshire) and bluesman Guy Davis, whom Thom was managing. Our conversation turned to Steinbeck, and Thom shared how he was inspired to pursue the arts after watching *Of Mice and Men* as a 14-year-old self-described "theater brat." He still had a signed publicity photo from that 1972 community theater production, held in a barn in Summerville, New Jersey.

A clear starry sky lured us outside to watch emerging bats while we lingered over cognacs and Cuban cigars. As the family wound down with popcorn and a favorite movie, I drifted in and out of consciousness on the pullout couch. It had been a very full and somewhat surreal first day on the road.

Day 2: White Mountains to Maine

I was awakened by night owl Anna and a chattering crow at first light and lay for a while peering out at the trees and an old barn off in the woods. After everyone had arisen, I appointed myself chief pancake maker, whipping up a batch of flaky, silver dollar-size treats made with blackberries, nuts and raisins. As mourning doves visited a feeder outside the dining room window, I scanned the local *Valley News*. In a column titled "Half A Bubble Off Plumb," Editor Tom Hill humorously dwelled on the amazing flexibility and durability of the English language, "a ground-hugging sports car that can handle any turn and twist in the road." He built his case around the phrase "okie-dokie" and supported it with other "punchy rhymes" like "fancy-schmancy, flower power, hanky-panky, heebie-jeebie, helter-skelter, hokey pokey and mumbo-jumbo." The article would have had great interest to Steinbeck, a keen observer of the nuances of language.

The paper also yielded an item about videotape taken by a Czech immigrant of the first plane striking the World Trade Center on September 11, inspiring Thom and Evy to recall that morning. By chance, they turned on the TV to look at news, something they rarely do, catching the first tower in flames and the second plane hitting. Thom lost two friends in the attack, including his high school class president and the brother of the founder of Speakeasy, a club in Greenwich Village that was a focal point of a 1980s folk revival.

Late morning, I was ready to go and, as I repacked my gear in the van, Thom told me that the reclusive author J.D. Salinger lived in nearby Cornish. I'd often heard of people trying to locate him but did not want to be one of those.

Evy carefully wrapped and placed a few items of pottery that I'd bought from her into a Harpoon beer box then I leapt into the arms of another great, mild day. My aim was to move on up through the White Mountains and into Maine, with Skowhegan or Bangor the endpoint. This would bring me within striking distance of Deer Isle.

The roller coaster-like nature of the hills on my route out was lulling. Students at a local college, on their lunch break and relaxing in the sun, eyed me with curiosity as I lazily drifted past. In Lebanon, services were just concluding at the Methodist church and the town's only gas station was closed. Further on, I sought a paper, mistaking a gun shop for a corner store, but, ultimately, found both gas and reading material at a nearby mini mart.

Here, I thought of another family trip that began just across the river in Quechee, Vermont and led us to the far northwestern reaches of the state. At the outset of this winter voyage, we sampled local grog, watched pottery being handcrafted, broke bread with good country folk in a café setting and gazed at deep gorges and icy falls. Mid-state, a farm on the far side of a covered bridge offered thick maple syrup and chunks of cheese, Ben & Jerry's dished up creamy ice cream, and hot cider fetched from a Cabot outlet warmed our insides. At the state's cap, a former stagecoach stop heated by a cast iron stove became a home base for treks into Burlington, where we welcomed in the new year with all-day music performances around town and fireworks above Lake Champlain. Like a blanket just out of the dryer, Vermont's great appeal is its simple, down-home warmth and charm.

These images faded as I trundled on and noticed at Grafton signs urging me to "Explore Ruggles Mine." Heeding them, I wound along a twisty, crumbly paved road to a dusty, dirt trail, then up another steep paved road that seemed to go on forever. Just when I began to question if the detour had been a good idea, I arrived at the summit and a spectacular overlook.

A young cashier collected a steep sixteen dollars from me for a self-guided tour and another dime for a paper bag into which I could place minerals blasted loose from two spots in the site. According to a provided brochure, "The Mine in the Sky" atop Isinglass Mountain was founded 200 years ago as a commercial production site for mica, used in lamp chimneys and stove windows. Years later, feldspar and beryl mining began. Sam Ruggles, his family and their descendants hauled their lodes by oxen-pulled wagons to Portsmouth for shipping overseas.

The mine could be accessed through a tunnel bored through the peak of the mountain, which opened up to a fantastic quarry with more cavities in it. Echoing through the chamber were the tap-taps of handheld picks that fellow visitors had rented to chip away at the rock walls themselves. I scavenged from the piles of loose rock all around, gathering specimens of mica, feldspar, quartz, garnet, tourmaline, pyrite and uraninite. As I picked, I wished my son Evan, a passionate rock collector, were beside me.

Without a light for guidance, I boldly crept through a 75-foot long pitch-black tunnel, feeling my way along the cave wall, then, re-emerging into the open, visited with a man who was perched on a rock reading a paperback while his two sons clambered about. Back when he was in his late 20s and his wife found herself jobless, he left his own job, which he hated, and they went on a seven-month adventure around the world. And here *I* had fancied *myself* the grand adventurer.

As it was nearing mid-afternoon, I trundled back down the mountain and continued on my way, spotting in Danbury my first farmer-on-a-tractor caution sign and — of all things — an ostrich farm. Meredith offered RV campgrounds and all sorts of boating opportunities on gleaming Lake

Winnipesaukee. A Chevy with license plate "VIRGIN" was my escort through Center Harbor, where separate signs warned about both a DEAF PERSON and a BLIND PERSON. I thought it oddly coincidental that there should be the two in the same general area.

Squam Lake was where "On Golden Pond," starring Kate Hepburn and Henry and Jane Fonda, was filmed. Down 25 East, there was a "Moose Crossing" sign, the first of many to come.

In Tamworth, I asked after Grammy-nominated folk singer and author Bill Morrissey, whose CD I'd listened to at Thom's and with whom Thom was loosely acquainted. A clerk at the Village Store passed me a phone book to find his listing, but it was unpublished, and her call about him to a friend went unanswered. We assumed he was "out of town on a gig" as he hadn't been in in a couple of days for his usual paper, beer, bread and chunk of scrapple, the latter an Amish pork sausage. According to a local calendar, "The Bold Men of the Mountain," in which the subjects were mostly nude and in which Bill was featured (thankfully not nude and only bugling), Morrissey was drawn to the area by the breathtaking view of nearby Mount Chocorua. I bought a soda and began my climb through the White Mountains.

Here, Steinbeck encountered an egg farm, bought a dozen and asked permission to camp beside an "eager stream." The farmer, "a spare man with a Yankee face," granted it and asked for a look at his vehicle. Steinbeck agreed, and after straightening up — the cabin had gotten trashed as it rocked about — and a meal of corned beef hash cooked over a low flame, he entertained him. Over coffee spiked with 21-year-old applejack, they talked about Russian premier Kruschev's address to the U.N. and how presidential election activity was going in these parts. Late night, after the farmer's departure, he read passages of William Shirer's "Rise and Fall of the Third Reich." Rest did not come easily — "roosters were crowing before I went to sleep" — as he mulled over the evening's conversation. It had been far more illuminating than his experience at a roadside restaurant would be the following morning. There, "customers folded over their coffee cups like ferns" uttered a series of "laconic grunts," burped or simply said nothing at all.

Chocorua connected me to 16N for the ascent and, just north of Albany I saw my first logging truck. Camper after camper and a large group of motorcycles passed in the opposite direction, no doubt heading home after weekending in the mountains. I expected the passage here to be steeper and a strain on my aging van but the mountains were rolling and easy.

North Conway plays host to the annual World Mud Bowl Championships, wherein teams from across New England meet to compete in two-hand touch mud football games to raise money for local nonprofit organizations. Though the bowl date had passed, the town was teeming with tourists, bound for any number of restaurants there. On the outskirts, a huge warning: "BRAKE FOR MOOSE. IT COULD SAVE YOUR LIFE." A 35-year-old muscle car with the plate "OUR-68" served as a blocker should one of these shaggy, antlered mammals decide to barrel across our path.

As the sun started to slide down in the sky, I entered the impeccably well-kept White Mountain National Forest. Ahead of me, clouds actually sat on the mountaintops, the climb was more strenuous and the air noticeably cooler. I wished to stop to enjoy some of the attractions but also wanted to make the Maine border and reach a KOA campsite near Skowhegan by nightfall. It was a difficult goal to stick to, as the sights became more and more visually inviting and I entered Mt. Washington State Park.

Gorham, 87 miles west of Portland, put me in touch with Route 2E as the sky turned a brooding gray and the birch trees rustled uneasily. The smell of leaves burning in an oil drum, a smell I'd always mentally associated with camping, filled the air.

A very understated sign, "State Line Maine," tempered by an equally overstated sign warning out-of-towners about the state's TOUGH drunken driving laws, signaled my exit from New Hampshire, though I was still in the White Mountains.

As Steinbeck made his own way into Maine, he remarked on radio fare, becoming "aware of more and more advertising for Florida real estate" the further north he pushed. A fan, as am I, of "weather rather than climate," he wondered how long an Aroostook County man would be able to stand the sunny south before missing "the shout of color, the clean rasp of frosty air and smell of pine wood burning" that define his native state.

At intervals, the author pulled into "places of rest" to exercise Charley, heat up his coffee and contemplate the scenery. At one such stop, he relaxed to enjoy a volume of "The Spectator" by Joseph Addison, suggesting that the latter likely influenced his own prose style. "A rather stout and bedizened woman" and her "rather stout and bedizened Pomeranian of the female persuasion" interrupted his reverie. Spying the petite pooch, Charley made romantic overtures, was promptly repelled by its master and responded by nipping at the woman. In seeking to separate the canines, Steinbeck sustained a bite from the pooch and it took brandy to restore calm. The event dampened his day plan, ensuing rain made it soggier and Steinbeck drove hurriedly eastward.

In Bethel, 60 miles shy of Skowhegan, I tried to phone ahead and make a camp reservation, but my phone wasn't picking up a signal in this sparsely populated area. On the radio, however, I was able to tune in a Bears-49ers game, which San Francisco was dominating at halftime. At a pause, I heard that my own New York Giants had played the Rams, winning their NFL season opener.

A hilltop crest afforded a fine overlook at Rumford, distinguished by a great iron train trestle and a distant factory, steam drifting from its active smokestacks. I needed gas and, as daylight faded, pulled into Gould's Exxon in Dryden. Milling about at the pump were several young men in work boots, jeans, tees and caps. A teen approached them and, in a thick accent, asked one, "Can I keep the change? It's only a dollah fifty anyhow." Dressed in my khaki shorts and boat shoes without socks, and sporting short-shorn locks, I must have looked like an alien to them.

Nightfall came while I continued seeking my destination and, in the dark, I almost didn't see two farmers atop their John Deeres pulling giant coils of hay on trailers along the roadside. Given the close call, I thought it best to refresh with a food stop in Norridgewock, finding a pizza joint to accommodate me. These establishments appeared to be a common denominator in Maine towns, along with Civil War memorials showing a single soldier atop a pedestal.

A bearded bear of a man in a sleeveless t-shirt at the counter recommended a meatball sub as a quick and hot meal solution and guided me with very detailed directions to the camp, only miles away now. For reading material while I ate, I eyed a copy of *No Umbrella*, billed as "A

Reader For River People" serving Maine's Upper Kennebec Valley. I asked a chesty young waitress in a black tee, sleeveless like the counterman, if we were, in fact, in said valley. Though she admitted to being a lifelong area resident, she wasn't sure. I assumed so as the small paper was published in nearby Bingham and recognized that the irreverent, laid-back biweekly was devoted to the state's river sports community and thus featured paddling-related fare. The editor's note encouraged readers, "When you're sitting 'round the wood stove as the cold wind and snow beat on the clapboards outside" this winter, to jot down and send in their favorite warm-weather river memory.

Another reading focus, *Coffee News*, offered this quote from Earl Wilson: "If you wouldn't write and sign it, don't say it." Good words to live by I ventured.

The counterman wished me a safe trip and soon I was pulling into a campground at Canaan just up the road. The camp's co-owner checked me in and, after learning of my journey, we stood talking for almost an hour. She admitted that it was a full-time job and that most camp owners only stay at it seven or eight years.

Ultimately, in a golf cart, she led the way to a camp space and bid me goodnight. In my small RV, surrounded by other hulking, bus-sized RVs, I felt minute and a little out of place, but I was sure the feeling would pass the more familiar I became with this campground experience.

Day 3: Deer Isle & "Bah Haba"

My night's sleep, the first in the van, was not sound. It took some getting used to arranging my six-foot frame diagonally across the space with which I had to work, measuring 5-1/2 feet each way. I ended up pulling my knees up in a fetal position and lying on my side. And though my sleeping bag was cozy, I still couldn't drop off, hopped up from Mountain Dew had at dinner, conversation with the campground owner and excitement about my first solo campout.

At 2:30 a.m., I found myself up typing on my laptop with the only TV station I could tune in, the Worship Channel, on in the background. By first light, I was dragging, but a hot shower in a private compartment in the main building helped bring me around. Tuning in the ideal shower temperature, like adjusting the vertical hold on an old black and white television, was my only bathing challenge.

It was time to debut my, as yet, virgin RoadTrip grill. At first, I thought that a hose component was missing, but located it and, with a silent wish for luck, ignited my compact stove. It fired right up and, quickly, I poured a blob of egg batter on the griddle surface. Discovery #1: Make sure your grill is level before placing food on a cooking surface. The blob ran through an opening and down around the burner. Discovery #2: Remember to pack a spatula. With none in tow, I used a plastic fork to tend to my scrambled concoction. Discovery #3: Placing bread on the grill surface to brown is more effective than using a pop-up bread stand, but don't let it sit too long.

All in all, the morning experiment was pretty successful and I enjoyed the eggs, toast and even cereal, using Evy's pottery, at an adjacent picnic table. Though it was nippy out, I was exhilarated and thoroughly enjoyed the sound of a light breeze shuffling through the leaves of the birch trees around the campsite.

A woman of retirement age wandered past walking a black mini Charley and said, "I'm glad I don't have to eat *my* breakfast outside." I replied, "Oh, I could eat it inside but I'm really enjoying the morning." She smiled at my folly and returned to the propane-generated warmth of her Greyhound bus-sized RV.

While I ate, I read accumulated newspapers that included *USA Weekend* featuring a story titled, "After 9/11." It was written by Dr. Tedd Mitchell who wrote that he had always considered himself 100% Texan until the terrorist attacks. Since then, he considered himself, like millions of other Americans, he supposed, "at least 1% New Yorker." He talked about the range of feelings he'd experienced since then, from fear of and overcoming fear of travel to determination to prevent another attack, while urging compassion in our everyday lives.

In the pages of *The New York Times* magazine, the Nordic-looking, bronzed women modeling the new DKNY, Gap and Prada fall fashions helped me feel a little warmer in this chilly climate.

As the rising sun shone on my picnic spot, I watched a 30-foot Gulfstream Ultra Supreme towing a Jeep Liberty nimbly navigate out of its space, around a tree and off out of the campground. It was time for me to go, too.

All packed up, I went to turn the engine over but found the battery dead. Had I left the radio on? What had drained it? The topper was that I hadn't charged up the portable Jumpstart system I'd brought with me. I went to summon the campground owner's fiancé, a former native of Shelburne Falls I discovered, and bought a pre-paid phone card in the process to solve my no-signal phone dilemma.

Walking back to the van to meet him, I passed a young Mennonite couple — she with a bonnet on her head and he in a crisply pressed baby blue shirt. They waved hello. The sighting made me feel like Jim Carrey in "The Truman Show" in which all the activities around him are coordinated and filmed to make better reality TV fare. Was someone in some control room in my little world whispering into a headset, "OK, cue Mennonite couple in 3, 2, 1…" I later learned that they were on their honeymoon and taking a month to travel around New England. As it was later explained to me, the Mennonites are a bit more progressive than the Amish and drive cars, versus relying on horse and buggy.

Later in the morning, I had planned to meet up with aforementioned seafarer Walter Billings of Little Deer Isle down on the coast, but wasn't at all confident the meet would happen. In a phone call to Walter a few days before, he'd told me that he'd been in and out attending local wakes and funerals and might not be available. And though I now had the phone card and could use it with a pay phone, I was unsuccessful at raising him. Deciding to just wing it his way, I got on the road mid-morning.

As Steinbeck toodled into Maine, he noticed that all the summer attractions, "the hot-dog stands, ice cream parlors, curiosity shops and deerskin-moccasin-and-glove places, were all shuttered and closed." As we both knew, Vermont is as popular in the warm months as it is in the cold, serving as a shady haven for "refugees from the sticky heat of Boston and New York." He remarked on the abundance of antique shops, with enough wares "to furnish the houses of a population of fifty million." A fan of junk, Steinbeck admitted to having "half a garage full of bits and broken pieces" that he used for "repairing other things." I had witnessed first hand the handiness of which he'd written and could imagine his delight tinkering in these shops. I recognized, too, that his attitude was an old-fashioned one and that modern folks neither have the time or the inclination to repair their belongings; nor are there many resources left that offer repair services. We have become a wasteful society and our landfills are choked with the evidence.

Moving east, I defied the little voice in my head and took the campground owner's advice to go ogle author Stephen King's house in Bangor, a hop that took me through pretty farmland and along I-95 for a short spell. The dwelling was what one might expect of a horror writer: a blood red Victorian with off-color white trim, surrounded by a black, wrought iron fence. The main gate leading to the front veranda featured a spider web-like pattern and mini bat-winged gargoyles atop the posts. Several other structures, including at least one garage on top of which was a large radar dish, lay behind the house at the end of a long driveway. I toyed with going up to the door to say "hi" but noticed a PRIVATE PROPERTY sign on a tree and thought better of it. Instead, I went around the corner to a video rental place, and asked the counterman what he knew about him. King was, not surprisingly, a customer and on occasion rented horror films, including those based on his own novels.

Steinbeck had also made a Bangor stop, to overnight at an auto court advertising winter rates. He had tired of taking sponge baths from a bucket and, more to take a hot dip than anything else, rented a room. It was all done in plastics, from curtains to lamps, as was the adjoining restaurant where he had a meal served by a listless waitress. She sucked the energy out of the room and grayed his mood, leading him to retire to his "cell" where he tossed back tumblers of vodka and lay deep in hot water, "utterly miserable." To his great relief, a sighting of the Aurora Borealis, in a "star-riddled sky" while out walking Charley before bedtime, salvaged the evening.

A stop at Luttrell's Corner Exxon for a fill-up and I was back on track for Walter's, startled at first by the low pass overhead of a large, flat-gray colored Air Force jet coming in for a landing at a nearby airport. It was around this area and on the way to Deer Isle that Steinbeck got thoroughly lost. I could understand why given the frustrating signs I, too, encountered: posted arrows without directions and a confusion of north with east and west with south or any combination thereof. He got lost again around Ellsworth and, in fact, spent much of the day lost. At one point he stopped to ask a "majestic Maine state trooper," who was "granite as any quarried about Portland" and "a perfect model for some future equestrian statue," for directions. The cop wordlessly pointed across the open water, with an additional swing of his chin to show where Steinbeck should cross. The cop's name, I would later learn, was Wentworth "Wimpy" Wessel and he was still a Penobscott resident.

Route 1A brought me down by Frankfort where I gazed upon the ever-widening Penobscot River, an outlet to Penobscot Bay and the Atlantic Ocean beyond. Once again, I found myself following a vanity plate, "MOONFLR," attached to a Honda Civic. A hippie driver perhaps?

On 1E approaching Bucksport, I pulled into a "scenic turnout" to view the waterway. A plaque told me that, in 1779, it was the site of the largest combined infantry-naval operation undertaken by the American colonists during the Revolution, but that it met with disaster when 2,000 colonials failed to capture British-held Fort George.

A middle-aged couple dressed in black motorcycle gear and driving a Harley was standing rail-side admiring the view. From Winchester, Tennessee, they were on their way to Bar Harbor. They were also considering going to Nova Scotia, which I think I persuaded them to do based on my own travels there. In turn, they told me where I might enjoy an "awesome steak" in West Virginia near the Blue Ridge Parkway.

On 15 South, I was yet again pursuing a custom plate, "4WAY399," on a Ford Aerostar from California. I couldn't fathom the meaning on that one. I pressed on, munching Tostitos from a bag at my feet.

Through Blue Hill, homes were few and far between and the road beaten to heck by winter weather. Unfortunately, because of its condition, it was also under repair by work crews in a number of sections, which made the going slow. I swapped out one custom plate for another, "DEARS," on a SAAB.

Near Sedgwick, I did my best to ignore signs for Live Lobsters and the Sow's Ear Winery, to keep to my mission, and soon crossed over a high-arching steel bridge spanning a sparkling blue channel to Little Deer Isle. A helpful woman at Sisters Little Market on the far side managed to get Walter on the phone and mapped out a route to his house for me.

Walter's wife, Evelyn, who had a brush in hand and was painting the garage, greeted me. She explained that the painting task had been Walter's until very recently and that they were expecting a vinyl company to appear shortly to see to the house, a gray clapboard Cape Cod. This explained the contractor sign, "Maine-ly Vinyl," out front.

Dressed in a blue plaid shirt, gray trousers and boat shoes and sporting close-cropped white hair, Walter emerged from the house and led me into the kitchen, which was decorated with photos and paintings of boats and harbors. One boat photo was of his former charge, the *Brilliant*, since taken over by the Mystic Sea Scouts. Another was of the *Chaperone*, a Navy air/rescue craft that he'd captained, that could do 60 knots thanks to two big Packard engines. There was also a black-and-white photo of the 78-foot *Mercantile*, a schooner that he had worked aboard in his teen years that carried pulpwood. Built in 1914 by the Billings Brothers (Walter's dad and uncles), it was still sailing as a cruise boat in Camden, Maine, a testament to local craftsmanship.

Above the kitchen table was a large framed depiction of the Billings family tree, traced back to the 1500s and possibly Huguenot roots. Walter was one of seven children, though one of them died during the great flu epidemic of 1919. He told me that his brother liked to say "the family didn't come over on the *Mayflower* but, after all, someone had to catch the lines!"

For ten years, beginning in 1948, after he and Evelyn wed, Walter lived on Mill Plain Road in Fairfield and was responsible for towing Lightning class sailing craft to regattas on Long Island Sound. The new interstate put him out of that business as boaters began putting these craft on trailers and towing them up by car instead.

Still standing in the kitchen, he showed me an album depicting the West Coast home of his old boss, Briggs Swift Cunningham. Located in Rancho Santa Fe, north of San Diego, it was an extravagant, hacienda-style place, with huge vases, large horse statues and several pools. The home itself covered well over an acre Walter guessed. Cunningham's neighbor was Ray Crock, the founder of McDonald's.

The photo album also included color postcards of Briggs' racecars, 72 of which were purchased by Miles Collier Jr. to put in his museum in Naples, Florida. One of the cars, a 1931 Bugatti Royale, was purchased from Miles by an investor for a whopping $9.8 million, at the time the highest price ever paid for an automobile.

Other cars depicted included Gary Cooper's Dusenberg, a 1912 Mercer 35C "Raceabout" (one of Briggs' favorites) and a 1910 American "Traveler," a four-cylinder underslung that had springs that went underneath the axle. It was a fantastic collection to be sure.

Moving into the living room, Walter then showed me two cherished books: "Cunningham: The Life and Cars of Briggs Swift Cunningham," which Briggs had autographed, and "A Picture History of the America's Cup," one of only 99 copies, signed by 12 of the winning captains. He handled the volumes with great care and obvious reverence. As to how Walter had connected with the Cunninghams in the first place, the skipper of the *Brilliant* had heard from locals about his sailing abilities and hired him in 1946 after Walter got out of the air force. Though clearly a man with a great love of the sea, Walter had been on a boat only twice since retiring from yachting in 1989. Steinbeck would have delighted in speaking with him at length and hearing his many stories.

The hour was growing late and I had yet to see Deer Isle and, though Walter had had no information to offer about Steinbeck's visit, he knew someone locally who did. I said goodbye to Evelyn, who was gardening by that time, and followed Walter in his Mazda pickup along Deer Isle Road to see Neva Beck. She had been a friend and neighbor of Eleanor Brace's, with whom Steinbeck had stayed.

Steinbeck was actually reluctant to visit Deer Isle as it was off his intended route, but persuaded to by his agent, Elizabeth Otis. She had a great fondness for the area and made annual visits to see her friend Eleanor. Naturally, Steinbeck got quite turned around finding Eleanor's "great old house" but was happy to have once he did. He found the area almost indescribably strange in a wonderful way, an "island that nestles like a suckling against the breast of Maine."

To me, the smell of the sea, mixed with the scent of wildflowers that grew along the roadside, was intoxicating, and around every bend was a delightful postcard scene. In short order, Walter deposited me in front of Neva's place of business, "The Periwinkle" gift shop, full of postcards, Maine-type gifts and hand-sewn, treasured "Winnie the Pooh" stuffed animals.

Neva was living with her two children at her dad's dairy farm at the time of Steinbeck's visit. The farm was quite near Eleanor's so she sent the children over to get Steinbeck's autograph.

Appreciating my interest in seeing the house, Neva phoned Eleanor's niece, Brenda Gilchrist, the property owner. I got on the line, explained my quest and, though she had a guest coming to tea shortly, she agreed to a visit. Locating her home was like seeking the endpoint of a maze or following clues in a scavenger hunt.

I pulled up and parked in the very spot in the circular dirt drive where Steinbeck had moored his own RV and in which he spent his two-night visit, though accommodations in the house had been offered to him. A woman in her 80s sporting white straight hair, a top with a moose pattern, linen pants and sandals, Brenda greeted me at the front door. Her Corgy, Gabi, ran out from behind her to greet me, too, unlike her aunt Eleanor's mysterious gray cat, George (a female!), which skulked about the property during Steinbeck's stay.

We entered the house, a fantastic place designed and built in 1902 by Alexander Wadsworth Longfellow, the nephew of the author and Brenda's great-uncle. As we admired the architecture, Brenda explained that Eleanor, who was a typing teacher and in her mid-80s when she died in 1976, had lived in the house alone and, thus, welcomed Elizabeth Otis' summer visits. Eleanor was a reserved person apparently and knowing this, Elizabeth told her of Steinbeck's visit only at the last minute, leaving her no time to make up an excuse not to entertain him. Eleanor *did* call a friend, Madeleine Burrage, however, who lived in Wiscasset, three hours to the southwest, to come keep her company. For Madeleine, it was a mission of mercy. Though Steinbeck made mention of three lobsters at dinner his first night there, he did not mention the additional guest, much less Madeleine by name. Up until the day she died, Madeleine had been bothered by that fact. By naming her in my road tale, Brenda and I thought we might correct this injustice.

We walked through the house, past the rough wooden table where they had dined, out onto the back deck that faced the water, and to Trivet House, the small cottage where Elizabeth would stay when she visited. Brenda's uncle had built it in throw-together fashion when he was a teen — it was never expected to have lasted more than a season.

We found a renter inside, a woman who'd noticed an ad for a vacancy at the cottage in *Down East* magazine and secured it for two weeks. She was the last guest that Brenda would have for the year. The floor sloped this way and that and nothing was even, straight or insulated, which made for its appeal. Through the screen windows, you could hear the waves lapping the shore.

Back in the house, Brenda passed off one of several small books I'd noticed which featured a hand-illustrated picture of Gabi the Corgy on the front. Brenda authored and illustrated these books, mostly guides about the local area.

As she and Dixie watched me drive off, I thought about a letter Steinbeck had written Elaine the morning after the lobster dinner. He had "discovered [his] insulated underwear makes wonderful pajamas, toast warm" and said that he had repacked Rocinante, having initially "loaded it like a boat. This is wrong. Different motion." He'd also found that he gets "tired in the behind over two hundred miles," which he remedied with "one of those inflatable boatseats." He was beginning to recognize regional differences in language as well and the restless nature of folks, who looked "hungrily at Rocinante."

I lumbered back through the woods and onto the narrow road to the main and toyed with steering right, to the fishing village of Stonington, the southernmost point of this peninsula where Steinbeck had purchased a kerosene lamp from a hardware store. While curious to see if the shop was still there and what its operators knew of the visit, I also wanted to see the three-story, 91-year-old barn-like opera house there that had recently been restored. The structure, or at least the present smaller version rebuilt out of the ashes of a fire in 1910, had been the cornerstone of culture in the village in its heyday and enjoyed a colorful audience because of the ships that would visit there from foreign ports. Over the years, it fell into disuse, became an eyesore and even home to a family of raccoons. Since, it had become a draw for live summer performances.

I knew that Stonington was also the site of pink granite quarries from which rock was used for Rockefeller Center and the Brooklyn, Manhattan and George Washington Bridges in New York.

But the day was growing old, light was fading fast and I had to get moving, especially wanting to navigate these pitted back roads while I could still clearly see them. Heading back the way I'd come, I passed over the bridge and near to where Steinbeck had stopped to ask the policeman directions to Deer Isle. Through Sedgwick, then Blue Hill, I went, winding my way northeast to citified Ellsworth and along up to Bar Harbor. Fun parks, mini golf, the Acadia Zoo, farm markets, blueberry stands, trading companies and even a Frisbee golf facility lined the road there.

At the Hancock County-Bar Harbor Airport, Columbia Air offered lighthouse flyovers while, up the road, lobster barbecues were going great guns — flames and smoke flicking up from large metal grates. The familiar KOA camp emblem came up in my headlights and I pulled in to the office. After some fumbling on the part of the cashier there, I got myself checked in and was led to a waterfront campsite, which I eyed with great satisfaction. Looping back to the camp entrance, I noticed a modem hut, hooked up my laptop and tried to dial up e-mail, but AOL had no local port and this hub wouldn't permit a long-distance call. A clerk came to my aid, allowing me to tap in through an office computer that connected me to my inbox and half a dozen messages. The majority were from my wife, who hoped I was doing well and reported on family activities, haircuts and bank transactions.

In a similar manner, but by pay phone "three times a week from some bar, supermarket, or tire-and-tool cluttered service station," Steinbeck had checked in with *his* wife, reestablishing his "identity in time and space." It was a reaffirming feeling: "For three or four minutes I had a name, and the duties and joys and frustrations a man carries with him like a comet's tail. It was like dodging back and forth from one dimension to another."

Packing a man-sized hunger (and thirst), I ventured into town, finding the road instantly familiar from a previous area visit. That foray saw stops at factory outlets and taffy shops in Kittery and Kennebunkport, blowholes at Acadia, and Nubble Light in York. It was also the launching point for a crossover to Nova Scotia via a new high-speed catamaran, for a weeklong tour of the Canadian peninsula. The adventure was perhaps one of the finest that we'd ever enjoyed.

On the main drag this particular evening, Geddy's advertised "The Best Tail in Town" and live music. It fit the bill perfectly. A friendly, golden-locked waitress sat me down and made recommends as to dinner fare and, soon, a Shipyard Pumpkinhead Ale and 12" Italian pizza appeared. The blend hit the spot and a guitarist and singer supplied a fitting background. Needing the facilities, I noticed that the mens' room door was marked "Outboards" and the ladies' room "Inboards" and that the urinals inside had coaster-like resting places for beer bottles.

Back at my table, I mentioned to the waitress that I was traveling around the country by myself and she said, "Oh, like John Steinbeck in 'Travels with Charley.'" Not only did she know the book, but also the stops he'd made in the area!

A café mocha at The Opera House up around the corner was a welcome cap to dinner and, just across the street, Donahue's Eatery & Spirits, allowed me to do some newspaper reading. In *The Bar Harbor Times*, photographs of license plates bearing Maine-related custom messages — like "ACADIA" and "BAHABA" (a Mainer's pronunciation of Bar Harbor) — were displayed. The Coast Guard Station in Southwest Harbor was busy barbwire fencing itself in at the directive of the Department of Homeland Security. The "Calls of the Wild" column noted that animals are starting to fatten up for the winter, most noticeably the deer, bear and woodchucks. A photo of a gas station sign showing fuel priced at $2.01 a gallon was captioned "OUCH!!!" Home prices in Hancock County had climbed almost 28% in 2002. The hawk-watching season had begun at Acadia National Park. And singer Warren Zevon's latest recording, "The Wind," topped Amazon.com's best sellers list — a posthumous honor given that he had recently passed.

A trio of young people walked in, we got into conversation about vodka brands and I joined them for shots of the same. They toasted "Nostrovia" while I toasted "Carpe Diem," explaining that it was a Latin expression translating to "Seize the day," my operating motto. One of the women, a blonde with a slight cold, spoke about the inferiority of non-Russian vodkas, mentioning that a shot of Absolut had killed a man in her hometown of Krasnadar. Her friend, a brunette from Stavropol, took interest in my little notebook and read a few pages. The male in the trio, the only U.S. resident of the three, inspected El Rucio, which I'd parked in front of the Opera House. They all taught me Russian phrases and helped pass the evening.

Day 4: Down East & Houlton

Sleep came more easily during the night, likely due to the alcohol intake the evening before. Nevertheless, I was still up before the whales, at 4, and reveled in the sight of a full moon reflected off the calm waters of Western Bay. Using my Coleman power inverter, a unit that plugged into the cigarette lighter and had outlets that you can put a standard plug into, I worked at my laptop, making sense of my scribbled notes of the past 48 hours. As I typed, the moon turned a murky yellow and dropped behind the tree line on the far shore and a rose color worked its way up into the sky as the sun took the moon's place.

Around 6:30 a.m., when I was sure other RVers around me had started to rise and my thumping and bumping would not disturb them, I emerged from my wheeled cocoon to put clothes and toiletries together and pad to the shower building. It was quite cool and not much warmer in the shower compartment, particularly as the space above was open to the rafters so didn't help contain heat. The hot shower, which I quickly leaped into and speedily mastered the controls, was a good thaw out. Unfortunately, I'd forgotten to bring my towel from the van and so had to dry off using a 10" x 10" square washcloth. I was glad to get back to El Rucio and even gladder that she started right up, and let her engine heat warm the interior, and me. By this time, the sun was up and just over the trees to the east, bathing my campsite in golden light. I set my washcloth out to dry and considered my day plan. Rather than pull all my breakfast gear out and since the van was already warmed, I decided to get food on the go. On the agenda was Cadillac Mountain, blueberries, the Maine coast and, with luck, Houlton for an overnight, stops that were along Steinbeck's path to northernmost Maine. First, though, a stroll along the waterfront was in order.

I gingerly stepped from rock to rock, avoiding snails that clung to them here and there, peering in tide pools for sea treasures and creatures. The water gently licked the shore, the smell of a wood fire was hanging in the crisp air and a hint of pine just caught the nose. It was nirvana. As I sauntered back to the van to depart camp, one overnighter standing nearby was telling another about having seen the Northern Lights, an experience I hoped to have.

At the front office, as I dropped off postcards, I noticed a note tacked to a bulletin board, "Pie Lady Coming" and a date. The clerk told me that the reference is to a woman who travels through selling pies. "She calls [her service] 'A Moveable Feast,'" the clerk said, a reference to Steinbeck contemporary Ernest Hemingway's literary masterpiece. What a novel way to earn a living I thought, no pun intended.

In contrast to the simple pie-woman, a Lay's truck pulled up out front and I couldn't resist telling its young driver that his company was one of my sponsors and that I had Tostitos and salsa on board. He was clearly amused.

A final stop at an Exxon across the road provided fuel, a squeegee to clean off the 12-dozen bug splats that had formed a Jackson Pollack-like arrangement on my windshield and *The Ellsworth American*, an unusually sized (16" W x 23" H) daily promoted as "Maine Owned, Maine Managed Since 1851." I paused to read that the Blue Hill Fair was underway, offering pie-eating contests, fried dough and goat judging. Karaoke nights were in danger of extinction at the Blue Moose Bar in Blue Hill due to an outcry from neighbors about the noise level. Grilled salmon, chicken and mussels were on the menu at Blue Hill's Down East Feast. The Winter Harbor Lobster Boat Races were marred by a confrontation between fishermen and U.S. Coast Guard officers.

Following a green Voyager with the plate "GO JO" back into Bar Harbor, I passed hotels, motels and mini golf places, arriving ultimately at the intimate headquarters of the Wild Blueberry Association of North America, run by husband-and-wife team John and Jean Sauve (pronounced So-vay). A month or so earlier, I'd read an item about blueberry burgers — the sweet fruit a boost to the nutritional value of the burger — and the WBANA's support of their development. Through the association's website, I connected with John and hoped to catch the tail end of the harvest.

They welcomed me in and filled my arms with wearables (including a blue cap, the same color as that which Steinbeck wore in his travels), and we spoke of the wonderful world that is blueberries. A double for Hugh Hefner at a quick glance, John had worked for Friendly's Restaurants for a quarter century, as VP of National Marketing in his last post, and struck me as very promotion savvy. He tumbled into the blueberry business by chance through a client contact and he and Jean moved up to Maine from Massachusetts to establish the association. Coincidentally, he had a copy of my dad's marketing book on his office bookshelf! It seemed the hand of fate was at work again.

After a quick look at the van, John steered me to Jordan's Restaurant up the street. A strong endorser of the fine berry, owner Dave Pane, a good-natured guy in his 50s, shook my hand with his batter spattered paw and proceeded to cook up a two tier, plate-sized stack of some of the heartiest blueberry pancakes I've ever enjoyed. These are the kind that just drink in syrup and beg for more. Around me, sturdy, homegrown waitresses scurried to and fro, balancing five or six plates of food at a time along outstretched arms. Fellow patrons, perched at the counters on tall, mushroom-shaped chrome and red vinyl revolving stools, sipped coffee, their cups continuously topped off to keep their brew steaming. This was no fancy joint, just good down-home dining. Dave liked it that way and I did, too.

For the balance of the morning, I sat at a table at the Opera House, where I'd stopped for a coffee the night before. As I checked e-mail on my laptop, I became very aware of the place as a crossroads of the world. The owner, a tall, pleasant woman with a sweet, Southern drawl and cheerful, "Y'all need help?" greeting turned out to be from New Iberia, Louisiana. We determined it was on my intended route and she shared the address and phone of her parents down there, that I might pay them a visit.

The self-dubbed Opera House's "espresso jerk and piano player," Ron Gamble, heard about my trip and let on that he'd been working on his own travel-oriented book, a guide to getting around on a small budget. Ron was also the director of the local youth hostel.

A bearded, red bandana-topped café worker told me of his own Steinbeck inspired around-the-country travels following his graduation from college. Among his experiences, he labored as a field hand out west and had an opportunity to see "Rocinante" up close, a pleasure I highly anticipated.

A couple bearing British accents strolled in and I learned they were from the Cotswolds area in England, but living and working temporarily in Columbia, Maryland. Another couple entered, seeking directions to an area site. They were from Freiburg in southwest Germany, near the home of my German ancestors.

I could have spent all day here making new acquaintances and hearing about world travels but time had a bad habit of continuing to tick and it was growing late. With much to do, I hopped in the van and went and scaled nearby Cadillac Mountain, Acadia National Park's highest elevation and, at 1,500 feet, the highest point on the U.S. Atlantic Coast. According to a plaque at the summit, "If you stood here alone at dawn, you might be the first person in the country to see the sun's first rays." I let the breeze waft over me and the sun beat down as I looked out over lichen-encrusted pink granite at Frenchman Bay. To my right lay Seal Harbor, the Cranberry Islands and the open sea. Named after one-time island owner Antoine de la Mothe Cadillac (who later founded Detroit and after whom the automobile is also named), the peak was one of the most inspiring I'd ever stood atop.

Downshifting my way to the mountain's base, I started heading back north to Ellsworth and then east along Scenic Coastal Route 1. Here, the population was sparse, the trees many and the conveniences few. But the occasional peeks at Frenchman, Dyer and Pleasant Bays were fantastic.

In this area Mainers call "Downeast," I passed the Schoodic Section of Acadia National Park, following a RAV4 with the plate "TUPPY 2." On the radio, stations, like one calling itself "The Bear," played only country. I settled for an international public radio station supported by GBH in Boston and the BBC.

Approaching a small post office in Harrington, I remembered I had an envelope to mail. It contained a set of car keys I'd found on a lip under the hood of the van when I went to charge the battery yesterday morning. I guessed that they belonged to my van dealer, so wrapped them in a note to mail. For a return address, I put "Lauterborn somewhere in the U.S.A."

The counter girl helped me determine postage due. It was a more complicated process than one would have thought because of the bulk of the envelope, and so was rated differently. I hung in the balance with anticipation as to whether I might be paying 49¢ or 60¢. The transaction even required a consultation with a supervisor, who was dressed very neatly in her uniform like an old-time airline stewardess, with her blonde hair "boofed" ever so carefully. I asked the counter girl what one does for fun in these parts and she said, "Oh, lots. Bicycling, boating down Big Little Falls..." She added that she didn't really know beyond that as she works six days a week and is an Ohio native. I mentioned I was heading toward Calais, pronouncing it "Ca-lay," and was quickly told that the place name is said, "Cal-las," like a rough patch of skin. Climbing back in the saddle, I heard a cow mooing in a lot across the road and a weather report on the radio noting that temperatures "up north" would be dropping into the 50s, with a chance of frost possible.

Wild Blueberry Land, a giant blue orb of a structure, stopped me in my tracks at Columbia Falls. Inside, the doors, floor mats, display cases, counters, signage and even recycling bins were also blue. Filling every shelf and counter were juices, spritzers, cream sodas, smoothies, pies, jams, honey, tea, syrup, soap, candles, vinegar and chutney, all made with the mighty blueberry. I also noticed a can of something called "Road Kill Stew" with a label declaring, "It's got to be good; it's from the hood."

A round-bottomed woman walked in and declared, "I think it would be pretty neat to live in a giant blueberry." I wondered if that was true and asked the young son of the proprietor, who sat near the counter, "How do *you* like living in a giant blueberry?" "I don't," he replied. "There's nothing to do." "I won't let him cook," the owner added, smiling. "Maybe you can paint some more things blue," I suggested to him, then bought a blueberry scone to eat on the road.

Further on, I passed the aptly named Blueberry Hill Experimental Farm run by the University of Maine, Stephen King's alma mater. Blueberries grew low to the ground within fenced borders. In Jonesboro, on the side of a red barn, I spied a hand-painted wooden American flag with the word "Remember" on it. Obviously, 9/11 had an impact even in this remote place. In the middle of nowhere, an asphalt lot devoted to Demolition Derby events, according to a sign on a fence, popped up. Machias was a sprawling place where a branch of the U of M and Blueberry Ford were located.

In Whiting, I turned off the main towards Quoddy Head, falling behind a pickup with the plate "KYOTE" and a bumper sticker "I'm a Coyote Hunter." A desolate road brought me to Lubec, billed as "The Easternmost Town in the U.S.," settled in 1785. The sights here were classic downeast Maine: lobster traps, fishing boats and weather-beaten farmhouses.

After navigating a moody scenic stretch, over a rise I saw the oft photographed Quoddy Head lighthouse, the object of my detour, shining in the late day sun, its candy-stripe tower a cutout against the deep blue Atlantic behind it. From a raspberry bush amidst clumps of wildflowers around the tower, I plucked a few ruby red berries, popping the sweet delights in my mouth.

Retreating to Route 1, I was now seeking a place to stay and eat and perhaps have a beer. Leaving the coast behind and pushing north like I was now doing, Steinbeck noted having "forgotten how much of Maine sticks up like a thumb into Canada." As notable was how quickly the season changed and how apparent the struggle was between man and his environment here. Observing deer that strayed onto the roads and marks of bear, it appeared to him that nature was winning. He also remarked about the abundance of hunters and their careless ways and tied a red Kleenex to Charley's tail so that he would not be mistaken for a buck deer.

Perry, near the 45th Parallel Picnic Area, proclaimed that it was "Halfway between the equator and the North Pole," but lacked dining and camping choices. In contrast, Robbinstown offered the Hilltop Campground overlooking Passamaquoddy Bay. With the manager, I negotiated rental of a grassy spot behind a Monaco Windsor 330 turbo motor coach. With a motorcycle trailer behind it, the vehicle was 32,000 pounds of luxury living. The couple attending it looked familiar and I realized that I'd seen them at the KOA in Bar Harbor. They'd pulled up on their Harley and inquired about storage for their coach, but the camp didn't offer it. I remembered them only because they were a strikingly handsome couple.

He was a former Pan Am pilot back in the late '60s and he and his bride produced two beautiful southern belles, one a former model and the other a waterski champ. They invited me into their vehicle, which featured a slide-out living room that they happily demonstrated. Over a round of Busch beer, then red wine in pewter goblets, we spoke about our children, careers and the novel "Catch Me If You Can." The latter was of particular interest to him as its main character had masqueraded as a Pan Am pilot. We spoke about motorcycle travel too, given their bike and that the Harley Davidson Company had just marked its 100th birthday, a milestone celebrated with a big reunion in Milwaukee. He toyed with attending but shunned crowds for the road less traveled.

Hungry as a bear, I hopped back in my van and backtracked my way to a turn for historic Eastport, hoping to find something open. Well, it was sure historic but closed up tighter than a drum. Even the giant statue of a Gorton's-like fisherman holding his catch that stood by a row of tugs at the waterfront was tight-lipped.

Doing a spin around, I tried a restaurant back on 1 that had earlier been crowded, but found it closed to the public and six guys at a table inside playing poker. I thought to cut my losses and return to camp, but missed the turn, and by the time I realized it, I was in Calais — I'd pulled a classic Steinbeck! An Irving gas station and mini-mart set me up with fuel to continue on.

An inn advertising a restaurant and hot tub sounded great at that point, but, upon inquiry, there were no vacancies and the eatery was closed. Finally, adjacent to the border crossing into Canada, a pizza joint called Carmen's, still conducting business, threw its doors open to me. While waiting on a calzone, I looked at various wall hangings, including huge moose antlers and a greeting card from a Miss Maine hopeful.

On a whim, I decided to pop over to Canada to visit a bar in St. Stephen. Well, I did anything but pop. After light, mostly good-natured questioning by a young guard in a booth, I was directed to pull up beside a customs office and, to an officer inside, show the white ticket he'd given me. This officer was *not* friendly and gave me the 3rd degree to the nth degree. Where was I going? Where do I live? Where am I staying tonight? Do I know anyone in Canada? Do I have money on me? Am I carrying firearms? Potatoes? Beer? Just when I started to get disenchanted with the whole idea of visiting, he let me go. But these folks weren't done yet. A burly, no-nonsense female officer then gave my vehicle a going through. She was no doubt challenged by all the materials I'd managed to cram into my living space and didn't try to be too thorough. She did upset my cargo, though, which required some straightening later. Once through the checkpoint, I stopped at the first bank visible and withdrew some spending cash. The machine spat out Canadian money.

The bar was easy enough to find but, from my vantage point, appeared to be a dump, and empty. Passing on it, I pressed on for a few more miles in this borderland void, finding it a strange, dark, eerie place that made me long for a safer haven.

High-tailing it back to the U.S. side, I bypassed a long line of trucks waiting for entry at the crossing I'd come through earlier and tried another passage point, a bridge over the St. Croix River, the latter forming the border between Maine and Canada in that region. Though I saw the customs buildings, I didn't see anything or anyone saying stop, so rolled through. The whoop whoop of an alarm sounded and two U.S. officials came sprinting out of their office after me. I immediately stopped, of course, and responded to a few pointed questions to their satisfaction. Though I'd indicated I'd be staying at the Hilltop Campground and, for appearance sake, turned back toward that way upon leaving them, I doubled back a few minutes later and continued north. I vowed not to try the Canada experiment again.

Now, however, I faced a dilemma. It was 11 p.m. and I was 80 miles shy of Houlton, my target. Should I go for it or find the closest resting place? What would Steinbeck have done? The former I decided and so made the mad dash along barren 1 North into Maine's most northern county, Aroostook.

By midnight, I was still 20 miles from Houlton and growing ever weary and considered overnighting in a small, unlit rest area — but a sign prohibited it and I had safety concerns. A well-lit motel lot or Wal-Mart parking lot was a second option, but I nixed that, too. After nearly colliding with a large stag that darted across the road, I settled on an Irving Oil Truck Stop in Houlton. There, beside some two-dozen idling trucks, their drivers catching Z's in their cab interiors, I pulled in, climbed back into my bed and exhaustedly fell to sleep. It was actually the best sleep I'd had in the van thus far.

Steinbeck's passage through the area was made along the same, dark, desolate road, a leg all the more trying and even frightening because of endless rain that "drummed on the steel roof of the cab." He pulled in beside a concrete bridge, and to combat the "terrible lonesome" feeling that had settled over him, lit up two burners on his stove and the kerosene lamp. Charley was restless, "growled and whined uneasily" and declined food. For his part, Steinbeck made two peanut butter sandwiches for himself and sat in bed writing letters home. As the rain let up, a stranger, whom Steinbeck confronted with a 30/30 carbine and long flashlight, approached. The man was simply headed home and, after he'd passed, Steinbeck dropped into slumber.

Day 5: To the Tip-Top of Maine

I awoke at about 5:30 a.m. at the truck stop in Houlton, the endpoint to I-95 in the U.S. and where, as it curls due east into New Brunswick, Canada, it becomes simply Route 95. Nature was calling and not only did the truck stop offer a bathroom but also individual rooms to shower in and even a small movie theater! The fee for the shower use was $5 U.S. Unfortunately, I only had Canadian money, the exchange rate was almost 3-to-1 and I ended up paying $12 for the privilege. For my money, though, it was well worth it.

Miracle of miracles, a cellphone signal had returned and I was able to make a call to an old acquaintance in the area, the cousin of a college pal. Nineteen years prior, he and I and another pal rendezvoused up this way for a night that ended with a run-in with border police. Suspected of being unscrupulous dope-smoking individuals, we were detained, questioned, probed and released. The visit was all part of a greater six-day trek that included stops in Hartford, CT, Framingham, MA, and Bangor, ME, before we each began our sophomore years of college.

My visit on this occasion would be radically different and rewarding. "Alene" received my call with great surprise and gave me directions from the truck stop. After straightening ourselves up, El Rucio and I rolled the short distance past a mill that turns timber into wood chips to her countrified log cabin, which sat on a good piece of mostly level land, accented by rows of flowers.

Alene's husband, a worker on a freight train that makes the run from north Maine to Searsport below Bangor, had been on disability leave for several months. He introduced me to his children, and then Alene appeared. She hadn't changed much and we talked a blue streak, sharing updates about our activities of the past two decades in the span of the few spare minutes she had. Then I patched into their phone line to check e-mail and set my sights on heading to the very tip-top of Maine to see where Steinbeck had enjoyed a lakeside stay and company of migrant workers.

Before pressing on though, I needed to focus on some paperwork and set up at the Dead River Exxon. I took a call from my wife, too, the first chance we had to speak in five days. She reported that youngest son Phillip had decided that I wasn't coming back and that elder son Evan was being indifferent. We hoped to remedy these feelings with a phone call in the evening, service permitting.

A farmer atop his John Deere 3050 sidled up to the pumps for a fill-up — a sight you don't see every day — as I began to detect the distinct smell of propane in the air. The odor was being carried on the breeze from a filling cylinder a heavyset female station attendant was operating for a customer. All the while, big logging trucks rolled by.

The *Houlton Pioneer Times*, flagged as "the only newspaper in the world interested in Houlton, Maine," captured my attention, too. Top stories: Police were searching for a flasher who had been exposing himself, a Class D misdemeanor according to Chief Soucy. The Military Street Baptist Church announced a 9/11 service. The Hogan Tire Company sponsored a burnout contest and car show. The Molunkus Valley Sno-Drifters planned to host snowmobile races on grass. And former German POWs, who were housed in barracks at what is now the Houlton International Airport, were returning for a reunion and ceremony.

My extended roost and occasional leap from the van to snap photos attracted the attention of a station manager. "You've been here for hours, taking pictures, hanging around – what's going on?" I told him my story, one I'd told dozens of times already and he listened, nodded and ultimately smiled, extending his hand and wishing me luck with my travels. I made a mental note to myself to be more aware of my actions, particularly in this post 9/11 world.

It was 2 p.m. when I finally pushed off and continued my progress north. On the open stretches of road, when there were farms and not forests lining either side, the wind battered El Rucio and I had to fight to keep her aimed straight. From intersecting dirt roads, clouds of dust were driven across my path. And all along the way there were busy potato stands, like one called Tater Time, vending spuds. Steinbeck, who had awakened from his soggy overnight to sun and renewed purpose, noticed the same as he sprinted along, seeing "more potatoes than you would think the world's population could consume in a hundred years."

Lining the front of a house in Monticello were two dozen men of straw, each dressed in a faded outfit and assorted headgear, identified as the "Hollow Men." In the driveway next to the display, a woman shoved logs into a woodchipper, pulling her hand away quickly on occasion as one caught in the blades.

A sign at a roadside market in Bridgewater advertised "Cheescake-BBQ-Pork" — an odd trio by any standards, and the sky, which had been bright and clear, began to look moody, matching the wind's tantrum.

In the wee town of Blaine, the sole lady manning the post office accepted my mail. "They'll be on their way in an hour and a half," she assured me. Mars Hill, featuring old, low-rise places, such as Al's Diner and a 5-and-10 called J.J. Newberry's, was aswirl in dust, making it look like a Midwest town during the Great Depression years.

A harvesting machine came along in the opposite direction, occupying three-quarters of the road. I gave it a wide berth. It was followed by a school bus that stopped to deposit a small girl at her snow-worn, modest house. She trotted up her drive with her ponytail and Barbie backpack bouncing behind her. Two dirty white horses, their heads down to munch grass and tails flicking back and forth, stood in a nearby field. One looked up as I passed, studying me with those sullen eyes that horses have.

Fort Fairfield boasted a Growers Exchange, Dairy Bar and Thompson's Redemption Center. I wondered if the latter was for bottles or for souls in this part of the world. A little boy sat in his father's lap on a riding mower — a must-have implement in these parts — and was instructed in its operation, information that would no doubt have future use. Further on, a snowmobile, anticipating winter when it would be put into action, sat idle in a front yard. Up the way was Presque Isle, where the Aroostook Micmac Indians, led by Chief William Phillips, operated a variety store and had been battling with state authorities for the right to sell cigarettes there, tax-free.

A small Catholic cemetery beside a field of withered, brown stalks held the long-dead members of families who continued to work and upkeep area farms. I stopped to read inscriptions: William Haley, a native of Enniscorthy, Ireland, expired in 1826. The McShea children, Ellen and

Owen, ages 9 and 13, died within a day of each other in 1858. Mark and Mary Mulloy, 3 and 4 respectively, died two and a half months apart in late 1862. William John Mulloy passed at 28 in the winter of 1882. Cecil Ray Parker nearly made 5 in 1902. That same year, wee Maggie Malloy passed at 5 months — "Baby we miss thee" was scribed on her stone. John McKenney had just turned 36 when he passed the following year. James Kelley, 72, a native of County Donegal, Ireland, shared a stone with his 18-year-old son. There was Michael Russell, a native of Tipperary. And poor Charlie and Helen McCarty, 9 and 11 months apiece, who died in infancy 2-1/2 years apart. Irish all, they'd come to this country to escape the famines and misfortunes of their native land only to find equally hard times and sickness here. I sensed the sorrow and the pain of young parents and tried to imagine what their lives must have been like. Horseflies, like guardians of the dead, mercilessly nipped at me, chasing me from the site.

At Caribou, I rejoined 1, proud that I'd deciphered oft-confusing signage that lays in wait for out-of-state victims fumbling with their road atlases, and soon came upon a brother and sister selling corn out of a trailer at the side of the road, 25¢ an ear. They claimed that the crop was the sweetest it's ever been and that they were raising money to attend college. I did my bit to reward their enterprising efforts, paying twice the rate for a half dozen.

A Swedish-inhabited area bore the name Stockholm, which was immediately followed by Van Buren. Planning to prepare dinner for myself, I asked a Rite-Aid counter girl there for guidance on local fishing. "There's perch, trout...salmon if you're lucky," she replied, also suggesting places where I might collect other supplies, like meat, in case the fish weren't biting. I bought a bottle of Merlot and a corkscrew and moved along to Sauciers IGA down the road for steak, standing in line behind a French Canadienne stocking up for the cold weather with 16 frying chickens. The young, doe-eyed cashier who put the frozen fowl in a box pointed me to a place where I could buy a fishing license.

The purveyor of same was Peter Ouellette, an Acadian with a trading post on Champlain Street. His family came from France in the 1600s and had lived in this area ever since. The license came with a tub of nightcrawlers and some tips about where I might be luckiest fishing. Another patron, sporting a hunting cap with a deer on it, got in on the conversation to add a comment about local game. He recommended a 30-odd-6 to bring down a moose or deer. Peter cautioned me to not leave food out at my overnight spot lest it attract bear, then sent me along with a wish of "Bon Chance."

It was in this area, perhaps at the edge of Long Lake, that Steinbeck met up with his own band of Canucks, migrant potato pickers resting for the evening. He was downwind of their camp and the aroma of soup drifted to him. Based on the smell, he formed the impression that they were good people and orchestrated a meeting using Charley as his go-between. Six of them joined him in the cabin of Rocinante and they sipped beer and aged Cognac. After the loneliness of the previous night, he was glad "to be surrounded by warm and friendly but cautious people."

Down the road apiece, I passed a historic Acadian Village with a French flag flying from a timber. A flock of geese warmed themselves in the setting sun beside a fence-enclosed pond. I decided to change clothes here from my "city" attire to more of a backcountry look to better blend in and be less obvious as an out-of-towner.

Reaching Madawaska at 7, I got my bearings with the aid of a local out fast walking. The area offered neatly manicured lawns and compact little homes and appeared, for this region, to have a hopping little downtown. I docked curbside and leaped ashore to explore the surroundings.

A karaoke club with pool tables seemed to hold the most promise. Sporting a bejeweled, exposed mid-drift, the bartender set me up with a local brew and allowed me to pester her with questions about Long Lake and camping facilities. My intention was still to camp by the lake as Steinbeck had and try my luck at fishing. But now I was thinking that a grilled cheese sandwich from the local pizza joint and delaying fishing until the morning might be the easier way to go at this point.

I was also eyeing the bright lights of Edmundston, across the St. John River in Canada. Though it had been a hassle crossing at Calais and I'd sworn I wouldn't try to breach Canada again, I thought, perhaps, that I'd fare better here. With only a couple of minor inquiries aimed my way, across I went.

Edmundston was, in fact, the busy place I'd expected it to be but didn't have a hook to keep me there, despite the six or so drinking establishments I noted. So, like my earlier crossing, back I came, seeking the comforts of the karaoke bar once again. A woman there dominated the sound system, but no one seemed to mind as she had a fine set of pipes. The place bounced to the beat, the neon signs glowed, and the beers went down easily — a happy spot in an otherwise desolate way station.

In good cheer, I bid goodbye to the place and followed a hand-drawn map to the west, to Flat Mountain Road in St. Agatha and the Lakeview Camping Resort. A dirt road led me to the crest of a hill where I inched by a shuttered office, followed a perimeter road around stationed RVs and tucked El Rucio into a spot under a clump of evergreens. Though I'd figured the owner wasn't awake to record my arrival and planned to settle up in the morning, he *was* aware and, presently, approached in his pickup. He was actually looking for another vehicle that had pulled in but welcomed me nonetheless.

Taking advantage of Mother Nature's natural cooling abilities, I placed my cooler and some bagged food on a picnic table at my spot. Then I removed my bar smoke-tainted clothing and draped it beside the foodstuffs. For a short while, I tried to read but sleep beckoned me and I crawled into bed, my nightlight a big full moon framed by a few puffy white clouds in a bluish sky.

Day 6: The Call of the Moose

My night's sleep topped my truck stop nap and I awoke to see the sun come up over the horizon that was New Brunswick. The sun's glow illuminated puffs of steam that hugged the surface of the St. Croix River and the little houses that lined its bank on the U.S. side. I stepped out of El Rucio to stroll a short way on the perimeter road of camp to take in the view, hearing a group of crows in the trees carrying on a conversation.

Realizing it was September 11th, the 2nd anniversary of the terror attacks on our country, I flipped on my TV, at which I'd barely looked to this point, to tune in news. I found, instead, a children's program all in French and brushed up on the language I'd studied in high school. Unfortunately, I had learned a textbook version of French, which had little application for me in this region, as the accent and dialect of the Acadians was so modified. Still, where possible, I made my best effort to offer the odd phrase or word to Francophiles that I encountered.

I did manage to turn up a news station, WAGM-TV, which was just closing a segment with a composed still image of the American flag and Trade Towers, with the words "America Remembers" slugged across it.

Locally, people I'd spoken with said the event would be marked at church. In New York, families of victims were gathering at Ground Zero while newsman Harry Smith reported from the top of O'Hare's Restaurant. Debris had fallen on the eatery and set the spot ablaze when the South Tower fell. The station also carried a report of a new tape from Al Qaeda terrorist group leader Osama bin Laden, believed to be hiding along the border of Afghanistan, who warned of a greater attack to come against the U.S. In Washington, D.C., President Bush planned a moment of silence at the White House. Back home in Westport, a sunset service was scheduled at Sherwood Island State Park, where an oceanside memorial had been erected to honor Connecticut's 150 victims.

Though midday temperatures in Maine these last few days had generally been in the high 60s to low 70s, the early morning temperatures had been cold, hovering around 40. I was harshly reminded of this when I went to use the camp's bathroom/shower facilities. The restroom structure was an unheated pine cabin mounted on cement-filled oil drums and had wood floors with slats 1/8" apart. In the toilet area, when I dropped my drawers to sit on the seat and my backside made contact, my heart almost seized. I experienced the same shock emerging from the shower when cold air seeping up from below connected with my wet skin. Needless to say, I dressed quickly and returned to my site.

Breakfast was my next order of business: pancakes with raisins and apple and banana chunks in them, with hot strips of grilled ham on the side, all topped with Vermont maple syrup. As I prepared the meal, the mustachioed camp owner pulled up. "Beautiful morning, isn't it?" he remarked cheerily. I agreed, though he added that it wasn't like this at all during the summer, when it rained most of the time and made for his worst year in four years. He not only owned the campground but the adjoining Lakeview Restaurant and 800 acres around it.

When he heard about my journey to this point, he shared his own experiences traveling with his wife in the southwest, recalling, in particular, the deplorable conditions in which the Navajo Indians lived. I'd seen the scrubby, barren lands that they'd been corralled on, too, and we agreed that these proud people, who once called all of America home, had gotten a bum rap. He added that Native Americans up here had met the same sorry fate.

After he moved on, I received another visitor, a French Canadian man walking his Cockerspaniel. He was raised in nearby Keegan and had come up from Florida by himself in a 34-foot Gulfstream RV to visit friends. He'd also come to see a woman but discovered from a town clerk that she'd died two years ago. Oddly enough, he had worked in Plainville, CT, where I'd bought my van and also in Milford, CT, operating an automatic screw machine that pumped out parts for M-16s and chainsaws, among other items.

We spoke of the noisy crows around us and he related the story of a friend who kept losing watches and spare change to one that was hoarding them in its nest. "They'll go for anything shiny," he said. Just then, a V of Canadian geese flew past, headed north.

About my intention to fish, he said he used to ice fish on the St. Croix for a species he called a "Smelt." He added that when the river freezes over, one can walk from the U.S. side right into Canada. I thought that must make for some security headaches but he said the border patrol monitors it by flying their helicopter up and down.

As we spoke, I packed up, bid him "adieu" and sought out Gary Babin's Meats & Groceries where the cashier tipped me off to a local fishing hole. A road around the perimeter of Long Lake led me past a tumbledown red house, onto a dirt road and out along a land bridge that cut the lake in two. Midway, I parked El Rucio in a pullover, drew out my fishing equipment and, with one of Ouellette's nightcrawlers fastened to the end of my line, began casting, balancing atop some large rocks. Occasionally, I rested on the bank, which was covered with wild daisies, clover and thistle, and sipped at a beer, enjoying the light breeze, sun glinting off the rippling water and the sad call of a loon. For a good hour, the spot remained tranquil until the buzz of a chainsaw across the way and gutteral croaks of three long-billed birds that had come to roost at the top of a nearby telephone pole shattered the calm. The combination of these interruptions, my luckless casting and selfishness of the fish gods was telling me to pack it in.

As I moved off, now midday, my mind drifted to thoughts of Steinbeck's 1962 Nobel Prize acceptance speech and how it seemed to relate to his "Travels with Charley" quest. Humbled by the honor, he talked about the greater role of the writer. He concluded that, "The understanding and the resolution of fear are a large part of the writer's reason for being." More so, "He is charged with exposing our many grievous faults and failures, with dredging up to the light our dark and dangerous dreams for the purpose of improvement." Further, "The writer is delegated to declare and to celebrate man's proven capacity for greatness of heart and spirit — for gallantry in defeat, for courage, compassion and love. In the endless war against weakness and despair, these are the bright rally flags of hope and of emulation. I hold that a writer who does not passionately believe in the perfectability of man has no dedication nor any membership in literature." I believe Steinbeck really did fancy himself somewhat of a Don Quixote, off to fight the good fight.

The trees along the road back up to the main in Madawaska were beginning to show off their fall colors, bearing red, gold and orange leaves. Attracted by the lowest gas price I'd seen in days ($1.76 per gallon), I pulled into a Mobil and tanked up. At the register, a sign offered used videos, 3 for $10 — I loaded up with a half dozen.

At the office of the *St. John Valley Times*, a local weekly, I stopped to speak with a reporter. She snapped a photo of El Rucio and me curbside, then darted off in her pickup to cover a breaking story at the local high school. I remained a while to eyeball this week's edition of the paper, finding many colorful, region-specific stories. Notably, a 46-year-old man, paralyzed from the neck down in a car accident, was riding his electric wheelchair across the state to drum up support for stem cell research. Author Jack Schneider was conducting a signing for his book, "Allagash River Towboat," an adventure story about logging on the Allagash. The 2003 Little Maine Potato Queen helped send off the reigning Miss Maine in her quest to become Miss America. The Madawaska Fire Department, organized in 1928 with 16 volunteers and no fire station and staffed with active firefighters with surnames like Savoie, Michaud, Jandreau, Clavette, Lagasse and Pelletier, marked 75 years.

Pushing off, I tuned in Willie Nelson crooning "America the Beautiful," then, passing Saint Luce church west of Frenchville, flipped over to a

French music station. In Fort Kent, the historic blockhouse fortress that lends the town its name was a brief stop. Though it was closed, I was able to peer in through a plexiglass window at the wide oak flooring and narrow staircase leading to a second level. Gun holes, spaced every six inches, lined each side on both levels. An adjacent sign declared that Fort Kent is the beginning of U.S. Route 1, which runs 2,209 miles to Key West, Florida.

With some difficulty, I found Route 11 South and put the pedal down, aiming to reach a campsite while it was still daylight to cook up my steak and corn. Steinbeck had come along the same way, thinking about the sites he'd seen and the fact that, big towns up here were getting bigger and villages smaller. "People who once held family fortresses against wind and weather...now clustered against the busy breast of the big town." His assertion remained true as I observed.

As Steinbeck had done at Arthur Rogers' farm in Deerfield, MA, he sounded his truck horn — or "cattle caller" as he termed it — on a wood road to signal four lady moose crossing ahead. Simulating "a bellow like a Miura bull," it had the effect of not scattering the mammals but attracting them. He stomped on his "accelerator and got the hell out of there fast."

But for the occasional flash of civilization, this area was indeed logging country and, often, there were only trees for miles. Some roads were just being laid, in fact, with huge CATS moving load after load of rock, kicking up dirt that got in every nook and cranny of El Rucio.

At Ashland, the road threw me a curve and I had to ask a farmer stopped beside the Ashland Logging Museum for help. "Go back where you came from, make a right at the bridge and then a right at the light." I was about to u-turn when he added, "Unless you don't want to stop in town, then go straight and bear to your left. It'll run right into 11. Ya' can't go nowhere's else."

On a wide-open rural road south of Ashland, I noticed a neatly mowed stretch of property with bric-a-brac displayed in clumps all across it. On one set of planks were old teakettles. On a fence post, saw blades, cast iron skillets and an old, red Dietz No. 2 blizzard lantern. A table under a tree strung with orange, yellow and green party lanterns featured a small TV next to five moose skulls, an odd contrast. At the front of the property was an old Empire State stove, two lawn mowers grown over with grass, a black hand-pump and a big Howe scale with capacity of up to 1,000 pounds, meant for potato weighing. A red birdhouse sat on a porcelain toilet. A collection of electric irons, bottles and jars sat on a picnic table under a covering. More skulls, some with skin and fur still on them, sat atop a metal grate at the driveway entrance. Flies buzzed around them madly as they rotted in the late afternoon heat.

I walked up to the door of the property's small trailer-like house and, though I heard a radio playing inside, the door was padlocked. A neighbor, who sported a MACK truck cap and spat at intervals, had noticed me prowling the property and came walking up. I asked if the things were for sale and was told they were — by the owner who lost a leg in a 'huntin' accident.

He guided me to a dirt road that led around back to more oddities: a birdhouse and "Speed Limited 3 1/2 M.P.G." sign nailed to a tree. Aluminum bowls and baking pans secured to another tree. Three trees with skillets nailed up them, some 30 feet high. In a clearing, a homemade shack identified as "Lula's Den." More skillets. Pitchforks. A Coke machine. A shopping cart. Hubcaps nailed up trees like the skillets. It was all so bizarre and disturbing and, yet, highly whimsical. I extracted myself after a self-guided tour and pressed on.

On Canadian radio station Radio One, I heard how firefighters in Toronto were gathering in memory of 9/11 to show solidarity with their New York brethren. Secretary of Defense Donald Rumsfeld spoke at Arlington National Cemetery.

El Rucio soared along roller coaster roads and hills south of Knowles Corner just west of I-95. Steinbeck noted, Maine is "just as long going down, maybe longer" as the route up. As my eyelids started to droop and the dinner hour approached, I concurred. Thus, at Patten, when I saw a sign for Baxter State Park, a site Steinbeck said he "could and should have gone to," I, too, took a pass and moved along. He had dawdled and so had I and I needed to retreat from the state as he had. But, again, that steak and a relaxing evening, instead of one spent driving, had appeal. So I decided to sprint a bit more down the road toward a finish for the day at Millinocket.

Remembering that my new Coleman inverter had gone on the blink, which made working with my laptop a challenge for any great length of time, I stopped at a hardware store in Patten for a 25-foot extension cord that I could plug in at camp. At the same time, I had a dupe of my van key made in case I locked the only other set inside.

I overheard the clerk, who accented all his sentences with "jeez" or "becripes," tell the owner that he was taking Sunday off to attend a NASCAR race in Louden, New Hampshire. "That's ok, you'll pay for it," he joked. If it had been a week earlier, I could have attended, too, I thought, having passed near there.

For his own part, the owner was headed to an Art Garfunkel concert at the University of Maine. He gave me guidance to Millinocket, mentioning that a paper mill had closed there, causing the town to dry up, but that Patten's mills, including one devoted to veneer production, were still going strong. Steinbeck called these mill towns "knots of worms" and found them choked by a "howling hurricane of traffic." I couldn't agree but, then, Steinbeck was always complaining about traffic.

Shooting along 11 still, I passed a dairy farm on a rise that framed some two dozen cows against the background of three mountain peaks in Baxter State Park. From left to right, the peaks included Mt. Katahdin at 5,268 feet, Traveler Mountain at 3,541 feet and Horse Mountain at 1,589 feet.

On a back road, I came to a marshy wetland on the left and paused to admire it, half hoping a moose would come splashing through as I'd seen 200 yards off I-95 a number of years ago on a rainy return from northern Maine. Mosses and grasses hugged the water top. The bare stubs of trees stood at odd angles to one another. Splashes of red in the foreground contrasted with the lushness of evergreens in the background.

Inspired to try my luck fishing, I leapt out of the van, grabbed my rod and tub of nightcrawlers and stood atop a drainage pipe at the water's edge. At the first sign of a ripple, I cast and, bam, fish on, a small brown trout. It waited patiently in my hand while I removed the hook from its lip and released it. Another toss and, pow, another fish on, a slightly larger trout. Successive casts yielded no less than ten trout, the largest, however, measuring only eight inches.

All the while, I marveled at the setting, overflowing with life and activity. Dragonflies played tag. Water bugs skittered. The sleek bodies of the trout slipped through the murky water. Two loons whooshed in like seaplanes, folding up their wings and cruising to a stop in the water.

More joined them, the combined sound of their approach like a gust of wind. And my moose? It was out there, and surely had company. In the distance, I could hear one call another and heavy splashes at the far edge of the water. All the while, the only traffic that passed was three or four vehicles, including a passenger car that slowed down to eyeball me. I was glad to have this woodsy paradise to myself. As it grew dark, I finally pulled myself away, my hands smelling of fish and insect repellant and my head returning to thoughts of steak.

My final stretch of the day brought me to Katahdin Shadows Campground, in Medway near Millinocket. It was not a KOA but seemed to meet that standard. I backed into a space and immediately got busy making dinner, spontaneously crafting a meal combination that would be a feast compared with previous nights' fare. In a skillet went slices of tomato from Massachusetts, onions and peppers from Connecticut and cubed steak from Maine, sautéed together. In a separate pot, corn from Maine boiled, followed by Connecticut pasta. The skillet's contents went over the pasta and the corn; toasted bread and beer complemented. Feeling quite kingly, I dined in the comfort of the van, watching a Bond film until my lids got heavy.

PART FOUR

Westward Bound

Day 7: A Sprint to Lancaster

I rose at 5:30 a.m. to a misty morning and strolled to the main camp building to use the men's washroom, labeled "Bucks" (the ladies room was dubbed "Does"). It was heated and the showers were clean. Walking back to my site, I spied at the side of the dirt road two rabbits, one black and the other black and white, munching the grass, wet with morning dew. Their cousins, of varying colors, and numbering more than a dozen in all, joined them in the clearing.

Thinking quickly, I rummaged in my cooler for spinach, placed several leaves on a plastic plate and set it on the ground, making clicking sounds to attract the furry foragers. The offering drew some interest, particularly from a small black bunny with a patch of fur missing at the back of his neck. Given that his coloring was the same as Steinbeck's poodle, I dubbed him Charley, and, for befriending me, gave him an extra treat of some sweet raisins, which he ate right from the palm of my hand. Throughout breakfast — eggs with bits of red pepper, onion and ham in them — the brood, but most especially Charley who sat at my feet while I ate, hung around my site.

By 8:30 a.m., I was packed up and ready to go but needed to dump my trash and pay my bill. The camp owner was switching out a propane cylinder and filled me in on the rabbits. It all started with a domestic pair, he said, that did "what rabbits do," adding, "and the kids love 'em." To settle up, he steered me to his wife, who was seated in the office with two other women conferring over a jigsaw puzzle.

Life had dealt the couple some left hooks, but they were still on their feet and living with their son in a turn-of-the-century house on the Penobscott River. She said it bends and sags and refuses to stand straight and, during some renovation work to shore it up, they found curious things in the walls like a book with a bullet hole through it.

As I munched on some free apples from a basket and scribbled in my little notebook, the office cashier brought me a poem written by her dad, a paper mill employee and "not a writer of any sort." It captured the essence of the area and was obviously a special treasure for her.

I paid my tab, purchased some needed supplies and used the balance of the morning, which had become gorgeous, to check in with the world and get a reminder of life responsibilities. It was midday before I was off again, shooting down 11, following a dusty pickup with a rifle hanging upside down in the back window. Everywhere there were signs welcoming hunters, and others rating the potential of forest fires. Today, thankfully, the fire potential was only "moderate."

The road to Brownville was a challenge. Pitted, slanted and twisty, it tried to pitch and buck me like a new colt being broken in and I had to hang on for dear life, cussing the whole way. I stopped at a convenience store for caffeine, standing in line behind a hunter in camouflage gear wearing a *Northwoods Sporting News* cap.

Reaching Milo, I finally made my big turn west, picking up 6/16. I thought it would be appropriate to have some sort of western entertainment to mark the occasion and pulled into the Pleasant River logging camp to pop a CD of a "Gunsmoke" radio production into the van's new player. The recording was one of six road trip-themed CDs a family friend sent me from Burbank, CA. Originally broadcast in 1952, this particular selection was classic, corny old radio featuring tough talkin' U.S. Marshall Matt Dylan, various grizzled louts and forced, amateurishly manufactured sound effects.

Lowes Bridge, a big old covered structure spanning the Piscataquis River, deserved a pause. A young couple that had stopped to enjoy the site, too, had made their way to the opposite bank and were picnicking on a large rock. Farther on, where the road was particularly bad, threatening to shake poor El Rucio apart, a trio of young teens on 4x4s came shooting across the road.

Mid-afternoon, I came upon a shimmering body of water called Kingsbury Pond and decided to take a break and do some fishing, perhaps to catch something worth eating. Standing upon a fortress-like cement platform, below which a grid filtered pond water into a stream behind and below, I tossed my line in. The moment I did, a catfish appeared on the surface of the water. It was so still that I thought it was dead and had floated to the top. But it was indeed alive and looked me right in the face, as if it were sizing up its competition. So there we were, that catfish and me, ready to do battle. He swam below to take up a position and I fired the first shot, executing my finest casts and trying to entice him with a fat nightcrawler. To inspect my weaponry, he sent a scout, a small perch, which I hauled out and tossed back, saying, "Take that, lackey!" More raiders were dispatched and they stole my booty in a sneak attack. Reloading, I made another foray as more soldiers gathered and volleyed. But still my chief foe, that whiskered, black-eyed Darth Vader of the deep, stayed hidden. Even a mallard, which swam over to see what all the commotion was about and helped me spot the lurking submariners, was no help. The duel ended in a draw with the only casualties being the brave nightcrawlers who'd given their lives for the cause.

Skowhegan, which I reached just after 4, tied the knot in the lasso I'd thrown at Maine, and Route 2 was my passage out of the state. I hit it hard, clawing my way back to New Hampshire and its northern treasures. Left behind were the long, lonely stretches of road, the lumbering logging trucks and the secret fishing holes, to be replaced by rolling green hills, the smell of manure and white steepled churches.

As Steinbeck came back through this area, he noted "the foliage of the White Mountains had changed and tattered." Of course, his timetable was a couple of weeks behind mine and snow had already begun to arrive. To me, the landscape was still as brightly accented by fall color as it had been on my earlier breach. He "barreled on across the upraised thumb of New Hampshire," seeking "a bath and a new bed and a drink and a little human commerce," setting his sights on the Connecticut River.

El Rucio and I needed fuel and the Oosoola Exxon and mini mart in Norridgewock called to us. Just outside the store, a woman at a small table offered raffle tickets for a chance to win a hunting rifle — a fundraising effort for the local American Legion Post. Inside, as I stood at the counter waiting my turn to pay, her Highness, the County Teen Queen, rushed through, her sash crossing her bare middle and a tiara perched on top of her head. She was a jeweled, gum-chewing blur who departed as quickly as she'd arrived.

I stayed on for pizza, sitting windowside to watch locals stream in and out. A family of three pulled up in a Pontiac and ordered drinks and a hot dog for their blonde-haired, blue-eyed little girl. Her father, dressed in jeans, with a pack of Marlboro sticking out of one pocket, a white t-shirt and Dale Earnhardt "3" NASCAR cap, walked into an adjoining room to peer at a display of fuel-carrying, miniature die-cast trucks. I joined him and he remarked that he worked on one marked "LIQUID CARBONIC." "You drive it?" "Naw, that's liquid death right there. I just work around it." Meanwhile, his wife, a heavy-set woman in a tank top, had gone back outside to give their Bison-Friche a quick run in the parking lot.

Looking ahead at the map, I thought I'd make a run for Lancaster, NH, where Steinbeck had found his Connecticut River and experienced an eerie overnight at a camp spot. The ride was made more enjoyable by back-to-back, hardcore Johnny Cash ballads on the radio, a tribute following news that the legendary country singer had passed on at age 71.

Just shy of the New Hampshire border, I spied a deer grazing in a large, open field as the late Frank Zappa's "Joe's Garage" emanated from the tune box. I'd seen Zappa perform at the New Haven Coliseum a decade ago where he sang a line I oft quote: "Don't eat the yellow snow; that's where the huskies go." Zappa gave way to the Doors classic "Riders on the Storm," a ghostly song that mirrored my low-key mood and the gray silhouettes of the White Mountains as I returned to New Hampshire. Gorham was lively this pass through and, I imagined, was a real hopper during ski season given all the lodging choices.

Sprinting to Lancaster on the long Route 2 stretch across New Hampshire's cap and encountering the occasional warm, inviting little motel, I felt like I was in another place, a desert road in the Southwest perhaps. The outline of the trees against the blue night sky lent itself to mystery and yet an inviting serenity.

At the bottom of a long descent through the Great North Woods Region was Israel's River, named after early settler Israel Glines, and Lancaster, a town that had a good feel like an old flannel shirt. Like a moth to a flame, I was drawn to the Double SS, a big, wide spread of a bar one flight up. A beefy bar back named tipped me off to a couple places I might try for information about Steinbeck, destinations that would have to be left to the morning.

Tonight was Open Mike Night and a spunky brunette had assumed the stage. She strutted around while belting out a string of country tunes. As we all listened, a couple carrying an amp, guitar case and gym bag joined the scene. A crazy line dance tune came on and she and three friends jumped to their feet to participate. They were all celebrating the impending marriage of one of the girls in the group, whose ceremony was scheduled for 6 p.m. tomorrow. I mentioned to them why I was in town and received a half-serious invite to crash the party.

Following a round of pool and a beer, I moved on, thinking to find another watering hole, perhaps in Whitefield. But I had grown tired from the day's travels, so promptly located Roger's Family Camping Resort and Motel on the east side of Israel's river. The lights of the main office were out so I just drove in, located a spot and prepped for bed.

Day 8: A Clue Hunt in Lancaster

I arose at just after six and walked up a short length of paved road to a bathroom, upon which a simple note, "Friday Night, Candy Bar and Bingo, 8:30 p.m.," had been tacked. The shower stalls were tiled and looked moderately clean so I gave one a whirl, hoping for the best. In the camp's effort to conserve water, however, it had restricted flow so much that it barely dripped from the showerhead. Just to get a washcloth wet was a challenge. I lingered only as long as I had to, then returned to El Rucio.

The sun was up over the treeline by then and the mist that had hung in the river valley below had burned off. Songbirds twittered and I laid my damp towel on a picnic tabletop to dry, brushing aside acorn shell bits left by a feasting squirrel. From my spot, the view of the Presidential Range, with peaks named Madison, Adams, Jefferson and Washington — the latter the tallest and highest mountain in the Northeast — was impressive.

On the far side of town, along the Connecticut River, Steinbeck had found "a row of neat little white houses on the green meadow" and a "small, compactly housed office and lunchroom." In a letter to Elaine, he wrote that it was four in the afternoon (early for him) when he arrived and, though the cabin operator advertised vacancies, no one ever appeared to assist him. He thought about taking a numbered cabin key from a pegboard in the office and just showing himself to one, but resisted. For dinner, he had planned to make his "famous Spanish rice" but, instead, had lima beans, walked Charley, "read a little Robert Graves" and hit the sack. The oddness of the situation troubled him and made for a restless night spent in his camper. The following morning, still with no sighting, he made a long breakfast, eyed the river and went and attended services at a "John Knox church" across the river in Vermont, catching a riveting sermon delivered by a minister with "tool-steel eyes and a delivery like a pneumatic drill."

Determined to locate the place at which Steinbeck had stopped and perhaps the church as well, I directed my first inquiry to the proprietor of the camp, with whom I went to settle up. She suspected that I might be referring to the "Country Kettle" on the Vermont side of the river, though I was fairly sure the cabins were in New Hampshire. I thanked her and descended back down into Lancaster.

My next stop was the Great North Woods Welcome Center where a volunteer there guessed that the site might be Munce Truck Stop, where she thought there had once been white cabins. To confirm her suspicion, she put me on the phone with a longtime local resident, who ventured the same and added that a minister, the late John Cornelius, had owned them. A second call to the local historical society had a matching result.

The editor of the local *Lancaster Herald* later discovered that Cornelius and his wife Margaret had, in fact, sold the cabins and campground, named Whip 'O Will, to Fred and Velma Treffrey on November 12, 1959, so the latter were actually the owners when Steinbeck went through. Sadly, 93-year-old Velma just passed.

Though aimed for the Truck Stop, I couldn't pass up a small crafts and food fair on the way out of town. There, I bought a brick of Farmstead Cheese, eliciting a goat call from a passing postman, though this cheese was made from cow's milk. I picked up some chocolate nut bread, spicy herb mustard and blueberry lime jelly, all of which were made with produce grown in the seller's garden. I also bought bread & butter pickles, so named because farmers would enjoy them as a side on a slice of bread with butter. To provide warmth on the cool autumn nights to come, I negotiated a wool blanket buy with an émigré from Koburg, Germany, then spoke with a woman selling magnets depicting local wildlife.

Overhearing me tell of my travels, an elder couple who owned a farm in nearby Jefferson took a look at El Rucio, comparing it to their Dodge RAM Horizon camper.

Finally, just out of town, I came to the famous truck stop and guessed that it had to be Steinbeck's resting place. There was the idyllic river and the steel bridge he referred to but, of course, the cabins were gone, replaced by a convenience store, gas pumps and a 56-site campground. At the river's edge, I stood awhile contemplating the scene then went and spoke with a young, pleasant cashier who said that there were plans, actually, to re-incorporate cabins into the truck stop site.

A truck driver who hauls paper and groceries tapped into our conversation and offered to lead me by car to a couple who might know more. He said their house was "right up on the hill here," which I took to mean up behind the truck stop. But we ended up going back through Lancaster town center and along 3 South a couple of miles to an old white house on a hill.

These kindly folks welcomed me in and, though they didn't know me from Adam, offered me a fresh-baked cookie. We sat in their cozy living room and I tested their recall about the cabins and suspected owner. "If he had had a pair of horses or a cow, I might have known him better," said the gentleman, who was pushing 90, as the couple's 150-acre property had included an active dairy farm with, at one time, 100 milking cows. As their gray and white cat lazed and yawned in the big chair beside me, I commented on how lovely their hilltop home was and that I wasn't surprised they'd been here all their lives. To that, the woman offered, "They're going to take me outta here feet first." She noted they spent their days watching visiting wildlife: wild turkeys, foxes, moose, bears and "coy dogs." As we concluded our conversation and I rose to leave, I received another cookie as a parting gesture.

Back at the truck stop, I bought ice and then connected with the owner of a local trucking business. He recalled eating clams at the lunch counter when the Rev. Cornelius owned it and said he went to school with one of the minister's sons, David.

I mounted the steel bridge — known as Rogers Rangers Bridge after Maj. Robert Rogers who fought in the French and Indian War — and expected to hear steel plates clank under my tires, like they had clattered when Steinbeck crossed. But those had long since been paved. And there I was in Vermont, rolling in as Steinbeck had.

A first pause was a "collectables" business, where the elderly owners were seated on the porch. With a big round cat nestled in an old baby carriage beside them and a black Lab plush toy they called "Hey You" propped on a chair by the entry door, they watched traffic, and life, go by. They didn't know about Steinbeck's visit but did share that the cabins were knocked down to make way for the White Mountain Zoo. The latter was driven out by townspeople who protested the keepers feeding live cows to the tigers that were kept there.

At a later date, the *Lancaster Herald* editor confirmed the zoo era and added that a Rev. Clinton White, a radio evangelist, had later used the site for sermons. On a hilltop overlooking Lancaster, in fact, White built a cathedral, using timbers from an old railroad roundhouse in Island Pond, Vermont. He also initiated a theme park called Bible Land, where he was going to bring in animals two by two, but there was a flood at the site, which nix'ed the plan.

Coincidentally, the editor's daughter, a young graduate of the University of New Hampshire, had embarked on a cross-country journey with a girlfriend around the same time I had. She had headed in the opposite direction, though, going south along the coast and down Alabama way, where the two attended a University of Alabama football game. He gave me her cell number in hopes that we might connect on the road.

I never did see the church at which Steinbeck had stopped and moved along to St. Johnsbury, billed as a place "where rivers and people come together." An antiques shop there had a fine assortment of literary works. I purchased a few volumes including Steinbeck's "The Winter of Our Discontent," which he'd completed just prior to his U.S. tour. Noting my interest in two other volumes, the owners threw in on the house Charles Dudley Warner's "In the Wilderness" and Quincy Adams Sawyer's "A Story of New England Home Life." A shop dog named Ruby, named after the Beatles' song "Ruby Tuesday", looked after me as I moved along.

Crossing signs for everything from ducks and snowmobiles to moose and trains marked Route 15, my path to the northwest corner of Vermont. In Hardwick, I paused to satiate a thirsty El Rucio and, as I operated the pump, looked over at an old auto showroom called TUCKER CARS. In the window was a red Chevy BelAir convertible, circa 1955, with cat paw prints in dust covering the hood. The site made me think that some cataclysmic event had happened, freezing the place, and the whole town for that matter, in time.

Wolcott was a remarkable pass-through as seven of the ten buildings that comprise the town were painted dark brown with a yellow and red stripe across their middles, and a BUCK'S designation: Buck's Furniture, Buck's Antiques, Buck's Used Furniture. Evidently, Buck was a big wheel around here.

Morrisville brought a distinct smell of skunk, an odor I was used to given the frequency of the visits of these black and white foragers in my own area. In the parking lot of an Ames department store there that had gone bust, a couple was selling apples. Stopping to inspect their produce, I mused with them about the warm weather. "I'll bet you wish it could continue," I said. "No, snow's good for the economy," came the reply. I bought a three pound bag of the McIntosh variety, shined one on the leg of my jeans and munched it as I continued on.

Near Fairfax, a huge red barn advertised BOOKS, FURNITURE, COLLECTIBLES and CLOTHING on its side. While picking out a kids' sand sifter to adapt as a colander, small electric heater to plug in at campsites and Bill Morrissey's book "Edson," I caught snippets of conversation from other browsers. One complained about a chipmunk that was eating sunflower seeds she had put in a feeder and intended for birds. Though she'd greased the feeder's pole with butter, the striped rodent was still conducting successful raids. Another couple wowed over a large stuffed bear, planning to give it to their pet, which the woman described as "that stupid dog." She urged her husband, "Git it. It'll freak 'im out bein' bigger than he is."

As I mounted El Rucio to rejoin 104 North, a property owner walking across the lot from the main house to the barn handed me a fresh-picked tomato. It was so juicy that, when I bit into it, seeds and pulp dribbled down my chin. An old, rather well abused GMC truck complete with a cabin on the back, like Steinbeck's, sat by the exit wearing a "FREE" sign on its windshield.

Having now seen a gaggle of Vermonters and, more specifically, their assorted, unregimented attire, I thought about an article that *Times* contributor Valerie Frankel had drafted after an informal study of Vermont style. Folks she polled offered descriptors like "unpretentious," "unadorned," "understated" and "unaffiliated." Labels, she concluded, had no place here. What was important was authenticity, being a native. As Edward Koren, a Brookfield native put it to Frankel, "Who is and who isn't a native is the great divide."

Approaching Interstate 89 North, there was a distinct farm smell that never failed to remind me of an elementary school class trip to upstate

New York's Catskill Game Farm in the Adirondacks, by which I'd soon be skating.

On a high flat of land near the Swanton exit, I could see for several miles in any direction, giving me a conquering, top-of-the-world feeling that buoyed me to Swanton Center. There, goods for sale on a town green included books with western themes and a video of British comedy, additions to my growing on-board media library.

Lake Champlain, from my approach, was not the impressive body of water I thought it would be and I passed quickly over it, stopping at a service station to clean off all front-facing surfaces of the van and the extensive bug mural that had again accumulated.

As Steinbeck provided no detail about his travels between Rouses Point and Niagara Falls except to note that it "rained cold and pitiless" and that he was going to hug Lake Ontario, I decided to get creative with my route. This included attempting another crossing into "Maple Leaf Land".

Looking our best, El Rucio and I pulled up to the Canadian border crossing and had the most congenial of chats with the guard who was only permitted to identify himself by his badge number. He even brought me a lovely color map and guided me with detailed directions to Saint-Jean-sur-Richelieu, or St. John's. "Merci et bon nuit," I said and crossed in, finding the route rural and lined with cornfields and wooded areas. It was an altogether more enjoyable crossing than the ones to Edmunston or New Brunswick had been.

Following 223 North, I sighted three hot air balloons, then a single-engine plane towing a glider, in the distance beyond some silos. As the sun dropped from the clouds and lit up the horizon, I noticed four young boys, each sporting hockey jerseys, bouncing on a trampoline in the front yard of a roadside property.

Soon enough, I was in festive Saint-Jean and found it hopping with busy bistros, people strolling and, curiously, the main drag, Richelieu, lined with stacks of tires. Apparently, there had been a car race held in the streets here earlier in the day. A sponsor tent was filled with leftover revelers and I fell in with them, enjoying "poppers" and a new beer called Bowes and, coincidentally, eating Frito-Lay chips.

Mid-evening, I crossed back to the U.S., picked up VT 78 to take me over Lake Champlain and sailed by a "Welcome to New York, the Empire State" sign, marking another border crossing.

I was a high-speed express train on a track to parts unknown, blowing down the highway, slicing through the tar black night. Getting weary on this maniacal push, I pulled up at a town called Chateaugay where a bar on the main drag was rocking and rolling. People were sitting outside on a landing, a band was firing things up inside and I was being drawn in by the revelry. A round of "Genny" Light and some conversation with locals made me feel human again, though when a drunken patron went down with a thud, whacking the back of his head on cement, I figured it was time to go.

For the life of me, I couldn't get the interior lights of the van to shut off. This, of course, attracted the attention of a patrolman who followed me for a spell, testing my driving skills. I passed, he turned off and I dashed to a service station to see if I couldn't resolve the interior light dilemma. With much feeling of embarrassment, I asked the clerk for help, who looked no more qualified than I to analyze the situation. But didn't he just turn my light switch a notch and it solved the problem?

I slunk away and continued on, only to be pulled over by the Rooseveltown Police. It was, after all, 2:30 a.m. by this time as I was making my insane dash for Massena. Doing 59 in a 35 was the offense, but the officers were understanding enough to give me a get-out-of-jail free card.

The Massena International Campground became my endpoint and, thinking on my feet, I decided to use the washroom first before finding a spot. It was immaculate and even had music piped in overhead. As I brushed my teeth, I sang along to a Blondie tune, "That man from Mars has stopped eating cars, now he only eats guitars." As unobtrusively as possible, I crept to an open space using only my parking lights as a guide, though El Rucio's engine lowly growled. With a relieved sigh, I curled up in my cocoon and dropped off.

Day 9: A Family Reunion in Syracuse

Working on only four hours of sleep, I rose, surveyed the flat, hedge-lined, rectangular campground and hatched my day plan. I would shower quickly, eat some leftovers down the road and continue my drive southwest, with a goal of being in Syracuse by mid to late afternoon to meet up with my folks, who were attending my dad's 52nd high school reunion there.

I made three discoveries upon reaching the washroom: 1) I'd used the Ladies Room last night. 2) There was no shower. 3) The campground is on a river (the Raquette, which flows out of the greater St. Lawrence River, which skirts part of the top of New York State and, in turn, joins Lake Ontario). I stood at the sink and washcloth bathed, spraying an extra dash of cologne in critical areas, while crooning to a piped-in tune, "Give me the beat boys and free my soul, I wanna get lost in your rock 'n roll and drift away…"

SeaWay bowling alley and the Massena Arena advertising "Shinny Hockey" marked the main drag going west. Stewart's, a chain store where we would buy milk and ice cream when I was a boy growing up in Schenectady, came up on the left. The Grasse River, its surface perfectly still, reflected a cloud-tinged early morning sky and trees along its banks.

I had traveled 2,000 miles to this point, met some amazing, hearty souls and seen many unique sites, and remained excited to see what lay around the next corner.

Past Louisville, three-dozen black-and-white cows grazed in a pasture. A yellow tractor, with a small American flag attached to the rear of the seat, sat in a clump of tall grass. Cylindrical bales of hay sat like breakfast rolls in a bright green field.

South of Morristown near the Jacques Cartier State Park, I pulled to the roadside to have a cup of juice and eat a tub of leftover scrambled eggs. A squirrel at the top of an evergreen dashed from limb to limb readying its nest for the colder weather to come.

The coastal route provided a scenic overlook where, in the shade of a tree near a bramble of thistle, I gazed out over the wide expanse of the St. Lawrence at the far shore of Brockville, Canada, in the province of Ontario. Further down river, a blindingly white lighthouse and red, clapboard keeper's dwelling stood on a small island in the channel. Norah

Jones' drifting, lazy, mellow tune "Don't Know Why" played on the radio, fitting my mood perfectly.

In the Alexandria Bay area, the inlets lining the road were filled with tall, even sea grasses. As ever, I wanted to pull off and fish, like one shirtless guy sitting atop a bucket was doing.

Suddenly, I had a dilemma: Jump on the interstate for the quick ride to Syracuse or continue on the scenic shore route and make a later arrival. I decided to split the difference and take the shore road to Cape Vincent, then, back in Brownville, catch the highway. To my amazement, I had a cell signal again so radioed mom and dad and checked in at home.

The 1,000 Island Bait Store offered a fishing license for $15 and its proprietor advised me on bait. "They've been catchin' 'em with nightcrawlers," he said then guided me on the type of fish I could expect to catch — Bass, Pike, Pickerel and Musky.

Inns and motels on the route down were numerous and all bore mariner-related names: Clipper, Sand Bay, Millens Bay, Buccaneer, Island Shadows, Willow Shores, Featherbed Shoals.

Remembering I needed a net to haul in a larger catch should I get one, I called in at Clayton's Bait Shop. The young counterman, who was wearing a Syracuse Orangemen tee, helped me to a low-cost aluminum number that would do the trick.

The air near the cape smelled wholesome, a blend of manure and lake, and a manufactured jetty of rock and concrete seemed the perfect place to sit and drop a line. The sun felt hot at my back but the breeze was cooling. After several casts and some interest, I got a hit and pulled in a 5" smallmouth bass. He swallowed the hook deep and it took a little maneuvering to remove. I dropped him back in, he got his bearings and returned to the depths. My next cast hooked a cousin, just slightly larger than the first. Another, equal in size, got on the next drop. Overhead, seagulls coasted on air currents while powerboats skipped across the lake.

Two men and a gangly young girl joined me down the way, baited up and dropped. The girl caught a small bass on her first cast. It expired as the men struggled to get the hook out and they laid it on its side on the concrete.

From the blue-green water, now rippling more feverishly as the wind kicked up, I pulled #4, again, of equal size, and returned him unscathed to his family. One of the guys down the way snagged a decent-sized largemouth that had fillet potential. I hoped he had a big brother lurking below me.

Two more snags and I was ready to make the dip down to Syracuse. Collecting up my gear, I had a quick gab with a couple from Watertown, who mentioned that their last name is French and that he has roots in Grand River, Canada, where "just about everyone's named Bourque."

Near Rosiere, a sign drew my attention to the Pleasant Valley Buffalo Ranch and Sundry. It seemed too compelling to pass up. Paula Bourquin, sporting a sunny yellow polo and a personality to match, greeted me at the Sundry and guided me to frozen buffalo patties and sausage, as well as dried buffalo jerky. Lower in bad fats than either beef or chicken, the meat had appeal to me given a history of high cholesterol in our family.

Up and around the corner was the actual buffalo farm with some 250 head of the wooly beasts (the largest herd in the state), grazing on hay and swatting flies with their tails. There, Paula's husband, Chuck, awaited me. He was feeding the herd chopped corn from a silo and remarked that they eat a half a ton a day. An impressive figure to be sure but he said the same number of cows eats three times that. He had been inspired to own buffalo after attending a convention in Georgia hosted by Ted Turner, who announced at a pinnacle moment, "I'm done being a bullshitter. I'm going to be a bullraiser."

Chuck talked about some of the challenges. "A wild, big bull will stand there and give you those beady eyes, then take you right out." In fact, the first time he tried to take one of the bulls to be slaughtered, the animal put a two-inch gash in a tractor tire that cost several hundred dollars to repair.

I was behind schedule and dropped the pedal again to zoom toward Syracuse. My windshield wipers decided to go haywire and refused to be turned off, much like the interior lights the previous night. I kept moistening the windshield to keep the wiper blades from sticking and burning out the motor. Picture it: Blowing down 81, wipers going, spray going, and me probing and fiddling with buttons on the dash.

When Oneida Lake came up, I felt like ripping the blades off and throwing them in the water. But, then, as suddenly as the mad wiper episode began, it ended. Perhaps I'd passed through a strange, electromagnetic Bermuda Triangle. And maybe I was just lucky to have emerged alive.

From 81, I hopped to 481, following a purple, restored and souped-up 1932 Ford Coupe with the inscription "Johnny B. Goode" on the back. This led to Route 5 and the Craftsman Inn.

There was Dad on one of the porches and Mom, who had been worrying about me for the past couple of hours, rushing out to meet me. We exchanged hellos, they inspected the van and then we powwowed in their room.

It was decided we'd have dinner at Weber's (one of my grandparents' favorite haunts) then, in the morning, I'd grab a log of great German bologna from Liehs & Steigerwald. With a little ketchup on it, the latter was always a treat on visits to East Syracuse, where my dad lived as a boy. As to overnight accommodations, staff threw open the doors for me with a room for the night. Glad to have a real bed and shower and space to move around in after living in the van for seven of the past eight days, I could also keep an eye on poor El Rucio, who would have to stay out in the cold by herself tonight.

The shower was everything hoped for and I used all of the free toiletries set out on the sink counter. On the way to dinner, we toured the area and spoke of Dad's reunion of fifty-five surviving students of Eastwood High School's Class of 1953. Eight of these, including Dad, were the tightest of buddies and all showed.

His alma mater, Eastwood High, had been converted to the Charles F. Todd Eastwood Heights Retirement Home. On a pathway in front, a white-haired woman in a wheelchair stared off into the distance. His elementary school, Arria S. Huntington, and Sunnycrest Park, led us to his boyhood home, behind which stood a towering pine that his sister had planted as a seedling.

The pharmacy where he first worked as a soda jerk was now occupied by a furniture store. His boss Ephraim Bodow's son ended up running WQXR radio, "The radio station of the New York Times." Around the corner, a "very German" cemetery came up, a site that many of his classmates visited on the second day of the reunion.

We found Liehs & Steigerwald, "A family tradition since 1936", on Grant Boulevard, though it was closed for the day. When my grandfather, known as "Fred", first moved the family to the area from Albany in 1944, his mother Lena walked into the place, inspected their sausage making process and gave her ok for the family to shop there.

Dad pointed out a plant with a big smokestack, labeled Crouse-Hinds, in nearby Salina (pronounced Sah-line-uh) and said it was where all the traffic lights in the world are made. Heid's was a classic old drive-in that served "coneys" (white hot dogs) and Onondaga Lake was where the boys would lure the girls to neck on the pretense that they were to watch "nighttime submarine races."

Ultimately, we pulled up to Weber's Restaurant & Haus of Reubens at the corner of Danforth and First North. It was your down-to-earth, no frills place with green vinyl tablecloths and steel-frame chairs with green backs and seats. On a narrow shelf around the top of the wall, there were plates depicting scenes from the old country and beer steins. Below these, beer trays, featuring brands like Moore & Quinn's Diamond Ale, Old Milwaukee and Huberle's Congress Lager, hung.

A round of Franziskaner Weiss bier that came in 20-ounce glasses, enjoyed with pumpernickel bread topped with Otto's hot 'n spicy Bavarian mustard, whet our whistle. While I told my folks of my travels to date, more beer and our entrees arrived — fat, white knackwurst, sauerkraut and warm German potato salad "like grandma used to make," Dad noted.

Over the feast, we exchanged Canadian border crossing stories and it came up that my grandfather and Uncle Jack, tile setters during the Prohibition Era, got the contract to tile the customs offices. The tile boxes would go up full of tile, but return full of Scotch!

After Weber's, we took a drive around the North side, seeing the stadium that used to be home to the Triple A International League baseball team, the Syracuse Chiefs. They had been renamed the Syracuse Sky Chiefs so as not to offend the local Indian population.

I saw the Muench-Kreuzer Candle Company, commonly referred to as "Munch Krunch", a world-famous operation that supplies the Vatican. We passed the Bada Bing go-go joint and the large brick home of the old Porter Tool Company, with a little red house on top containing its elevator machinery. The CNY Regional Market, once the City Market, a retail and wholesale produce warehouse, came up on the right. Then back along the shore of Onondaga Lake we went, past an old French fort and Griffiths Stadium where the Catholics played six-man football.

We returned to neon-lit Heid's, beside which was Sweet Treats, an ice cream purveyor. The girl inside, with "eyes like Natalie Wood," Mom thought, and wearing a "Stood in Line At Heid's" t-shirt, served me mint chocolate chip ice cream in a sugar cone. We ate at an outdoor table then returned to the inn where I passed out on the king-sized, quilt-covered bed.

Day 10: Indians & Racecar Drivers

My night's sleep was sound but short as I woke in the middle of the night to work on sorting through some paperwork. My parents, who had an early morning flight back to their home in North Carolina, had already left. In just my "gutchies," I sat at a bedside table in a chair padded with pillows, with the curtains to the outside drawn tight to prevent distraction, composing and editing my notes to date. I sought to keep on top of capturing and regurgitating everything I'd seen and done in a timely fashion.

Outside, a gray day with rain in the forecast was evolving, the same weather Steinbeck had experienced when he pushed through. Following a shower, I read a copy of the local paper, Fayetteville's *The Post-Standard,* which had been deposited outside my room. It spoke of a man who'd bought the exclusive development rights to build waterfront housing along the entire length of the state canal system. In local news, an Elbridge girl proudly displayed the 21-pound, 40-inch long Musky she had caught in Otisco Lake. Local papers like this one had provided me with a great barometer for the mood and character of an area and I looked forward to seeing more like them.

Two ladies from housekeeping paid me a visit, asking if I wanted service. But seeing how I'd spread myself out across the room, they decided to come back after I'd checked out.

Dad called from the local airport. They'd missed their early flight and were delayed getting out on a later flight due to runway construction in Newark that was backing up air traffic. He mentioned that the Craftsman had a wonderful free buffet, so I wandered to the lobby. There, I met a cleaning person from the local Onondaga tribe. A brown-eyed brunette with a kind, radiant face, she moved off the reservation "to try something new." She said the reservation is still run according to tribal customs, with elders and faith keepers, but that they are no longer self-contained. For food shopping and other supplies, they travel to nearby Nedow. When I inquired about touring the reservation, she said that I could just drive right in and speak with anyone. This was not the case when my dad was growing up here, when the state police guarded the entrances to keep locals from harassing the tribe.

For now, I enjoyed my breakfast, consisting of a cup of coffee, orange juice, toasted raisin bagel and blueberry muffin, eaten at a small table in the dining nook. The lobby itself was warmly decorated like a mountain lodge, with oversized wood and leather furniture. On one wall near a sofa was a framed print of an 1852 painting of an English foxhunt by J.F. Herring that bore the quote, "Delightful Scene! Where all around is gay, Men, Horses, Dogs, And in each smiling Countenance appears Fresh blooming Health and universal Joy." Another painting, by "J. Mather", showed a turn-of-the-century country lane in autumn. Above a gas fireplace, a plaque was inscribed, "The lyf so short, the craft so long to lerne." On another wall, small artworks done in the giclee (pronounced "jee-clay") style, a digital print process, showed flowers, forest scenes and the front of a red tractor amid tall weeds. A pot-bellied maintenance man crossed my path to wind the mechanism of a grandfather clock housed in a veneer cabinet.

I thought to call my namesake, Mike Lauterborn, in Rochester, the owner of Lauterborn Electric and a racecar driver, to set up dinner. Then I reunited with El Rucio and off we went, headed to the reservation. Route 481 South yielded to 81 South which led me to the Onondaga Nation Territory. At a cigarette retailer, the counterman guided me to an access point and introduced me to one of the chiefs, a short man with black hair tied back in a ponytail, who happened to be standing by the counter. He didn't have time to speak with me but said I could drive through.

My first glimpse of the reservation was of modest, trailer size houses, in front of which residents milled. I pulled up to the Powless Craft Shop and introduced myself to the owner. Her shop featured many handcrafted items, including bolos, necklaces and leather bracelets, all made by her six daughters, son and others in the community. A large majority of these featured animal emblems carved from deer bone. She explained that the animals — turtle, deer, eel, bear, wolf, beaver — represent the different clans in the tribe, each of which claims a common maternal link. She was a bear, so her children are all bears. It is forbidden to marry within your clan, she explained, as this would be incest. Marriage outside the tribe was also discouraged in order to keep labor, commerce and tradition strong and intact. However, many of the younger people, she said, had been leaving the tribe for greater outside opportunities.

One of her daughters, in fact, moved from the Onondaga reservation to Canada, but to an Oneida reservation there. The Oneida and Onondaga are part of a Six Nations Confederacy (called the Haudenosaunee) along with the Mohawk, Tuscarora, Cayuga and Seneca, and all share a common language, Iroquois.

Thinking that I needed a mascot to watch over me and be my road guide, I bought a necklace with a wolf pendant made of bone. As I was paying, a very tall, blue-eyed blonde, who looked Irish except for her high cheekbones and straight nose, entered the shop. A Pawnee, she had relocated nearby from Texas so that her husband could pursue environmental science and forestry studies at a local college.

Jokingly, she explained that, "The Pawnee were the bad guys in 'Dances with Wolves'" and were centered in Oklahoma. She said she was from the wolf clan and her Indian name means "white bird" as she had the palest complexion in her family. She was interested in the beadwork at Powless, but also wanted to know more about the Onondaga nation and culture. We wandered up the road together to an information center, noticing EMTs pulling up at a nearby house to attend to a young man who'd had a diabetic attack. Kristen said that many Indians have diabetes, a result of the gradual transition to a richer American diet.

At the Center, a pair of language teachers were developing a teacher curriculum for Onondaga language instruction. To date, the language had been unwritten, so they were creating standards to represent oral words.

The communications liaison for the tribe's council of 14 chiefs (each of whom represent a clan) joined us to share information about the size, scope and customs of the Onondaga nation. We learned that the tribe was 1,500 members strong, that residents receive free health care through a federally funded health center on the reservation and that clan mothers select the chiefs, who are chosen for their honesty, the respect they command and show, leadership ability and language.

The liaison taught us a phrase, "Nya wenha Skannon" (pronounced Nya-way-ha Skan-noo) which means, "I'm thankful for the light within you." It was both their greeting and way of saying farewell. "Skannon" alone means "peace."

She shared a booklet, too, titled, "Neighbor to Neighbor, Nation to Nation," which gave us additional information about the Onondaga. For instance, "Onondaga" is really an Americanization of the original tribe name, "Onundagaono", meaning "The People of the Hills." "Haudenosaunee" means "People of the Long House", which refers to how people were meant to live together as families in the same house. One of the original pacts between the Nations and colonists was called the Two Row Wampum that essentially declared that the two groups would co-exist as brothers, but govern themselves independent of one another. The Nations, for instance, heed what they call the Great Law of Peace, which defines the functions of their Grand Council and how disputes can be resolved to maintain tranquility.

I was particularly interested in an official communiqué the liaison had written in response to 9/11. She noted that on the morning of the attacks, the tribe gathered at their Longhouse to support one another and lift each other's spirits. She observed that, "In the midst of all the sorrow and fear, families were drawn closer together, people were forced to take time out." Things like money, materialism and malls were suddenly unimportant and "bird life regained the skies as airlines shut down." Overall, the Nations sympathized with the families of the innocent victims of the tragedy and extended their prayers for peace.

My visit to the Onondaga Nation took much longer than I'd planned but was highly fascinating, as I had not experienced Native American culture to such a degree before. Because of the great passage of time, I headed straight for the New York State Thruway going west, the quickest route to Rochester. El Rucio bucked and jumped like a new colt eager to get going, my new wolf pendant suspended and swinging back and forth from the rearview mirror. I reasoned that a wolf is part of the canine family and thereby related to Charley, so named my pendant wolf Charley Skannon or Charley Peace. Though it rained some in the morning, it had been clear and sunnier since, and I savored the flatlands between Syracuse and Rochester.

Along the way, I hit my first tolls since leaving home nine days before. For these occasions, I had reactivated an EZ Pass tag and affixed it to my windshield. As I sailed through the first gate, I said a little prayer, hoping the issuers had gotten my account straight and it would work. With great relief, it did, flashing "EZ Pass GO." I wondered if the technology, had it been available, would have interested Steinbeck or if he would have preferred to pass change to a live person, in hopes of catching a snippet of conversation.

The fine weather, unfortunately, gave way to a storm that had rolled in off Lake Ontario and settled on Rochester, turning the sky a charcoal grey. The drops came down big and hard slowing up rush hour traffic that had just begun. I was almost spitting distance from Lauterborn Electric and owner Mike was waiting on me.

A couple of times before reaching Mike's exit, I passed over the Erie Canal, a marvel of engineering that had a great impact on the state. To gain easier, faster access to the land and resources west of the Appalachians, New York Governor DeWitt Clinton, in 1817, convinced the State legislature to put up $7 million for the construction of a canal 363 miles long that was 40 feet wide and four feet deep. It would run from Buffalo on the eastern shore of Lake Erie to Albany on the upper Hudson River. Initially, it was known as "Clinton's Folly" but in the years following its completion in 1825, it quickly proved its worth. Eighty percent of upstate New York's population have settled within 25 miles of the Canal.

Dressed in jeans and an orange company t-shirt, Mike met me at his workplace. I immediately noticed that he had an amazing facial resemblance to my grandfather as a young man. I followed him up to his office where we took a seat and he showed me a photo of his dad. A general woodworker mostly, he resided in Florida. Mike's office was filled with some of his dad's wood creations, including a toy truck, miniature horse and his desk.

Mike told me about a cross-country trip he and a buddy had taken in the summer of 1972 after completing their electrical contractor apprenticeships. It was three months long and passed through Denver, the Rockies, Las Vegas, San Diego, Tijuana and San Francisco. They made the long stretches in a Chevy van and used Mike's Triumph chopper, "a basket case motorcycle," for day jaunts.

I thought Marlene would find it amusing to speak with two Mike Lauterborns, so we dialed her up to say hello. Then we hatched a plan to have dinner, an authentic German meal at a joint called Rohrbach Brewing Company in Ogden. Mike lead the way in his big red line truck, used for installing telephone poles.

At dinner, Mike talked about Rochester and it being the HQ of Bausch & Lomb, Xerox and Kodak. I also knew that the city had hosted the 85th Annual PGA Championship back in August. Shaun Micheel made an incredible shot on the 18th hole to capture the coveted prize, the Wanamaker Trophy, the first tournament win of Micheel's career. In fact, he became only the seventh player in PGA history to win a major before winning any other tournament.

Mike and I spoke of his racing experiences, which took him to different towns and states every weekend, up to 20 weekends out of a year, sometimes two races a weekend. When *not* racing, he attended races or sponsored another driver. He also maintained the lighting at some of the local racetracks. Back in 1993, in fact, at a race at the Can-Am track in Thousand Islands, the lights on the backstretch went as Mike's car was about to go out. He got out of his car, grabbed his tools from his truck, shimmied up a pole and fixed the system. To this day, he's remembered for his take-charge action at that event.

Our Rohrbach's meal choice was "Just East of Buffalo Style Wings", billed as the BEST WINGS IN ROCHESTER, prepared "kind, agonizing or somewhere in between," with celery and blue cheese dressing on the side. We went the medium route, still hot enough to paralyze the tip of my tongue, while glancing at weather reports on a nearby TV showing the approach of Hurricane Isabel, a threatening Category 5 rushing toward the east coast.

Our wings were followed by the State St. Schnitzel — tender pork loin fillets lightly seasoned, breaded and griddle fried golden brown, served with sauerkraut and German potato salad.

We spoke about why Mike never got married. "Women take the lumberjack out of the man," he reasoned. And why he didn't have kids: "Don't want no ties to nothing."

Mike picked up the tab and led me to his apartment/warehouse where his two race cars and other equipment were kept. In short order, Mike's longtime friend, "Joe", joined us. Joe was a drag racer and recalled a notable regional racer, Shirley "Cha Cha" Muldowney, the first female drag racer. She had kept her car at a BP station on State Street in Schenectady, just around the corner from my elementary school. Joe remembered seeing her in 1966 at the Indianapolis Raceway Park summer nationals and joked, "She was having a hell of a time getting her shoulder harness around her tits."

Ham radios became a topic when Joe and I discovered that my grandfather and his dad had both been operators and enthusiasts. In fact, they had built their own first radios out of Quaker Oats boxes when they were kids.

Joe told me, too, about his own big cross-country trip in Summer 1963 after graduating from a heavy equipment school in Idaho. He decided to pursue a job in Alaska that would start on a particular day and if he didn't make that date, the job would go to someone else. In his '55 Chevy pickup, he started driving the Al-Can Highway. He had been driving for two days when he hit a rock that had been dislodged in a landslide, broke his front axle and was essentially stranded. A flatbed truck picked him up and carried him and his truck to Seattle. He got a new front axle put in but, by that time, had missed the Alaska job opportunity. With no other plan in the works, he decided to just start driving, getting around by working in gas stations, as a short-order cook, operating heavy machinery — "anything and everything." As we spoke, a Conrail train out of New York headed west blasted its horn as it passed nearby.

Mike's office décor was amusing, including a photo of Ms. Dirt (an acronym for Driver Independent Race Tracks) Motorsports, Jana Holmes, clad in a teeny red bikini and identified as "Parts Peddler of the Year". Another photo showed the van Mike drove cross-country, labeled "1972." Elsewhere, there were motocross shots and a 1993 Kodak Film Racing Team photo.

The garage was once a two-level chicken coop Mike converted, with an upstairs office that contained more colorful wall ornaments, like the following sign: "WANTED Good Woman. Must Be Able to Clean, Cook, Sew, Dig Worms and Clean Fish. Must Have Boat and Motor. Please Send Picture of Boat and Motor." This just about illustrated Mike's philosophy to a "T."

As he had some car maintenance to do to get ready for an upcoming race, I darted to a bar in North Chili (pronounced Chai – lie) to catch some Monday Night Football. The place had a sports theme with framed sketches of sports heroes on all the walls. This night, the Giants were facing the Cowboys at Giants Stadium, and though New York had a home field advantage, they were getting beaten and soaked by rain.

Half a dozen people sat at the bar, including a brunette with smoke blue eyes and a tongue piercing. She told me about working as an alcohol abuse counselor and raising a daughter whom she had at 17. There was a group of firemen there, too, drinking Labatt's ("Blues") and watching an episode of "Choppers," a reality TV show revolving around a family that custom builds bikes in nearby Orange County.

Talk around the bar was of a 150-unit apartment complex planned for a large field nearby. It would replace a water tower that had been a hangout for high schoolers who would allegedly go there to "smoke pot and drink and occasionally set a couch on fire." The fear was that they would have nowhere else to go to fraternize. Perhaps, I thought, that was a good thing given their choice of activities.

The often off-color banter and beers were welcome on this drizzly night. I trundled back to Mike's after midnight, crawled in my van parked next to Mike's utility truck and was out like a tranquilized bear, stuffed with beer and German food.

Day 11: The Home of Wings

At 4:20 a.m., the blare of a horn and thunderous sound of a diesel train, one Mike had told me to expect, stirred me from my slumber in Mike's driveway. It had stopped raining at this point and the chirp of crickets filled the air.

As I'd been so busy with travel-oriented tasks, I finally set up my cell phone's voicemail and checked any messages that had accumulated since leaving home. While offering communication benefits that Steinbeck hadn't had, devices like this one and the laptop and other electronic equipment I carried on board had their challenges, too. At the same time, I tried to plot on my road atlas my expected position any given day over the next week or so.

Mike tapped on the van window around 7 a.m., giving me the go-ahead to use the shower in his apartment above the garage. Accessed by a narrow ladder, his loft was the epitome of bachelor pad-dom. The bathroom featured guy stuff like bottle openers and a sign that said NURSES OFFICE. On the sink counter, a small black-and-white TV piped in the news.

Cereal and juice was breakfast after which I mugged for a few pictures with Mike. We both wore Lauterborn t-shirts and his mom served as our photographer. She reminded me of my Irish grandmother — a petite bottle of pop with a sweet, good-hearted personality. Mike also applied a decal of my/our name to my driver's side door, then I was off.

Up 259N, I crossed a steel bridge over the Erie Canal at Spencerport, made a brief supply stop then moved west on the Lake Ontario State Parkway, with that massive body of water off my right elbow. Deciding to get close up to the lake, I pulled into the Hamlin Beach State Park. A long stretch of waterfront with several manmade jetties, picnic tables and a few stationary grills, it reminded me of an oceanfront. The clear water, and lack of a salt air smell, of course, was the tip-off. The urge to fish snuck up on me, so I took pole in hand and tried a few casts. But a snag-up on a rock and no signs of activity other than some small silver baitfish that moved in schools with the current soon told me to quit. Besides, the nightcrawlers I'd had on board had expired and were stinking pretty high. I dumped my tub, cut my losses and kept going.

Fields of goldenrod, corn and spinach and a pickup truck pulling a trailer piled high with heads of cabbage were my visuals. There were also many orchards: peaches, apples, and blueberries. From a lot in Olcott next to Camp Allen, a community of small cottages, I looked out over the far-reaching water and monitored a man fishing from a jetty to see if he would fare any better than I had.

Under way again, I passed the Willow RV Park and thought how nice it might have been to have camped lakeside the previous night, but then I saw how crammed together the campers were and nix'ed the notion. The Robert Moses State Parkway led me to old Fort Niagara, a structure with a history spanning more than 300 years, at the mouth of the Niagara River. Seven dollars bought me access to sixteen points of interest. These included storehouses for food and powder, gun batteries, lookout towers, a bake house, log cabin and the "French Castle." Built in 1726, the latter was the oldest building in North America's Great Lakes area. Surveying the scene from the South gateway, I watched a young woman running after her two dogs that had spied a rabbit and given chase. A staff member dressed in a soldier's uniform of the period strolled across the quad after concluding an educational session. A herd of tourists, in badly matching outfits with cameras around their necks, arrived on a school bus and spilled through the main gate. Men fished off boats in the waters around the base of the fort.

It was time to see the crown jewel of the area, Niagara Falls, known as the "honeymoon capital" because of its popularity as a wedding destination. Until recently, many of these ceremonies were held at the Niagara Wedding Chapel, which offered packages ranging from Basic to Super Deluxe.

I turned south onto 18F following the road through Youngstown past many grand, columned homes set back from the street. Lewiston was very well maintained and inviting but I dared not dally and leave the Old Girl waiting.

Mike had suggested I see the falls from the Canadian side. After getting lost in Medina and finally reaching this same point by the seat of his pants, Steinbeck had wanted to do the same, then "creep across the neck of Ontario, bypassing not only Erie but Cleveland and Toledo." Feeling "an uneasy sense of guilt," he approached Canadian customs, where Rocinante was searched and he was questioned. When the guards encountered Charley, they asked Steinbeck if he had a certificate of rabies vaccination for him. He did not, so they advised him to get one or U.S. customs would not allow him back into the country. To obtain a certificate would mean backtracking 20 miles or more, which Steinbeck was not willing to do. He boiled inwardly, cursing governments in general and the rules that they generate. Toward the guards, though, he showed respect and they, compassion with him. They even served him a cup of tea and Charley a half dozen cookies.

Steinbeck had no choice but to u-turn back through U.S. Customs. Though he hadn't crossed the border, he was again questioned about the certificate and a phone number he'd scratched into his passport at a moment when he was unable to find a scrap of paper to write on. Ultimately, he was allowed to pass, viewing what he could of the Falls as he pointed himself toward Pennsylvania. That night, he and Charley "stayed at the grandest auto court" he could find, "a pleasure dome of ivory and apes and peacocks and moreover with a restaurant, and room service." He had Scotch and sodas and soup and steak, and Charley had raw hamburger.

My border experience, in comparison, was easy. The guard asked where I had been and my intended destination and wished me a good day. An overlook on a perimeter road provided a view of two stepped rows of nine transformers respectively that crackled from the electric current passing through them. Ahead was a great dam with 12 breakers, below which green-blue waters churned.

I passed up a tourist-infested butterfly conservatory, floral clock and botanical gardens to stop at a nature area. There, the view, combined with the strong breeze and bright sun, was more spectacular and the river rushed by more furiously. Further on still, a point showed a wide turn in the river where it had carved away the bank. Wires from below led to a cable car and station on the far side.

Another overlook gave a better view of the earlier fork and the cable car station I'd seen from the other side. Here, swollen tourists stuffed themselves with nachos, pizza and hot dogs.

My anticipation grew as I saw a sign, "The Falls." Suddenly, there She was, with tons of water gushing down and kicking up an incredible spray in two main points. This was not my first visit to the Falls. My folks had taken me here when I was small and we donned rainwear to walk through an underground tunnel to see them from behind. I remember the feel of the spray in my face as I felt it now, walking down from a hilltop parking spot beside a new casino under construction. But, certainly, the site did not have the effect on me then that it did this visit. Steinbeck, perturbed as he was and no doubt viewing them from a limited perspective, was less declarative about the scene, noting that it was "very nice...like a large version of the old Bond sign on Times Square."

From my vantage point, to the left was the Rainbow Bridge connecting Canada to the U.S. and city of Niagara Falls. Ahead, the "modest" American Falls. To the right, Horseshoe Falls, the grande dame of postcard legend. Gathered to take in the view with me were peoples of the world

— black, brown, white and yellow. Though the languages they spoke were all different, the look of awe on their faces was universal.

Like rain, the spray settled over us and soaked our skin. In the water below, a tour boat, the Maid of the Mist VI, passed under a rainbow and neared the base of the Falls, plunging on until it was in the thick of the rapids and mist. I watched it battle the current, struggling to hold position, while the blue raincoats of its passengers, American and Canadian flags and small "MM" banner fluttered in the wind. The thundering water was so foamy at the rocky base that it looked like so many tons of milk rushing over a pile of chocolate chips. Overhead, on the U.S. side, a white hot air balloon, anchored by a long tether, hovered.

Very close to where the water races by and disappears over the crest, some 2,200 feet wide, I felt dizzy. I could not imagine the brave (insane?) souls who, over the years, have climbed into various watercraft to tumble over the edge, no doubt bracing for the bone-pulverizing smack that would follow. I would later be amazed to read about a 40-year-old Michigan man, Kirk Jones, who, a little more than a month after my visit, plunged over the Falls without any safety device or container and survived, with only a few broken ribs. Shortly thereafter, he joined the Toby Tyler Circus, to sign autographs, wash elephants and take down tents, as the attraction toured border towns in Texas.

Seeking to recreate my childhood visit, I purchased a $7 ticket from a woman with a missing front tooth for the "Journey Behind the Falls" tour, formerly called "The Scenic Tunnels." Recommended to keep clothing dry, a yellow, trash bag-like slicker became my costume and, with a group, I descended 125 feet in an elevator to the tunnels below. The sudden rush of wind and spray that greeted me instantly recalled the past. The Cataract and Great Falls Portals, along another tunnel, put me behind the falls to witness the 34 million gallons of water per minute flowing past.

After purchasing a postcard to mail home, I crossed an iron bridge headed back into the U.S. Questions by the border guard at my re-entry point were few and above board. My route out of the Falls area took me directly beneath the big, white hot air balloon I'd seen from the Canadian side and onto 190 South. Having never visited Buffalo, home of the Bills (always the bridesmaid, never the bride when it comes to Super Bowl contests), I decided to drop in to have a classic Buffalo experience. Exit 14 brought me right in by the water and, noting a few men fishing, I drove up and parked.

Two brothers were casting to the accompaniment of a custom-mixed jazz CD emanating from the open hatch of their black Chevy Blazer. They weren't having any luck catching anything and studied me when I dropped in to see if I might have a more sure-fire technique. I didn't as it turned out, but it didn't matter in the long run. We'd made a connection and were soon sharing bait, drinking beers, talking about our respective travels, comparing cool tools and making plans for the evening. They were taking a break from their construction business back in Arizona to manage their dad's club here in Buffalo. Both were raised locally but relocated to Arizona after one earned a football scholarship out there.

Spotting a scuba diver returning from exploring the waters off the pier, we went and talked with him. He told us he logs 70 dives a year in the area and told us that there was, in fact, a load of bass at this waterfront, but that they feed on crawfish, not nightcrawlers or smaller fish bits like we'd been using. He described how the bass were feeding right out of his hand, making a slurping sound to represent the crawfish going into the bass' mouth. Besides the sea life, there was an abundance of treasures, including bullets, car parts, shoes, nets, lures and more.

When I asked where I should go for dinner, they agreed, "Anchor Bar." Off I went, trying to feel my way to the establishment.

I half expected to cross trails with Buffalo's only bike messenger, Mike Rizzo, a former computer programmer who replaced his routine office job with a cell phone, delivery sack and Xtracycle bike. He regularly clocked 200 miles a week circling the five square mile downtown area and had become a beloved Buffalo fixture.

Founded in 1935 by Dom and Teressa Belissimo, Anchor Bar offered good tunes, license plates on all the walls and Jen, a tall redheaded bartender, daughter of the founders and lead guitarist in a band called the Voodoo Dollies.

According to legend, Teressa's son, Dominic, and some of his friends came by Anchor late one evening, seeking a snack. Teressa had some chicken parts that she'd planned to use in soup, but thought them too plump to waste that way. She deep fried them in a spicy sauce instead and served them up. They were so enjoyed that not only did Dom and his friends continue to ask for them, but others began to as well. The buffalo wing was born.

From my corner-of-the-bar perch, I chatted with two sisters and their mom. One sister, a straight shootin' blue-eyed blonde, was on loan from Florida, up this way to help plan her sister's wedding. A third sister, also a bartender at Anchor, was in on the planning. They all steered me to the wings and, soon, an order of 10 appeared. Because I'd asked for a medium hot sauce, I heard a "candy ass" comment from the stool squatter next to me. Eventually, the messy nature of the food required a bathroom visit to hose off, where I was treated to a unique paper towel experience — motion activation wherein a specific length of towel is fed to you as you pass your hands beneath the dispenser.

Back at the bar, Jen was showing off her tattoos to some patrons. I looked on while leafing through *Night-Life* magazine, which listed bars in the area bearing Irish and Italian names like Rory O'Shea's, Milligan's, Caputi's, Anacone's, Eddie Brady's, Eddie Ryan's and Fugazi's.

Hoping to meet up with the brothers from earlier in the day, I moved down the street and around the corner to their dad's place and pulled up a stool at the bar. It was a low-lit joint with colored light strips here and there, R&B-like D'Angelo, Stevie Wonder and Toni Braxton in the CD juke, and Molson Ice ads and a Bills game schedule on the wall. Unfortunately, the lads never appeared, so I pressed on toward Erie on 190. Weariness soon took over, forcing a stop in the parking lot of a Tallyho-tel in Hamburg to snooze for a while.

Day 12: Cleveland Rocks

Around 3, I woke up in the van, still in the hotel lot but eager to keep going. So I steered back onto 90 and began seeking coffee for my *own* fuel tank.

The Angola Travel Center featured a breezeway over the highway connecting to immaculate bathroom and food facilities, including a Lavazza coffee stand. The counter girls each wore the company's uniform of black pants, a white button-down shirt and black apron with the company emblem. Some chit-chat revealed one was on a work/travel program from the Czech Republic; the other was studying to be a state trooper. I mentioned my Anchor Bar stop for wings and the future trooper countered, "If you want the absolute *best* wings, you've gotta go to LaNova Pizza and order the BBQ style." While we were speaking, I watched six identically dressed Amish men enter the complex one after the other, in a line like ducks, and dart to the restroom.

Rolling again, El Rucio, the truckers and I — and an odd deer or two — owned the road again and my forward progress was rapid. At 4:45 a.m., the "Pennsylvania Welcomes You" sign emerged from the darkness. A Connecticut writer, David Agostino, had dubbed Pennsylvania "the best sports figure producing state in a per capita sense." Supporting this assertion, he offered the likes of NFL quarterbacks Johnny Unitas, Joe Montana, Dan Marino, Joe Namath, George Blanda and Jim Kelly. In golf, he served up Arnold Palmer. Wilt Chamberlain and Earl Monroe topped his basketball category. In boxing: Larry Holmes. Tennis: Bill Tilden. Racing: Mario Andretti. The state has also given rise to Heisman Trophy winners Tony Dorsett, Leon Hart and Ernie Davis. Was it something in the water? A lucky gene pool? Good eats? It made food for thought.

I was just nicking the state, unfortunately, and while I thought of stopping in Erie — the state's only port and a shipbuilding center during the War of 1812 — it was still dark and there'd be nothing open for several hours. So I aimed for Cleveland, bucketing along "U.S. 90, a wide gash of a super-highway, multiple-lane carrier of the nation's goods," as Steinbeck termed it, along which "trucks as long as freighters went roaring by… delivering a wind like the blow of a fist." He did not like being on the highway, explaining that "these great roads are wonderful for moving goods but not for inspection of a countryside." He marveled at the new service areas, "dining palaces" where one could obtain from a vending machine "handkerchiefs, comb-and-nail file sets, hair conditioners and cosmetics, first-aid kits, minor drugs such as aspirin, mild physics, pills to keep you awake." He was equally "entranced" with the new automatic beverage dispensers.

As to the long-distance truckers he encountered, he gave them great credit, describing them as "a breed set apart from the life around them." Pursuing the thought, he tried to calculate the expense of energy involved with operating a truck and made comparisons between truckers and sailors.

As I had in Houlton, he, too, discovered the joys of truck stop showers, and mused about how we occupy our minds as we drive long distances.

I was reminded of a place in Erie that one of the brothers in Buffalo had recommended: the Steak & Lube, a racing-themed place where I could expect "nice girls and good steak." But it was barely even breakfast time, so I would forego it. On the radio: "Here I go again on my own, goin' down the only road I've ever known, like a drifter I was born to walk alone…"

As I neared the Ohio border, I "drafted" a truck for a while like I'd seen my dad do so many times with his own vehicles when I was a kid. Drafting is when you closely follow the rear of a truck so that the truck bears the brunt of wind resistance and you take advantage of fuel economies. At dawn, I passed beneath the "Ohio Welcomes You — to it all" sign.

Truck stops rule, no question about it, like the Flying J Travel Plaza in Austinburg, Ohio. It offered an excellent shower, which cost $6.50 and from which I didn't want to remove myself. Then there was the wide inventory of items for sale, which I noted while standing in line to get my shower deposit back from the cashier: electronics, stationery, toiletries, confections, music, magazines and more. An Amish couple, in traditional gray blue and black attire, picked up and purchased a personal organizer, Altoids and aspirin and went away in a car driven by a non-Amish gentleman.

In the van again, I stumbled on owner manuals that had come with my vehicle and learned that it was assembled in Ocala, Florida, sold to Orange Ford in Albany, New York, and purchased by a Bennington, Vermont woman. The original standard vehicle price was nearly $26K but with options (13" color TV, VCR, sport top, accent lighting, heating/AC), the price kicked to almost $29K. Exterior color: Willow Green with light gold trim. Interior: "Antelope" colored fabric and Brazilian walnut wood fixtures. Van height: 7 1/2 feet. Width: 6 feet. Length: 17 1/2 feet. Highest point in the interior: 5 feet. She was a big girl with enough creature features to accommodate me while I journeyed, and now I knew her intimately.

I also plotted out my day route and plan, with intended stops in both Cleveland and Toledo and a goal of crossing into Michigan for the overnight. I recalled that Cleveland had been the point of origin of an eight-state blackout back in July — specifically, the loss of a 345,000-volt power line that was part of the Erie loop of transmission lines that circle Lake Erie and Lake Ontario. Power was out for days there, resulting in Mayor Jane Campbell issuing a warning to Cleveland residents to boil their drinking water. Fifty members of the National Guard were also put into action to help distribute some 7,600 gallons of drinking water. Operations of assembly plants run by General Motors, Ford and Daimler Chrysler were affected, idling thousands of workers.

Hungry and needing to check e-mail, I visited the plaza's restaurant, treating myself to a fixed-price, sit-down buffet breakfast and tapping into its Internet portal. Rather, I *tried* to tap into its portal. The local hub wasn't responding. So I contented myself with reading the local paper, *The Plain Dealer*. On the front page was a photo of the 105 m.p.h. Hurricane Isabel snapped from the International Space Station. Coastal residents from South Carolina to New Jersey were bracing for the storm's arrival, due to hit land the next day. In sports, the Cleveland Indians, with a record of 4-11 in September, were nearing the end of the season and it couldn't come sooner for them in the words of the reporter.

Getting back on the road took absolutely forever but was time well spent in that it resulted in tickets to the Rock 'n Roll Hall of Fame and an Indians night game. But my having motored through much of the night finally caught up with me 30 miles west of Cleveland where a pause for z's was necessary. Refreshed and going again, I noticed how much the landscape along 90 resembled upstate New York. Dissolving the thought, a RAV4 with the plate "BUBBA W" shot past.

Barreling along the outskirts of Cleveland, I saw not only the skyline but also the Lake Erie waterfront and long rock jetties jutting out. My intended exit put me near the Cleveland Browns football stadium, which loomed ahead, and the Hall of Fame, as well as a small airport. The pairing with the city to the left made quite an impression. I swooped down in front of the stadium, crept past it and the equally grand Great Lakes Science Center and the Hall of Fame, to a lot adjacent to the U.S.S. Cod World War II sub and museum. According to an elder man manning the site's admission booth, the boat was brought here in 1959 as a training ship and funds were obtained to open it as a museum. It did not have any guns on it and the torpedo tubes were welded shut per a longstanding treaty with Canada that stipulates that there must be no man of war permanently based in the Great Lakes by either country unless express permission is obtained. The clerk himself served on the SS-192, "The Sailfish," in the South China Sea. Sixty days after the A-bomb was dropped on Hiroshima, he walked the streets of the Japanese city. The bomb itself did less damage than the fires that resulted and the streetcars were back in service when he visited. A motor machinist's mate 2nd class, he began his work at this sub site six years prior. I mentioned a similar craft and facility we have in Groton, CT, and he remarked that the sub he served on was scrapped there. To amuse themselves on board, he and his mates wrote letters, played cribbage, watched movies, read books or listened to Japanese propagandist "Tokyo Rose."

Steinbeck did not care for submarines, noting that "their main purpose is threat" and, in fact, had personal experience with them while "crossing the Atlantic on a troop ship." As he coasted above, "the dark things lurked searching for us with their single-stalk eyes." Equally troubling was the memory of "burned men pulled from the oil-slicked sea." He would likely have avoided this sub memorial.

Without similar associations, I climbed down through the aft hatch and peered up the length of six torpedo tubes, gradually working my way astern, looking at all the quarters and tight areas within which the sailors lived and worked. One had to admire the courage of the men who subjected themselves to this naval life.

From the sub, I moved on to the Hall of Fame where a marketing person received and pointed me to an appropriate starting point. As we walked, he related some of his close encounters with rock celebrities, including U2, to which the current main exhibit was devoted.

Throughout the hall, I saw incredible memorabilia and music paraphernalia: photos of Elvis, John Lennon, Mick Jagger and Bob Dylan. Black and whites of early influencers like guitarists T-Bone Walker and Les Paul. There was Pete Seeger, in a knit cap with his banjo, the folk legend whose 50th birthday I'd attended at his home along New York's Hudson River. Spotlighted sound booths offered the opportunity to tune into all the various rock genres through the years. In one, an elder man bounced his baby grandson up and down to the beat of "Johnny B. Goode." I found myself starting to bounce along, too, as did others, as we drifted from area to area.

There was video footage showing rock's powerful effect on America's youth, and the backlash from parents and other morals watchmen. There were the outlandish outfits of personalities Britney Spears, David Cassidy, Christina Aguilera and Mandy Moore.

Items devoted to teen music idols filled five wall-mounted display cases. Album cover art decorated the perimeter of a circular hall within which Pink Floyd's "Money" resonated. There were autographed guitars, 45s, photos, hats, jackets, instruments and pianos. Janis Joplin screamed and shook on a monitor to the right of a poster promoting Country Joe and the Fish, who had played at my high school in 1979, singing his anti-Vietnam war songs.

There was the instantly recognizable American/Union Jack Flag cape that Mick Jagger wore on the Stones' 1981-1982 tour. And ZZ Top's red 1933 Ford Eliminator Coupe, which I remember from their "Legs" video, the centerpiece of an open passage.

Personal letters displayed under plexiglass gave insights into the troubles and behind-the-scenes lives of rock legends. I was particularly amused to read a typed letter dated October 1970 to the Florida Probation and Parole Commission by Admiral Morrison on the matter of his son, Jim, who would become the front face of the legendary band The Doors. Admiral M declared having strongly advised Jim to "give up any idea of singing or any connection with a musical group because of what [he] considered a complete lack of talent in this direction."

In the same case was Jim's Last Will and Testament in which he bequeathed all his worldly possessions to his common-law wife Pamela Courson. Close by, a handmade Christmas card to his folks: "A cool yule and a frantic first to Pop and Mom." The P.S. — "This is all I could afford" and "You better get me something."

I took particular note of the Led Zeppelin exhibit, as the band's tunes would strangely air on my car radio when Marlene and I were courting and would set out on a date.

Here was Madonna's bustier; there, the late Nirvana lead Kurt Kobain's guitar. There was so much more to see but the hour had grown late and I had to cut my losses. I passed under the suspended cars from U2's "Zoo" Tour, exited and returned to El Rucio, aiming for "The Flats". Its cobblestone streets and waterside location instantly reminded me of Fulton Fish Market in NYC.

Walking along a cement path beside the Cuyahoga River, I looked over at an outdoor bar, concert stage labeled "Scene" at which loud sound checks were occurring, traffic passing on a bridge, and a train in the distance crossing a steel trestle. A plaque by the riverside told me that Cleveland was named after Gen. Moses Cleveland who first surveyed the area. He only spent three months here before resuming his law practice in Connecticut, and never returned to Ohio. Another plaque marked the site of the beginnings of the Standard Oil Company, founded by John D. Rockefeller.

Two eight-man crew boats tacked out towards the mouth of the river, pursued by a motorboat. An old log cabin was identified as once belonging to Lorenzo and Rebecca Carter, the first permanent family in the area who settled in the early 1800s.

A low-lit joint with thumping dance music displayed a free buffet, which became dinner. From there, it was back up to the Odeon, a concert space where a crowd was gathering. Seeking to get a pass to see the evening's performance, I tracked down a sponsor rep and he took care of me. As the show wasn't scheduled to begin for a couple of hours, I darted across town to see the Indians play, courtesy of the team's media rep.

Ontario, a wide boulevard, served up a parking spot and I walked along past Gund Arena to Jacobs Field, the setting sun lighting up its face. It was truly a beautiful sight and, while I had no personal connection to the team, was always one to root for the underdog. With a Miller Genuine Draft in a plastic collectible mug in hand, I settled into my seat and play began. The Kansas City Royals were at the plate, 3-year veteran Jeff Westbrook on the mound. KC was up and down quickly and the unusually named centerfielder, Coco Crisp, led off for Cleveland. But it was Ben Broussard who got things going, scoring for Cleveland on a Victor Martinez single.

Between innings, a couple near me, from Lima, Ohio, "where they built the tanks that rolled into downtown Baghdad," told me that the namesake of the field sold the team to Larry Dolan, a local businessman, its current owner. As we spoke, a giant, pink-beaked mascot, named Slider, walked by, eliciting catcalls.

A vendor offering Jacobs Field Salted Peanuts sold me a bag. When I told him to keep the change, he said in a booming baritone, "I'm a man who appreciates that. Welcome to the she-ow." In the distance somewhere, a die-hard fan, who reportedly attends every game, whomped on a Tom-Tom drum. I recalled him from "Major League," the Hollywood production about the team.

In the second inning, Indians infielder Travis Hafner put one over the fence in right, about 390 feet. The crowd erupted in cheers and the digital display flashed, "It's Outta Here!" At that moment, my media host came and joined me, filling me in on more of the stadium's history: The Indians' original facility, built in 1932, was called Municipal and located on the site that's now the Browns' stadium. When Municipal outlived its usefulness and was pushed into the lake to make a reef for fish, construction of the new field, named after brothers Dick and Dave Jacobs, began. The stadium apparently holds a major league record for most game sellouts in a season: 455. Renowned players of the past include Bob Feller, Larry Doby, Rocky Colavito and Herb Score.

In the 5th inning, Indians' outfielder Alex Escobar contributed another solo shot straight up the middle, lighting the stadium up with cheers, music and fireworks. I'd picked the right night to see the down-on-their-luck squad, but also wanted to return to the Odeon.

The promoter's signature got me past the guards at the showplace gates, and there, commanding the stage and hypnotizing the masses, were the five warriors known as Sevendust. Headgear in the crowd: Knit hats, baseball caps and bandanas. Accessories: Lip rings, belly rings, eyebrow rings and tattoos in all places. The sound: Hard yet soothing rock, sharp chords, authoritative voices. The atmosphere: Live, on, pressed to the stage, heads bobbing and smatterings of air jamming. The beer: Bud and Michelob headlining, Coors Light and Rolling Rock in step. Attendee numbers: Three to four hundred.

As they played, I scribbled, not the only one at the task. A writer/photographer from *The Free Times*, the local alternative paper, had notebook in hand penning away. We were a curiosity to those around us. In an adjoining room, a CD/tee shirt stand was doing brisk business, folks milled about drinking and photos of past Odeon performers adorned the walls. These included Fairfield's own John Mayer, Sammy Hagar, Marilyn

Manson, Henry Rollins and MOBY. In short, some of the industry's hottest commodities were represented here.

A spontaneous mosh pit erupted back in the other room, with hardcore fans smashing into each other like rams seeking domination over the herd. Lead singer Jean quieted them with his own rendition of Prince's "Purple Rain," which sent hands up in the air to sway back and forth. A guy with a tee shirt, "FAILED MUSICIAN," nudged me to throw my arms up, too, and hard-patted me on the back as I complied.

The road was calling me again, I climbed in El Rucio and was off, leaving friendly Cleveland behind. But not before going by the ballpark to catch the final score of the game: 9-1, Cleveland!

Before long, Hunger was nudging me, so I pulled roadside for a mini feast of cheese, Tostitos and water. As I sat there, Hunger's sister, Sleep, joined the party, urging me to recline in the drivers' seat. Because this was not a dedicated stopping area, I attracted the attention of an Ohio state trooper who came up behind me, lights flashing. He appreciated my circumstance and directed me to a proper pullout a half-mile further along. Here, I picked up with my slumber, drowning out the sound of passing freight trucks with some very good jazz scared up on a local Ohio radio station. The air temp was a balmy 67.

As I neared Thomas Alva Edison's birthplace in Lake Erie Islands and located it on the map, I decided it was worth exploring. A toll collector agreed, recommending Port Clinton with a visit to East Harbor State Park in the morning.

I crossed the long-stretching Thomas A. Edison Memorial Bridge on Rt. 2 over Sandusky Bay into Ottawa County and diverted toward Lakeside on the Lake Erie Circle Tour. But, somehow, I managed to end up in Marblehead. There, I didn't notice that the speed limit on a 600-foot-long section of road had changed to 25 from 35 and rolled on through at 35. Suddenly, there was a Marblehead police car behind me that duly pulled me over.

"Do you know what the speed limit is back there?" asked the policeman. I admitted that I didn't and, to myself, decided that I couldn't give a hoot it being two o'clock in the morning with my eyes about to fall out from exhaustion. "It's 25, and you were doing 35." I thought to myself, at 35, I was creeping along as it was, and I was the only car on the road. Besides, even if I was the mad speed demon for which he seemed to peg me, it wasn't likely that I would have the opportunity to endanger anyone.

"License, registration and proof of insurance."

I produced my license and, as I did, he asked me if I had just come in and where I was headed. As to my other documentation, it was in the back, in my stationery box. He told me not to bother with it, a sign he was softening I hoped, and had me just quickly state the name of my carrier. I passed his test and, as it turned out, I'd missed Lakeside. According to the policeman though, East Harbor would be better for my purposes anyhow. He released me with a surprisingly good-natured warning and even directional guidance.

Unfortunately, my contact with the law, and bureaucracy, didn't end there. Finding the East Harbor State Park entrance, I pulled up to the office and, as it was dark, started to push past. Suddenly, a policeman who resembled Wilford Brimley, who was sitting in his patrol car behind the office, called out, "You have to self-register."

When I asked how I do that, he pointed to a long list of instructions posted on the backside of the office — the last place I'd expect to look! Bleary-eyed, I backed up, got out and started to read. Did I want electric and water or a "primitive" site without? Noting the price ($24 and $16 respectively), I chose primitive, particularly as I only planned to be here a few hours. Then I had to provide details about my length of stay, license information and home address, and enclose a check, which required some digging to find, in an envelope. Finally, all documents in order, I put my check and form in the provided envelope, sealed it and slipped it into a slot.

I found a set of sites labeled "A" near the restrooms and as I pulled in under the trees, frightened a plump raccoon, which scurried into the brush. In only minutes, I was collapsed in the back of the van and out like a light.

Day 13: Lake Erie Pit Stop en Route to Detroit

I awoke after 8 to see a squirrel with an acorn in its mouth running through my site. It was another fantastically warm and bright day, though in Toledo it was foggy, delaying school openings. In North Carolina's Outer Banks, Hurricane Isabel, downgraded to a Category 2, was starting to thrash the coast. The TV was plastered with those at-the-scene reports wherein the reporter stands like a dope in the rain and wind, yelling at the top of his lungs while the camera jiggles and shakes for effect. Of course, there's always a dramatic title to go along with the report such as "Storm Watch 2003" or "Isabel: The Fury" or some such nonsense.

A park representative, whom I mistook for the owner, approached on a golf cart. Actually a maintenance worker, he told me about the camp features, which included a beach, and local fish, namely Perch and Catfish, which could be caught with nightcrawlers. He added that the camp would be closing for the season in three weeks, which got me wondering if I'd have problems finding open camps further north and west.

My experience in the bathroom was like a visit to the wild kingdom. In the toilet stall, a small green grasshopper and white moth were my companions. Likewise, a small black beetle that ultimately washed down the drain, and a large, hearty black cricket shared my shower space.

Stopping at the office for ice and a map, I heard tell of a guy who'd been through recently on his own adventure. He had traveled 3,600 miles by bike, a trek highlighted by 19 flats, four near-death experiences and the birthing of seven puppies by his canine partner.

The map led me to one of the most delightful spots I'd been to on this trip — a strip of beach on the lakefront that one might easily mistake for ocean. Picnic tables stood behind a cement seawall, waiting for sandy bottoms. Gentle waves, pushed along by a friendly, constant wind, lapped the shore. Clean sand made a soft carpet underfoot. Seagulls stood like sentries keeping watch. A little girl in her two-piece swimsuit frolicked and tumbled by the water.

A white-haired woman came and perched on the seawall to share the view. She explained that she was waiting on a young woman to whom she was planning to sell a dog cage. When I said how ideal the site was, she agreed and said she'd been coming here for 33 years. From the Cleveland area and an Indians season tickets holder, she referred me to a few more picturesque sites up the coast. She also invited me to come visit her and her husband on their turquoise houseboat nearby. For now, though, I was very content to enjoy some breakfast and catch up on some writing here.

Along the lip of my cereal bowl, a ladybug walked in an endless search for a terminus. She changed direction several times thinking she had found a better way. A couple of bees took interest in the blueberry lime jelly I was spreading on two slices of bread. Orange juice filled my new Indians mug, which had held beer last night.

To my right, down the beach, a young woman in a bright pink bikini set up her gear. To my left, another young woman seductively posed beside shore grasses for her male companion, who was seeking to take her photo.

In the *Sandusky Register*, which flapped in the breeze and threatened to take flight as I leafed through it, I noticed that B.B. King would be appearing at the local State Theatre. The "Trout & About" column informed that the Angry Trout Fish and Steakhouse Tavern recently reopened. *Lake Front News, The Lake Erie Vacation Guide Since 1933*, promoted the 17th Birthday Celebration of Port Clinton. A local chiropractor agreed to provide adjustments to drivers participating in the Sunoco World Nationals of Drag Racing in Norwalk.

After breakfast, I removed my shirt to enjoy the sun and set up my portable table and camp chair in the sand — an open-air office, in effect, for my writing purposes. More folks appeared over the course of the two hours I was here: A couple who set up a little blue pop-up tent for their infant son, seniors come to survey the lake and a pair of couples with a dog and a baby.

Returning from a bathroom where I went to wash out my bowl and mug, I walked barefoot along the water's edge to more closely experience this little paradise. Ducks bobbed in a shallow pool. An elder couple, squatting on a blanket with a cooler by their side, listened to a portable radio. The woman in pink I'd seen before waded in from the surf, a raven-haired tot by her side. As she rejoined her blonde friend, sitting with another child, I struck up a chat with them.

"Gia" was the woman in pink's name and she had a colorful background. Her South Korean mom was in a "girl gang" and they would often make "runs" on the U.S. military base in Seoul. "They had a thing for the GI's," Gia said. Her mom met Angie's dad, of European and American Indian stock, during one of these friendly assaults, and they married and relocated to a base in North Carolina, where Gia, and a kid brother, were born. When Gia was a toddler, they moved to Ohio and her dad began working post-service in a steel mill.

Gia followed her dad's lead in terms of military service, training as a nurse in Missouri, transferring to Texas then getting stationed D.C.

She met her future husband and they had their daughter, she received an honorable discharge to care for her family. Her path led to part-time nursing, from which she was taking a little time away at this beach.

Gia's companion, "Anita", worked at the locally based International airport and was on duty the morning of 9/11, boarding an Orlando-bound flight, spookily between gates 9 and 11. Suddenly, the TV sets in the bar across from the gate started broadcasting news of the attacks. She was standing with a "redcoat," who had a walkie-talkie and was able to connect to more inside information. That's when operations started calling all planes back, ordering passengers to deplane and for the airport to be evacuated. Holding back tears and trying not to fall apart, Anita managed the deplaning process at her gate as thousands of people, hugging and sharing cellphones, started moving toward exits. In the sky above, passengers of the doomed flight bound from Boston to L.A., that terrorists had seized and pointed at D.C., struggled to wrest control of it from their captors. Ultimately, the passengers forced the aircraft down in a field in eastern Pennsylvania. The crash killed everyone aboard but prevented a more devastating disaster and loss of life in the nation's capital. In the days following, she and fellow employees made poster-sized sympathy cards for American and United staff that had been affected.

It was mid-afternoon when we knocked off. The girls and kids had been great hosts and made an ideal place that much better. They led me out to Route 2 West (passing a cop who yelled "slow down!" at us though we were only doing 20) and, with a wave, I was gone.

Toledo, a place about which no Ohio person I'd met thus far had anything good to say, was 40 or so miles down the road. "Toledo's a good stop if you've gotta go potty," one Ohio-bred person commented. I was not encouraged, but wanted to give it the benefit of the doubt.

On the way out of the area, I passed the 200th Red Pony Air Squadron base and Camp Perry army training facility, both for reservists it appeared. Off to my right, in Caroll Township, loomed an enormous nuclear reactor, the Davis-Besse Nuclear Power Station. This was the closest I'd ever been to such a place and, frankly, was anxious about it. I particularly feared, though, for the families and vacationers in the area who would be in harm's way should anything ever happen.

I saw a large hand-made sign, "Tractor Accident, Info Wanted," in front of a house beside a cornfield and could only assume that the field's tender had been in some sort of altercation with a passing vehicle. Tom Repp, executive editor at *American Road* magazine, called then. Our chat spanned an hour while he interviewed me about my travels thus far and brushes with Steinbeck lore, and we hatched a plan to meet when I reached his Washington office.

Continuing on, I whizzed by a pumpkin farm, a place selling Amish-built furniture and an ice cream shop with a sign that stated, "Scream 'til dad stops the car." Sweet corn, tomatoes, watermelon and peaches were the crops of choice advertised along the route.

At the dinner hour, a roadside joint in Maumee Bay, on Toledo's fringe, made a good stop for wings. Though they came with blue cheese, they were sans celery and not batter dipped as they were at the Anchor Bar in Buffalo. But I realized that that was like comparing an acorn to an oak.

I got chatting with a landscaper next to me, asking him about Detroit."I don't care for it," he said, adding, "Fast pace, bad sections, traffic." Yet, this was the Motor City we were talking about, home of Detroit Steel. Like Toledo, I would not accept the outside opinion.

My curiosity about the city had been peaked and it became my target, but first I needed to make a Wal-Mart supply run and find somewhere to clean up. The chosen big box, in Oregon, Ohio, had a middle-aged guy, with a ponytail and American flag-emblazoned leather jacket, astride a motorcycle, out front. Just inside, a retiree, wearing the store's trademark blue vest, greeted me, "Good evening sir. Welcome to Wal-Mart." He set me up with a cart and away I went.

A tall, blue-eyed salesgirl with a mane of straight brown hair helped me get my bearings and even passed off a store map. Visits were made to automotive, housewares, sporting goods and electronics, while great care was exercised to avoid packs of Midwesterners that spilled from minivans into this ultimate chain emporium.

The route Steinbeck traveled through Ohio was primarily 20, with passes by Madison, Cleveland and Toledo, "and so into Michigan." He made no Detroit stop, choosing to be like a passenger in a tour bus, pressed to the window, rolling past. In this way, he mused on a number of topics, including the new, aluminum-skinned mobile homes, many of which he saw coming out of the manufacturing centers, being hauled to trailer parks. He termed them "shining cars long as Pullmans" which "sit down in uneasy permanence." He interviewed the people who owned them who "were not only willing but glad and proud to show their homes" to him. One of these owners, I discovered in a letter he'd written to Elaine, was a "square-jawed, crew-cut, National Guard officer" who operated a trailer park that Steinbeck had pulled into for the night. The man lived in "a red trailer about the size of our house," the author remarked. He wondered about the apparent lack of roots of these owners, a question that was met with a question in return: "How many people today have what you are talking about?" He concluded that, "Americans are a restless people, a mobile people, never satisfied with where they are as a matter of selection" and surmised that we'd inherited this tendency from our European ancestors.

He regarded poor Charley, whose fur had become balled and dirty, and the promise he was breaking to Elaine to keep him "combed and clipped and beautiful." He noticed an "enormous increase in population" in the area and the "vitality" of electricity everywhere. It struck him "that people were more open and more outgoing" in this region, too, though I'd found people receptive wherever I'd gone. Their level of interaction, as I'd observed, depended on how you approached them, and what topics you breached.

Toledo, as I rolled into its heart, showed itself as a strip of auto dealerships, discount stores and fast food chains. And I did stop to use the "potty," at a K-Mart bathed in blinding fluorescent light. Sometimes you *can* believe everything you hear.

Beyond, I found myself adrift in a sea of concrete, barriers, orange arrow signs and turns and detours so sharp I held onto the steering wheel for dear life. The jump to Detroit on 75N was more of the same, with the brand of man burned into the landscape. In the middle of it, a blue sign: "Welcome to Michigan, Great Lakes Great Times."

A welcome center came up and offered a few maps, recommended sites and other information, including a slim pamphlet provided by *Michigan History* magazine, a treasure trove of factoids. I learned that Michigan's name comes from two Chippewa words ("michi" and "gama") that mean "large lake," it became a state in 1837 and its present-day coat of arms, among other elements, features a Latin phrase that translates to "If You Seek A Pleasant Peninsula, Look About You." As to state symbols, the flower is the apple blossom, the bird is the American robin, the fish is the Brook Trout and the tree is the White Pine. I also gleaned that much of the soil in the state is of a gritty composition called Kalkaska sand, that 350-million-year-old fossilized coral called Petoskey stone is common, Mastodon skeletons have been found in over 250 locations, and the state led the nation in lumber production from 1870 to the early 1900s.

I was not without pre-existing state knowledge, aware that it was the top U.S. grower of blueberries, the French were the first to claim it, former President Gerald R. Ford grew up here and Lansing is its state capital. Of course, Michigan was also #1 in the country for auto manufacturing: Ransom Olds, John and Horace Dodge, David Buick and Louis Chevrolet all founded operations here.

While all this was highly noteworthy and fascinating, for now, I needed to know where I could find a cold, frosty beverage and some folks with whom to mingle. A trucker passing through gave me an inside tip: Greektown, a section of Detroit.

Several exits short of the Motor City, I detoured for gas at a Mobil, located just down the street from one of ExxonMobil's major fuel storage facilities as well as Ford's Stamping Plant, where parts are spit out for its autos. Noting the low per gallon price of $1.69, I filled El Rucio, the first time I'd done so. She drank $53 worth of regular, about 32 gallons in total.

To get a second opinion on Detroit bar references, I consulted two men lounging in the station office — a Trenton police officer and a Dearborn-raised Lebanese cashier. Their recommendation was the city center near Comerica Park where the pro baseball team, the Tigers, play.

Asked if he was descended from a family of cops, the policeman replied that his dad actually worked for Chrysler, but his uncles were on the force. Then, noting his Irish heritage, I wondered if Detroit had many Irish residents. They both said it was a melting pot.

The Comerica Park area seemed like the way to go, so I hopped to locate it. The MGM Grand Hotel came up first, followed by a stream of commercial structures. Seeking some directional help, I called over to the driver of a Detroit yellow cab. He was delivering a fare near my goal so had me follow him. Off Woodward Street, El Rucio found a comfortable rest spot while I set out on foot.

The Town Pump Tavern, across the street from a firehouse, was crowded and loud and everything a good bar should be. Bells Oberon, made in Kalamazoo, quenched the thirst and soon I was in conversation with two patrons, one from Troy and the other from Sterling Heights, a AAA Trip Tix employee and bartender respectively. They described themselves as "kindred spirits," "good girls with no drama" and "true friends, no fake shit, no bullshit."

They tipped me off to 5th Avenue, a bar in the Comerica Park complex. Its top level provided a spectacular, larger-than-life vista. Panning from left to right, I noted a searchlight probing the cloudy night sky atop Comerica Park, with statues of a tiger and lion perched on its rim. The State Theater promoted an upcoming gig. Its twin, the Fox Theater, was lit up with a grand marquis. There was a bar called Hockey Town and farther right, St. John's Episcopal Church, with a banner strapped to its roof: "Pray Here For The Tigers & Lions." Good marketing and a thoughtful appeal I mused.

Two lasses at the bar banged back shots of an apple-flavored liqueur and vodka concoction called a "pucker f*cker." They told stories of their misspent youth and said about Detroit, "It's not a generous city" and is "rough" and "hard" and that it operates on a "love it or leave it" proposition. "It's a learned love, just like black licorice."

As last call was announced, I chased a tip to the old-style elegant Ramada Downtown, checking in around 2:15am. Twenty miles from Detroit Metro Airport and in the heart of Detroit's Central Business District, it was originally opened in 1927 as the Detroit Leland Hotel. This same district also contained the Fisher Theatre, Michigan Opera Theatre, Music Hall, the Second City Comedy Club and a few casinos.

My room was a palace compared with previous accommodations — a four-room suite complete with bathroom, bedroom, a king-sized bed, living room, cavernous closets and a kitchen with stove, refrigerator, pantry, cooking utensils and window-side breakfast nook. I dropped on the bed like a falling tree for a couple hours of shuteye.

Day 14: Detroit City to Lake Huron

Rain greeted me in the morning. From the kitchen window, I looked down on cars and trucks inching along with their headlights on. A trolley-style bus rounded a corner. People trussed up in rain gear made their way to work. Lights blinked at the top of the DTE Energy building. Traffic, from which there seemed to be a constant hum, passed on the highway in the distance. A black police car with gold pinstripes patrolled a local street. El Rucio, in the lot below where I'd parked her last night, stood safe and sound behind an iron fence and card-access only security gate. A white postal truck made its deliveries, moving building to building.

A hot shower in a deep tub and a couple servings of coffee made with the in-room appliance and poured in a Styrofoam cup helped me fight a feeling of sleepiness that was sneaking over me like the gray clouds that passed over the city. These measures allowed me to sit in the breakfast nook and read and write — something I'd struggled to make time for throughout my journey thus far. In my lap, I held a skillet from which I ate heated leftovers and, because tomato sauce was involved, I removed my white shirt so as not to spot it. So there I was, shirtless, eating linguine and sausage from a skillet, browsing literature and surveying the Motor City from my 14th floor suite. Life was grand.

The *Metro Detroit Guest and Resource Guide*, a hardcover book provided with the room, yielded a splashy ad for the new Motor City Casino, "The pulse of Detroit." Another slick, blue-hued ad was for Casino Windsor, just over the border in Canada. An article profiled Hong Hua, a Chinese restaurant named best of 2002 by a local magazine. There was an MGM Grand ad boasting that the place had 2,700 slot machines, 80 game tables and four restaurants. Greektown Casino weighed in with 90 tables and over 2,500 slots.

The free *Metro Times* served up its Best of Detroit list of bars, restaurants and personalities. Among these were 89X DJ Kelly Brown shown astride a Harley, hometown sax player James Carter, club scenester Stirling, Young Soul Rebels record store and label co-owner Dave Buick, and U.S. Rep. John Conyers, described as an "idealistic hell-raiser."

The Detroit News profiled 73-year-old Dick Kughn, the former chairman and CEO of Lionel Train Co. He'd amassed a huge private collection of cars, toys, model trains and related items, including a 1,500-square-foot Lionel train layout and a touring sedan once owned by actor James Cagney. The Detroit Shock, led by center Ruth Riley, captured the first WNBA Championship for Detroit. More than anything, these resources had given me a great snapshot of the city, its inner workings, the things that make its heart beat. But to really feel it, I needed to get on out and hit the streets.

Cobblestoned Michigan Avenue was the thoroughfare I chose to lead me to the Henry Ford Estate in Dearborn, a must-see area attraction I ventured. It took me through what appeared to be old Detroit, past the old Tiger stadium, run-down Roosevelt Park, seedy little hole-in-the-wall bars, Motown Custom Cycles and the old Senate Theater. Of course, there were also half a dozen Ford auto dealerships, tucked next to places like the Sunset Strip Topless Lounge, several Coney Island food stops, Sophia's Bakery, the Venus Club and an ancient Montgomery Ward.

Emerging from this combat zone, the pastures became greener and well-heeled thanks to Mr. Ford and his investments here. There was the Henry Ford Centennial Library, Ford Community Performing Arts Center, the Ford HQ, a United Air facility and the University of Michigan Dearborn Campus, which Ford helped fund with a donation of $6.5 million.

An estate tour, joined by a whole gaggle of employees from the Southeast Michigan Community Alliance, had just begun when I arrived and off we trotted. The white limestone, castle-style home, called Fair Lane, donated to the state in 1957, was surprisingly cozier than I'd imagined, furnished with Oriental rugs, large cushy chairs, marble fireplaces and family photos.

Ford was known to have strolled the residence carrying a book of Ralph Waldo Emerson verses, which guided much of the way he lived, did business and raised his son, Edsel. A dining room with a large brass chandelier above a mahogany table entertained the likes of Charles Lindbergh and Dizzy Dean. The kitchen continued to be a working one, and staff hurried in and out of it. An airy, sky-lit, wide room with an arched ceiling like an airplane hangar once contained a swimming pool, but was filled in after Henry's wife, Ethel, died.

The comfortable library, where I was suddenly asked by the group to introduce myself and explain my journey, held books about nature,

Kipling, WHO'S WHO volumes and medical and science journals. I quickly scanned for Steinbeck books but was told a great portion of the classics had been sold off.

My favorite room of the house was the Field Room on the bottom floor. Cypress logs provided main support and a stone fireplace declared "CHOP THE WOOD YOURSELF AND IT WILL WARM YOU TWICE," an indication of Ford's focus on efficiency.

One of the more unique aspects of the estate was a 300-foot tunnel through which heating, cooling and water pipes traveled. At its far end, the generator room, "The heart of Fair Lane", was filled with 1914-era state-of-the-art breakers, gauges, circuits and huge generators. Through the windows of the room, I could see the River Rouge gushing past at the back of the property.

Our tour concluded in a brick garage, the central focus of which was a black, gleaming 1916 Model T Touring Car, top speed 42 m.p.h. Standing beside it, I thanked our guide, adding, "You're very entertaining." To that, she said, "I'm only as entertaining as the stories," which was very much my philosophy as related to my book writing.

I'd wanted to tour the nearby Henry Ford Museum but it was already late afternoon and a storm appeared to be brewing. So I exited Detroit to head north into the Lake District as Steinbeck had. There, he admired the "rich and beautiful" countryside, describing it as "handsome as a well-made woman, and dressed and jeweled." He thought about regional speech, too, fearing that it was "in the process of disappearing, not gone, but going" due to the impact of television and radio and, as he continued working his way west, said he "did not hear a truly local speech until I reached Montana." My own findings conflicted with that.

Emerging from Detroit on I-75 North, I got sucked into the first traffic jam of my trek, an accident related tie-up. It seemed an appropriate time to make a dinner stop and Marinelli's in Madison Heights called me over. Its sign was the magnet — Pizza, Pasta, Ribs — my three favorite food groups. In the bar area, no less than 11 TV sets carried sports programming.

The bar manager allowed me to pester her with questions about the immediate area and her connection to it. By day, she was a local ad agency project manager assigned to the Chrysler account; Marinelli's supplemented her income.

Dinner was a grand production, making me feel almost kingly. My main dish was sirloin steak, beside which were nestled vegetables and delectable red potatoes. Containers of olive oil and balsamic vinegar came on a condiment caddy with a basket of assorted bread, pile of butter packets and large dish of fresh salad. The entire fare was placed on a tray that clipped to the edge of the bar so I could enjoy my meal without having to stretch to get at it.

With my ear to the room, I heard one guy ask another, "Did you have a good day?" "Define good." "You still got your job." "As far as I know." The snippet was a vivid indicator of the uncertainty of the local economy.

I aimed to make a run for a campground near Linwood on Lake Huron, so rejoined the now freely moving interstate in my quest. Near Pontiac, named after an Indian chief, I screamed past Daimler-Chrysler's HQ, the Walter P. Chrysler Museum and the Palace Theater, thinking about my son Evan whom I'd spoken with earlier. His teacher had received a first e-mail from me with a day-to-day snapshot of my trip thus far. Evan reported that his classmates thought what I was doing was "cool" and he seemed more upbeat than when I first left. Phillip told me about a fire drill he had at school.

The storm that hit North Carolina was on my mind, too. Mom and Dad, two hours inland from the coast, reported high winds, rain and "tree salad," a milder event overall than past hurricane experiences like "Fran" in 1996 when they lost 22 trees on their property. The area between North Carolina's Outer Banks through the mountains of West Virginia and Pennsylvania was a different story, however. There, Isabel came ashore with 100 mile-per-hour winds, claimed at least 31 lives, left millions without power and caused massive flooding and wind damage. President Bush signed disaster declarations for North Carolina, Virginia and Maryland, authorizing a full range of federal assistance. Some of the more dramatic illustrations of the storm: Dead fish on the George Washington Parkway. Water as high as first-floor windows in Alexandria, Virginia. A Comfort Inn in the Outer Banks with portions of its back walls missing. Hotels and houses in Hatteras physically moved off their foundations to other areas on the island. In D.C., Congress and the city transportation system shut down and President Bush retreated to Camp David.

A giant mural of Jesus, erected by the Dixie Baptist Church, posed the question, "Are you on the right road?" Near Lansing, traffic slowed to look over at a car that was certainly not on the right road and, in fact, had detoured into a field. I flew by Flint (where, in late July, Buick had celebrated its 100th birthday), blew past Bay City and landed in Linwood, site of Hoyle's Marina and campground, my target.

Thinking ahead to breakfast, I stopped for eggs at a Mobil with a mini mart. The counterperson wouldn't allow me to split the carton but was good enough to give me leads to three watering holes in town: Peggy's Pub, the Village Inn and Linwood Hotel. As I passed them, the first appeared dead but the other two, adjacent to each other, glowed with activity on this chilly, windswept, dark night.

The camp office had already closed so I u-turned and returned to the bars. The Linwood offered a mean pizza, of which I made a mental note, but it was the Village Inn that had that certain friendly hook. The end of the bar became my temporary residence and, while a DJ in the corner cranked some old classic rock 'n roll, I made a first contact.

"Wanda" and I spoke of Bay City, birthplace of pop star Madonna reportedly and home to the singer's grandmother. It was also apparently the home of the Bay City Rollers, an old-time women's roller derby team. The area had been a hotbed of recent police activity when it was suspected that the remains of ex-Teamsters boss Jimmy Hoffa, who vanished near Detroit in 1975, were buried outside a local home.

Around us, pool matches, karaoke and general revelry was happening, and the tunes, consistently classic, helped transport the mind and spirit. One selection, "Funky Town," seemed an apt designation for Linwood, as it was clear its residents knew how to have a good time. As for the décor of the place, it related to the Red Wings and housed awards for achievements in local events like a "Beer Bash" softball match and annual Chili Cook-Off.

The DJ, who learned of my trek, thought I should have a CD for the road so passed off a compilation of NASCAR-related take-off songs, adding a personal message for me on the inside of its jewel case. The inscription: "To Mike, Wish you the best of luck on your adventures and always remember — when sailing on life's trouble waters, look for the rainbow's end."

She referred me to a place down the way, aptly called Roadside, where her boyfriend was also DJ'ing. I filed into a main karaoke area and set myself up at a front table to watch events unfold. Off the bat, a young woman who was engaged to a military cop in Kuwait due to return home in two months, got up and sang "Jezebel." It seemed an odd choice given her circumstance. As inconsistent, she puffed away on a cigarette while claiming to be majoring in Phys Ed and Health at a local state university. Her soon-to-be sister-in-law, whose husband was also in Kuwait, came over with an American flag and placed it in her hand as a guy belted out Toby Keith's "Stars and Stripes." A song called "Tootsie Roll" came on next, which drove "Jezebel" to abandon her drink and join her pals on the dance floor. Together, they made their tootsies, um, roll. The song was followed by "Get Your Freak On," which led to more body parts getting limber.

As the day started catching up with me, I found my way back to camp. The restroom was locked but camp spaces had running water and electric, making it possible for me to brush my teeth and use my laptop. A "Late Show with David Letterman" re-run aired in the background which, in this foreign setting, gave me a temporary connection back to things familiar.

I awakened briefly in the middle of the night and, stepping barefoot out onto the grass beside the van, regarded the brilliant sky, with a perfect crescent moon and twinkling stars clustered around it. I felt as if I'd leaped into a painting.

Day 15: Looking for Wolverine

My sleep had been very sound and I woke, as usual, with first light. A chill hung in the morning air as the sun came up and colored the horizon a pastel pink, making the many watercraft that were dry-docked at this marina/campground pop against it. As I strolled near them, a flock of mallards bobbing there became animated, popping their heads up to look at me. A fellow camper walked a black Lab, which barked occasionally as it spotted a rabbit or squirrel. Another stoked a wood fire, its scent drifting in my direction. After pecking away on my laptop for a couple of hours and regarding other campers stirring and preparing breakfast, I pulled up my stakes and moved on.

My best guess told me that Steinbeck had camped beside this very lake, Lake Huron, though his only mention of his overnight was "sitting alone beside a lake in northern Michigan." It was not an organized camp that he found but more of a roadside pull-in and, it turned out, private property. A "young man in boots, corduroys, and a red and black checked mackinaw" pulled up in a jeep and, in a "harsh unfriendly tone," told Steinbeck he was trespassing. But Steinbeck defused him with an offer of a cup of fresh-made coffee with "a dollop of Old Grandad" in it. The man stayed on to enjoy it, squatting "cross-legged in the pine needles on the ground." The man even guided him to a spot behind pine trees where no one would bother him. They drank some more "whisky together and had a nice visit and told each other a few lies." Steinbeck showed him some of his fishing tackle, "fancy jigs and poppers" he'd bought at Abercrombie and Fitch, and even gave him one along with some "paperback thrillers" and "a copy of *Field and Stream*."

This "guardian of the lake", as Steinbeck described him, invited him to stay on as long as he liked and they fished together the following day. Steinbeck's impression of him was that he was lonely, with a "prettyish blonde" wife "trying her best to live up to the pictures in the magazines" and get out of "the sticks." Their fishing excursion yielded no catch, though Steinbeck said he generally had "no desire to latch onto a monster symbol of fate and prove [his] manhood in titanic pixine war," though he admitted to liking "a couple of cooperative fish of frying size." Steinbeck politely refused a lunch invitation, growing anxious to meet his wife as they'd arranged to in Chicago. So instead of proceeding further north in Michigan, he u-turned and headed south, then west, on the "huge toll road that strings the northern border of Indiana," bypassing Elkhart, South Bend and Gary.

Not having explored northern Michigan, particularly the farther reaches like Sault (pronounced "soo" for those of you at home) Ste. Marie, I broke from his route. My plan was to head to the very top and then drop south to Chicago through Wisconsin, keeping to the shore and traveling through Green Bay on Lake Michigan.

Since the restroom had not yet opened for the day, I moved right on out of camp, passing the previous evening's haunts to join Rt. 13 headed west. A "Huge Yard Sale" sign at a home beside a hubcap vendor's shop captured my attention. Topping makeshift tables in the front yard was everything from clothes and flowerpots to tools and switch plates, all boxed or Ziploc bagged and impressively categorized. "It would've been more organized but the wind was kickin' up this mornin' and we couldn't keep nothin' down," the owner commented. I purchased a screwdriver set, marked 25¢, for a dollar, in humble tribute to their efforts.

El Rucio needed servicing and the assistant service manager at Dean Arbour Ford in Pinconning was only too glad to fit us into his busy morning schedule.

While I stood by, a guy in a camouflage shirt, who was having his Coachmen camper serviced and noticed my CT plates, initiated a conversation. As he was from the area, I asked him about the Wolverine Camper Company in nearby Gladwin. He didn't know of it, but gave me directions to the town. As to my plans for Sault St. Marie, he suggested I try a fishing spot by the "powerhouse" for Atlantic salmon, Coho (a type of salmon) or Pink Salmon ("best eatin'"). "You can catch 'em with Cleos or check with the locals," he advised. For an overnight, he suggested a casino parking lot. As for himself, he was headed up to his cabin in Deer Park to open it up for bow hunting season and cut firewood for the winter.

On the van service front, bad news came: El Rucio not only needed transmission service (the fluid was black), but new front brake pads and, chiefly, rotors. It would be a couple of hours at least for all the work to be done. I accepted the loan of a silver Taurus and motored over to Gladwin, stopping briefly along M-13 at a service station. At the pump were 33-pound bags of corn kernels, used as turkey feed. From there, I went rural past cornfields, signs for canning tomatoes, beef jerky and deer carrots, and woods and farms.

As it was noon and I hadn't had a scrap of food to that point, Kelly's Place, a rural country diner in the town of Wooden Shoe, pulled me aside. Promoting "Home Cooked Meals Including REAL Mashed Potatoes And The Best Walleye Around," the waitress took my order for a "Big Man's Breakfast" and brought hot coffee and o.j. These were good country folk gathered here, dressed in jeans and work boots mostly, with caps on their heads and flannel shirts on their backs.

The owner was also unaware of Wolverine, but did provide some background about the restaurant. Known originally as Mary's Dutch Shoe, it was more recently the Saw Mill. As to décor, it was Indian-oriented, with many woodcarvings, cattle skulls, antlers and fur pelts displayed. She didn't have a particular reason for the décor choice, noting, "I just liked it." She planned to remodel soon but I commented that she shouldn't change a thing. There was a warmth, glow and family feel about the place that made it magical.

In short order, my meal arrived. It was a fine arrangement of scrambled eggs, sausage, ham slices, big thick toast and strips of bacon — the kind of appetizing, filling breakfast that I hoped it would be.

Folks continued to file in and out, including a young mom with a blue hat that declared in large letters, "BOUNTY HUNTER." Another patron wore a #88 NASCAR hat. Still another sported a roofing company hat and camo pants. A pair of hunters filed in, their caps and clothing marked with orange patches to make them more visible to other hunters. I offered them seats beside me as I was alone occupying a table meant for four. Just past the middle-age mark, the pair told me of the hunting excursion they had earlier: out for Grouse with 12- and 20-gauge shotguns. They bagged a Woodcock, about which they noted, "They're a little strong tasting and sometimes the dogs won't retrieve 'em 'cause they're oily."

The two had been friends for 30 years and done their own share of traveling in that time. Back in the summer of 1970, "Lem", a 22-year-old hippie who got out of being drafted because of allergies, threw his sleeping bag and Coleman stove in his Ford van and took off going west. He went through Wisconsin, Minnesota, the Black Hills of South Dakota and Glacier Park, out to L.A. and San Francisco, to the Berkeley area. He stayed in California three to four months and took in shows like Vanilla Fudge at the Fillmore East. In the fall, he returned home by way of Lake Tahoe, past the Sequoias and Redwoods, and back across the top of the U.S. The following year, he sold his van and used the money to buy a bus ticket back west. That time, he spent two to three weeks in Colorado and in the Arches of Utah. He added that he went to Woodstock, too, in 1969, which for him was all about beer, wine, free food, drugs and "little girls swimming naked in the river."

"Gordon" had experienced a different sort of journey, from Detroit to Anchorage to Guam and finally Vietnam when he was drafted into the infantry. He arrived in 1968 just after the Tet Offensive: "the real shit when everything broke loose." He was stationed in the mountains between North Saigon and Laos. Returning through Oakland, CA, he stayed six weeks with a friend's sister until he ran out of money and came back across the U.S., too.

I moved down the road to both the Gladwin Historical Society and Chamber of Commerce for information about Wolverine but, because it was Saturday, both were closed. Lucky for me, an elder woman was strolling by who knew where the company was and its owners and gave me directions. Sure enough, on 18N, I came across it, seemingly shuttered. My knocks at the door of the main building, a well-worn aluminum structure surrounded by old-style RVs, went unanswered and a phone call or two dead ended.

Frustrated by the roadblocks I'd hit but glad, at least, to have found Wolverine, I drove back to Ford, settled my bill and got back on track planning to run the length of the field to Sault Ste. Marie by nightfall. With fresh ice in the cooler and a topped-off tank, I swung out onto the interstate and engaged the cruise control to let El Rucio do the driving.

Farms and silos plotted on low rolling hills was the scene through West Branch. Forestland took over from there and two squirrels, in separate suicide dashes across the road, took their chances in front of El Rucio.

Higgins Lake in Roscommon was another strong candidate as a Steinbeck campsite, especially as he had u-turned near here to head back downstate. Against all my convictions and yet hungry, I picked up a satchel of fast food as Don McLean's "The Day the Music Died" battled with Norah Jones' "Don't Know Why" for radio air time. A sign in the wilderness: PRISON AREA – DO NOT PICK UP HITCHHIKERS. Good advice that.

Like in Maine, more signs marked the 45th Parallel, the midpoint between the equator and North Pole. Near Cheboygan, yet another promoted "the world's largest crucifix." Though it sparked my curiosity, I took a pass after spying, from a rise, the amazing terrain ahead and Lake Michigan. "They call me Mellow Yellow" had me bopping as I neared the Mackinac Bridge and spied a billboard: Man-Killing Giant Clam, Sea Shell City. It included an illustration of the imposing 500-pound crustacean.

With the sun almost down, I crossed the five-mile long Mac Bridge with its wide, incredible vistas. For 75 years, its development was discussed before construction finally began and it opened in 1957. Five million vehicles a year traverse it over to Michigan's Upper Peninsula, notably the setting for Longfellow's "Hiawatha."

At a quarter past seven, I landed in Sault Ste. Marie noting immediately that it was prosperous and quite commercial with many hotels, restaurants, bars and stores. Up by Lake Michigan, the area grew more intimate with small inn-type places and ice cream shops. I pushed on to the other side of the river, Ontario, but not without a wash-up. Smelling like a rose after a gas station sponge bath, I made the crossing over St. Mary's River.

The border guard on the far side was to the point, limiting his questions to ten, and granted me entry. Though it was a Saturday night, Queen Street was deserted so I kept puttering along, for miles actually, out of the commercial district and through a tidy residential area. I was feeling inclined to return to the states until a music space known as The Eastgate stopped my forward motion. A door tender promised it would be crowded later; I killed the intervening time with a beer at a bar across town.

Circling back to Eastgate, I spotted a hostel and wondered about taking a room for the night. The desk manager showed me the saddest looking hovel you could imagine, with a small sink, two simple beds, flat-out exhausted carpeting, one chair, no wall décor and only dim lighting. I'd had nicer college dorm accommodations. In fact, my van interior seemed like the Ritz in comparison.

A crowd had gathered at Eastgate by this time and hip hoppers were spinning on their heads. This wasn't really my thing but a thirst drove me to the bar, where I hovered until the venue shuttered at 2 a.m. precisely. The parking lot of the Casino Sault Ste. Marie became my home for the night.

Day 16: From the Soo to Milwaukee

The few hours of sleep that I got were very restful, surprising to me as the casino's parking lot lights were bright and penetrated my sleeping compartment. A blast from the horn of the Algora Central, a 15-car diesel engine-pulled passenger train bound for upper Ontario, jolted me awake. Pushing up the blinds, I noticed a flock of seagulls tearing apart a Styrofoam tray of Chinese food that had been left in a bag on the ground. Other motorhomes and RVs that I'd seen when I pulled in last night had gone and various casino workers were arriving for the day shift. Casino security, circling in a "courtesy shuttle" van, was itching to have me move along, given the numerous passes it took near me. After straightening up, brushing my teeth using a bottle of water to rinse both my mouth and the brush, and a splash of juice, I was away.

The goal for the day was to find that fishing spot by the powerhouse and drop anchor for a little while, weave my way down to Green Bay and get some laundry done. My two-week supply of clothing was exhausted and the oversized bag I'd been using for "dirties" was bulging and straining at the zipper.

The seagulls stared after me as I put on my fish radar, hunting for a salmon breakfast. A police officer I flagged down pointed the way to the powerhouse (the Francis H. Clergue Generating Station, a hydroelectric plant) and suggested I should have spoons or plugs with which to fish.

A few short blocks away, I found a dozen fishermen lined up close together along a fence beside the Sault Ste. Marie Canal, a Canadian national historic site. They had eight- or nine-foot spinrods and were dropping their bait into a swirling area and letting it sink and rest on the rock bottom. I asked this one fisherman, who had already pulled out two large Chinook Salmon that were laying on the grass in the morning sun, what he was using as a lure. "Spawn" was the reply — Salmon eggs in fine orange casings — with long lead "pencil" sinkers to keep the bait stationary on the bottom. I had neither and fumbled around first with a pink, feathered lure then with a long, silvery rubber worm. The going was slow and snags — on rocks, bushes, fence and other lines — were frequent.

When I lost a lure to the depths and after he had caught his fourth Chinook and decided to quit for the morning, he mercifully offered his leftover egg casings, a three-way link and even some small hooks that he bent slightly with pliers to better set in the fish. "Working" this spot for three years, he was taught by one of the guys down the row. Now the student had become the master. Someone gave him a cold bottle of Heineken about which he said, "Eh, look here. Breakfast of champions." He enjoyed it with a Canadian cigarette brand called Studio while showing me where to drop in, how to let it drift toward the powerhouse and how to reel it when I felt a hit.

When I told him of my journey, he pointed to an old Schwinn bike lying on its side and said, "That's my ride. I go from here to home and home to the mall and that's all." His green windbreaker, with "CANADA" spelled across it, flapped in the light breeze as he tied a line for me, deftly working with his calloused hands and yellowed nails.

When I climbed over a fence to try and unhook a line, the main guy there said, "If they catch ya' down there, they'll give ya' a $130 fine, eh?" I climbed back up without incident as another of the guys caught a 12-pound Atlantic Salmon. In *his* opinion, the Coho were "the best eatin.'"

This continued until late morning when I lost the rig I had been given to the hungry rocks. I passed along my remaining egg casings to the guy fishing next to me, a trucker who at first thought I was in the same occupation. When I said I was headed to Green Bay, he gave me a very pointed route, citing both distance and length of travel in terms of time, too. "Not like you're keeping track or anything," I smiled.

On the way to the bridge back to the U.S., I passed the St. Mary's Paper company with its plant pumping out steam from tall stacks, the currency exchange center and a duty free store. Looking down from the high steel bridge as I crossed it, I could see all the various industry along the banks of the St. Mary's River, including the rear yard of the paper company in which was stacked hundreds of logs awaiting processing.

Traffic was backed up on the U.S. side, with two lines of cars bumper to bumper seeking entry. When I reached the guard, he asked a couple questions then directed me to pull the van over by an inspection booth. He asked the same of two young guys with goatees, traveling together. "It's the beards," I remarked, pointing to my own. "It's the age," came the reply. There, another set of officers ran my license against FBI records and poked through stuff in the van. Satisfied that I was not an evil-doing terrorist or wanted for arms smuggling (or even leg smuggling), they let me go through.

Missing the turn for 28W but finding a Mobil station, I filled up, got ice and made myself a tasty turkey and Vermont cheddar sandwich from cooler fixings. Then, along tree-lined 28, I pulled over in front of a snowmobile crossing sign to catch a wink or two. The passing of big rigs, which dominated traffic here, shook El Rucio.

Plowing through the Hiawatha National Forest, I passed a powder blue Buick Riviera, circa 1966, with the plate, "ORIG GS," referring to the car model. "I don't own the clothes I'm wearing, and the road goes on forever, I've got one more silver dollar, but I'm not gonna let 'em catch me, no, not gonna let 'em catch the midnight rider," I sang aloud with the radio.

In Gulliver, on 2W, which would take me into Wisconsin, a sign for an outdoor home accessories dealer called "Birdbath and Beyond", a play on the popular chain Bed, Bath & Beyond, gave me a chuckle. In Manistique, the center of a region known for its world-class trout rivers, I got my first look at the northwest end of Lake Michigan. Like before, I had trouble accepting that this was a lake and not an ocean. It deserved closer inspection.

Lake Michigan Beach was a collage of sand dunes, tall beach grasses, waves, gulls, even a small lighthouse at the end of a jetty. Gull tracks and driftwood led to a stretch of rocks filled with tide pools, which I stepped through and around. In one spot, someone had taken a number of rocks and built a semicircle shaped wall. Further on, I teetered along the length of a fallen, weathered tree that had washed ashore. Returning to my starting point, I recognized that the rock here had once been one whole mass, as it still was in places, and that it had broken up into individual parts over time — a shattered lakebed in which I expected to find evidence of prehistoric shore-dwelling beasts.

Noticing a couple taking individual photos of each other with the lighthouse as a backdrop, I stepped in to snap them together, then turned an eye to the local paper, *Michigan Outdoor News*, "The sportsman's choice for news and information." It detailed several prize fish catches: a 51-inch, 37-pound Muskie caught in Lake St. Clair; a 1-pound, 8-ounce Bluegill pulled from Chippewa Lake; and a 5-pound, 22-inch Largemouth Bass nabbed in Oceana County. Wolves had been preying on cattle in Engadine in the Upper Peninsula. The walleye population in Lake Erie was diminishing. Ticks infected with Lyme disease were turning up in Lansing. A 15-member U.S. Fish and Wildlife Service crew was warring on parasitic Lamprey in Sodus.

Around Ensign, I tuned in a live NASCAR race, this one being run at the Dover Downs International Speedway. Ryan Newman, Elliott Sadler and Dale Earnhardt, Jr. filled the leading spots. The event inspired me to pop in "Drivers of the Track", the CD the DJ had given me. The songs were pretty dopey, like a primer for racecar drivers. Very frequently, the term "boogity boogity" was used. While the CD was not to my liking, I still appreciated her gesture.

The name of a bar, the Breezy Point Bar & Grill, south of Escanaba, reminded me of a stretch of beach with the same name in Queens, New York, on Long Island Sound. In the summer of 1982, I spent a Saturday out there with an Italian girl I'd met through our department store workplace. I'll never forget the family meal we shared, my first in an Italian household, that began with ziti, salad and bread, which would have been ample but continued with sausage and peppers, slices of beef, chicken in a red sauce, clams, homemade wines and sinful desserts. It was an early lesson in cultural difference.

As I switched over to the Green Bay Packers Radio Network to catch NFL game results from the day — happily finding that my Giants were topping the Redskins 14-3 — I heard that Earnhardt had hit a wall in turn 2 and had to be helicopter transported to an area hospital. For a moment, I was reminded of his dad's fatal collision in a similar manner.

Just shy of the dinner hour, I hit the Wisconsin state line denoted by a log structure that said, "Welcome to Wisconsin — Recreation, Industry, Agriculture." This was the 10th state I'd visited in 3,670 miles traveled over 15 days, with three Canadian provinces breached as well. With only 45 miles to Green Bay, I knew I could make the stretch and would seek out a hotel room with a good, very needed shower, a hearty meal and Internet service.

A "V" of Canadian geese soared over an Ireland green field while a Packers-Cardinals game, already in 4th quarter play, popped on the radio. Local business showed support for the home team with GO PACKERS GO signs.

At 6:30, I turned off for downtown Green Bay, seeking to fulfill my agenda, following a station wagon bearing the plate "LTL DOC" from the Oneida Nation. A girl walking along with a cell phone guided me to the core of Green Bay — the West Side where the bars, stadium and hotels are located. On the way, I passed over a couple of major bridges and by some factories and car dealerships, finally reaching the area shadowed by Lambeau Field, home of the Packers.

As I pulled into The Bar, a wide-open, noisy sports tavern adjacent to the stadium, the game had come down to the last 10 seconds, with the Packers behind 20-13 and in possession of the ball on the 8-yard line. QB Brett Favre rolled to the right, aimed for a receiver in the end zone but had the ball intercepted — a disheartening defeat.

Inside, the majority of locals were deflated by the loss, including "Mae", a blonde wearing a "Rebel Rider" t-shirt who mentioned that she *and her mom* had "partied" with the Packers following a regular season game against Dallas back in '96. The team gathered at their regular hangout and they all drank Crown Royale whiskey out of champagne glasses. This line of conversation led to her mentioning her various past beauty contest honors, *both clothed and unclothed.* Of all the people I could have chosen to speak with, none could have been more colorful.

Needing to fuel up with dinner, I ordered the Wisconsin Cheese Steak, a sandwich with shaved prime rib of beef topped with sautéed peppers, onions and Swiss cheese on grilled Texas toast. It seemed like the ideal choice in this neck of the woods.

From there, I exited Green Bay and aimed for a KOA in Fond du Lac. The closer I got to the site, however, the nearer I got to Milwaukee, on my direct route to Chicago. The beer town won out.

One thing I was glad to realize was that I'd gained an hour due to crossing into the Central Time Zone. I'm not sure at what point the transition occurred — likely in northern Michigan as I moved west.

The term "road rage" defines an act of aggression provoked by one driver against another. On this trip, I'd redefined it to refer to that period of time when I'm reaching the end of my physical ability to focus on the road. It's when the eyelids get heavy and threaten to snap shut. When you become hypnotized by the lines on the road and start to see more lines than those that exist. When your vehicle starts to drift to the shoulder. When I would hit that phase, I would get maniacal — yelling, shrieking, even slapping myself in the face to try and stop my body from shutting down. I hit this wall near Sheboygan and couldn't get over it, so landed at a Mobil for some hi-test White Chocolate flavored coffee and a brownie wedge. It and a call home to hear Marlene's familiar voice as rain started to come down hard helped restore my energies and let me complete the 50-yard dash to Milwaukee.

The city and general region had always had appeal to me, particularly because of its beer roots. It was also the site of the infamous sausage assault back in early July at Miller Park where the Brewers baseball team plays. The customary sausage race, between four team employees dressed, respectively, as an Italian sausage, hot dog, bratwurst and Polish sausage, was being run between the sixth and seventh innings around the infield-warning track. As they passed the opposing team's dugout, Pittsburgh Pirates first baseman Randall Simon slugged the Italian sausage with a bat, sending it and the 19-year-old girl inside tumbling into the hot dog. Simon was apparently "just trying to get a tap at the costume" and didn't mean any harm, but was taken away in handcuffs. Battery charges were not filed but Simon was certainly "grilled" in the press.

As I noted earlier, the city's also the birthplace of Harley-Davidson and drew some 300,000 Harley owners for the company's recent 100th birthday celebration. The party began with fireworks shot from the roof of the Harley HQ and continued with exhibits of famous bikes (those belonging to Elvis Presley and Jon Bon Jovi), new product introductions, live music and food. A parade of 10,000 bikes through city streets capped the heavenly hog hoedown.

For generations, Milwaukee's been a center of German, Scandinavian and Polish cultures but has also embraced Africans, Asians, Italians, Irish, Russians, Mexicans, Arabs and Native Americans. As to architecture, gracing the city was a new Riverwalk along the west bank of the Milwaukee River, where crowds gather at pubs to drink local microbrews, and the futuristic-looking Milwaukee Art Museum designed by Spanish architect Santiago Calatrava, on Lake Michigan.

Breaching the city perimeter, I put my hotel radar on, deciding my target had to be classic, reflecting the city's history. I stumbled upon Hotel Wisconsin on North Old World 3rd Street. Opened in 1913, it was one of the city's first skyscrapers at 12 stories. With 500 guest rooms, it also defined luxury, though rooms were offered at "popular prices" of $1 a night and up. From his desk in Madison, Governor Francis McGovern pressed a button signaling the hotel's debut. Over the years, it has hosted both politicians and entertainers including Laurel and Hardy, Eleanor Roosevelt and Harry Houdini. The Circus Room, a club in its basement, saw the likes of greats from Glenn Miller and Benny Goodman to Bette Midler before a fire and resulting water damage shut it down.

Entering the lobby, I knew I'd made the right choice for accommodations. Its ceiling was of decorative plaster, featuring a state seal pattern. The walls were birch-paneled. Two large brass lighting fixtures and lamps on low tables around the room provided illumination. But the most notable highlight was the collection of old photographs of notable landmarks: There was Gately's Clothing in 1911. The Hotel Miller in the '30s. The grand Republican Hotel with its conical towers. The Hotel Gilpatrick, where an attempt was made to assassinate Theodore Roosevelt in 1912. The John Hinkel Building. The Western Union office in 1887. Steinmeyers Department Store. The Charles F. Stokes Bicycle Company in 1889. The Schlitz Palm Garden. The G.W. Ogden Co., which was razed to make way for the Hotel Wisconsin. The Tannhaeuser Building. One of my favorite pieces, though, was an 1898 Gugle Lithographic Co. print about four feet wide showing a color panoramic view of Milwaukee from City Hall Tower.

The night manager on duty was not only a databank of local history and knowledge, but familiar with "Travels with Charley." He set me up with a room, which the night watchman guided me to via the freight elevator, a classic metal structure built by the Rosenberg Co. of Milwaukee. The room was massive by today's hotel standards, measuring 21' x 25' with a chandelier affixed to the center of a 12-foot high ceiling. I flopped down on one of two double beds and fell right asleep.

Day 17: Rolling to Chicago

Up with a garbage truck passing in the street below, I busied myself all morning with real life responsibilities, emerging from my shade-drawn room not until noon to check out. At the front desk, the even-natured day manager fondly recalled growing up on the north side in his grandparents' house, attending the 21st Street Elementary and St. Galls High, and initially pursuing a nursing career. As to a good local eatery, the reco was Mader's.

A tall blonde of Lithuanian stock dressed all in black sat me down at the bar in the great, German castle-like establishment. Its décor included suits of armor, broadswords, brass trays, bugles, axes, intricate woodcarvings depicting early Bavarian beer festivals and the world's largest beer stein. The atmosphere had delighted a long A-list of Hollywood glitterati and politicos.

Into a 2-liter glass shaped like a boot, bartender Becky poured some fine Franziskaner Hefe Weiss then brought a dish called the Bavarian Platter, comprised of grilled brat and knackwurst simmered in sauerkraut, served with a slice of Kassler Rippchen and a potato dumpling. It was delectable and, over the meal, I gabbed with a dot-com guy and his girlfriend, both from Chicago. Hoping to meet up in the Windy City, we exchanged contact information.

An attempt to coordinate an at-the-bar interview with the *Milwaukee Journal Sentinel* didn't pan, so I crossed the street to Usinger's Sausage Factory. In plexiglass cases in its marble-floored retail showroom were displayed all varieties of kielbasa, bratwurst, bologna, beef summer sausage and blood sausage. The smells were wonderful and made up for a missed Syracuse meat stop. While purchasing several logs, I was steered by a fellow visitor to a cheese shop at the corner. The Wisconsin Cheese Mart, housed in the first grocery store opened in Milwaukee, offered cheese, crackers and wine, floor to ceiling. After sampling some five-year-old cheddar, I bought half a brick and got on my way to Chicago.

A concrete roller coaster lifted me out of Milwaukee, past steeples, smokestacks and dense neighborhoods, depositing me in rush hour traffic headed south. Farmland, with a strong smell of manure providing the local fragrance, returned, interspersed with cheese emporiums, factory outlets and several state troopers. "The People of Illinois Welcome You" was my border greeting and a pleasant one it was at that.

Six Flags Great America popped up on my left, a maze of wild-looking roller coasters. An Abbott Labs facility, several posh hotels and a number of office complexes followed. Suddenly, there, on the horizon, was Chicago, its steel and glass buildings reflecting the sunset. Fullerton Avenue brought me in and I was immediately awash in bright light, from store signage, lampposts, traffic signals and oncoming headlights. What my Mom would describe as "neatsy" places — community theaters, bars, and hole-in-the-wall nooks — came up, giving way to the DePaul University area, related campus apartments and throngs of young people.

Gliding through a tunnel of trees with brick residences on either side, I pulled up and parked in front of the condo of my old high school classmate "Rose". Sporting a mane of reddish hair, she trotted out to meet me, slapped a parking permit on the inside of my windshield and we hopped in her ride to report to the bar at the Claridge Hotel on Dearborn Parkway, an area she described as one of the ritziest in the city.

This was her local watering hole and gathered at the bar was a quartet of friends: a Japanese guy who described himself as a "market timer," investing his money to support his main pursuit of music producing and songwriting; his girlfriend, a nightclub manager; a South African girl who worked as an au pair; and her partner.

Other than noting his accommodations, Steinbeck had not detailed his moments in Chicago, as they were spent with his wife. I suspect that partly this was to protect his privacy but he also stated that the reunion was a break in his continuity, "off the line, out of drawing." In his travels, he said, "it was pleasant and good; in writing, it would contribute only a disunity." As such, there were few paths for me to pursue here, only to invent. I decided that I would try and sample a broad range of experiences, from its nightlife and eateries to sports and transportation, and, naturally, seek to meet and learn about an array of local folks. The hope, as in other places, was to take a meter reading and understand how life's drama played out here.

We decided to take in the night air, so walked along bar-lined Division Street, chuckling at a great sign outside Butch McGuire's: "The Roast Pork Sandwich is Mighty." Oak Street Beach, like other lake beaches I'd seen, looked like an oceanfront stretch and, as we stood there, a wave smacked the sea wall and sent water over our feet. Its backdrop was the Chicago skyline, accented by The Drake Hotel lit up with a pink neon sign, the John Hancock building with two huge antennae on top, luxury apartments and the Bloomingdale building. The beach was a particularly popular summer hangout, where folks came to sun and juggle a la Southern California. Nearby, on Michigan Avenue, Oprah Winfrey keeps an apartment and often strolls down herself.

After popping into P.J. Clarkes and wondering if it was associated with the one in New York, we jumped back in the car and cruised LaSalle through the touristy River North area, known for its art galleries. Then it was over the Chicago River to the Loop, the Chicago Board of Trade building towering ahead of us. Cement blocks surrounded the Ralph H. Metcalfe Federal Building, placed there after 9/11. On that day, Rose was at work where classes continued but students with Pakistani and Indian backgrounds, their parents afraid of retaliation against them, were excused.

Gourmand, a factory space converted to a coffee bar in an area known as Printer's Row, featured psychedelic, Dali-like paintings, a movie screen and chalkboards listing its food and drink choices. At the counter, two young women hopped up on Skittles contemplated muffins and pastries. Others lounged in old chairs and couches, studying, reading, chatting or pecking at their laptop computers. Lazy, soft rock filled the room lulling and gathering everyone into its arms.

On the way back to Rose's, we eyed more sites: The large public library with illuminated gargoyles at its corners. The Art Institute, which, with its stone lions out front, looked much like New York's Public Library. Buckingham Fountain. The Millennium Park. The Wrigley building.

Gathering up some of my things from El Rucio, we walked up two flights of stairs and past her mountain bike to her condo space, a cozy, brick-and-black granite bachelorette pad. In one of four rooms, her billiards trophies filled a bookcase. Atop another sat a 3 1/2-foot-tall stuffed giraffe. As a girl, she'd begged her mom to buy the toy, which she referred to as "the Cadillac of stuffed animals," after noticing it at New York's famous toy emporium, F.A.O. Schwarz.

With my food supplies and belongings squared away, we relaxed on her couch, with Conan O'Brien's TV show on in the background, and leafed through a few compact photo albums. Some showed pictures of the students and teachers with whom she works, though the majority was of our fellow high school classmates, many of whom I barely recognized as they'd changed so much over the 20 years since our graduation. I could only imagine my dad's thoughts upon seeing his own classmates after the passing of 53 years. Any associations I had with these people, good or bad, suddenly ceased to be important, replaced by a keen interest in the career and life paths they'd chosen and how those choices fit with their personalities as I'd perceived them. Pointing to one photo of a group of eight, Rose placed her finger on each person's image and rattled off, "Divorced. Second marriage. Divorced. Divorced but engaged. Single, not working. Divorced. Single, not working. Married, the only one." We wondered why the divorce rate was so high among this sampling, my marriage of ten years and counting suddenly standing out as a shining example.

The effects of the coffee we'd had at Gourmand now worn off, we retired, I to nestle down on her couch in the warm interior of my sleeping bag for a sound night's sleep.

Day 18: Lincoln Park Lunacy

Rose had her job to go to and tried to quietly creep around getting ready, but my tendency to wake at the slightest sound, and at first light, had me up and writing. As she left for the day, she reminded me of various attractions in close walking distance. One I had great interest in seeing was the Ambassador East Hotel that Steinbeck referred to as an "elegant and expensive pleasure dome." His wife Elaine flew in from New York and they stayed there for a few days, a happy reunion and break in his journey, providing "a resumption of [his] name, identity, and happy marital status" and brief return to his "known and trusted life."

Recognizing his tendency to get lost and panic in traffic, he approached Chicago "long before daylight" and hired an all-night taxi to lead him to his hotel, much like the cabbie had guided me in Detroit. Though he was well known there, he suspected that his appearance "in wrinkled hunting clothes, unshaven and lightly crusted with the dirt of travel and bleary-eyed from driving most of the night" did nothing for his celebrity. He "had forgotten to bring a suitcase to transport" his clothes from Rocinante to his room in the same way that I had. I had solved my dilemma by carefully picking and choosing those items I'd need and placing them in several plastic grocery bags. In this hobo-like way, I'd appeared at the hotels in Fayetteville, Detroit and Milwaukee. Creatively, Steinbeck "found a clean corrugated paper carton and packed [his] city clothes." Then he "wrapped [his] clean white shirts in road maps and tied the carton with fishing line." To the bellhops, he "handed out [his] suits on hangers, [his] shoes in the game pocket of a hunting coat, and [his] shirts in their neat wrapping of New England road maps." Charley was sent to a kennel for the duration of the stay, a decision about which the dog "cried out in rage and despair."

Steinbeck found that his "room might not be vacated until noon" and, though understanding, he very much desired "a bath and a bed." I knew this desire well, having gone two days without a decent representation of either at one stage. So he piled up "in a chair in the lobby" to nap and wait on his room. The deskman wasn't thrilled at the spectacle and worked out a solution wherein Steinbeck could have the temporary use of a room, that a gentleman who had to catch an early plane had vacated, until his own room was ready. It had not yet been cleaned, which actually intrigued Steinbeck, an admitted and "incorrigible Peeping Tom."

Donning his detective hat, he dubbed the suspect "Lonesome Harry" and deduced from bits and pieces left behind that he'd come to Chicago on "a business trip with some traditional pleasures thrown in," namely a female visitor. He dubbed her "Lucille" and surmised she was a brunette who "wore very pale lipstick" and was nervous judging from the many cigarettes she half smoked. Harry, Steinbeck decided, was from Westport, commuted to New York, felt guilty about his transgression, drank too much and had an upset stomach. Steinbeck believed the rendezvous did little to make him less lonesome and that Harry probably hadn't had any fun.

Assuming my own detective disguise, I phoned the Ambassador East, now known as the Omni Ambassador East, to see what anyone knew about Steinbeck's visit. Leads to a long-time employee and a "select guest coordinator" went nowhere, unfortunately, so I spent the morning writing. Midday, after gobbling down an omelet, reading the *Chicago Tribune* and showering, I remembered that my laundry bag, a promotional item I'd received at a baseball game, was bulging at the seams and that I was down to my last pair of "gutchies." It was time to do some laundry.

Quite by accident, Steinbeck invented an ingenious method for laundering his clothes while on the road. In a large plastic garbage bucket with a cover tethered by a strong elastic rope inside Rocinante, he placed hot water, detergent and his clothes. As he drove, it jiggled around, agitating and cleaning the garments, which he then rinsed in a stream and hung to dry on a nylon line inside his vehicle. In this way, his clothes were "washed on one day... and dried on the next." For my part, I had neither the room nor the inclination to go to such measures, particularly as coin-operated laundromats were in such great abundance across the country — not the case in 1960.

Four blocks from Rose's was the most respectable LaundryLand. The place was a sea of washers and dryers, all with fantastic names, and a good third of them were in full operation: The Wascomat Junior W74 Double Loaders with their circular portholes standing guard up front. The gaping Speed Queen and Huebsch Originator Drying Tumblers along each wall. The yellow colored, top-loading Speed Queen Commercial Washers. The Wascomat Senior W124 Triple Loaders, the big brothers of the W74s. The squat UniMat 50 tumblers in the corner.

Overhead, three huge exhaust fans eliminated excess heat. A change machine exchanged bills for coinage. "Laundry aids", like small detergent packages, tumbled from a Model 125 Super 12. For entertainment, there was a Namco Classic upright video game machine featuring Pac-Man, Rally-X and DieOut. A Diet Rite machine stood in a corner ready to refresh laundry goers. Durable plastic laundry bags spit from an antiquated Vend-Rite Manufacturing Co. machine. Candy, in three assortments, was available to serve those with a sweet tooth.

This was laundry processing at its finest and, like riding a bike, I hadn't forgotten how to operate these beasts, deftly loading quarters, releasing liquids and sending them into action. In a molded plastic chair, a young apartment renter leafed through an *ELLE* spread across her lap. Another young Spanish woman talking a mile a minute on a hands-free cellphone walked her daintiest delicates from a dryer to a folding counter, reminding me that these are places where you check your modesty at the door.

After lugging my clean laundry back to Rose's, I pointed myself in the direction of where I thought Oak Street beach was located. Oz Park, with a clever sculpture of The Tin Man from "The Wizard of Oz" at one corner, was a site on the way. Amid clumps of wildflowers, park goers lazed in the sun or chatted. A small playground nearby was busy with kids, leaping, running and climbing on the play equipment. At restaurants like Glascot's, the Athenian Room, Hanabi and O'Hare's, people sat at sidewalk tables enjoying drinks and light meals.

Realizing that the beach would be too far to reach in a decent time, I set myself up in a park, to work at my laptop. A casually dressed, sunny blonde, who was a behavioral management consultant for business owners, was working at her own close by. I suggested that Chicago resembled New York, to which she replied, "The difference is that people in Chicago stay in town for the summer," to attend any one of a myriad of festivals or hang out at the beach. In the fall, she said, a fun time is dining at one of the outdoor cafes or hunkering down at a bar on Halsted. Though born in a suburb of Chicago, she was schooled in Davenport, Iowa, and recommended I go to Huckleberry's Pizza on my pass through there.

Rose had returned from work when I got back to her place and we agreed to hunt down a classic eatery: The Chicago Pizza and Oven Grinder Co. on North Clark Street, between Dickens and Webster, across the way from which the bloody "St. Valentine's Day Massacre" had taken place in 1929. A neat beam-and-wood paneled environment, the place had character, and friendly service to match. Our raven-haired, Irish/Scandinavian waitress and lifelong classical dancer sat us down and recommended a few fine dishes: a heaping chef's salad, paper-thin Mediterranean bread and a half-pound Pizza Pot Pie. The latter was quite unique, conceived by Attorney Albert Beaver, the restaurant's owner. Best described as "pizza in a bowl," it comes as cheese and meat sauce in a dish covered with a curved crust that is then turned upside down. The meal overall and the very tasty Hacker-Pschorr Weisse beer that came with it hit the spot. Even greater was the plié then relevé ballet moves we persuaded our waitress to perform for us.

The plan for the balance of the evening included finding other nightlife experiences and hunting for the coveted species known as the Trixie, which Rose defined as a 20-something, empty-headed wench known to travel in packs and drive Jettas, "its" car of choice. Its stomping ground was the Lincoln Park area, more popularly referred to as Drinkin' Park because of its abundance of taverns, and as we entered it, I was half-expecting to see a theme park-like entrance dubbed Trixie Land and ride with roll bars to come whisk us through it. Blocks into their habitat, we had spied neither powdered hide nor teased hair of a Trixie and I was beginning to doubt their existence. Then, at the corner of Lincoln and Fullerton, I had the dumb luck of parting a pair. Fine specimens standing tall and blonde, they were on the march to an ATM.

Failing to find a greater herd, we steered ourselves to a very busy sports bar showing the Cubs, who were up 6-0 against the Reds, on a big screen. Revelers were three deep at the bar, including a young woman whom we asked for a local libation recommendation. "Miller High Life, The Champagne of Beers," was her answer, sputtered between mouthfuls of a chicken sandwich that stood no chance against the Nebraska-bred brunette.

A pool table at the front of the place was seeing a lot of activity until two staffers walked up with a large slab of plywood, covered it over and turned off the Budweiser light hanging above it. It seemed to us like a Prohibition Era move, a veritable police raid, and was particularly perturbing to avid pool shark Rose. Noticing a Yankees-White Sox game broadcast then, I started cheering on New York. "No, don't do that! You'll get us thrown out," Sara cautioned, grinning.

The place was cramping our style and we thought a blues injection was needed, so traveled down the stretch to Kingston Mines. The doormen let us pass into the red-lit inner sanctum where we sat beside a fun couple from Utah. O.C. Anderson and his band were the opening act — "Twenty-five hundred pounds of blues" the emcee announced. Like oozing molasses, they launched into their set, spurring the crowd to jam. "I'm playing the blues for youse," O.C. announced. "If you like what you hear so far, we don't want you to say 'Oh, yeah.' We want you to say 'O.C.'" another urged.

A bucket of Goose Island brews accompanied our helping of blues, though a tasty side dish also seemed necessary. From the cook, I ordered up a half-slab of St. Louis style ribs, touring the place until they were ready. In a section of hallway dubbed "The Wall of Fame," like Steinbeck's own "Hall of Fame," hung pencil drawings of great blues men and women like Valerie Wellington, Eddy Clearwater, Detroit Jr., Ike Davis, Otis Clay and Jimmy Johnson.

After O.C.'s set, we moved into an adjacent room to hear Dion Payton and his 43rd Street Blues Band. "We pride ourselves on being completely accessible to the physically challenged and morally handicapped," said the ever-witty emcee, introducing them. After a set, we finally took our leave and padded back to Rose's, briefly participating in a street football game. It seemed the perfect end to a crazy evening.

Day 19: Sox Showdown

I awoke feeling the hair of the dog, as Rose departed for work, and spent the mostly overcast morning arranging to attend a trade show in town the following day, and writing, of course. At the same time, I re-connected with another old high school friend, "Norm", a commercial real estate financier. Always the life of the party, he had an infectious laugh and always knew where to find a good "kegger." He was planning on attending a White Sox-Yankees game at U.S. Cellular Field. With nothing but time on my hands, I decided to secure a ticket and try and meet up with him there.

At just after noon, I set off on foot to catch the elevated train, The El, walking past all the extremely quaint apartments in Rose's area, with their black iron fences, small neat gardens, brick and stone exteriors and wide, railed front steps. At a building site on Fullerton, construction workers with hard hats and Playmate coolers watched the girls go by like any and all construction workers I've known anywhere.

From a stationhouse vending machine, I purchased a CTA Transit Card — a slim credit card sized piece of plastic that you insert in a slot at the turnstile — and passed the time chatting with a business student waiting on the "Red Line". We spoke of Chicago people, which she didn't think could be categorized. "I don't buy into that whole thing about New Yorkers being mean and Midwesterners being friendly. I think people are the same everywhere."

The train carried me to the 35th-Sox stop and I followed a crowd up and through a breezeway over the highway, passing the scalpers and miscellaneous beverage vendors. The stadium was spanking new and emblazoned with White Sox signage.

The Public Relations department had left a ticket for me. Though rain had delayed the game start and a tarp was still on the field, I dropped into my seat, a Polish sausage with onions and mustard in my lap. When the game finally got under way, I enjoyed watching New York's Jason Giambi, then Bernie Williams, belt homers into the stands. A guy behind me also cheered. It turned out he was a lieutenant with a midtown-NYC Fire Department Engine Company who had taken some time off to do some cross country travel.

In front of me was another Yankee fan, though he was born only two blocks from the White Sox's old Comiskey Park home.

Unfortunately for us, in the bottom of the 6th, the Sox, behind 3-0, got a rally going, including a 3-run homer by Jose Valentin, to put the score at 5-3 Chicago. More hits followed in the same inning, the Sox with just one out. When the score reached 8-3, Yankee manager Joe Torre pulled pitcher Mike Mussina, five runs overdue as far as we were concerned. Joe replaced him with Antonio Osuna, which signaled to us that New York was writing this game off. The Yankees feebly answered with a run in the top of the 7th, which the Sox matched at the bottom of the same inning. That capped the game, with a final score of 9-4.

As I moved to the exit, a "South Sider", who'd taken interest in what I was scribbling, introduced me to "Mr. Chicago," Mike Sheahan, the Sheriff of Cooke County. Wearing a Duke University ball cap, Mike was "holding court" on the main level and everyone passing paid their respects. We spoke like we had known each other for years and, recognizing our common Irish roots, he shared a bit of Irish humor: "How does a South Side Irishman get to heaven? His funeral procession takes the Dan Ryan Expressway to the JFK Highway to O'Hare Airport and, from there, it's straight up."

We parted ways outside the stadium and I followed a pack chanting, "Jose, Jose, Jose, Jose" in celebration of the Sox win. The Red Line, which got increasingly crowded with each stop we made, whisked me back to Fullerton.

Upon arrival at Rose's, I spontaneously hatched dinner — the bratwurst from Milwaukee mixed in a red sauce with vegetables over linguine. It was a good home-based chow followed by a playing of Bob Marley's "Uprising" CD to get us in the spirit for our evening adventure — a visit to the Wild Hare reggae bar near Wrigley Field. I was fairly sure Steinbeck's visit had not included such a stop. But if I was to take Chicago's pulse, I really needed to see all sides of it.

We hit the bricks straight up Clark, a long stretch of eclectic restaurants, bars and shops, noting a pet store offering toy fire hydrants, two women mirroring each other with bobbed hairdos and long black dresses, and a French place where a trio crooned French songs. The classic Buca Italian restaurant, with "SPUMONI" in neon out front, had odd photos and artwork decorating every wall space inside. Our favorite items were framed photos of mock Miss Buca representatives from the early '60s: Donatella Plasky, described as a "graciously-proportioned brunette," Roxanne Campanella with the warning "Watch out, dangerous curves ahead" and Hazel "Butter" Bracco, billed as a full-time salesgirl at the Frederick & Nelson glove counter. Taboo Tabou displayed leather, whips and Bettie Page Christmas ornaments. BD's Mongolian BBQ was, in itself, puzzling. "Wrigleyville," the area adjacent to the ballpark, brought more diversity with Irish, Ethiopian, Chinese, Mexican and Jamaican eateries.

The Wild Hare & Singing Armadillo Frog Sanctuary Ltd. was, unfortunately, empty, needing more time to bubble. Though it seemed the evening was starting to stumble around the ring, Rose and I were determined to keep it from dropping to the canvas. As we started back the way we had come, "Barbie Doll," a 60-year-old peroxide blonde dressed in a Cubs teddy, rushed past us into a karaoke bar to shimmy and sing. Promising sign we thought.

Rose steered us to a hot dog place called The Wieners Circle, saying mysteriously, "Whatever happens, happens." The counterwoman, who'd just cursed at and hung up the phone on someone, recommended the Char Red Hot, a charcoal-grilled hot dog that came topped with warm onions, mustard, tomato slices and small green peppers. When I asked if the latter were jalapenos, the large woman behind the counter said, "Whatdya think they are, little dicks motherf----r?" Noticing that Rose wasn't ordering anything, the woman commented, "That's why she's a skinny little ass." We'd been subjected to live theater, café style, and had a great laugh about the interaction with other visitors seated outside.

Peering into the Galway Arms Restaurant and Bar, we spied a manly gathering of Pernaud liquor company representatives, some 20 men in all, puffing cigars and downing pints. NEO, a hole-in-the-wall at the end of a back alley with an indistinguishable, graffiti sprayed door, promoted "Medical Fetish Night", but the high cover charge and doorman in labcoat and rubber gloves gave us second thoughts about attending.

The night was now down for the count and, as we returned to Rose's, we realized we'd been nowhere, and yet everywhere. To wind down, we caught a TV documentary about Chicago's Soldier Field, an elegant columned oval opened in 1924 as a sports arena called the Municipal

Grant Park Stadium. Renamed in 1925 to honor soldiers that had died in WWI, it hosted football, world heavyweight boxing, political addresses and rodeos. In 1971, the Chicago Bears football team moved there after 50 seasons at Wrigley. Seven years later, renovation began to provide new lights, locker rooms, playing surfaces and spectator seating. Construction had just begun on a new Soldier Field, a monstrosity of a stadium designed to be state-of-the-art, though hiding the elegance of the original structure within which it sits. It was a sad symptom of progress.

Channel surfing later, I landed on a local show, "54321," on the Fox Sports Net Channel, co-hosted by an attractive woman named LeeAnn Tweeden. I realized that she'd been sitting down the row from me at the stadium this afternoon and that I'd actually spoken with her briefly as we were both waiting to meet up with people.

Day 20: So Long, Chi-Town

Rose had left for work by the time I arose, at which time I hopped right on e-mail. One task was to confirm flight information to and from Raleigh/Durham, NC, as I had planned yet another detour from Steinbeck's route. This particular one would allow me to attend a Saturday celebration of my folks' 40th wedding anniversary at the University of North Carolina's Carolina Club. My Dad had planned the event without my mom's knowledge and it involved family and friends flying or driving in from various points around the U.S. to attend. For my part, I would fly in tomorrow morning, hide out with a family friend and then appear at the party after it had gotten lift-off. Talk about journeys, this occasion embodied them all. The detour would also reunite me with Marlene and my boys for a brief spell, as Steinbeck had been reunited with Elaine in Chicago. For now, I would again take advantage of the morning quiet to read the paper and write.

Yesterday's *Chicago Tribune* detailed the Cubs win over the Reds that, with an Astros' loss, put Chicago in first place in their division. At the same time, the White Sox had their playoff hopes crushed with a 7-0 loss to the Yankees combined with a Twins win against Cleveland. That gave Minnesota the Central Division pennant and New York their sixth consecutive AL East title.

In the Business section, Donald Trump unveiled plans to build a 90-story skyscraper on the site of the *Chicago Sun-Times* building on the Chicago River. To be completed in 2007, it would be the city's 4th-tallest structure.

Old friend Norm, with whom I never connected at the stadium, checked in to declare himself "an ass" for having left his cellphone in his briefcase. We weren't able to coordinate another attempt. My contact at the Ambassador East also gave a ring. While unable to find any record of Steinbeck's stay there, he was able to say that the Dunffey family had owned the place, along with four or five other hotels, at the time. I thought I'd make the hotel a stop on the way to the Pier.

An overland trucker who lived across from the Wolverine company but was on the road when I tried to reach him, checked in and connected me to its former owner, Fred Renas, and Fred's shop foreman, Ron Hefner, who it was thought supervised the construction of Steinbeck's camper. According to Fred, Steinbeck had contacted GMC, and GMC, in turn, contacted Wolverine, in late 1959. The process "drug out" according to Fred but they did get the contract to build and outfit a cabin on the back of the GMC pickup. Fred recalled having to replace a window on the vehicle, too, which broke during Steinbeck's cross-country odyssey.

Besides having neighboring property, my trucker friend had his own story about and connection with Wolverine. Back in 1963, when John F. Kennedy was president and espousing fitness, he and a couple of his 20-something buddies, who fancied themselves weightlifters, decided to join the craze, planning a 150-mile, three-day hike. When the Gladwin Chamber of Commerce got wind of their idea, area businesses, including Wolverine, got behind them. Fred provided the loan of a brand new camper for the boys to use as a home base in which to change, sleep and take shelter.

Wolverine apparently had no direct contact with Steinbeck, according to Ron. It was GMC public relations man John Castle, a writer himself, who served as the intermediary. And it was Ron's brother Ken who actually worked on Rocinante, a vehicle that Pontiac, Michigan-based GMC Truck & Coach donated to Steinbeck in return for the publicity. In fact, when the trip concluded, Steinbeck appeared in a promotional video for GMC.

Early afternoon, I climbed out of my foxhole and started padding to the Navy Pier, within manageable walking distance of Rose's. A schoolyard was busy with kids kicking balls and tearing around while the Lincoln Park Zoo advertised its "African Journey" and a petting farm. In Old Town, populated with outdoor cafes, a Walgreen's helped me to film and more notebooks.

At Goethe and State stood the Ambassador East hotel. My connection met me and we stood in the green marble tiled lobby beneath the elegant crystal chandeliers and large arching mirrors, trying to imagine Steinbeck curled up in his wrinkled clothes on one of the couches there. When I asked if the place had changed much since Steinbeck's visit (or even since 1926 when the hotel was built), he said it hadn't. He also mentioned a guest room called the "Author's Room" where noted authors would historically stay. In it, there was a bookcase that held signed copies of visiting authors' books. We both wondered if any of Steinbeck's novels were among them, but couldn't access the space as a well-known music group was occupying it.

Lake Shore Drive, much like New York's FDR Drive, brought me east along Lake Michigan past all the luxury apartments. Purple asters, yellow mums and white violets lined the sidewalk along the opulent Drake Tower. Northwestern Memorial Hospital loomed large.

Emerging from a subterranean passage, I crossed through Jane Addams Memorial Park, where a lawn maintenance crew was hard at work, and found the Navy Pier on the far side. A Children's Museum, with a giant black spider affixed to the front, occupied the first block, followed by a shopping mall and Shakespeare Theater. Walking along the water, I admired the 150-foot, 4-mast Windy II sailing sloop, offering "an authentic Tall Ship experience" to all takers.

Ultimately, I reached the Festival Hall exhibit area to attend a sales promotion event. The hall was filled with vendors of everything from in-store shelving and displays to neon signage and electronic gadgets, and several attendee faces were familiar. After circulating through, I paused at an iron table in a café area to have a couple of hot dogs, eyeing sparrows that had somehow gotten into the show hall and were foraging for crumbs amidst the tables.

Planning to attend a post-show gala, I found an outdoor beer garden where a band of Beatles imitators were playing, a welcome time-killer. From a stationary bench by the water, I listened along, enjoying a chilly breeze and a view of Chicago's skyline glinting in the sun.

The Grand Ballroom, a dome-covered expanse, was the site of the gala, which included a silent auction, food and drink. The party was 1920s themed, with gaming tables. I browsed them, checking on players' progress. Some were up, some were down, but everyone was having a good time. With red-and-white poker chips in hand, I joined a blackjack game in progress. "Baby needs a new pair of shoes!" I cried. After a bit of gameplay, I split off to cash in my chips for raffle tickets. Unfortunately, none came up prizewinners, so I set out to return to the Lincoln Park area, finding myself walking in step with a Caribbean-born trade show worker. I dodged to a cab then, whose driver was an Indian fellow. These encounters and others here made me realize there was a great diversity of people in Chicago. It was a melting pot, much like New York.

As Rose was occupied, I was on my own to browse Lincoln Park again. The evening's tour began with a rail-thin blonde wearing a tank top — an odd choice of clothing as it was decidedly not tank top weather. The woman explained that she'd had to vacate her apartment because of a mold problem. All she had was the threads on her back and was staying on a friend's couch while looking for new lodgings.

I made a turn onto Belmont, steering into the Big City Tap. Like the Hotel Wisconsin back in Milwaukee, the sturdy tavern was full of old, sepia-toned photos of historic city scenes and people: Electric trolleys. A fleet of Chicago police cars from the '20s. Mayors "Big Bill" Thompson and Richard Daley. The Paradise Theater. Old Comiskey Park. Horse-drawn fire wagons. An 11-story auto parking elevator. The South Water Market in 1925. Wrigley Field in the '40s. The collection really brought home Chicago's history and was appropriately featured here in one of the city's longer standing establishments.

A while later, the Red Line shuttled me to Halligan's, which was noisy and smoky and had a film crew auditioning patrons for a beer commercial. I was done for the night and headed back to Rose's.

Day 21: A Detour East

Rose had set the TV to auto-awaken me at 6 and it did its job well. I quickly got organized condensing some weekend items into a couple of cases, thanked Rose for her hospitality and, with blistered feet from all the walking I'd done the day before, gingerly strolled to the train station up Fullerton. An Egg McGriddle and water served as breakfast.

The Purple Line was crowded with morning commuters, leaving standing room only, and even then there wasn't much space. Straphangers busied themselves with the *Wall Street Journal*, the *Trib* or the *RedEye*, the latter featuring the headline "PANICVILLE" referring to the Cubs' pennant chase. Though Sammy Sosa slugged out two homers last night, one of them pushing him past Mickey Mantle to the 10th spot on the all-time home-run list, Chicago still succumbed to the Reds 9-4 in Cincinnatti. The Cubs were due to return home tonight, a highly anticipated event that promised to fill the bars and streets around Wrigley.

At Clark, I transferred over to a nearly empty car on the Orange Line for the lift to Midway Airport, passing through dense residential areas, factory and warehouse lots fenced with barbed wire and scrubby trackside lots where squatters in makeshift tents had taken up residence. At the airport stop, the end of the line, a maze of corridors and an escalator led to Southwest Air check-in where I received a boarding pass and proceeded to a security area for pocket emptying and carry-on inspection. The latter required the use of a small wand with a swab on the end designed to pick up traces of explosives. Today's air travelers have come to accept this measure, random pat-downs and more intrusive invasions of privacy as par for the course. I think, too, that we live with any associated delays because of the extra peace-of-mind and safety they ensure.

Boarding was quick and my seatmate was a poli-sci grad out of USC bound for her folks' house in Palm Beach, Florida. More recently a public relations person for a politico in L.A., she had liquidated most of her belongings and planned to use the home base to figure out her next life move. She hoped to pursue p.r. but for societal good rather than economic gain.

We were in the air by 10 and my seat mate was asleep by 10:05, admitting to "narcolepsy when it comes to air travel." In no time, I was back on the ground, but in sunny, sweltering North Carolina. A home away from home, it had been a family retreat and holiday spot for nearly two decades, since my folks had relocated there from suburban New York.

This was my break in continuity, as Chicago had been Steinbeck's, but rather than keep my moments here under wraps as he did his, I thought it important to capture and regurgitate them. For, represented here was yet another way of life, individuals with unique values and new sites to see. No, the visit did not neatly follow the geographic trail I'd thus far pursued, but did it matter? Nor, in this exploration of America, could I omit this leg simply because a family reunion formed its center. Besides, the clandestine, offbeat nature of the gathering itself made an amusing tale.

Again, the anniversary party was a secret from my Mom, so on the premise that he was attending a faculty meeting, my Dad collected me at my gate and we crossed the terminal to wait on my brother, Dave, and his wife, who were flying in from California. Though it had been almost four years since I'd seen them, they hadn't changed a bit. Over his shoulder, my brother had slung an old Pan Am tote, a prop that would have later significance.

We traveled to Rick's Diner and Catering Company, a new restaurant in Durham, and, adopting a Peter Lorre voice, my brother ushered us inside. Seeking a Southern meal experience, I ordered fried chicken, served crispy and boneless with greens on a toasted bun. A round of drinks and overhead fans in our lattice-fenced outdoor space helped us keep cool in the heavy, 80-degree-plus air, markedly opposite to the chilly morning I'd experienced in Chicago. Over our meals, we spoke in general of road trip car difficulties, my unplanned delay in Michigan and the car keys I'd found under the hood of El Rucio in Maine.

Lunch adjourned and Dad, a professor of advertising at the University of North Carolina in Chapel Hill, took me by the school to make an office visit. Co-eds drifted by, turning heads as they crossed campus — it was a glorious day in this college community.

My "safe house" during my visit was the home of family friend Pat Johnston. Even more notably, the home was where singer James Taylor was raised and wrote some of his earliest, most inspired songs. On 25 acres of rolling land and offering over 3,000 square feet of split-level living space, the home had captivated Pat and her late husband, Jim, too, and was ideal as the meeting place for the new ad agency they'd formed in the early '70s.

Pat allowed me to set up shop at a large conference table in their front room at which I worked for an hour or two. Later, we dined at Acme Food & Beverage Company in downtown Carrboro, a contemporary eatery that offered black tables, funky red-and-blue hued artworks and "damn good food." With a Pinot Grigio, I enjoyed what I'd describe as a nouveau Southern meal of grilled Bartlett pear salad, herb-crusted pork tenderloin with potatoes au gratin, cappuccino and Jersey Queen peach crisp with a blob of vanilla ice cream. It was a decidedly fine feast with great company and, lazily, we drifted back to the house by way of Franklin Street, which was streaming with university students headed to the bars.

Deflating our mood, we learned later that author/personality George Plimpton had died at age 76 at his home in Manhattan. The son of a successful lawyer and ambassador to the United Nations who traced his roots to the Mayflower, George was schooled at Harvard, taught at Barnard and made a name for himself writing over three dozen books. I had known him indirectly through my Dad and an ad campaign my Dad's company, International Paper, had run, with Plimpton as a spokesman.

Day 22: Among Family

As is my wont, I rose with the new day, stumbling from the four-post bed that had been my resting spot for the night, to stand at sliding glass doors and watch Mother Nature dial up her dimmer switch. Then I relocated to my new roost at the conference table, on the wall behind which a clock in the shape of a bull terrier kept time, its tail swinging back and forth with the passing seconds.

When Pat rose, she sent me up the long drive to collect her morning paper, *The News & Observer*. There was the item about Plimpton but also a notice that British rock star Robert Palmer, whose music I'd enjoyed as a teen, had also died, succumbing at age 54 to a sudden heart attack at the luxury Warwick Hotel in Paris. Oddly, this occurred after a "calm night of dinner and a movie" with his girlfriend of 20 years. A resident of Switzerland in the latter part of his life, Palmer was best known for his 1980s hits "Addicted to Love" and "Simply Irresistible."

As I walked back to the house, I looked up into the branches of the pines, and at the bamboo — planted by Mrs. Taylor reportedly to hide a neighbor's garbage cans — and Beech trees that line the property. Squirrels shelled me with Beechnut husks as I kept my eyes peeled for the young, antlered buck that Pat said she often spots, but didn't encounter him.

Returning to my writing at the conference table, I began smelling breakfast cooking and helped put out placemats. "This table's like the Mad Hatter's Tea Party. We can just move down," Pat said, referring to the piles of newspapers, magazines, books and circulars that occupied one end. Indeed, the house was a warehouse of literary materials which Pat had been attempting to organize and catalog. Currently though, her project had been boxing up Jim's clothes for a local charity. He had amassed quite a wardrobe given that they had maintained offices in L.A., New York and here and needed to be prepared for any weather or occasion.

We sat to eat poached eggs and then strips of bacon in little bowls, rosemary toast topped with wild Swedish lingonberries, and tomato juice. There was kosher salt available to season the eggs for which Pat offered a ring of measuring spoons to administer it. "Oh, I never measure. I just use a dash or a pinch," I said. "Well, then, you'll find these spoons useful." They were labeled DASH, PINCH and SMIDGEN.

Returning condiments to the kitchen, I noticed some of the wall hangings there. A button: "He's Tan, Rested and Ready. Nixon in '88." A postcard: "Greetings from Siberia!" A sign: "Please do not annoy, torment, pester, plague, molest, worry, badger, harry, harass, heckle, persecute, irk, bullyrag, vex, disquiet, grate, beset, bother, tease, nettle, tantalize or ruffle the animals — San Diego Zoo."

I went for a little stroll around the immediate property to look at the house from all angles and the gated meadow where the Taylors had kept some 22 sheep at one time. Upon my return, Pat asked if I'd sprayed myself with repellant before taking my walk, as chiggers lurk in the grass. "They burrow into your skin and can really make your life miserable," she said. I hadn't and did my best job brushing myself off, but worried later with each little imagined itch whether I'd picked up some sub-dermal passengers. The midday hours that followed were spent pecking away at my laptop compiling my notes, while Pat busied herself with household chores.

Marlene, who had driven down from Connecticut with our boys, her mom and youngest sister, and stayed the night at her brother's in Norlina, checked in and was headed for us. It had been more than three weeks since I'd seen them all and, like Steinbeck, I was looking forward to reconnecting. The local bi-weekly, *The Chapel Hill News*, was a worthy time occupier, announcing the arrival of the Carrboro Music Festival and relating the odd story of a wedding guest staying at the Carolina Inn who had to be forcibly removed from the premises. He had been paying for his room with $1 coins, was harassing guests and carrying strange items — a safe and rope — around in a rented van.

The ultimate reunion was both joyous and tearful. Bills, mail and magazines were delivered, updates were shared and afternoon plans made. Pat led us on an area tour and, naturally, we fell behind a vehicle with a custom license plate, "UNC DUKE" — rivals occupying the same space. Evan told me about a new "wiggly tooth" and school tests, while I eyed Phillip's school papers and efforts to write the letter "B" and number "2."

We drove through the Finley Golf Course, then to the new SouthPoint Mall, a huge, crowded complex of stores in Durham County where the girls went to girl shops and the boys went to boy shops. Again, our congregating for the anniversary event was to be in the utmost secrecy to keep Mom in the dark, so we returned to Pat's where the ladies dressed to the nines, I donned my least crumpled attire and we convoyed to the UNC campus.

Stashing ourselves away in the Carolina Club's Peebles Room, we kept things to a dull roar while eyeing the hall with a small hand mirror, anticipating Mom and Dad's arrival. They came along soon enough and, as Dad steered Mom our way, we greeted them with a collective "Happy Anniversary" cheer, to my mom's great surprise. The "sting" had worked perfectly, and excited chatter, feasting on salmon and great celebration ensued. Highlights of the evening included Evan's tooth popping out and each of us telling how we'd become acquainted with the honorees. Most entertaining was Dave and Jill's "Flashback to 1963" presentation, a little piece of theater that the Steinbecks, with connections in that community, would likely have found entertaining. Dressed as a Pan Am pilot and stewardess, the duo employed such props as the tote bag that Dave had carried at the airport and other period items that played into their tale.

Our time at the Club expired mid-evening with hugging and best wishes and an invitation from Dad to have drinks back at the house. Presents were opened, bows worn on heads, beer and wine swilled — all the zaniness common to Lauterborn family gatherings and a festive cap to the day. The secret operation a wrap, we all remained at the house for the overnight.

Day 23: Southern Hospitality

After Dad's special pancakes, which Evan declared were "almost as good" as mine and included a customary heart-shaped one for my Mom, packing of vehicles was conducted, multiple photographs taken and farewells made. All too soon, Marlene, the boys and my in-laws were all returning north; I would stay another day in Chapel Hill then return to Chicago.

Sitting down to work on my laptop late morning, I discovered my A/C power supply unit was shot. On a trek out to locate a new one, my Dad and I ended up at a sports bar at a nearby mall. One in a chain of over three-dozen national locations, this was no ordinary sports-viewing destination. It offered no less than 20 TV screens showing 10 individual events, including NFL, MLB and NASCAR. To help patrons select which screen to watch and avoid arguments over channels, a guide to viewing was provided. I don't imagine Steinbeck was much of a TV watcher, and certainly there was nothing like this in his day, but even he would have been impressed by this setup.

We plopped ourselves down at a central bar, in view of screens showing the Bills/Eagles match-up, the only game that had interest to us. Our bartender/waitress brought us 20-ounce Blue Moons with slivers of orange on the lip, and sandwich platters. While eating, I overheard her try and entice a diner to do a shot and asked her after if she would join in if they took her up on the offer. "I already had my Power Half Hour, last night," she said. "Me and two girlfriends ran up a $75 bar bill in 25 minutes, drinking shots of 1800 tequila." I had to remind myself that the area is a college center and that this is what you do at a college age.

Upon returning home, I spent the balance of the afternoon working on my laptop, munching on pretzels and catnapping. As the sun filtered through the trees surrounding Mom and Dad's hillside glass house and reflected off the crystal and brass décor, Mom brought Dave and me curious, small bundles of old letters. Retrieved from my 89-year-old Welsh grandmother's home after she was recently moved to a senior care facility, they had been written to the family matriarch by my brother and me over a 22-year period, spanning 1976 to 1998. They were fascinating time capsules and relics, really, in this day and age when the practice of writing letters by hand has become almost obsolete, replaced by e-mail. Steinbeck's nearly daily correspondence seemed unimaginable to me — it had been an effort for me just to arrange the sending of postcards!

Still reading from the letters, we all climbed into Dad's "ark" of an automobile to travel to dinner. We were responding to an invitation from Tommy and Brenda Tapp, Jill's folks, who had a home in White Cross. Though a section of Chapel Hill and only 15 miles west of the cosmopolitan university center, the area was as rural as rural could be. Delayed in arriving at their single-level setback, we were, nonetheless, warmly welcomed.

As is my habit, I hovered in the kitchen to inspect wall hangings, often the greatest illustrations of a family's nature and personality. On the refrigerator, a mini mat, "Brenda's kitchen," and cat cutout, "Every life should have 9 cats!" Above a small table, a collage of country scenes with two photos of grandchildren tucked in the wood frame. Above the sink, a plate, depicting the Clover Garden Methodist Church on Route 1 in Chapel Hill. A wall hanging: "USA – My country, my home." A flower-bordered painting of a cottage bearing the message, "Within this house may love abide to bless all those who step inside." It was clear that God, country, family and felines all held special places here.

At the end of the room, there was a large print of a farm scene and, again, a photo tucked in the frame, this one of an old milk delivery wagon. The latter had particular significance to Brenda, whose dad Roger had been a milkman early in his career. Roger took a second wife a few years ago, a union that was celebrated at a local Hardee's, where he and his bride often met friends for meals.

Without further delay, we sat to the dinner table, a jerry rigged, banquet length job set up in the living room that was more than adequate for our purposes. Brenda had prepared a tasty meal of chicken pot pie in empty pie shells, and corncob halves, served with a side of salad, and wine that we had supplied. Dessert was strawberry shortcake. The setting was cozy and the faces of family members in photos all around smiled down upon us. Most notable was one of Tommy's mom, "Maw Maw," with a 76-pound pumpkin, or "punkin" as Tommy said she'd call it. The year of the photo, she had asked Tommy to get her a good-sized pumpkin and Tommy had seen the orange mammoth at the town hall. When the Halloween holiday was over, Tommy was able to take the gourd and delivered it, with some effort, to Maw Maw. She made 72 pies out of the beast, giving away all but two or three to friends and neighbors.

Following dessert, Chuck and Lisa and their 3-year-old snow-haired angel of a daughter, Brittany, joined us. Lisa is Tommy's daughter from his first marriage and they all live next door. Chuck, whose job is to move heavy construction equipment, came in limping, having tripped over a wheelbarrow recently and injured himself. Brittany just bounced through, a bundle of activity. In rural areas like this one, as I would see in many places across the country, families often took up residence near each other and benefitted from shared resources.

We looked at family albums, showing photos of Jill's brother, an English teacher in Thailand; her elder sister; and of Jill. The topic of my travels came up and Chuck mentioned a Sunday morning TV program in which the host throws a dart at a map of the U.S., travels to whichever place it lands on and interviews a person at random from the local phone book.

As we departed, leaving Dave and Jill there for the overnight, Tommy warned, "Watch out for the deer. They're out on the road this time of night." We sailed home in the ark without incident, singing along to the radio, "I've got a brand new pair of roller skates, and you've got a brand new key…" The latter was quite naughty we decided, but in a quaint, old-fashioned way.

Back at the house, when we turned on some outdoor lighting, we discovered a huge, intricate and strategically positioned web occupied at the center by what we determined was a large spider of the Orb Weaver classification. As it has poor vision, it locates its prey by feeling the vibration and tension of the threads in its web, then quickly rushes to the captive. We stood there in morbid fascination and watched winged creatures fly perilously close, and even through gaps in the web, until an unfortunate moth alit and stuck. The many-legged arachnid sprang into action, nimbly traversing the silky bullseye, biting its victim and rolling it over to devour it.

The evening closed with a call to Marlene, to check that she and the boys had had a safe trip home and to reiterate to each other how enjoyable our reunion, though brief, had been.

Day 24: On to Iowa

I awoke to the chirp of monster crickets, did an hour's worth of writing and sat with Mom and Dad for a breakfast of fried eggs and sausage patties. *The Herald-Sun* noted that an electrical failure in Switzerland put 58 million Italians in the dark. I wondered what 58 million Italians would do in the dark and thought that, if nothing else, they would make babies.

Dad raced me to the airport, tuned into local news radio. We heard about the passing of tennis great Althea Gibson, the first black star in that sport, who had lived for a time in Wilmington, NC. James Taylor chimed in on a commercial break, singing the University Mall's jingle. Coincidentally, we had just passed over the newly dubbed James Taylor Bridge spanning Morgan Creek. The sign marking it, a hot collectible, had already been stolen.

Traveling along I-40, we remarked on the road-widening project along its length. The work and other expansion and building projects reflected the continuing attraction the area has for retirees and young, tech-oriented professionals.

Rush hour traffic aside, we made quick time to the airport and Dad dropped me curbside. I collected my boarding pass, flashed my I.D. at a security person, again emptied my pockets of assorted belongings for scrutiny and settled in on my flight. My row mate was a busty blonde marketer of consumer package goods based in Chicago. Born and raised in Australia, she came to Ohio as a child when her dad was transferred to Akron. We spoke about our respective businesses as the plane lifted into the air — at rather a sharp angle, I observed with concern. A former Air Force serviceman, my row mate explained that the steep climb is purposeful these days, to avoid a possible terrorist strike by a ground-fired missile — yet another cause for worry in our danger-fraught society.

Around 10:30 a.m. (Central time), we swooped down out of the clouds and were discharged into chilly, overcast Chi-Town. Locating the Orange Line to The Loop was no problem and I was soon clacking across the city to the Clark Street stop.

Near me sat a very tan woman with brown eyes and frosted hair, wearing a grey sweat jacket with "UIC" on it. She had just returned from her hometown of Windsor, Canada, where I thought she must have snow skied or caught the sun, to get so brown. But she explained that her coloring was genetic, the result of the union of a Native American (Chippewah) dad and Italian mom. The "UIC" referred to her former school, the University of Illinois at Chicago. When I told her of my travels, she said she had only taken one big road trip in her life, to southern California when she was 16. She went with her parents and six-year-old sister, who constantly asked, "Are we there yet? Are we there yet?" even though they had thousands of miles yet to go. After three weeks in So-Cal, she was to return by car to Windsor, but had had enough car travel for one trip and flew home. I spoke of my adventures in Chicago and she asked if I'd seen the new Soldier Field. "Only on TV," I replied. She wondered how I could have missed it, adding that the debut game was being played there tonight, between the Bears and Packers. She'd obviously embraced Chicago as her second home.

We both hopped at Clark, where I diverted for the Purple Line. After waiting a long while, a kindly woman packing a stack of CTA cards informed me that the Purple Line doesn't run during the midday hours and led me to the Red Line for the ride to Fullerton. The sun, a quick change into a fleece jacket and sneakers, and fast stroll back to Rose's area helped warm me up. There was good old El Rucio waiting for me curbside and soon she was organized and ready to continue our journey west. She didn't seem to mind too much that I'd left her alone, unlike Steinbeck's Charley, who was a little miffed about being deposited in a kennel. At the same time, the dog was glad to see Rocinante, beaming with pride about his newly groomed appearance and "delighted to be traveling again." I, too, was excited, feeling that I'd been too long off the road and needed to re-attune myself with its rhythm. Steinbeck, in contrast, was apprehensive, not eager "to go through the same lost loneliness all over again."

As to his route, he headed northward into Wisconsin, which he described as a "noble land of good fields and magnificent trees." He was "unprepared for [its] beauty...for its variety of field and hill, forest, lake." Before laying eyes upon it, he'd imagined it as "one big level cow pasture because of the state's enormous yield of milk products." A lover of cheese, he noticed that "cheese was everywhere." He also spied a large distributor of seashells, finding the sighting odd as the state hadn't "known a sea since pre-Cambrian times." For the overnight, he stopped at a hilltop truck stop where "gigantic cattle trucks rested" and scraped from their cargo holds "mountains of manure," much to Charley's joy. The dog moved about "smiling and sniffing ecstatically like an American woman in a French perfume shop." While out walking later, they looked down into a valley that they found "carpeted with turkeys," a "reservoir for Thanksgiving." From there, he entered southern Minnesota.

As I'd done the climb up to northern Michigan and boomeranged down through Wisconsin to Chicago, I would head, instead, west to Davenport, Iowa and then north to Minnesota and rejoin Steinbeck's route near St. Paul. The plan decided, I set off for the interstate, immediately getting bogged down in traffic skirting O'Hare Airport. Eventually, I-90 yielded to 294 South and a sea of billboards for everything from Scotch and cars to strip joints and casinos. That road dumped me onto 55 South, which, in turn, popped me out onto 80 West.

I'd been to flat lands before but these were *the* flattest, with acre after acre of corn, the occasional steel silo, a water tower signaling a town, and truck upon truck hauling stuff. I set the cruise control — and would have hit a SNOOZE button if there had been one on my dash — and coasted across Illinois' forehead.

Actually, the blandness of the landscape gave me the opportunity to think about a general topic that had been percolating in my head: distracting activities that motorists get up to while they're driving. The thought was inspired by a recent traffic safety report citing some alarming statistics about drivers: More than 91 percent played with the radio or CD player — an average of once every eight minutes. Seventy-one percent ate or drank. Forty-five percent groomed themselves, something I could attest to, having often seen men shaving and donning neckties and women applying makeup, their vehicles coasting along nearly pilotless. Forty percent read or wrote, an offense that I must confess I've committed. And 30 percent used their cellphones. The topper was the Ohio woman who was pulled over for allegedly breast-feeding her baby at the wheel! From the reports, you would think we are all a bunch of nits, suffering from Attention Deficit Disorder. But the plain truth is that our lives are more complicated, particularly with an ever-increasing number of women in the work force than in Steinbeck's era, and we are expected to accomplish more in less time.

LaSalle, the largest city on this non-descript pass-through, got my attention for a minute. But only because state cops in unmarked Camaros were pulling speeders over. The Dixon/Princeton area identified itself as the hometown of Ronald Reagan. Stopping at a J&S Antiques just off the highway, I got word that Reagan was actually born in Tampico, "a nothing of a town" according to a counterperson, and raised in Dixon.

Nearing dinnertime, El Rucio and I crossed over the mighty Mississippi, glinting in the descending sun, and sailed on into a new state: "The People of Iowa Welcome You — Fields of Opportunities." I decided to head for Davenport's waterfront, on the way seeing ads for pork sandwiches and a digital display putting the air temperature at 56 degrees.

Over a rise, I found the Rhythm City Casino, a permanently moored riverboat that appeared to be attracting the blue hair set. The *Quad-City Times* building, Builders Sand and Cement Company and Iowa American Water Company came up soon after. Great homes lined the crest near Bettendorf, near which I pulled into the lot of the Isle of Capri, another riverfront casino. Inside, in large rooms on two floors, there were slot machines with names like Double Diamond and Cherry, piped-in Calypso music and more wheelchairs than you could shake a stick at. After helping push someone up a ramp, I made a fast exit and decided to plod on toward Iowa City.

Nature called so I pulled into Iowa 80, "The World's Largest Truck Stop." It lived up to its billing, with a cinema, Laundromat, arcade, gift shop, grocery, family den, at least 20 shower rooms and more. In the games area, six bearded Grizzly Adams types wearing Peterbilt hats cheered on one of their own who was manhandling a police chase video machine. Others lumbered to the Dairy Queen.

The West Liberty exit I was seeking, just 10 miles shy of Iowa City, finally came up and, there, off the ramp, was a KOA. The registration office doubled as a lunch counter called Mom's Kitchen where a very large man and woman, he hairless with one ear missing and a staple where it used to be, had just finished their fried chicken and mash. Another man sat at an adjacent table watching a woman on TV's "Fear Factor" trying to eat a large, live, multi-legged insect. "I don't think I could do that," he said aloud to no one in particular. "Mom," a hunched over woman who hobbled around the cooking area, had just made up a big pot of chili. I took a small container of it to go, which was provided with a Ziploc that held a plastic soupspoon, napkin and several Saltine crackers — very Mom-like accents. With a bag of ice added to the order and a camp map, I found my space, set up my grill and started making dinner, quelling my appetite with the chili.

It had come time to prepare my buffalo sausage and onto the grill top the four links went. Water for pasta boiled in a separate pot. When the sausage was mostly done, I sliced it up and further sautéed it with onion and pepper slivers, dumping all over the pasta in a large bowl. As the procession of trucks continued to roll by on the interstate, I ate my "gruel" in the van, enjoying the spicy flavor of the buffalo, orange juice to wash the meal down and the Bears-Green Bay game on the tube. Unfortunately for Chicago fans, who had come to see the team in their new stadium, Green Bay was beating up on them.

The wind kicked up outside, becoming quite ferocious actually, rocking the van from side to side and puffing up a tarp I'd used to cover over the grill. While watching my tape of British comedy, which I'd popped in after the game, I tired and scrunched up in my sleeping bag under my wool blanket, the first time the weather had warranted its use.

Day 25: In the Heartland

The temperature was in the 30s when I woke, still in the previous day's clothes, to the continued hum of passing semis and chirp of birds chasing each other through the nearby cornfield. Needing a restroom visit, I slipped on flip-flops and quick-stepped across the compound. A secret combination, provided with the camp map, let me into the very clean, though unheated, space, its cinder block walls decorated with stenciled pictures of moose, fish, pine trees and bear. Other features here were provided with particular purpose: The overhead light was motion activated to conserve electricity. A hand dryer ensured good hygiene and convenience. A roll of toilet paper was wedged onto a metal bar in such a way that the struggle to remove each length would make you think twice about wasting it.

Returning to the van, I got my portable heater going, trying to power it first with my new inverter. But the unit was indicating an overload, so I abandoned it for a good old extension cord plugged into the hook-up outside. Though the heat that the little unit produced was not as warm as I would have liked, it helped take the chill off and I was no longer seeing steam with each breath. I ultimately abandoned it, too, to run the van's own heater, which thawed me right out.

While letting the outside air temp rise before attempting a shower run, I occupied myself at my laptop for an hour or so. The wait helped some, the restroom combination hadn't been changed and the motion-activated overhead light detected me as before. As to the shower, it was very clean but highly sensitive, operating on a fine line between cold and scalding. Like a Swiss watchmaker, I tuned in the right temperature and, once locked, really started to thaw out. As I did, I gazed at the shower curtain with a KOA logo (half tent and half person) imprinted on it and thought that it has probably been a long time since a KOA camp saw a tent.

I may have indulged myself too long, for the light winked out, leaving me in darkness. However, my flailing to locate my towel, as the chill air met my skin, quickly re-activated it and I promptly dried, dressed and returned to my site. Noticing that I looked cold, the owner of the 30-odd-foot HI-LO Classic trailer in the space next to mine came over with his dog and a steaming cup of coffee.

The 67-year-old Scotch-Irishman had retired five years before and, since, he and his wife had been full-time RV'ing, with no home base other than a 39-foot camper back in Alva. They had adopted this lifestyle and new "carpe diem" approach to life after he overcame three types of cancer and his wife survived four bypass surgeries. He said his 93-year-old mother shared their life approach, though she'd just begun residing at a care facility after breaking a hip. He was pleased with the home, operated by Mennonites, saying it was immaculate and very accommodating, with daily menus and all. "There should be a special place in heaven for the people who work in these homes," he said. The story reminded me of my grandmother, who, though she had found herself in similar circumstances, remained unsinkable.

We parted company, wishing each other "Happy Trails," and I drove around to Mom's to see about breakfast. It was too cold outside, I'd decided, to prepare anything and I didn't want to lose the benefit of the hot shower or coffee.

A corn-bred woman was manning the grill this morning and produced for me two eggs scrambled, pre-cooked sausage links, hash browns and whole wheat toast: like paradise on a plate to me. For reading material, I commandeered a copy of the *Iowa City Press-Citizen*. A photo on the front page showed an Iowa City man covering his raspberry bushes with sheets to protect them from the first frost. An Amazing Maize Maze carved out of a cornfield in Princeton was attracting many visitors. Adventurer David Hempleman-Adams became the first person to cross the Atlantic solo in an open wicker basket balloon, traveling from Sussex in New Brunswick, Canada, to Blackpool, northwestern England.

With the staff, I spoke of famous Iowans: actor Ashton Kutcher whom I'd just seen on "That '70s Show", bandleader Glenn Miller, singer Andy Williams, actress Donna Reed and actor John Wayne. When I quizzed them about John Wayne's real name, they both answered in unison, "Marion Michael Morrison." There was no catching these two on their Iowa trivia. From a bookmark that Karen produced, we even learned Iowa facts. State nickname: The Hawkeye State. Bird: Eastern Goldfinch. Population: 2.9 million. Capital: Des Moines. Tree: Oak.

A postcard of a pig with upturned nose and the caption, "I Just Love The Midwest!" caught my eye and I decided to fill it out and send it to my family. As I paid for my meal, I passed the postcard to the grill attendant to be mailed, saying, "You're free to read it if you like." Her pink cheeks turned a little pinker as she admitted to a compulsion for reading people's postcards. In fact, she would even hold up the mail if she hadn't read them all, she confessed. I told her that I would do the same, as postcards capture a unique moment of someone's life, often preserved for a long time afterwards.

On that note, I fetched from the van the two postcards I'd bought the previous day and read the passage on the back of the one showing the Empire State Building. Dated Sept. 3, 1943, it was from Arthur Painter, a sailor stationed at the U.S. Coast Guard Training Station in Groton, CT, to his mother Beulah in Geneseo, IL: "Dear Mother, My chum and I was to N.Y. and say what a place. We managed to get a look at the city from the roof of the Empire State. And that roof, my dear friends, is really up in the air. Going up we made 86 floors in about 78 seconds. I thought that my shoes was [sic] still on the ground floor, 'Ha.' Well, how is everything back their [sic]? Tip top shape no doubt! Love Art." We shook our heads and smiled — a common passion for postcard espionage uniting us ever so briefly. "Have a good trip," she told me, and she meant it sincerely.

The experience there had awakened my interest in Iowa, which I'd written off as flat and corn-focused, like Steinbeck had at first dismissed Wisconsin. So, just up the road in West Branch, I stopped to see the Herbert Hoover museum. Hoover, our 31st president, was born here, and West Branchers were proud of that fact. The Hoover name dominated the town — from street and business names to banners and signage.

Born in a two-room cottage (on display at this site) in late Summer 1874 to parents Jesse, a blacksmith, and Hulda, Hoover's beginnings were humble but optimistic. "This cottage where I was born is physical proof of the unbounded opportunity of American life," a note outside the home declared. Inside, a guide, to whom I said, "My shed is bigger than this," greeted me. To that, he replied, "I've had people come in here and actually say how *large* it is. I guess it depends on which part of the country you're from." No matter which perspective you viewed it from, the home was intriguing, particularly the trundle bed. Really two beds in one, it featured a bottom section that rolled out from underneath. It was a smart contraption for a small space, though if both parts were occupied, there was no privacy to be had whatsoever. Still, a handy craftsman like Steinbeck would have thought it ingenious.

As I exited the cottage, a siren in town sounded. An approaching guide told me that it was a tornado warning system and is tested daily at noon. It's also sounded to summon the volunteer fire department. I couldn't imagine living with such a thing; though, if I were a resident here, I couldn't imagine living without it either.

I made one other stop in the complex, at Jesse Hoover's blacksmith shop. The combination of the chill air, clang of hammer on metal, snap of a little fire and scent of burning coal that I experienced there reminded me of South Wales, my Mom's birthplace — an ocean away.

At Iowa City, with a classic rock station on the radio and a herd of Black Angus grazing on a hillside off my port bow, I moved onto 380 toward the northern part of the state. The temperature had "soared" to 52 according to a digital sign outside the Nesper Sign Advertising Company. Cedar Rapids brought the Quaker Oats Company on the Cedar River (a tributary of the Mississippi), the Czech and Slovak Museum and a pen of miniature ponies.

Waterloo was a center for truck and trailer parts, construction, and asphalt and grout production. Its main sports complex, the Young Arena, advertised on a digital sign an upcoming Black Hawks hockey game. Just past it, I caught rural route 63 North, headed directly to Minnesota, shooting by manmade hills of asphalt at the Heartland Company.

Suddenly, something made contact with the windshield and stuck there. I pulled over to have a closer look and determined that it was some sort of very large-headed butterfly with black and yellow wings, and that it was its cranium, now smashed to a pulp, which had connected with the windscreen. I picked the carcass off the driver's side wiper, leaving an orange splat, and briefly considered bagging it for later identification. But, in its mangled condition, the alien specimen made me feel uneasy. I dropped it by the roadside and continued on.

The wind that had visited last night was back and forcing me to hang on tight to the steering wheel. I felt it especially when a truck would pass in the opposite direction. The air that would get trapped between our vehicles would literally smack and push El Rucio. Adding to the tension, I began to notice large boulders, one with a white picket fence around it, marking spots where motorists had been killed in road accidents.

Intact, though, we arrived at the headquarters of Featherlite Luxury Coaches & Trailers, appearing like an oasis in a corn desert. Outside, motor coaches and trailers stood in neat rows, gleaming in the sun. As prearranged, regional salesman "Dan", a self-described "farm boy", met me. Much like Steinbeck had been curious about trailer homes, this particular type of mobile accommodation fascinated me.

Apparently, big personalities need big vehicles. One of Dan's roles was to see that Featherlite's VIP clients' needs are met. His customers included racecar drivers, sports stars, actors and singers, who use the coaches to move about the country.

Randy took me through the Custom Service Center where a double-decker hog transporter and several motorcycle trailers were parked. Another area contained a mini Hummer, Dale Earnhardt Sr.'s #3 racecar, and Harleys that he and the company CEO had driven to the big Harley event in Milwaukee.

I finally had a chance to see one of the behemoths up close and personal when Dan took me aboard a new $1.3 million dollar, 45-foot long, H3-45 demo coach. It featured a granite floor with brass inlays, burl wood trim, acrylic laminate cabinets, a king-size bed, rear bathroom, two 42" plasma TVs, Bose surround sound and a video intercom system. We took our shoes off in reverence to pad around in it.

From farm boy to Featherlite, Dan had come a long way. We parted company, hoping to see each other again at a walleye tournament up north, and I pushed along toward the Twin Cities. A simple sign, "Welcome to Minnesota," protruding from a stone pillar, soon heralded my arrival in a new state. I bobbed and weaved as 63 did toward cosmopolitan Rochester, passing the Deer Park Speedway and, coincidentally, a Featherlite banner hanging there.

North of Rochester, free-roaming elk swarmed across pastureland. Feeling a bit like Steinbeck when he encountered the band of lady moose in Maine, I got out for a look. A female, turning grass over in her mouth, glanced over at me, and seeing no antlers atop my head, moved on. I wished I'd had some sort of cattle calling device to test its effect on the mammal. It would not be my only sighting of the species this trip.

Tired of driving and hungry, I took myself to a fancy steak place. But I took anything but a fancy meal approach, squatting at the bar for a plate of wings and pint of local beer, while a Cubs/Braves NL Division Playoff game aired in the background. Around me, Bud posters tied to the Vikings, NASCAR and the Twins adorned the walls. I had ordered a mild sauce to coat my wings, as is my preference, though the bartender mentioned a jalapeno sauce alternative if I dared try it. "Anyone who orders it, I tell 'em not to touch themselves or their woman," he grinned.

Steinbeck had not visited Minneapolis or St. Paul prior to his trip, nor was he able to during it, due to "a great surf of traffic" that engulfed him with "waves of station wagons" and "rip tides of roaring trucks." The flow carried him along and away from the area and he never found a sought-after destination, Golden Valley.

While it was too early to be spotting the metropolis, ahead there were suddenly bright lights and tall building-like structures. As I neared, though, I realized it was a kingdom-sized oil refinery complex, shining like a crystal palace. Beyond, huge planes bound for St. Paul's International Airport dropped down out of the sky. My entryway into Minneapolis, through the Financial Center, was impressive, though I had little opportunity to take anything in. Traffic shoved me past bars, restaurants, show palaces and go-go joints to a dark back street where a flatbed tow truck was plucking cars from the curb. Nearby, police cuffed and shoved two shifty-looking men into the back of their squad car. Having grown up in metro New York, I averted my eyes, not wanting the pokey-bound perpetrators to make my face.

A big, empty, fluorescent-lit public parking garage became El Rucio's shelter while I set out on foot. After a couple of unproductive forays into nightspots, I got a tip from a trio of giggling women for a place called DRINK. With a large, vertical neon sign out front, it wasn't hard to find, but was empty. Slightly more appealing was The Loon Café, across the street, which had the Cubs-Braves game on. I stooled it for a beer and Grateful Dead tunes, as Chicago took a 4-2 win.

All the while, I hoped that I would get a call back from a friend of my brother's in the area, a potential host for my stay here, but my messages went unanswered. Perhaps it was the night or the chill in the air, but whatever the reason, this Twin City, with its wide, cold boulevards and hungry tow trucks, was not doing handsprings to keep me here.

I was all set to drop in the van and move on when cool sounds emanating from a place called Fine Line Café reached my ears. A $5 cover admitted me to the brick-walled space, jam-packed with young people grooving and swaying to the evening's entertainment, Calexico, from Tucson, AZ. The feel here was upscale Greenwich Village, stylish casual. The sound was Cuban influenced with trumpet, bass, smooth electric guitar and maracas. The visual behind the band was a motion picture capture of old New York City, cable cars shooting back and forth on a cobblestone street. I was reminded of a club, 7 Willow Street in Port Chester, New York, where I met Marlene, which had an equally artsy feel.

An upper floor offered tables, black with pin spots above them, for more leisurely viewing, which seemed like a good perch for an observer like me. Cigarette smoke curled up into the lights and hovered in the air. As a loud, wailing segment captured the crowd's attention, a kind-faced brunette, who'd noticed me scribbling, asked what I was working on. Because the music was so loud, I replied via a napkin and, in this way, we continued communicating. It had to be one of the more unusual exchanges I've ever had.

A "farm girl gone corporate, "Abbie" worked in PR for a software company in Clear Lake, "where buddy Holly died." She didn't plan to stay in that field for long, though, and was busy working on a Masters in environmental policy. We debated about the music style in play here tonight. She felt it was Southwestern, with "echoes of cowboy melodies resonating in the Fender guitars and blaring trumpets." While it did get the spurs jangling, I thought there was a Spanish influence. "Think Malaguena," she offered, to which I commented, playing on the uniqueness of the name, "Some antibiotics and that'll clear right up." Fast on the uptake, she pursued, "I had it once. The rash never goes away."

As the napkins accumulated, I wondered if we were writing a separate book all by itself, a "great American novel" perhaps. Abbie thought our output was "more like a strange chat room for bar flies."

At midnight, the band was done, Abbie left for St. Paul and, I, with no lodgings or interest in hanging around Minneapolis, decided to keep going west. Ninety-four was my route and the posted speed limit was 70. I allowed for 10 miles extra and clicked on cruise control. Neon signs for places like Famous Dave's leaped out at me from the dark while a trucker ahead fought tiredness and to keep his truck in his lane. I was road raging with Jimmy Buffet's "Margaritaville", which leant a surreal quality to the moment.

Near here back in August, I remembered, Herb Brooks, the former coach that led the U.S. Hockey team to a win over the Soviet Union at the 1980 Lake Placid Olympics, was killed in a car wreck. More than 2,000 people gathered in his honor at the Cathedral of St. Paul and, when his coffin emerged through the front doors, former players held hockey sticks up high in salute.

At St. Cloud, I yanked the wheel right to visit an all-night convenience store in the Clearwater Travel Plaza. It was part of a whole complex that had shower rooms in an upper tier and a Nelson Bros. Bakery on the main. Seated in view of two TV sets, one tuned to an all-weather station and the other to Larry King's CNN talk show, I sipped coffee and nibbled at a strawberry turnover. The excitement I'd felt when I resumed my travels in Chicago had left me and been replaced by a cold hollowness.

As Steinbeck had done, I was moving north on the eastern side of the Mississippi, via U.S. 10. He'd also stopped roadside, but at a German restaurant. There, he had a terrible bratwurst, beer in a can, and sauerkraut that was "an insulting watery mess." To the waitress, he confessed being lost and asked for guidance to Sauk Centre, where author and friend Sinclair Lewis was born. The request brought the cook into the conversation and he and the waitress both wondered how Steinbeck could possibly have gotten lost here. Pointed the right way, he did manage to see the town, though very briefly, recalling Sinclair Lewis' friendship.

It was 3 a.m. when I passed an exit for St. John's University, intimidating foes of our local basketball team, the Fairfield University Stags. Flagging, I made a quick dash in and out of the "Middle Spunk Rest Area." The can of Coke the vending machine spit out was enough to get me to the aforementioned Sauk Centre. Considering a stay at the modest-looking Gopher Prairie Motel, I sounded a buzzer at the desk. As with Steinbeck's stop at the Whip O' Will cabins in Lancaster, there was no response. But rather than sit outside in my van and let the event trouble me for the rest of the night, I went across the way to try an AmericInn. It had vacancies, but the room rate wasn't reasonable for the short amount of time I'd be staying.

Pushing the threshold of my abilities, I fought near exhaustion and kept going, joining 71 North, a stretch of nothing so dark and undefined that I could see every star overhead, like pinholes in a large piece of black construction paper.

Suddenly, emerging from the blackness, a white sign advertising a roadside motel. I was good and ready for a simple bed, any bed, and drove right up to the little office. A buzzer by the door alerted a Dachshund and the Dachshund, in turn, alerted the owner, whom I'd rousted from bed.

He was a middle-aged man, maybe older, and appeared to have hurriedly pulled his clothes on. The dog, named Blade, barked a few more times as I entered, then, deciding I was O.K., retired to the back room with a snort. My credit card was run and a small key passed off, for Room #1, a wood-paneled hovel with a green shag rug, which smelled of smoke. The furniture was old and cheap and the bedcover and sheets worn, but the feature that I was most riveted to was the flyswatter with lime green paddle that sat on the side table. In my fog, I wasn't able to locate a thermostat to bring up the heat and, though the temperature had to be near freezing in the room, I simply dropped into bed, fully clothed, and pulled the covers up over my head.

Day 26: Detroit Lakes to Bismarck

A stream of passing trucks stirred me at 7 a.m. and, as I rose to use the bathroom, I noticed not one thermostat but two and quickly turned each up. Soon, the room filled with toasty electric heat that dropped me back into a slumber from which I didn't rise until after 9. The sun was well up by then and poured through the gap between the crooked, flower-patterned drapes, filling the room with golden light and changing my whole general mood.

Steinbeck had come right past this motel and may even have considered staying here. Instead, he continued "north on 71 to Wadena…and pounded on to Detroit Lakes," where he stopped late night on his way to Fargo, North Dakota. Wondering how Detroit Lakes got its name, he wished he had his W.P.A. (Works Progress Administration) Guides to the States — "the most comprehensive account of the United States ever got together" — which would surely have held the answer.

Indeed, the American Guide Series, as it was known, was the fruit of a program called the Federal Writers' Project, established by Franklin D. Roosevelt in 1935. The project supported more than 6,600 writers, editors and researchers during the four years it existed. The series consisted of volumes for each of the 48 states that existed at the time, plus Alaska, as well as smaller regional and city guides. Sadly, a great number of the plates used to print the guides were destroyed in the late 1930s when a Texas politician alleged that the W.P.A. was a Communist organization.

I turned my attention to the *St. Paul Pioneer Press*, a copy of which I'd picked up at the travel plaza. At the Hennepin County courthouse in Minneapolis, a 52-year-old woman shot her cousin and his lawyer who were involved with her in a legal battle over the settlement of her late parents' estate. "I hated to deal with her because she was so nuts," her own brother was quoted as saying. An orchard owner just southeast of Cleveland, Minnesota, had developed and patented a new breed of apple called the Stella and was betting the farm on its success. High hopes were being placed on the Twins who were a game into the AL Division series against the Yankees.

The free Twin Cities paper, the *City Pages*, reminded me that pro wrestler Jesse "The Body" Ventura had been Minnesota's latest governor. An ad for the Warehouse Nightclub in St. Paul, headlined "GET BUSTED", offered female patrons the opportunity to win free breast implants. Another item was devoted to a "child hatchery", called the Infant Incubator Institute, which existed in south Minneapolis in the early 1900s. There, prematurely delivered babies would further "cook" and grow, their care supported by fees paid by gawkers who came to view them through glass windows. Surprisingly, the majority of infants survived the process and rejoined their parents.

Late morning, I attempted a shower, finding the nozzle positioned at around the 5-foot mark, forcing me to bend down. If that wasn't bad enough, the water cut to a trickle while I still had soap all over me. Then, while I shaved, a fly played tag with my razor. But, again, it was a bright, crisp Minnesota day and, somehow, none of this seemed to matter. Checking out, I found a "Be Back At Noon" note on the office door, so slung my key through the door handle as Blade, ever the attentive watchdog, yipped inside.

In Browerville center, I was amused to find that Blade shared his name with the local paper, the *Blade Courier*. In the expanse between there and tiny Eagle Bend, I rolled by such rural sites as a turkey farm, the Clarissa Municipal Airport with its grass runway, the Canine Cattle Co., a pair of speckled gray horses standing in a scrubby field and an automobile graveyard.

Wadena was a cute place, with no building over three stories tall, but so busy with roadwork activities on its main street that it was necessary to detour around to catch 10 West. Along railroad tracks that ran parallel to 10 came an eastbound freight train that seemingly had no end, its cars double stacked with green or red containers labeled Evergreen and Uniglory. A while later, another train passed, a diesel locomotive marked BNSF (Burlington Northern Santa Fe) towing tankers full of corn sweetener. Yet another pulled by a purple Santa Fe diesel, toted containers marked HANJIN and YANG MING. I later learned that some 65 trains roll through the area a day, carting critical supplies to America's major distribution centers.

A large billboard at the town of Frazee (pronounced Fray-zee) declared it the home of the world's largest turkey. The pronouncement made me wonder what the townspeople would do with the billboard should the bird die and if they were fattening up a stand-in. Only then did I discover, with great amusement, that the turkey in question was a 15-foot-tall plaster statue, symbolizing Swift's Turkey Plant. Like an unsuspecting trout, I was lured into that one, hook, line and sinker.

At Detroit Lakes, I sought an answer to Steinbeck's 43-year-old question about how the town got its name. Jean at the Chamber of Commerce, as full of information as any old W.P.A. Guide, had a quick reply: The city was originally dubbed Detroit when a French Catholic priest camping by the lake noticed a sandbar at low tide that created a beautiful "strait," or "Detroit" in French. In 1926, because of postal mix-ups with the better known Detroit, Michigan, the city name was changed to Detroit Lakes.

To seek details about Steinbeck's stop here, Jean pointed me to the nearby historical society, where a pair of staffers received me. Unfortunately, they were unaware of his visit and, ironically, very glad for any information about it. In fact, to their knowledge, the only celebrities that had stopped in the city at any time were Bob Hope, who attended Sunday church services, and Jack Benny, who had a meal here. Benny's visit, in fact, was splashed across the front page of the local paper. One uptick: one staffer had a cousin back in Wisconsin who enjoyed "Travels with Charley" so much that she named her own poodle Charley.

On the road west again, I spied a digital readout at the First National Bank of Hawley on the Buffalo River. It flashed 46 degrees and 2:30 p.m. I was glad for electronic conveniences like this one, of which Steinbeck did not have the benefit, though only during the day and when it was temperate. When I noticed them in the evening, particularly very late in the evening when I was on a lonely road and half out of my mind with weariness, they coldly reminded me of my plight. At those times, they were like the face of a digital alarm clock that glares at you when you wake in the night and can't return to sleep. I would continue to see them all over the country, calling out Fahrenheits and Centigrades and the time.

As another locomotive hauling a long train of red and green Evergreen containers passed on the horizon, I turned in at a farm market, looking for something on which to nosh. Outside, plump pumpkins beamed in the sun and, inside, hearty looking tomatoes and gourds covered tabletops. From a large basket, I drew out two pounds of apples, placed them in a plastic bag and handed them to the attendant there, an old woman whose face, like a withered raisin, had shrunken into the hood of her camouflage-patterned suit. She was curt and bitter and devoid of pleasantries, bracing perhaps for the harshness of the colder months ahead.

In the lot out front, a woman struggled to stuff dry corn stalks around several bags of horse feed she had placed in the rear cargo area of her SUV. With my help, she managed, in the process mentioning that she had 10 horses and that they eat 20 bags of feed a month. I realized that I was getting to know quite a bit about the eating habits of various farm animals and imagined I'd make a good supply fetcher if I ever got the calling.

An indistinct retail block with your standard Wal-Mart, Taco Bell, K-Mart and Burger King signaled Moorhead, and led me to the state line where "The Episcopal Church Welcomes You to North Dakota" sign was posted on the Fargo side. Steinbeck had built up mythical illusions about Fargo all his life, calling it "brother to the fabulous places of the earth" and considering it the "east-west middle of the country." However, arriving in town, those illusions quickly dissolved. It was, in fact, "as traffic-troubled, as neon-plastered, as cluttered and milling with activity as any other up-and-coming town" of a comparative size, and he passed through quickly.

Stepping out to walk around, I found nothing of historical note either and the same ugly glut and tangle of traffic and signage. Following Steinbeck's lead, I traversed north-south running I-29, past tank companies, forklift sellers, car lots, trailer parts warehouses and oil and propane storage facilities, noticing what little greenery existed was sick and straggly.

A gas station in the process of becoming a BP was my fuel stop, but also a source for a long stick of Jack Link's Peppered Beef Jerky. It seemed the appropriate snack for these parts somehow and sustenance to keep on moving. Fargo, I'd decided, was an industrial wasteland and not worth dwelling on. But then I spotted Bonanzaville, a place where historical structures — a turn-of-the-century movie theater, firehouse, package store — and any shreds of importance from Fargo's frontier days appeared to have been placed. These were the objects of lore, the myth-making articles that Steinbeck had sought.

The site's event coordinator started me off in an exhibit area, where I gathered that it was William George Fargo, co-founder of Wells, Fargo & Co. and American Express, and a mayor of Buffalo, New York, who gave his name to the area in 1871. Born in Pompey, New York, he partnered with Henry Wells to bring express shipping, mail delivery and the Northern Pacific Railroad to the West. In those days, the towns of Fargo and Moorhead were raw outposts comprised of rough wooden structures loosely erected on muddy lands.

My host's great grandfather came to this area from Norway the year before Fargo was christened, crossing the plains from New York City. His wife died during the journey and he was left to raise his two young boys with a second wife, with whom he had "many more sons." One of the boys married my host's grandmother, a young lass who had come to work his wheat farm. "She was a warhorse who threw great parties that lasted three days and lived to be very old," she proudly told me. Her grandfather was equally a character — "a real dandy, never worked, hired people to do that." To reward his workers, he would collect them from the fields at the end of the day, take them into town "to raise holy hell and whore around" and pick up the bill. Back then, the area had "more whorehouses and bars than anywhere," according to my host.

As a young man, her grandfather also witnessed one of Fargo's earliest disasters, a fire in 1893 that claimed over 200 businesses and 140 homes. Sixty-five years later, almost to the day, a fierce tornado slammed into the area destroying 329 homes, killing 13 and causing millions in damage. Annual blizzards, rodent infestations and spring floods have added to the misery. The widespread destruction over the years is the reason few historical structures still existed and why the few that have survived have been deposited on this site. Had Steinbeck known of Fargo's difficult past, he would likely have been less irreverent. I was glad for the opportunity to set the record straight.

The center was closing for the day so I darted to I-94, which followed the path of the old Route 10 that Steinbeck had pursued out of Fargo. I was bound for the town of Alice to see what I could learn about his overnight there, under sycamores by the Maple River.

The exit came up quickly and, as I went over a rise to the south side of the highway, I was truly impressed by how completely flat, and beautiful, the land was. It was harvest time and the farmers and their crews were out gathering grain. Pulling to the side of the road, I marveled at the huge harvest machines, going back and forth, mowing down and shredding wheat stalks as they went. A farmer, seated at the wheel of one of the huge contraptions, noticed me looking on and waved.

Soon enough, I stumbled across the After U Bar, the only drinking establishment in Alice, and took a seat at the counter. "Beans" the bartender, a bearded guy with a black t-shirt and cap, served me up a right-priced can of Bud and indulged my questions about Steinbeck. He hadn't heard of the author's visit, but guessed that Dick Wadeson, who had lived near the river for all of his 70 years, might have, and got him on the phone. As he spoke to him, I looked around at the décor — a poster of a bikini-clad blonde with an "Ooohh Schmidt's" caption, a flyer advertising a basket of wings and pizza, Vikings' schedules, and NASCAR and Harley bric-a-brac. When Dick, my best prospect at that point, didn't know anything either, I decided to try and find the spot myself. Just down the road, there was the river and, beside it, a suspect clump of sycamores, overall a peaceful, eye-catching site that Steinbeck would have found appealing that was likely his campsite.

Though only mid-morning when he pulled in, he made dinner, let Charley wade, did laundry and contemplated "the nature and quality of being alone." He also drew conclusions about food as he had encountered it, regional newspapers, local radio and politics. Another RV'er, a man from the theater, joined him and they shared a drink and philosophized. The overnight was windy.

Open to camping at that time, today small signs note the spot as a waterfowl production and weed control area and forbid vehicles. Still, tire marks through the tall grass showed that several had made a recent passage to the site. I would not stay here but move along toward Bismarck, following the setting sun. It was so blinding, in fact, that I blew by a car not realizing it was the Barnes County Sheriff. The car's lights went on and I pulled to the side of the road. A policewoman, her blonde hair tied back in a ponytail, sidled up and informed me that the speed limit was 55 on this back road, and not 75. I apologized, produced my license and, when she asked me what I was doing around here, I told her of my afternoon. She smiled and nodded, ran a check on my registration anyhow, then pointed me back to the interstate.

A giant wind turbine standing some 300 feet high looked impressive against the now pink sky, a hue that made surrounding water surfaces look white, like ice. Though Steinbeck had guessed that Fargo was the dead middle of the country going east-west, he appeared to have been off, judging from a sign stating "Continental Divide, Elev. 1490" that appeared a couple dozen miles west of the town.

As Jamestown came up on my radar, James Taylor's "Fire and Rain" played on the radio, connecting me back to Chapel Hill for a spell. Hoping to find a good meal, I detoured, attracted by a red neon sign flashing "The Brass Rail." Part restaurant, part bar and part casino, it was busy with locals come to drink, play electronic darts and shoot pool. The décor was classic: busts of bison, deer and mountain goats; stuffed Canadian geese and ducks hanging from the ceiling; bearskins; and football gear. Asking if this was the place to be, a scruffy young can kicker who seemed raring to start a fight, belched, "Friday's better, if you want a f-ing load of people and f-ing rich bitches from the f-ing college, Jamestown, up on the hill."

At a big oval table in the center of the room, I perched to eat a personal-sized pizza and leafed through area papers. In Fargo's *The Forum*, North Dakota State University President Joe Chapman was trying to decide if alcohol should be allowed in the Fargodome parking lot before Bison football games. North Dakota wheat production was up 46% from 2002 and was at the highest level since 1996. Williston, ND residents awoke to a temperature of 15 degrees yesterday morning, a record. The Harney School in Tioga, a country school that can accommodate kindergarten through grade eight, had only *one* student enrolled this year. The Twins beat the Yankees in their AL Division series opener.

In *The Jamestown Sun*, a Golden Valley couple was displaying hay bale art along the road and Bismarck area American Indian tribes were readying to celebrate "First Nations Day" with drum groups and tribal dancers.

In my mad way and even though it was after 8 p.m., I decided to make the sprint to Bismarck, chasing its glow through the black night. Like a boxer, I danced around its perimeter, trying to get a handle on her, sizing her up: Commercial. Established. Hotels. Chain restaurants. Neighborhood pockets. Then, a very welcome sight: Starbucks. Though it had just closed, the counter girls inside sensed my desperation and served up a tall hazelnut coffee from an urn that they hadn't yet emptied. It came with advice as to the area "in" spots for the night: a chain restaurant and Pirate's Cove.

I had my doubts about the former but tried it anyway, occupying a seat next to three giggly girls who grew in size from left to right. The sorry thing was that this could have been any chain spot, anywhere, as it had no unique features. It was the type of place that Steinbeck would have despised. Pirate's Cove called.

More of a dance club, the Cove was unique and much livelier and, I estimated, about half full of Native Americans, their bronze faces smiling broadly and black hair flowing down their shoulders.

I spoke a patron of mixed heritage — Sioux, Dacotah and Irish. She was raised on the Sioux Reservation south of the capital and was writing a book about her experiences. She and her circle of friends, led by a jolly character named Honey Bear, lit up the evening, leaving me with a happy glow that carried me to a KOA campground in the hills overlooking the city for the overnight.

Day 27: Moose Steak & Boxing

Steinbeck did correct his assessment of what he considered mid-country, but to Bismarck, counting the Missouri River, which he came upon "in amazement," as the midpoint. He noted the differences in terrain here: "On the Bismarck side it is eastern landscape, eastern grass...on the Mandan side, it is pure west, with brown grass and water scorings and small outcrops." After viewing it, he moved along to the Badlands, a decision I had likewise decided to make.

Working on four hours of sleep, I slipped out of the KOA before sun-up and hit the dusty trail, literally, finding a gravel road near Crown Butte Lake that ran parallel to 94. It took me past simple homes, grazing cattle and beautiful rolling hills matted with the brown, straw-like grass to which Steinbeck had referred. The sun rose at my back, lighting the sky up as orange as the pumpkins I'd seen at the farm market yesterday. I wondered if, of all people, Hal Rosenbluth was watching this sunrise from his ranch in Linton, south of Bismarck. According to *The New York Times*, Rosenbluth sold his travel management company to American Express, bought 3,000 acres there and was looking forward to drinking "cheap whiskey" and sitting "on a rocking chair and looking out at the grassy buttes."

I'd seen the "World's Largest Turkey", and now, at New Salem, I was treated to "The World's Largest Cow", a wooly-mammoth-sized figurine on a hilltop next to which "NEW SALEM" was spelled out with white rocks. On the spur of the moment, I leapt off the highway to take a local road south towards South Dakota, a more scenic diversion from Steinbeck's path. A pair of ring-necked pheasant dashed across the road at a bridge crossing. Nearby, Black Angus lowed in a valley. Paved road turned to gravel again past the wee sleepy hamlet of Almont. Low barbed wire fences marked property lines.

Passing some brown-and-white cows, I tooted my horn. Again, Steinbeck's cattle caller would have come in handy here as my own horn succeeded only in casually raising heads, which turned in my direction as I rambled by. Another set of pheasants, a quartet this time, rushed to the roadside and flapped off across a field, their wings beating the brisk morning air. Clipping along and kicking up a napalm strike of dust behind me, twice I was surprised to find cars suddenly on my tail.

Reaching a paved road, Route 21, I questioned whether my detour had been wise, particularly as my gas supply was low, and decided to zig rather than zag, heading west toward the Little Missouri National Grassland. In Carson, "Cowboy Country", passing drivers waved hello, glad perhaps to encounter someone, anyone, on these sparsely trafficked backstretches. Perhaps, though, this was a long-held habit adopted from frontier days, when one rider would spot another coming across the plains and seek to determine orientation: friend or foe? I was only too glad to return their greetings.

Seeing a wind-abraded sign for the Carson Community Cemetery, I detoured over a rise to explore it, eager to know about the people that carved out lives here. As I began to read headstones — Grandma Nutz, born in 1863, was 95 when they placed her here; Helmuth Heil, a private in World War I, was 60 — I realized that a majority reflected German surnames: Kuntz, Deichert, Wingenbach, Schlosser and Heinz among them. They were hearty stock all, and most long-lived, with strong backs and determination to farm this harsh land and raise their families upon it. With only a brief sample of the climate, I was glad to return to the warmth of my now dust-encrusted van, my hands stiff from the cold and ears and cheeks red from the steady, biting wind.

On a hillside near Heil, a log cabin with a green roof reminded me of those I'd built many a time as a child with my Lincoln Logs set. Further on, in Elgin, Wade's filling station offered fuel I now so greatly needed. In front sat a smashed-up red and blue car with the name "General Lee" and flames on the side, resembling the hot rod Bo and Luke Duke had driven in the long-running television show "The Dukes of Hazzard." The station owner said that her son had driven it in a local derby and received "best paint job" honors for it.

Across the road was the humble office of the *Grant County News*. Its publisher, Duane Schatz, took interest in my story and led me into a side room to chat. On the walls behind him was a large McLaughlin Livestock Auction calendar, a photo of a boy holding a dead pheasant upside down by its legs and a stuffed mountain lion posed on a branch. In a larger workspace, there were other stuffed trophies, of a bison, coyote, rainbow trout, fox, turkey and sizable stag, many of which Duane had shot himself. There was even a mythical jackalope, as well as an impressive collection of box cameras.

As we admired everything, Duane briefed me on local history, noting that, in 1864, General Custer came through from Fort Lincoln with 5,000 troops and camped just south of town. The men were fed with deer, buffalo and grouse (called "prairie chickens" then), shot in the wild. He spoke of the mysterious Medicine Rock, too, where the Sioux brought their sick and wounded to heal.

Now 65, Duane "trapped as a young person on the farm to make a living," served as Elgin's mayor for 12 years ("$750 a year for peacemaking") and had published the newspaper for 40 years. He had wanted to visit Alaska for some time but, "at 65, the hills are getting harder to climb." In an outstanding show of generosity (and to make some room in his freezer), Duane led me to his house nearby and gave me several packages of meat — moose, deer and lamb included — some of which had been seasoned by a butcher in Carson. Then he guided me west to Dickinson, where he said, referring to the landscape, "Things are really gonna happen."

I had taken a copy of Duane's fine publication, labeled the "Official Newspaper of Grant County, North Dakota", and eyeballed it before getting back underway. It was highly entertaining, filled with small town chat and news, and I digested every word.

One item concerned the "first-ever reunion" of people related to Andrew Krause, who came to America and settled in this area with his wife and six children in 1913. In all, 66 cousins attended, traveling from Pennsylvania, Arizona, Texas, Oregon, Colorado, Nebraska, Wyoming, Illinois and even Japan. They visited local towns and the gravesite of Grandpa and Grandma Krause, ate "lots of food" and reminisced.

The 33rd Annual Oktoberfest Celebration was held last weekend in New Leipzig, despite a chill in the air and brisk wind. Mrs. Bruce Parsons, who writes the "Leith News" column, humorously suggested her bean soup might have caused the gusts, though quickly added, "It wouldn't be North Dakota if the wind didn't blow." The event was quite the time apparently: Friday, there was a German supper catered by the Leipziger Hof. Saturday began with a hot breakfast, Kiddie Parade (kids wore costumes and "each received a $1 gold coin for braving the elements") and Grand Parade with antique cars and tractors. In the afternoon, attendees gathered in the Community Center for "German goodies" — fry bread, fleischkuechla, knoephla soup, borscht soup, kuchen, snow cones, pie, and pigs in a blanket — then browsed a flea market and eyed a Soap Box Derby held on a hill by the school. Junior and Adult Tough Man Competitions, a Nail Pounding Contest, Biggest Grasshopper Contest (the winning entry was 2 1/2 inches), Fireman's Pit Barbecue (offering pork and beef), German heritage-themed Musical/Variety Show and Biergarten Dance rounded out the day.

Bert (who "continues to work in the brick business") and Ramona ("loves her cooking, baking, canning and going on daily walks") Ternes of Raleigh celebrated their 50th anniversary. After a polka mass at St. Anne Church, the couple went by horse and buggy to a social club for their reception.

Jill Friesz, in her column titled "The Farmer's Wife", mused about fall and wondered how her two-year-old son, Evan (!), was "going to react to scarecrows, pumpkins, gourds, corn cobs and dried leaves throughout the house."

Dean Meyer shared thoughts about the orneriness of Shetland ponies: "Deep down in their souls, Shetland ponies are evil. They appear nice and cuddly, but…go under small trees, scraping their rider off…step on a youngster's foot as he goes to mount up." However, once a Shetland is broken in, Meyer said, "I don't think there is anything cuter than a little kid, with his hat pulled down over his ears, a stick in his hand, trotting along on [one] and being a cowboy."

Elgin True Value's bowling team had the highest scoring group game at the most recent competitions at Our Place Lanes. The Classifieds offered "first cutting alfalfa and mixed hay in big round bales" and "year old egg layers."

While Elgin's citizens and those in surrounding areas were locally focused, they were not isolated from the goings-on of the outside world. Fort Yates, ND resident Marine Corps Pfc. Kyle American Horse had just shipped out for duty with the 1st Stinger Battery in Okinawa, Japan and North Dakota State University had just hosted a biosecurity training program to help area residents identify incidences of agroterrorism and animal diseases.

This was classic small town life, and in an area that was still very much a wild frontier, despite these glimpses of civilization. One where intersections had no signage — you looked right or left — speed was virtually unchecked and no services were available for miles and miles. I found myself doing 80 as I left Elgin and, yet, was passed by a grain-carrying truck doing close to 100.

Entering Burt, a most unusual event happened. A small, white bird sailed in front of and collided with a smack against my windscreen, somersaulting backwards over the top of El Rucio and landing on the asphalt in my wake. It was killed on impact and I was helpless to do anything about it. In more than 20 years of driving, I had never had such an encounter. It would trouble me for the rest of the day.

The sun glinted off a row of silver, cylindrical grain silos, like giant coffee cans with their labels removed, in Regent, dubbed "The Friendly City." Beyond, the land on both sides of the road, the grasses shorn to nubs, was flat as can be, with the exception of distant purplish buttes that rose out of the heartland desert — the landscape features to which Duane had no doubt referred.

Of the Badlands, Steinbeck said, "They are like the work of an evil child…such a place the Fallen Angels might have built as a spite to heaven." He had two encounters here, the first with "a man leaning on a two-strand barbed wire fence" who had "a .22 rifle leaned beside him" and "a little heap of rabbits and small birds." The second visit was with an old woman in a small house that gave him a drink of water and was "hungry to talk." Ultimately, Steinbeck, ill at ease about the landscape, "went into a state of flight, running to get away." Yet, no sooner had he started to flee, then the late day sun brought out the magic of the place. He was even encouraged to stop for the night, "near a thicket of dwarfed and wind-warped cedars and junipers." There he admired the night sky — "lovely beyond thought" — made a fire of dead cedar branches and listened to the sounds of screech owls and coyotes.

Now re-connected with 94 West, near Medora I drove up to the Theodore Roosevelt National Park Visitor Center. The namesake of the park first came to the area 120 years ago to start a cattle business with two other men. The following year, he created an open-range ranch. The more time he spent in these parts, the more he became aware of the near extinction of buffalo for their hides and widespread wildlife destruction. As such, when he became President in 1901, he obtained an O.K. from Congress to create five national parks and 51 wildlife refuges, including this one.

An oasis in this wild country, the park contained petrified forests, hiking trails, a length of the Missouri River and protected grasslands. At a viewing station, from which I gazed upon conical buttes with red lignite tips, a plaque informed that the landscape is in constant transition due to hard rain that attacks loosely cemented clay and sandstone. The scene reminded me of a stretch between Flagstaff and Page in Arizona's high country.

Setting off on a 20-mile loop through the park, I happened almost immediately upon a shaggy old bull buffalo grazing by the roadside. Inching past him, I stopped at a pullout up the way, where dozens upon dozens of prairie dogs popped in and out of holes and called to each other like squeak toys. Bill Murray's efforts to destroy the wee beasties in the film "Caddyshack" came to mind, while, on a more serious note, I wondered how much of a problem the rodents must be to area farmers. To look out at the valley below, I stepped across their encampment, treading carefully to avoid the occasional cow pie land mine and cacti obstacle. My presence caused a shrill, collective squeak and much diving into foxholes.

As I retreated back to the van, a passing motorist told me about a herd of bison up ahead and, sure enough, there were the great brown mammals noshing on underbrush. The largest male, the apparent protector of the group, kept a steady eye on me as I rolled by.

Corner after corner, bend after bend, afforded another incredible view and opportunity to learn and explore. But I was anxious to see Montana and made a fast exit back to the interstate, passing a coal carrying train on the way. The National Grasslands and the towns of Beach and, remarkably, Home On The Range, were my parting looks at North Dakota before reaching the big, blue "Welcome to Montana" sign.

"Of all the states, it is my favorite and my love," Steinbeck declared. "The Queen of the World...a great splash of grandeur... rich with grass and color." He noticed a "slow-paced warm speech" and that "the frantic bustle of America was not in Montana." About its towns, he perceived them as "places to live in rather than nervous hives." Indeed, there was an easy, calming influence here and the roads in were big, wide and smooth. The land rolled and desired to be trod upon and ridden hard. The sky was a grand paintbrush stroke of blue. The trees were gold and orange. And the channel of the Yellowstone River, which I spied at Glendive, was broad and slung low.

It was time for some "Tim Tunes" to complement the glorious scenery and, feeling quirky, I chose Roger Miller's "King of the Road," closely followed by Johnny Cash's rapid-fire "I've Been Everywhere."

A trio of hunters in camo suits with an eager dog in tow had just pulled into a CENEX gas station when stopped in Terry for a recharge. Into one of those big RAM trucks, they loaded an 18-pack of beer and bag of ice, "headed north for elk." Across the street, the big screen for the Prairie Drive-In stood idle and in disrepair.

At a pizza joint called Roy Rogers, not affiliated with the singer or his restaurant chain, neatly dressed ladies sat proper in one room and their men sat stone-faced at the bar in the other. A sign at the rear of the latter threatened, "I've got PMS and a loaded gun. Any questions?" It spoke very fittingly of the large woman manning the taps.

The local high school's football team, the Terries, was out on their field doing a post-practice stretch while the Yellowstone Bean Company was in full swing across from the shuttered Rialto Theater and Bud & Bette's Bar. According to Susan at Terry's Landing (its motto: Good Food and Friendly Faces), where I ultimately decided to eat, Bud died seven years back and Bette tried to run the place herself. She fared well for about four years until she got real sick, too, and the doctor told her she had to give up the business. As to the drive-in, its owners had just decided to up and sell, despite doing brisk business. Susan had her finger on the pulse of this town all right, though given that its population hovered around 900, it wouldn't have been too difficult.

When I mentioned that my near-term destination was Seattle and asked how long it might take for me to get there, she wasn't sure, having only ever gone as far west as Spokane. But looking at a map, we guessed that it could be done in 12 hours, at a constant clip. For now, I would shoot for Billings, some 179 miles off.

Lunch was Santa Fe chicken, a decent piece of meat on a store-bought roll with a thin pickle slice on the side and, as I tucked into it, I listened to four men holding court at an adjacent table. Their topic was tomatoes, introduced by one with scars from a bad burn on his face. Nonchalantly, I tried to pick up bits and pieces of their conversation while a fly danced in the front window under the glowing neon OPEN sign.

As a freight train clanked past the café, shaking its walls and the very foundation of the one-room Prairie Baptist Church next door, I resumed my voyage. There would be little further dallying and, soon, I was rocketing by Miles City, a destination for boot buying and gambling surrounded by camel humps of land.

Forsyth, near Rosebud, known as "Home of the Dogies," was a splotch of a town lined with places like Lucky Lil's Casino, Kum & Go quick-mart, Big Sky Auto Service & Café and country radio station KIKC. I stopped to use the facilities and fill up there, noticing that I'd traveled 5,500 miles to this point.

Near Carson, where Steinbeck had detoured to see Little Big Horn, the sun was sitting on the road and the bugs were thick, making it virtually impossible for me to see. The orange orb finally took the plunge as I raced past Conter's Spotted Ass Ranch, and a girl in a silver SUV with the license NEEDABUS cruised by. My ability to see did not improve, forcing me to pull over. The windshield was plastered and if I could have located my snow scraper, I would have employed it. Instead, I used paper towels and water from my thermos and scrubbed hard. It made things clear enough to handle the last few miles to Billings, my stop-to-be for the night.

A place where Steinbeck had treated himself to a hat, Billings was a most welcome sight. At the same time, it was a challenge to navigate and, as I attempted to turn off to a hotel, I somehow found myself on an adjoining highway headed in a completely opposite direction. Turning around wasted a whole bunch of already limited evening time, so I nix'ed the hotel to see the town.

So I wasn't going in totally blind, I sought destination guidance at a truck stop that doubled as a liquor store and casino. "Downtown," and a point in its direction, was the feedback, and so to downtown I went, finding activity at the Babcock Theater on 2nd Ave.

Its marquis screamed "FIGHTS!" a great come-on promoting a Bob Lacoure's Club Boxing event with seven three-round matches, a good value for the $10 price of admission I thought. Soon, I was sitting in a crowded, rowdy theater watching two boxers trading blows in a tight ring onstage. Between rounds, bikini-wearing ring girls, at whom fight attendees threw wadded dollar bills, took laps. Each "donation" was acknowledged with a wiggle of the posterior.

Nick "The Giant Killer" Holt, in the red corner, stood his ground and picked his punches, getting the win against Tanner "Cuddles" Ketchum. At the break, most everyone ran to the bathroom or to get a beer from one of two bars. I followed the crowd to the upper tier, where I spoke with a boxer whose fight had been bumped and a curly-haired Cheyenne woman tending bar who gave me a tip for a post-fight spot, The Wild West Saloon.

When fighting resumed, I witnessed Eli "Torpedo" Chavez put away Brendon "Twang" Brown then chatted with some teenie boppers who were trying to decide on a plan for the rest of the evening. When I heard the mention of drinking and pot, I wondered if their parents knew, or even cared, about their whereabouts.

Crystal "Fire" Marshall, a female boxer trying to get herself psyched up at the back of the theater, seemed like she needed a pep talk as she was about to fight her first public match. However, when she climbed into the ring and quickly put away her opponent to the enthusiastic appreciation of the crowd, I recognized that she was doing just fine on her own. The win seemed to have inspired a heavy-set guy in the front row, who, in his splashy Bermuda shirt, stood up and started gyrating. Security quieted him and we all broke for intermission, the place emptying to the street. A thick haze of smoke hung under the marquis, making it near impossible to see.

Two beefy guys, Ted "The Rabid Carebear," with a clean-shaven head and chunk missing from one eyebrow, and Carlos "Wild Man" Navarro, who entered the place like Rocky Balboa to "Eye of the Tiger", were the main event. They came out swinging furiously, particularly "Wild Man", until he stumbled, screamed out and went down, writhing in pain. He'd snapped his left ankle like a toothpick. The fight was called, the theater emptied and I went looking for The Wild West.

As I searched, I passed Casey's, a bar around the corner where many patrons had gone, and "Wild Man", who was hopping down a side street, a big wrapping around his foot and a cigarette in his mouth. Expanding my search, I moved to the western part of town where umpteen casino and package stores were located. Still luckless in finding Wild West, I settled for a restaurant/bar called Gusick's.

Though I wanted a meal, the restaurant side was empty and I didn't care to sit by myself. When I asked if I could eat at the crowded bar counter, I was told I could, but would have to dine from a Styrofoam to-go container. Something about mixing bar and food operations I guessed. However they wanted to work it was fine by me.

It was late, I was now full, and Billings, though a bit off-kilter, didn't seem like such a bad place to settle for the night. Seeking a decent hotel, my choices came down to the C'mon Inn and the Fairfield Inn, which faced each other across a parking lot. Though the former was creatively named, I favored the latter because its name mirrored my hometown. I also liked the fact that I could drop in its hot tub, though it was past midnight. The latter felt heavenly but I was a little uneasy about a security camera trained right at me and finished up after only a short while.

Figuring that coffee would hit the spot, I visited the lobby to help myself, finding the night clerk lounging in front of the TV lost in a Keanu Reeves movie. Little did I know then that she would be the real star of the evening when, two hours later, she decided to have a late-night popcorn snack and, underestimating the power of the microwave, set it on fire. The smoking appliance set off the hotel alarms, jerking me from what had begun to be a solid, much-needed rest. I quickly thought about what would be important to gather: Boots, jeans, sweater — check. Laptop. Car keys. Wallet. Filled notepads. It was a fast assembled though complete inventory and I groped my way downstairs, my eyes and brain struggling to adjust.

Other guests, in various states of dress, joined me, all looking like deer caught in the headlights. We milled about and tried to keep warm while the poor night clerk, who was managing to keep her cool, got instructions over the phone to open the main level windows and doors. After quite a bit of time, we guests, sensing the danger had passed, began to return to our rooms. Only then did a lone police officer show, followed later and, at that point, a good 20 to 30 minutes after the initial alarm, by a single fire truck. No firepersons even got out to look at the appliance but just u-turned and went away at the cop's say-so.

I'd observed all this from a table in the lobby where a yogurt, small container of milk and copy of the *Billings Gazette* had become my comforts. The news this day: Sixty-three-year old South African writer J.M. Coetzee, whose books relate the stories of innocents oppressed by history, won the 2003 Nobel Prize for Literature, 41 years after Steinbeck achieved the feat. And a 300-pound black bear broke into "Late Show" host David Letterman's house in Choteau for the third time, was captured, and released in the Flathead National Forest just south of Glacier National Park, 50 miles south of Letterman's ranch.

Day 28: The Last Stand & a Two-Step

My sleep had been cut to four hours due to the surprise fire drill, and my day began with the rumble of a freight train passing at the rear of the hotel. Make no mistake — the room was terrific and the bed comfortable, I just wish I'd had a longer time in it. The idea of soaking my road-weary body in the hot tub again had appeal so I got started that way, followed by a continental breakfast in the lobby's sunny dining area. There, I saw many of the faces that had evacuated their rooms last night including a couple and their three boys from Woodby Island, WA. They were headed to New Orleans and had been on the road 18 hours to this point, towing a trailer behind them.

When a weather station on the overhead TV mentioned that there had been a first snow in Michigan's Upper Peninsula, I was glad to have left home when I did and looked forward to high temperatures in the 70s over the weekend in the direction I was headed.

Checking in by e-mail with my life back home, I learned about bills due, that the lawnmower wheel had fallen off and that the bathroom ceiling was peeling. As I replied, a quite familiar Burlington Northern train passed, carrying car after car of grain.

When I finally checked out at noon, the day shift clerk very graciously comp'ed my room in light of the evening's inconvenience. She also shared the hard fact that Yellowstone National Park, which I'd wanted to see today, would be closing at 4 p.m. and that it was a four-hour drive from here. Seemingly knocked out of the picture, I decided to focus instead on the Yellowstone Art Museum here in downtown, and on Little Big Horn.

With some bobbing and weaving, I was able to find the museum. There, the resident café owner and barista gave me some quick detail about the featured exhibit, marking the upcoming bicentennial of Lewis and Clark's expedition. "A big deal" in Montana, the team essentially "discovered the state," which it took them a year to cross. When I mentioned that I'd wanted to see Yellowstone, my host said that he was traveling there tomorrow morning to bike it from the western part of the park to Old Faithful and back, a 60-mile circuit.

With the expert accompaniment of a piano being played elsewhere in the building, I began my tour, admiring paintings of the region from the 1800s by Scotsman Walter Shirlaw, New Yorker Ralph Blakelock, Rhode Islander Charles Bird King, Baltimore-bred Alfred Jacob Miller and German Albert Bierstadt. All had traveled through the region, accompanied expeditions or helped survey the Northwest, and these were their impressions. More paintings, of buffalo hunts, river encampments, Yellowstone scenes and Indian reservations, filled another area. A class of chattering 5th graders from Eagle Cliffs Elementary came through, assigned the task of finding a favorite painting to discuss. A third room featured dramatic portraits snapped by David Francis Barry of Chief Sitting Bull, his son Crow Foot and daughter Standing Holy.

The most phenomenal room to me was one dedicated to the stories and illustrations of Will James, described as "A Western Icon." Done in carbon pencil and oil paint, they depicted horse corralling and herding on his ranch, the Rocking R near Pryor, Montana.

The source of the background music was a Yamaha piano being nimbly tickled by Asaph, a black gentleman in a white linen jacket, crowned by carefully straightened hair. He'd played at the Northern Hotel and had a gig at the hospital as well as doing Fridays here at the museum.

Noticing the large office of the *Billings Gazette* across the way, I went over and gabbed with a reporter there. He was, predictably, on deadline and didn't have much of a chance to talk, but had read Steinbeck's book and asked questions that showed knowledge of it.

When I mentioned that I was about to head through the Crow Indian Reservation to see Little Big Horn, he told me about a story the paper ran in mid-July about a 19-year-old Marine from Crow Agency and his return from duty in Iraq. One of 48 young men and women the tribe sent to fight, Lance Cpl. Leon Pretty Weasel Jr. was welcomed home at Billings Logan International Airport by no less than 150 friends, family and veterans, "all with black smudges on their cheeks as a sign of his victorious return." The paper reported that, "His Whistling Water Clan fathers smeared his cheek with a victory smudge and placed a wreath of horsemint atop his head." After Dale Old Horn announced Pretty Weasel's arrival over the terminal's public address system, Barney Old Coyote, the soldier's clan grandfather, a WWII veteran and the most decorated soldier of his tribe, sang him a praise song. In addition to the smudges, the clansmen were adorned with headdresses of eagle feathers and beat drums. Many travelers that witnessed the event had tears in their eyes as Pretty Weasel, who had been burned on his arms pulling a fellow Marine to safety after a munitions dump exploded, was paraded by.

In an email to me sometime later, the reporter put his own two cents in about Billings, describing it as "an odd place, a dusty cow town getting swept up in the Western money boom. We have filthy rich New Yorkers sitting in coffee shops next to old cowboys with shit on their boots. We've got movie stars buying up hobby ranches and driving up the cost of land so that fourth-generation Montanans descended from homesteaders can't afford to live here anymore. And, we've got rich, young, pretty L.A. and Seattle refugees dining in martini bars across the street from boxers beating the hell out of each other in front of a crowd of chain smokers." He added that the Babcock Theater, "on other nights of the week…has hosted come-to-Jesus revivals for a very different crowd."

The images of Yellowstone that I'd seen at the museum convinced me that it had to be part of my experience, and I resolved to accommodate it first thing in the morning. But first, Little Big Horn trumpeted, which I planned to access via 90 East through the Crow Indian Reservation.

On the rise before Big Horn County, I looked out over the land that, if you blurred your vision, seemed like a desert, with so many moguls and dunes. The difference was that *these* were covered with that bleached grass so common in this region. As to trees, you could count them on one hand. And around them, a coal-carrying train snaked, moving along like a sidewinder. Houses were also few, until Hardin that is, when a community, which included the Big Horn Historical Society, suddenly appeared. The society, like Bonanzaville back in Fargo, had preserved a cabin, church and barn from frontier times on its property.

I switched over to a parallel road that the Crow here seemed to prefer, their brown faces a blur as we shot by each other, and steered into Crow Agency or "Crow" as the locals call it. The hub of the Crow nation, the town was a scrappy place dominated by a long building where the tribal elders meet, ornate Little Big Horn College and a park with a basketball court where a group of kids played. The group studied me, an uncommon sight around here I was sure, as I walked across the road to the Apsalooke Trading Post, which sold everything from lug nuts to lunchmeat. One of the proprietors proudly told me she was named after a rodeo queen and recommended the Shake & Burger Hut for a bite to eat. With a copy of the *Big Horn County News* and a bottle of water tucked under my arm, I took her advice.

The Hut was an intimate place, with pressboard walls, chairs with red vinyl seats and a menu offering Mexican food and Indian tacos. From the owner and cook, I ordered a bean and meat burrito and soda and struck up a talk with a young couple of high school age. I was surprised to find that they were not only married but had two girls, aged four months and one year respectively. They told me they usually pass their time at the "rec" center, rodeos and the annual Crow fair or powwow, the latter open to everyone and featuring food, crafts and dancing. As no alcohol is permitted on the reservation, locals tend to go to Hardin. When I breached the topic of Crow culture and customs, the owner stepped into the conversation and suggested I go to the Little Big Horn Battlefield to speak to a certain park ranger there.

Up the road, through big iron gates and past a tollhouse I went, making the same approach that Steinbeck had. Reaching a cemetery where hundreds of white grave markers stood, the author stepped out to remove his "hat in memory of brave men." Similarly, I strolled between these same headstones, devoted not only to soldier and Indian scout victims of the battle here, but to soldier victims of other conflicts over the past century.

As the park was, unfortunately, closing for the night, the ranger, whom I found inside the visitors' center, directed me to meet him at his home back in Crow. We sat in his gated yard with a scrawny black cat circling us and he was only too glad to open up.

About the infamous battle, which occurred June 25, 1876, he related that it essentially took place along the road that extends 4 1/2 miles past the visitors' center, with a first stage happening near the cemetery and second at the end of the road. General George Custer and 12 companies of the 7th Cavalry, come to rout the Indians from their homes, arrived in the Wolf Mountains, known as the "Crow's Nest," and looked out over the valley. In the distance, they could see a fine mist that, when the sun rose higher, was identified as smoke from teepees on the plains. Six hundred and forty-five soldiers started down the mountain, leaving one company behind to escort an arriving pack train. The soldiers split into two groups, one commanded by Major Reno who was to cross a river and attack a village, and the other led by Custer. They came up against as many as 2,000 Sioux, Cheyenne and Arapaho, and 260 soldiers and scouts were "annihilated."

Though he looked predominantly Native American, my new ranger friend admitted that he was more English and French than anything. Still, his interest in the Crow was committed. He continued, saying that the Crow had foreseen the future and recognized that the white man was here to stay, and adapted to that fact. The Laramie Treaties that settled the conflicts between the Indians and U.S. government provided Federal health care to the community and stated that they could make their own laws and govern themselves. Up until two years ago, a tribal court handled the latter. Now a legislative body with lawyers ran the show. However, the way the Crow leadership is structured is unchanged, with a Chairman, Vice Chairman, Secretary and Vice-Secretary holding the top spots. To be Chairman, a person must speak the Crow language, reside in Crow Agency, be at least high school educated, have a clean police record and be at least 25 years old. A new hierarchy is chosen every four years and tribal police enforce the laws amongst the Crow, numbering about 10,000.

It was growing dark when we concluded our conversation and I headed back to Billings, that big sun in my face again. This time I respected it, though, and for my patience was treated to a swirling celestial soup at sunset. Back within city limits, I ran a squeegee over the entire length of El Rucio then reported to Stageline Pizza for a sausage pie. Though not really an eat-in joint, I sat at a table there and read the paper I'd bought earlier.

In the news, the Legislature the ranger spoke about voted to establish primaries in six districts — Mighty Few, Valley of the Chiefs, Reno, Black Lodge, Valley of the Giveaways and Arrow Creek. Voting were representatives with surnames like Crooked Arm, Little Light, Not Afraid, Goes Ahead, Medicine Horse, Plain Feather and Bulltail.

A continuing drought was cause for extreme fire danger in much of south central Montana, in counties like Big Horn, Carbon, Musselshell, Stillwater, Sweet Grass, Treasure and Yellowstone. Lodge Grass High School celebrated Native American week with Crow Flag songs, prayer, word identification challenges, handgames, a chili feed, football game and teepee building races.

Seventy-nine-year old Crow Agency resident David Bravo passed. As a young man, he broke horses, hunted in the Big Horn Mountains and took part in arrow throwing events and Sun Dance ceremonies. He was given the name Baakakaa'xxinneesh for guiding two elderly people to safety during a blizzard. In WWII, he served in the infantry and then worked as a ranch hand.

The name Wild West came up again as the place to go in town and I just had to find it this time. The pizza folks gave me specific instructions and I finally located the elusive nightspot, sharing building space with Surfin' Joe's. Greeted at the door by a guy in a black cowboy hat and red shirt and immediately hearing country music, I questioned whether I would fit in here and enjoy myself. The place was also pretty empty though it was past 9 p.m. "Just wait, 10:30 and you won't be able to move in here," said the red shirt. I was doubtful but took a seat at the bar beside two other guys watching slides showing past nights here. It looked like it lived up to its billing but I would have to see for myself. More people trickled in as I gabbed with a waitress who wore a black hat, rolled up black t-shirt and low-slung black jeans, looking a bit like Debra Winger in "Midnight Cowboy."

Soon the place was a sea of cowboy hats and teased hair, with music running the gamut from songs with lines like "He drinks tequila and she curses in Spanish" to top-40 pop. Like the movie "Coyote Ugly," a string of women took to the bar counter to strut their stuff to win cash awards.

I took it all in, the evening faded to black and I camped for the night near a sugar beet factory, the sound from the trucks on the interstate lulling me to sleep.

Day 29: At Beartooth's Summit

I woke to see two large rabbits, one black and one sandy colored, hopping about and realized that the date marked one month I'd been on the road. I guessed that I'd be another month-and-a-half going around, putting me back home in mid-November. The time had gone quickly and, I expected, would continue that way. For the moment, I focused on my immediate goal: Yellowstone. Chomping at the bit, I put El Rucio in gear and left crazy, fun Billings behind.

The route to the park held unique sights: A giant figurine of a cowboy standing beside a casino. Many ranches, their entrances identified with the ranch name carved or burned into timbers forming a frame. Joliet locals in orange safety vests collecting trash from the roadside — much like my boys and I had volunteered in past years to clean up our beach. The carcass of a deer struck by a passing vehicle. One-stop shopping for "Beer and Ammo." The Carbon County Sheriff in his pickup truck. A llama farm. This was really beautiful country and if I wasn't so magnetized by coastal areas, I thought that I might consider living here.

South of Joliet, an owl swooped past in front of the van and flew over a pocket of self-absorbed Black Angus. Fall had fallen here, the trees a bright yellow or burnt orange. Nearing the mountains, resorts became abundant, each trying to top its neighbor with beefed-up promises of hot tubs and other conveniences.

A vulture took a leap of faith in front of the van, narrowly missing becoming a hood ornament. Three closely grouped deer standing in a clearing seemed to blink, anticipating a collision. Nearby Red Ledge had the authentic look of the Old West except for the wild-haired, leather-trussed bikers gathered there.

Intersecting the Custer National Forest, the Beartooth Mountain Range, like breathtaking bicuspids rising high into the air, was carpeted dark green with pines. Down the faces of most, boulders loosened by rain had slid and tumbled, smashing against and splintering trees that held the rest in check or crashing to the roadway.

I actually got quite fearful that the misstep of some small animal would bring a ton of rock crashing down upon me. It was no surprise to see some rock faces cemented over, to prevent further erosion and ensure the safety of travelers, and to know that the passage is closed in the winter. Continuing my ascent, the only signage I noticed up here warned of ROUGH BREAKS where the road had slumped and threatened to collapse.

Rock Creek Vista Point brought an almost 360-degree view of the range. I walked to the end of a path that looked out over the valley and, standing by the rail, felt like I was at the prow of a great ship asail on the high seas.

At an alluvial plateau streaked with snow, a large "Welcome to Wyoming, Shoshone National Forest" sign was posted. On its backside was "Welcome to Montana, Custer National Forest," a greeting to travelers headed the other way. On the tundra adjacent to it, a man packed and threw snowballs. I passed on the pleasure to collect specimens of lichen-covered rose quartz, digging the chunks out from amidst frost-burnt grasses.

The last push to the West Summit, 10,947 feet above sea level, was marked with tall sticks to show the path of the road for the benefit of plows when the first heavy snows come. Seeing snow up here already, I could no longer resist the temptation to play in it and stepped out to toss a few snowballs at a rock target.

As it was noon and given the top-of-the-world location, I was moved to break out my grill, dig out a couple moose steaks and cook them up with onions and peppers for lunch. A couple of good old boys from Arkansas who pulled up behind me came over to see what I was cooking. I traded them some cuts for a Busch beer. They had not, nor had I, tried moose before — "all we got is whitetail where we come from" — and we agreed it was like a tender cut of beef. "It don't get no better'n this," one of the lads said. Too true I thought.

Sitting in my camp chair in the sun, I tore into my meal and regarded my surroundings. A short siesta in the van followed, which would have been a longer siesta if I didn't have to get back down Beartooth *and* visit Yellowstone. Around 1 p.m., I began the descent, which was much more gradual than the climb had been, winding down by clumps of thistle; crystal clear, ice-cold lakes; and more crags and rock outcroppings than you could shake a walking stick at. Suddenly, there were magnificent buttes ahead of me, which grew as I approached. Then, another surprise, a grey coyote stalking a rodent in tall grass by the roadside. I regarded him and he regarded me, then I moved along through spindly columns of pines down past serene Beartooth Lake. To my left, two hunters wearing orange vests and carrying rifles in hand combed through a marsh, and a sign came up: OPEN RANGE, EXPECT COWS ON THE ROAD. I didn't see a one, however.

There was a turnoff for Cody, named after William "Buffalo Bill" Cody to whom I'd long known I was distantly related, followed by a babbling brook. And if it wasn't babbling, it was sure speaking at a high volume. I pulled up beside it and thought I'd just stick my landing net in the neck of a narrow channel and scoop a fish out. But, like the purported cows, they were on a tea break.

Now back in Montana near the Gallatin National Forest, I went by a camp that offered guided fishing tours. The latter was very appealing, particularly as I hadn't been able to spot any on my own, but I let it go.

Cooke City was a manufactured tourist town, with overpriced Indian arts and crafts at a trading post and packs of sightseers roaming about. Still, it had its charm, particularly the Soda Butte Lodge, where I even considered getting a room. Instead, I popped into an adjacent Exxon and bought a six of Moose Drool Brown Ale (brewed by Big Sky in Missoula) and a postcard of the Beartooth Highway pass, which I sent to the crew back home.

At long last, I reached Yellowstone, which I accessed through the northeast entrance and station house where I presented my National Park Pass for the very first time. The rangerette, with eyes as green as the surrounding pines, guided me about the roads, and open campsites, something I was considering. Toddling down the road, I was welcomed back to Wyoming and then found myself in a wide-open expanse where a lone bison drank from a stream. Further on, this same body of water was populated with fly fishermen, making me wish I'd had a kit with me.

Having come through Beartooth with all its steep drop-offs and views, I have to admit to being less impressed by Yellowstone, as its roads were much gentler and established. Steinbeck felt like he had to go to the park, lest his neighbors say, "You mean you were that near to Yellowstone and didn't go?" His opinion of national parks — of which there were 388 — was that they "enclose the unique, the spectacular, the astounding" and are "no more representative of America than is Disneyland."

In this place he called a "wonderland of nature gone nuts," Steinbeck discovered that Charley was a potential bear slayer. Spotting one less than a mile inside the park entrance, Charley "shrieked with rage. His lips flared, showing wicked teeth...he screeched insults at the bear." A little farther, two more showed, producing double the effect. "He became a primitive killer lusting for the blood of his enemy." This continued to happen to the extent that Steinbeck "turned Rocinante about, and retraced [his] way," foregoing staying the night in the park. He ended up retreating all the way to Livingston, Montana, where he checked into "a pretty auto court" and had dinner in a restaurant and where Charley, "totally exhausted," dropped to sleep.

At the spot where the fishing was furious, I pulled in and asked a returning quartet about their experience and, lacking a fly kit, if I might be able to simply scoop up a trout — Cutthroats here — with my net. "We walked across the bridge and saw about 50 down below, but when we got out in the water, they spooked," said the youngest, a sandy-haired kid from Missoula. As to using a spin caster, only fly rods were permitted.

As I perched on a large boulder for a moment, a woman from Cody came to sit beside me and asked if I'd seen any "woofs," her way of saying wolves. I told her I hadn't, but hoped to, planning to camp here. "You should go to Mammoth Springs," she advised, adding, "The elk are buglin.'"

On the go again, I saw a herd of some 20 bison on a plain, trees scorched and blistered from crown fires that swept through in 1988, the base of a petrified redwood and a huge elk laying in the sun beside the Yellowstone National Park Chapel. The latter did indeed bugle as I approached, a sound I likened to one you might make howling through a long paper towel tube.

Mammoth Hot Springs brought scores of elk, making themselves quite at home in and around a general store and hotel there. The actual hot springs, denoted by Liberty Cap, a dormant tower, was otherworldly in the late daylight and gave off a pungent, earthy phosphorous smell.

When I remounted, I found El Rucio had developed a wheeze and was cutting out when I depressed the accelerator. This is not a good development in a national park on a Saturday night at dusk. My best guess as to the problem was a clogged fuel line or dirty air filter, though I couldn't get a confirmation on that from the guys at the Mammoth gas station, as they were just gas pumpers. I thought I'd put in at the Mammoth Campground and figure out a plan of attack in the morning, but it was full. Then I considered the hotel, but thought it best to seek advice from the visitor center. "Except for the bathroom," the center was closed I was informed by a couple sitting on the steps watching a bull elk escort his harem. There were here in the park area celebrating her birthday and staying in Gardiner at the North entrance to Yellowstone on the

Wyoming-Montana line. I decided to head that way, see how El Rucio performed at a lower elevation and, if all was well, keep going.

As I came down out of the mountain pass, I spotted a self-wash station large enough to accommodate El Rucio and thought a bath might do her some good. Using a spear gun-like apparatus shooting high-pressure water, I sprayed her down from nose to tail, rinsing away weeks' worth of dust, dirt, bugs and crud.

The effect seemed to be positive as, by the time I'd reached Carbola, she was already running more smoothly. There, a deer, one of dozens sprinting about in wide-open fields, vaulted itself over a barbed wire fence and crossed the road behind me. Its neighbors, Black Angus and horses, like a crowd at a gymnastics competition, coolly regarded the hijinx.

Reaching Livingston, where Steinbeck had stopped and bought a jacket, I reconnected with 90 West and aimed for Butte, near the Flathead Indian Reservation. But to be able to hit that target, I needed a caffeine infusion. Bozeman City served up hi-test cappuccino while, for extra measure, Whitehall slid me a large Coke.

In Butte, Steinbeck bought a Remington bolt-action .222, a rifle he said he "didn't particularly need…second-hand but in beautiful condition." He also found a telescopic sight to go with it and, while he waited to have it mounted, "got to know everyone in the shop and any customers who entered." One of these was Bill "The Silver Fox" Baltezar, self-dubbed "Watercolorist of the True West." (Baltezar later contacted me through a newspaper to share that the shop was Phil Judd's Sporting Goods, a place that "sold everything from fishing tackle to dynamite." He said he watched "the lanky stranger as he strolled in and walked back to a rack of old guns," describing him as having "worn and yellowed teeth" and "jeans, with suspenders and a belt — the belt for insurance." He noticed that "a beard covered his chin, masking his humble features, and a cigarette hung from the corner of his mouth." Baltezar immediately recognized that the stranger "knew guns," as he turned them over in his hands and admired their barrels.)

Steinbeck indeed purchased the Remington, saying to shopkeeper, Judd, "I'll take it, just the way it is," and requested the scope, adding, "My eyes ain't as good as they used to be." As the scope was affixed, Baltezar and Steinbeck stood outside talking in the noon sunlight. The author sought directions from him, too, taking a well-used map from "an inside pocket of his thread-bare jacket" and asking him to "mark the way to Polaris." Baltezar advised him about flyfishing on the Big Hole River, to do some "varmint hunting" to try out his rifle and to be sure and bathe in the springs at Elkhorn in the Valley of the Grasshopper, a sacred Indian healing place. His last image of Steinbeck was of the author gazing at the distant mountains and remarking about how much "he loved the sea, the smell of fishing boats, and the taste of salt spray." Baltezar guessed that he was a sailor, the disguise that Steinbeck had worked to effect, until shopkeeper Judd ("a big mountain man") read Steinbeck's name off the check he'd given him and said, "I'll be goddamned." By that time, Steinbeck had already pulled away.

The son of a copper miner from Austria, who "got the rotten jobs" at the local mine and died of silicosis at age 51, Baltezar had heard of Steinbeck but, to that point, hadn't read any of his work ("My wife's the book nut"). He also hadn't known about Steinbeck's past in Salinas, California, where Baltezar moved in 1967. At that time, the copper miners in Butte had gone on strike, a situation that lasted nine months. "Things really went to hell," Baltezar, who ran a dental laboratory at the time, said. "When people don't have money, they don't get their teeth fixed, don't get their eyes fixed." His sister, one of his 13 siblings, saw an ad in a San Francisco paper seeking a dental lab technician at the Community Hospital in Salinas. He applied and became one of 26 technicians on staff at the facility, "the biggest lab between San Francisco and Los Angeles." He and his wife, Dorothea, settled in town in a house they bought for just shy of $30,000.

Though he didn't meet Steinbeck again, Baltezar had a small part as a drunk crossing a street in Director Harvey Hart's 1980 film production of Steinbeck's novel, "East of Eden." Featuring notable actors like Anne Baxter, Timothy Bottoms, Jane Seymour and Lloyd Bridges, the movie was filmed in and around Salinas. He said the producers re-created Soledad Street, "a bad block with whorehouses," as it was in the old days, changing storefronts and temporarily removing any modern accents for the event. It was amusing, he said, to see "all the classy people in town and those of us who were ham enough to participate" playing extras. His daughter, Michele, 16 at the time, was in the film, too, one of four girls who get into an argument at an ice cream shop in the little town of Spreckles outside Salinas as you head toward Monterey.

About Butte, he said it once had "more bars and Catholic churches than you could count" and that the typical resident was Roman Catholic, Irish and a Democrat, much like the south side of Chicago. During WWII, Butte had a peak population of 72,000, a figure that had since dropped to half that, though he said, "It's coming back."

I didn't stop in Baltezar's birthplace, choosing to press on to Missoula, which reared her wild head at 11:30. From three bleary-eyed college girls parked in a car drinking wine outside a service station, I quickly got the good word on a place to go, a split-level joint up the way. Though it had a band, it was a little sedate and greatly overshadowed by another night spot that was busting with folks to the point that people were spilling out onto the sidewalk. I joined the masses, jostling my way to the bartender for a beer. Near me, a guy who was incoherent from drink was maintaining his vertical stance only because of the people next to him. Others weren't as lucky — at least three patrons toppled as I circled the place, creating a domino effect as they fell against others.

Seeking the scoop on the Big M, as I'd dubbed the town, I chatted with a University of Montana alum who offered that it's a unique town because of all the nightlife in easy walking distance and its energy. This weekend was the height of energy, it being U of M homecoming, which accounted for the crowd. Earlier in the day, the Missoula Grizzlies beat Cal Poly 17-14 in their football match.

About the nearby Flathead community, he said that it was quite diluted. Tribe members have the right to sell their property and have in great numbers. As a result, the reservation has become 70% white. Those that sold out apparently resettled in Missoula suburbs like Great Falls, which this particular guy called home. He, too, suggested I visit a couple of other establishments for a "local feel."

Embracing that, I walked around the corner to a lounge that was as homegrown as a place can get, with a shrieking, rowdy band a floor up, a crowd to match and exposed timber walls covered with hundreds of staples from past fliers and posters. The cacophony of sound was more than my eardrums could tolerate so I relocated to a burger joint, walking into the middle of a yelling match between two women.

A place called Rhino's had the head of a black rhino busting through one section of brick wall and was less crowded and volatile than the other spots, so I slid in at the bar beside a threesome of students. One, who was part Menomonee Indian, was well acquainted with "Travels with Charley" and, oddly enough, one of her best friends was named Charley.

At last call, I exited and turned the corner to El Corazor, one of these metallic-sided diners on wheels, serving up Mexican food. The beef enchilada with rice and beans was recommended and served up hot and sloppy, just the ticket to warm the belly on a chill night. A few exits west of a row of hotels and gas stations, the Missoula KOA became my camp spot, and I tubed myself into unconsciousness.

Day 30: Missoula to Seattle

I was done with Montana, eager to cross through Idaho, see Washington and connect with Tom and Rebecca Repp at *American Road* magazine. They'd been featuring news capsules about my journey in the fine monthly and agreed to host me in Seattle.

Seeking to wash up after my usual four hours of sleep, I drove up 90 apiece to a travel center. When I learned it was $8 for a shower and "sheeshed" about the outrage — the going rate in my experience was $5 or $6 — the clerk said, "I know, a little pricey. At least I'll give you the Cadillac." The Cadillac was shower room #5 and more like a Chevy, with pine slat walls, a shower stall that could have benefited from an acidic grout cleaner and ceiling that needed a paint job. But it was also large and all mine for the ten minutes I needed it.

It did the trick of resuscitating me and, for breakfast, I tapped the cafe next door for the "Driver Combo": three scrambled eggs, a thick slab of ham, sausage, bacon, hash browns and toast. Turning my table into an office space, I plotted my day's travels, did some reading and made phone calls. Notably, I buzzed traveler-in-spirit Liz Ehlert, learning she was in Albuquerque, New Mexico, but headed this way. We figured our best bet to meet up was still in California.

A middle-aged woman squeezed into the booth across from me, remarking, "I'm not getting fatter. These booths are getting smaller." A trucker who looked like a modern day Wyatt Earp, with a handlebar moustache, 10-gallon hat and pointed Western boots, ambled through, looking to fill a silver coffee thermos he carried in one hand. An announcement, "Church services will be held in the movie room at 9 o'clock," was heard.

My reading materials of choice this morning included *Yellowstone Today*, a seasonal paper I'd picked up at the park yesterday. It came with a yellow flier, "WARNING: Many visitors have been gored by buffalo." It went on to state facts about the beasts, namely that they can weigh up to 2,000 pounds, sprint at 30 m.p.h. and are wild, unpredictable and dangerous. The paper further admonished calling elk by using buglers or imitating their calls.

More *YT* discoveries: Yellowstone was the world's first national park, established in 1872. If charged by a bear, *YT* advised the use of pepper spray to diffuse the situation. Old Faithful, which I'd missed seeing, erupts every 92 minutes, expels up to 8,400 gallons of water per eruption and has a water temp of 204 degrees. Fires in 1988, started by both humans and lightning, claimed 793,000 acres and killed 300 large mammals.

Movin' Out, a free "journal of the trucking industry" that I'd picked up here at the travel center, showed a photo of an Indianapolis trucking company's cab memorializing the victims of 9/11. It also profiled professional trucker Arnold Wass, who began driving when he was 17 and was still driving at age 80. Over his 63 years in the industry, he has logged nearly six million miles. Asked when he was going to give up driving, he replied, "When they make me, I guess." There was also a photo of another unique individual, Robert E. Harris, the nation's last practicing circuit-riding preacher, astride his horse. His ministry would take him to towns throughout western North Carolina and rest areas along the interstate there.

The *Daily Inter Lake*, "Serving the Flathead since 1988," noted that Montana has the second-highest suicide rate in the nation, and that a conservation-minded Ferndale man was building his home using straw bales for insulation, the advantages of which were non-toxicity and lower energy bills.

Studying my atlas then, I noticed that I was about 80 miles south of Glacier National Park, the site of huge wildfires during the summer.

Like the Yellowstone fires of '88, these were sparked by lightning igniting already bone-dry timber.

I was also about 120 miles southwest of Fort Benton, an area that Lewis & Clark studied extensively, recording 178 plants and 122 animal species then unknown to man. These included wild sage that tasted like chamomile and scores of Bighorn Sheep, trout, Black-Billed Magpies, Pronghorns and Spruce trees, the latter 36 feet across at the trunk. Today, the Eden they'd described is just a vestige of its former self. Pollution has choked rivers, and many species, such as the Carolina Parakeet and passenger pigeon, are extinct.

These sites would have to wait for a future day for me to experience them. In fact, I was closer to the Idaho border than either of these places.

Pine-covered mountains lined my exit from Montana and my only stop was in Hagen for gas and to de-bug. I had intended on purchasing supplies, gathering several items and placing them on the counter of the gas station's package store. Somehow, though, I managed to get distracted and left without them, only realizing what I'd done after getting miles down the road. By that time, it was too late to go back. I wondered if the clerk there was still waiting for me to resurface.

Down the backside of Lookout Pass and through the Panhandle National Forest I traveled, reaching a colorful "Welcome to Idaho" sign. Besides breaching another state, my crossing marked entry into the Pacific Standard Time Zone, so I pulled to the side to set my watch back another hour. That made me feel less anxious about the time I lost at the café.

About this top third of Idaho, which he referred to as an "upraised thumb," Steinbeck noted driving "through real mountains that climbed straight up, tufted with pines and deep-dusted with snow." It snowed, in fact, as he went through — "a light gay snow." As to the underbrush, he described it as "thick and very green, and everywhere was a rush of waters." While he was enjoying the setting, he was becoming concerned about Charley, who had been "having increasing difficulty in evacuating his bladder."

Midway through the state, Steinbeck stopped "under the ridge of a pass…for gasoline in a little put-together do-it-yourself group of cabins." Besides offering fuel and accommodations, the place served as a store, repair shop and lunch room. He decided to stay the night in a cabin, which turned out to be "uncomfortable and ugly" with a lumpy bed, dirty yellow walls and an "aroma of mice and moisture, mold and the smell of old, old dust." A naked bulb hung from the ceiling and kerosene stove heated the room. The proprietor's son, "a young man of about twenty", named Robbie, befriended him, wanted to hear all about New York and invited him to family dinner. After "bowls of bubbling navy beans and fatback" and ham, Steinbeck retired for the night. Charley's condition, which he addressed with Seconal to relax Charley's bladder, made sleep difficult and, the following morning, Steinbeck "drove hell for leather for Spokane" to locate a vet.

Idaho, to which I'd traveled over 6,400 miles to reach, represented my 17th U.S. State. I didn't know much about it, other than its designation as a potato capital, and didn't know what to expect. So, to capture some local color and the supplies I still required, I stopped in historic Wallace, in the shadow of the highway. An Exxon, where a 43-inch, 25-pound Pike was mounted on the wall behind the cashier, filled my order. And while the town looked inviting, with many antique carriers and jewelry vendors, it was Sunday and closed up pretty tightly.

Back up on the highway, I noticed the word "silver" beginning to appear everywhere: The town of Silverton. Silver Mountain Recreation Area. Silverwood Theme Park. Silverhorn Motor Inn. Silver Valley 4H Club. Then I remembered that Idaho is known as the "Gem State" and this all made sense.

With the exception of a couple of rises, I seemed to be ever descending through Idaho. My favorite sight was the overlook of Lake Couer d'Alene, a broad and beautiful body of water that had yielded the Pike I'd seen back in Wallace.

Early afternoon, when the road had flattened out and mountains faded into the background, I crossed into state #18: "Welcome to Washington, the Evergreen State." A digital display flashed 76 degrees, quite balmy and unseasonable for "inland Washington" this time of year the local radio disc jockey observed. The state, in fact, had recorded over 50 consecutive days of temperatures over 70 degrees the past summer. A transplant from the south, the deejay had been told to prepare to be wearing scarves, gloves and a coat by this time. As you can imagine, she was thankful that she did not need these articles of clothing and for the extended bout of good weather, as was I.

At the City Center exit for Spokane (pronounced Spo-can), I spilled out by a Frankie Doodle's Restaurant, offering "coffee still under a buck." Up ahead was Gonzaga University, with its respectable basketball program, a general store selling guns and ammo, umpteen furniture stores including one with an inflatable purple gorilla on the roof, and a comic books shop.

Two missions were on my agenda here: To call the Repps in Seattle to give them a heads-up about my visit and to try and find out which veterinarian Steinbeck visited to get help for Charley. On Mission #1, I was successful in reaching Becky Repp and informed her that I'd likely reach Seattle by dinnertime.

On Mission #2, a phone book at a Chevron station on Division Street connected me to a local clinic and a vet on duty. He said that there would only have been a small handful of practitioners in Spokane in 1960, and that a couple were still alive. Of the two he had in mind, one seemed to fit the descriptions Steinbeck had applied: "One more good reason for a good home book on dog medicine," "if not elderly, pushing his luck," and "shaking" as if hungover. The vet's manner had been poor and uncaring, Charley sensed it and Steinbeck got "snappish" because of it. Sensing Steinbeck's irritation, the vet ultimately gave Charley "something to flush out his kidneys," diagnosing the problem as "just a cold." With haste, Steinbeck "took the pills and paid [his] bill and got out of there."

It was a sore topic all around and I decided it was to no one's benefit to press for an identification of the physician. Besides, I was anxious to see the city by the sea that I'd long heard so much about, to smell the wonderful scent of the ocean from which I'd been deprived for a month and to take in Seattle insider experiences. Steinbeck felt the same, having grown up along the Pacific, and imagined, still far inland, the smell of "the sea rocks and the kelp and the excitement of churning sea water."

There was extra weight in my accelerator foot as we barreled west and I gazed with refreshed spirit at the flat grasslands, rugged black rocks and cool, olive-colored lakes surrounding us. And, like in the Midwest, there was a whole lot of hauling going on, though all by transport trucks or pickups. Masses of hay, timber, cattle, horses and boats went by in either direction.

In a fact book for the states I had stashed at arm's length, I was surprised to learn that Washington leads the nation in apple production, for, to see the landscape I was seeing, you'd have trouble swallowing that tidbit. It's also the only state named after a president.

Tiredness caught up with me a third of the way into the state, around Schrag, where I found a gravelly pullout suited to a late afternoon nap. When I plied my lids open again, the sun was lower in the sky, bugs were hovering around my door and Seattle was 200 miles off. Travel resumed, brown grasses turned to green grasses and a heavy, hanging farm smell became noticeable in the air. Small compact blocks, then whole hangars of hay stood covered with white tarps. Irrigators rolled across fields adding a just-rained scent to the now midland bouquet. Periodically, tall cypresses formed property divisions.

There was a brooding majesty to Frenchman Hills as we reached the spot, and awesome serenity to Wanapum Lake — named after the Wanapum Indians who lived along the water from Beverly Gap to Pasco — as I viewed it from the Wild Horses overlook. On its far bank, the Ginkgo Petrified Forest held over 200 varieties of wood.

At dusk, we entered the Wenatchee State Forest, now 70 miles southeast of Seattle, with its white pines stamped against blue gray mountains and a light gray sky. Six-thousand-foot-tall Snoqualmie Mountain towered over us as we hurtled through a mist filled valley. Formidable fortresses of forest pocketed the cool, early night air. We were in a downward spiral on an asphalt flume expecting to be shot like a cannonball from some gaping egress at the base of this great range.

True night came on like octopus ink fanning as it would through water, enveloping everything in its path. If not for the taillights of cars ahead, there would be no light.

The flume put us in a low, wide, smooth tunnel that rolled us into an alley and the brightly-lit Seattle suburbs. There was another tunnel, bigger than the first, then a wide "S" curve, a cement jungle, glass-and-steel Seahawks Stadium, City Center signs and the great pearl itself.

I had no prior notions of Seattle unlike Steinbeck who remembered it "as a town sitting on hills beside a matchless harborage — a little city of space and trees and gardens." As such, he was shocked to see "tops of hills shaved off," "highways eight lanes wide," "high wire fences" and "the yellow smoke of progress."

Glancing around, I realized I was in the Chinatown/International area of the city, several blocks square, jam-packed with bakeries, restaurants, karaoke bars, noodle companies and other establishments serving the Asian community. After some circling, I asked a couple strolling along the street for a restaurant recommendation. "Honey Court Seafood," they said in unison.

It was a large place and had seen a lot of traffic judging by the well-worn industrial carpeting. Live lobsters and crabs squirmed and writhed in tanks in the entry. I was quickly seated beside a table of seven, and watched their chopsticks precision deliver payloads of prawns, rice and scallops to their hungry mouths. To warn her infant daughter about a spicy food, a mom in the group taught her to say "hot," which she repeated perfectly and to much amusement.

At the recommendation of the waitress, I ordered salt and pepper squid as an appetizer, supplementing it with a main entrée of prawns, snow peas and scallops on a bed of steamed rice. To wash it down, I added a Tsingtao beer. When the food arrived — an abundant salvo to be sure — a Vietnamese girl at the next table, who later introduced herself as "Thien", looked over and exclaimed, "Damn!" As it was much more than I'd expected and more than I could handle on my own, I offered my squid to them, which elicited a collective giggle. It appeared that they were going to refuse out of politeness until the girl's grandfather, not one to be shy, stood up, stepped over and collected it, scooping half the squid onto their plates. Since I'd been giving, I thought it wouldn't be an imposition to pass off a piece of paper seeking their suggestions on "Three Things I Should Do In Chinatown Tonight."

"I can give you ten things," said Thien's friend, "Mai". She started scribbling: Eat pho (beef noodle soup, pronounced "fuh") at Little Bit of Saigon on Jackson Street, watch fish being processed at Pike Place Market, visit the Bruce Lee Museum (he was a Seattle native) and hit the Purple Dot for late night food. She seemed so informed about the local scene that I asked if I could hire her as a guide. She agreed and we exchanged contact information.

As I did not have room for even the remainder of the squid, Mai suggested we give it to a homeless person sitting outside of the restaurant on the sidewalk. It was a thoughtful gesture and I believed that I would be in excellent hands the next day.

When the group left, I poked at my prawns while thumbing through a couple of free papers I'd picked up inside the door. The *Northwest Asian Weekly* reported that a dragon sculpture coiled around a traffic light in the area must be removed, as it is a liability according to the city. Propaganda from China's Mao Zedong era was becoming a sought-out collectible. Asian girl band the Buttersprites, pictured dressed as nurses with red crosses on their hats, were scheduled to play a local benefit. Paradorn Srichaphan, the world's 11th ranked tennis player, was profiled as a self-dubbed Asian ambassador.

The *Filipino American Herald*, which was celebrating its 34th anniversary, discussed the effect that 9/11 has had on immigrant populations in terms of their being targeted for unjust searches and deportation.

Involved in the reading and watching other patrons as they came and went, I ordered another beer and mulled the recommendations Mai had made. While good, Chinatown was closing up for the evening, and these attractions were not available at this hour. Seeking a game plan, I turned to two Asian women near me and they suggested a lounge in the Capital Hill neighborhood. It was an easy ride and, happily, a funky, cool destination. Black was the "in" attire and R.E.M.-like tunes the backdrop in this two-level coffeehouse.

Fetching my laptop in, I ordered a mocha coffee and plopped down at a high counter perch beside a modelesque woman studying Near East art. Just outside the window from us, three beatnik-looking types sparked up hand-rolled joints. In the distance, the awesome Space Needle, where I would be dining with the Repps tomorrow night, stood guard over Seattle.

My "model" counter mate suggested I walk a few blocks to Broadway, saying I'd see "outlandish, liberal things" there. Off I went, padding uphill, past vintage clothing shops, used vinyl sellers, and funky book places, to the target. There, I noted a couple of gay joints, then other places full of folks of many different makes and persuasions, all wearing their various colors without reservation or hesitation.

U-turning, I walked down Pike Street, past the Convention Center and big hotels, to the Farmers Market on 1st Avenue. This appeared to be the red light area, with a mix of go-go bars, comedy clubs, adult shops, and transients — the seedy side of the Seattle bun. I hooked through here, too, before walking the few blocks back to El Rucio.

Given the high rates of the city's hotels, even on a Sunday, it became necessary to figure out a cost-effective accommodations plan. At that point, it was a toss-up between a Wal-Mart lot and a KOA, with the camp winning out. Located about 10 or so miles south of Seattle, down I-5, it offered a quiet spot facing a bluff, where I bedded down for the night.

Day 31: The Needle in the Sky

I was up at 7 and broke camp a half hour later after a solid shower. The road the camp was on was choked with rush hour traffic that curled past misty meadows of horses to an equally congested I-5. The slow-moving tangle of carbon-emitting steel reminded me of my old commute from Fairfield to Stamford on the I-95 corridor, particularly since the radio carried shock jock Howard Stern's morning show, broadcast from New York City. Four lanes wide, I-5 was still a better road though, and I got to see the sites that had been cloaked by darkness last night: the official-looking Seattle Tacoma International Airport, Amtrak railroad line, the Port of Seattle, ferries shuttling back and forth to Victoria, Canada, and the city skyline.

An ad message that interrupted the Stern show announced that rock band Aerosmith was coming to the White Snake River arena, while a sports news clip noted that the Seahawks lost their football match yesterday. There was nothing classic about this station like in more intimate, off-the-beaten path areas, making me long to return to the jazz beats at the previous night's lounge.

The interstate spit me out in the Capital Hill area again, and soon I was seated at my familiar window perch watching upwardly mobile young professionals in neatly pressed clothes filing in for their coffee injection on their way to their city workspaces. These folks most likely included the very same individuals I'd seen on the town last night flirting with alternative lifestyles, now trading their vinyl, leather and piercings for conservative corporate disguises.

In the spot where the pot smokers had camped last night, an old guy in a sheepskin-lined denim jacket and blue knit cap was holding court. A patron near me said, "He's got something to say about everything." Indeed, people just gravitated to him. Noticing a young guy showing the coffeehouse king his all-in-one camp tool, I went and got my Gerber knife from the van and joined the proceeding. The multi-instrumented wonder garnered nods of approval all around and, as the group examined it, I related how I'd used it to cut up moose steak in the Beartooth. This led to talk about other areas I'd traveled to and those I still planned to visit.

Still needing to tap the 'net, I went up the street to a small Internet café with seven computer stations, and brought up my e-mail. There, Mai met me and led me to a parking lot where I transferred to her car. We shot downtown to the Farmers Market, which Steinbeck called "the old port" and that I'd seen last night. He'd walked around here, in fact, admiring "the fish and crabs and shrimps…on white beds of shaved ice and…the washed and shining vegetables arranged in pictures." The transients, which Steinbeck called "vague ruins of men, the lotus eaters who struggle daily toward unconsciousness by way of raw alcohol," were now gone, replaced by scores of vendors. They offered paintings and drawings of Seattle scenes, hand-knit beanie hats, mountains of fresh fruit, stacks of King Salmon reclined on ice mattresses, succulent vegetables, and bizarre comic books like *Alice in Sexland* and *Bondage Fairies.*

At a bath salts booth on a lower level, we met up with the two friends that had dined with Mai and her family last night. Both had unique backgrounds: Thien believed she was half-Vietnamese and half-Caucasian, though not completely certain as she was adopted. Arya was both white and black, or "an inside-out Oreo" as Thien jokingly termed it. As Arya was manning the booth, she wasn't able to join us, but passed a bath salts packet to me on the house. Thien, on the other hand, was free, and, soon, we three were sifting through button bins at a collectables shop. Negotiating a "group discount," we walked away with more than a dozen, featuring slogans such as, "I did not escape, they gave me a day pass," "I think, therefore I'm dangerous" and "Beer, it's what's for dinner."

Tumbling back into Mai's car, we drove to Thien and Arya's apartment in ritzy Belltown, where Thien had planned to prepare a special Asian appetizer. The 900-square-foot place was decorated to a large degree with items the girls had recovered from the building trash, including leather chairs, tables and even paintings, like one of Rio de Janeiro. On their refrigerator was an Angelina Jolie "Got Milk?" ad, which Arya called "Ange-tina Jolie" because of Thien's resemblance to the puffy-lipped actress.

The secret snack turned out to be steamed shrimp dipped in a sauce of pepper, salt and lime juice, and then banh thec (pronounced bun-tek), a pod of rice, peas and banana leaf. As we ate, I heard about Thien's background growing up as one of the only Asians in Coeur d'Alene.

Our tasty treat was followed by a visit to Alki, the shoreline opposite Seattle. There, we gazed across the water and looked at our feet and watched the boats pass. It was an everything's-right-with-the-world moment, or as a t-shirt at the Market declared, "It's All Good."

Mai then took us by Camp Long, where she thought I could rent a space for the evening. Ten rustic cabins surrounded by hiking trails, horseback riding, ponds and climbing opportunities were available. But what was truly noteworthy was a red book on a tabletop just inside, marked "Phenology Notes: Record your sightings of flora and fauna at Camp Long." Opened to a page, I read: "Sept. 16 - Saw fox near bridge by golf shed." I turned to another section: "Red back salamander found under log (very mossy log)." Another page: "Saw a great blue heron at the pond." It was a running record of the natural workings of this particular biosphere. I picked up some literature for later consideration, including a reservations number, and rejoined the girls.

Our next stop was Pacific Garden restaurant on King in the International District. It was one of those places that you know about only by word of mouth, and within the Asian community — and I felt privileged to have this access. Mai did the ordering for us: Beef Chow Fun, Fried Rice and Fried Chicken. Three generous dishes soon arrived and we tucked in. We gabbed away as chicken grease and rice tumbled down our chins and coated our fingers. I noticed a brass statue of a fat Buddha in the corner. Mai informed me, "You rub his belly and he brings you a lot of money." We three felt like fat Buddhas when we finished our meals.

The occasion was as great as our afternoon adventure in Seattle. Mai returned me to the van, we all hugged farewell then they led me in the direction of the Space Needle, like a small plane takes a glider up into the air and releases the tether. I rode John and Denny Streets down their roller coaster lengths, with hills as steep as in San Francisco, as the Needle seemed to grow taller ahead.

Rain, the weather for which Seattle is more known, started to come down. It was a shame, as it would greatly reduce my Needle-top view of the area, to which I was looking forward. The precipitation brought another problem — a leak in the roof of El Rucio, which allowed water to drip onto the front console. To fix it, if only for a while, I jammed a washcloth up into the gap between the roof interior and windshield and placed a towel on the console to catch any drips that might get through.

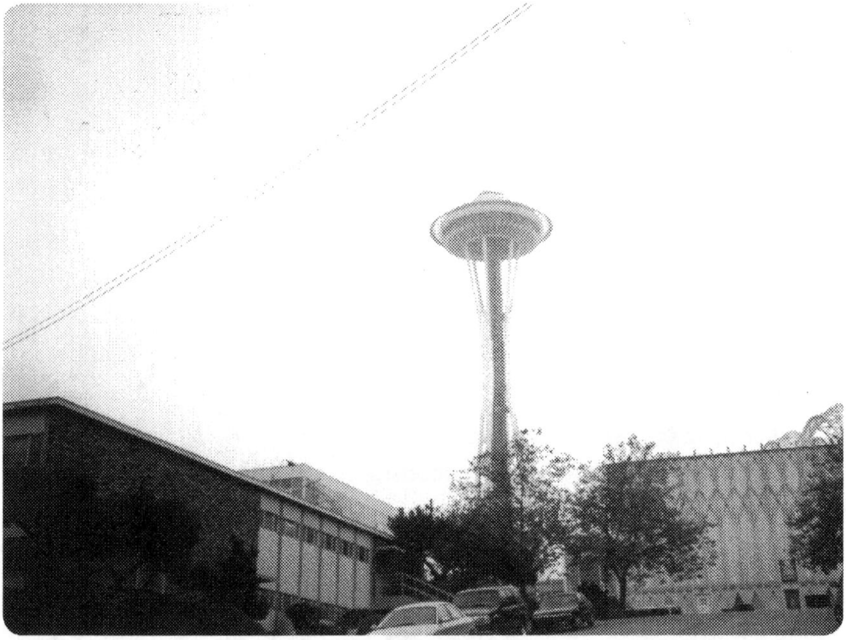

With the Space Needle as my aim, I changed into a neat outfit and alit on foot, entering the gift shop at its base. Walking up behind a nattily dressed couple, I inquired, "Tom? Becky?" I'd guessed correctly, we exchanged hellos and stood talking awhile before Becky reminded us of our dinner reservations.

Up the west flank of the structure we went, ascending at a rate of 5 m.p.h. It was a 1 1/2-minute climb to the Sky City restaurant, 628 feet in the air. The observation level, with its 15 high powered telescopes, was another 18 feet up. Built upon tons of concrete and rebar, the tower is a remnant of the 1962 World's Fair, which my Dad had worked for General Electric.

The restaurant itself revolved at a speed of 285 feet per hour via a one-horsepower motor. This afforded diners a complete, 360-degree look at the city. We took seats window side and talked about their background, spent partly in theater, including studying under playwright Sam Smiley at the University of Arizona. Steinbeck's "Grapes of Wrath" was actually their first production there and, to enhance their roles, the actors pinpointed the Joad family's stops on a map and read up about those areas.

When Smiley retired, Tom began teaching theater history at the University of Washington. He penned two books about Route 66, too, before making a choice of taking over his dad's sprinkler design business or pursuing his interest in America's roadways. It was an easy choice — "the sprinkler business wasn't very creative" — and *American Road* magazine was launched in May 2003.

We spoke of Seattle in general. Tom remarked that it "doesn't know it's a big city yet" and that it had "a sprawl and traffic problem." Historically, it was the home of Thomas Crapper, who invented the toilet. We spoke of Tacoma, too, and Tom asked if I'd smelled the "Tacoma Aroma," a hovering odor produced by paper mill emissions.

Dinner, meanwhile, was superb: salmon with vegetables and a fine Merlot, with a brownie, ice cream and mocha coffee for dessert. It complemented the company and the view. We dropped back down to street level, browsed the gift shop, then, after they gave me a few tips on additional Seattle attractions, parted.

Away I went again and, on a whim, decided to shoot up to Vancouver, despite the rain. It was not a Steinbeck stop but one I'd always wanted to make, in accordance with my overall mission. Rolling up 5 and even with a large dose of French Vanilla coffee in my system, I had to pull in at a filling station in Lakewood to rest my tired eyes. The slam of a car door that pulled in beside me set me back into action and I resumed my mission.

The rain continued to come down, hard at times, and the road was slick and black, begging me to travel her if I dared.

The border checkpoint was a wide expanse and the guard was brief, moving me on with a "bye bye." I clawed my way the last few miles to Vancouver, in the province of British Columbia, passing the Cecil Hotel, a few small restaurants and several namebrand inns before finding the ROXY. It was full of folks and featured a band that knew its way around several cover tunes. I did the circuit, ordered up a beer and threw myself onto the dance floor to shuffle my feet a bit.

Unfortunately, I'd barely begun to experience the place when last call was announced and the lights came up. By then, the streets had fallen under the control of drunken British Columbians, the homeless and a pack of working girls. They all accosted me in one way or another as I moved down the way to a pizza place on the main. It offered lukewarm slices of pizza topped with vegetables, ham and pineapple. I sat and took in the spectacle of a trio verbally accosting every person who entered. A foursome, that found themselves in the middle of the escalating volley, was greatly amused. I told them that while you had to pay for the pizza, the comedy was free and that the next show starts at 2. I even offered to rent them my seat, the best in the house at that point.

No sooner had I said that than a bearded wino walked in and started playing "Oh, Susanna" on a harmonica. A haggard looking woman nearby began stomping her foot and clapping in accompaniment and, when he switched to a Dylan tune, she got up in his face to dance and whoop. All the while, her male companion inexplicably chanted aloud, "Cheese crust, plain pizza" over and over. The chorus, enriched by the laughter and supplementary stomping of other patrons, was a cacophony of Canadian craziness that I didn't dare look to top, so turned in for the night at an inn on Nelson Street.

PART FIVE

South to Steinbeck Country

Day 32: Vancouver's Beautiful B-Side

The morning, as I observed it through my tall hotel room window, framed by floor-to-ceiling length leopard print drapes, looked dreary. But as long as it wasn't raining, I thought, my day plans would be doable. By e-mail, I sent a greeting to my eldest son on the occasion of his 8th birthday, an event I was sorry to be missing, and confirmed with my brother that my engine troubles up in the Beartooth may have been altitude related, the thin air affecting the fuel mix.

It was nearly noon before we got going, behind schedule as usual, and, as we moved north from the inn's parking lot through a busy commercial and transportation center, I noticed that Vancouver was a very different place by day, bustling with shoppers, business people and visitors. Except for some of the traffic signage that has that international look I'd seen in Europe, it didn't feel like Canada. And, here, like Seattle, there were many Asians, both Oriental and Indian. In fact, we stumbled across the equivalent of Seattle's Chinatown around Main and Hastings, seeing noodle companies, importers and restaurants, all with an Asian slant. It seemed as good a place as any to hop out and pad about, to pester people with questions about area attractions.

An elder gentleman with a distinctive Cockney accent suggested sites like the Gastown historic district, the view from the Pan Pacific Hotel, a hike to the top of Grouse Mountain and a side trip to Whistler, a world renown ski resort. A slim Oriental waitress suggested Robson Street for shopping, English Bay Beach and the Capilano Suspension Bridge. A stunning brunette, who was studying to be an air-show pilot and hauling around a bulging backpack of thick books, guided me with directions.

I mulled their suggestions over a burger, fries and coffee but ultimately decided to stumble around the city in my own way. Following cobbled Water Street around to Georgia, we passed the columned Vancouver Art Gallery with its flowers and spouting fountains out front, tall office buildings housing financial services, towering glass luxury apartments, a marina and horse-drawn and motorized trolleys. Breaching Stanley Park, named after English aristocrat Lord Stanley, I looked across the harbor at the city, eyed an oxidized statue of 18th century Scottish poet Robert Burns and saw massive motor yachts idling at the Royal Vancouver Yacht Club. A grouping of painted totem poles carved from red cedar by the British Columbia Indians depicted real and mythical events and each animal carving had symbolic meaning: eagle = air, whale = sea, wolf = land and frog = air/sea link. While studying them, I spoke with a Taiwanese man who was driving an older model van like my own and we compared features. He was visiting the area from El Paso, Texas, where he worked for a DVD manufacturer.

A West Coast Air seaplane lifted off from the harbor as I continued along the park loop to Prospect Point, where, in July 1888, the English steamer "Beaver" was wrecked. A family of raccoons ran across my path as I stopped to look out across English Bay to Lions' Gate Bridge. Further ahead, a large, hollowed cedar tree more than 18 feet across defied the elements and served as a backdrop for endless visitor photos.

Ferguson Point, where the Teahouse Restaurant, once Lord Stanley's estate house, was located, offered yet another skyline perspective and craggy beach walk. There, I met up with — I kid you not — Neil Armstrong and his wife Marjorie, a delightful pair from Alberta. They were walking their Kerry blue terrier, Tara, named after the plantation house in "Gone with the Wind" and a virtual duplicate of Steinbeck's Charley.

The Armstrongs had had some terrific life adventures together. One of the most memorable was a nine-month worldwide voyage they began in early 1984. They traveled through Asia, South America, Africa, the Middle East and Eastern and Western Europe. In London, at a café where they sought a meal, the staff, noticing the name on his credit card, mistook him for the astronaut. He played along and signed some memorabilia.

I re-boarded El Rucio and ambled Denman and Robson Streets, completely lined with high-ticket shops and crowded with pedestrians. With a #10 bus, powered by overhead wires, as my lead, we passed over the high arching Granville Bridge and hooked down and around to Granville Island. Seeking more specific directions to the marketplace, I got the attention of a long-legged Chinese girl strolling by. She had a pleasant face and I hoped that she would be accommodating. Not only did she guide me, she agreed to allow me to thank her with a tea at an adjacent Starbucks.

We sat on wire chairs at an outside table in the shadow of the bridge and traded information about ourselves. A table setter at an area restaurant, "Lan" hoped to save enough money to take some art classes. About Vancouver, she said, "It's a beautiful city but very reserved."

She agreed to be my guide at the market and we walked beneath the bridge onto the island to the venue, visiting a postcard specialty shop and fruit and seafood stands. Passing through to the waterfront ferry dock, we sat on a bench and shared focacia and sourdough bread, tossing crumbs to greedy seagulls that gathered at our feet. On the water, crew boats, tugs, water taxis and Canadian geese trundled past.

Night was falling and a chill settled over us. The seagulls felt it, too, and sought out chimney pots from which warm air was rising from market kitchens. I saw Lan off at a bus stop and strolled across the road to an Indian restaurant. The hostess welcomed me with a smile that drove away the chill that had settled in my bones. In the kitchen, two ladies in colorful saris prepared wonderful smelling soups and entrees while, in the doorway, another, her doe-brown eyes welling with tears, peeled onions.

Supper was a feast of Mulligatawny Soup (vegetable broth with lentils and spices), vegetable samosa (pastry puffs stuffed with spiced potatoes and peas), bhuna chicken (cooked with fresh tomatoes, sliced onions, green pepper and spices), roti (whole wheat flaky bread) and Kingfisher beer. The spices in the food, though "medium," fueled my thaw-out and fired up my moving-on urge. With a to-go package in hand, I hit the street, rain soaking my clothes as I dashed back to the van. Once again behind the wheel, I really got going. At 10:30, I reached the Peace Arch at the border, nearly tearing my axles off on the speed bumps. A pair of very accommodating guards processed me and, from there, I imagined the only thing that would slow me down was me. And slow me down I did, at Bellingham, Washington, where I started to see double. A large lot behind York's Exxon, where a line of trucks was already parked, offered shelter and the opportunity to sack out.

Day 33: Chuckanut, Hendrix & Me

As the truckers fired up their hulking cargo carriers, so did I, around 4:30 a.m., pausing to refresh myself with a sponge bath at the Exxon bathroom and to fill El Rucio. Parked beside a Border Patrol truck, I heard from the station's overhead radio the tune "Travelin' Man", an appropriate ballad with which to begin the day I thought. From the adjacent Northwest Cruisin' Coffee Kiosk, I snagged some caffeine and a warm raspberry scone. Chuckanut Drive, an 18-mile scenic detour, was in my plan as the kickoff for the day. Should I wait until sun-up to see it? "I think you wan'noo," the barista suggested. A couple of exits down, near the start of the trail, I pulled into a Chevron to have my breakfast and wait for first light. It came, but so did showers.

I set off on the wrong foot but was quickly rescued by a motorist I flagged down. We pulled up along a side street and he drew me a little map, noting, "It should be an awesome day to see it." He also suggested I tour Bellingham, saying that once people "land there, they never leave. It's just the nicest town. On any given day, I can windsurf, golf or go skiing."

Though the rain had slowed when I hit the Drive, the wind had kicked up, making for tempestuous, moody conditions, maybe the ideal viewing climate I thought. As I scaled the road to its hip, the trees lining it lifted their skirts to bare the tuft of an island centered between the shores of a well-sculpted bay down off to the right. Soaked and lashed by the unharnessed waters around it, the island appeared to quiver in fear. As I clawed further, the bay widened and the heartbeat of the sea raced while, around me, the wind moaned and gasped and tossed leaves around with abandon. The whole scene panted with life and glistened with precipitation and, as I slid down the backside of the curvy route, I paused at intervals to regard it with wonder.

Ultimately, I spilled out onto a calming plateau of green fields, trimmed with sea grasses and trod by milking cows and speckled ponies. An alpaca farm, hawk perched on a wire and several potato farms followed. Then, at Burlington, the Drive and I parted company and once again I coupled with 5 to continue south.

The rain began anew and picked up in intensity, forcing the wipers into action at their highest setting. They slapped furiously at the wet in a valiant effort to keep my field of vision clear. Seeking momentary refuge and help finding other attractions, I darted to a visitor center in Marysville where a pair of helpful ladies outfitted me with maps and information. Remembering a supply need then, I crossed the parking lot for a close encounter with a Wal-Mart. Par usual, a retiree inside the door, a gentleman wearing a company vest decorated with pins, wished me a "good morning" and helped me to a department. On the way, I was privy to a store meeting, wherein employees and a person dressed as a clown were gathered. They were just concluding their session with a cheer. "Give me a W…give me an A…give me an L…" a team leader prompted, eliciting appropriate responses. Then there were concluding cries of "Who's #1?" and "Who comes first?" followed by the response, "The customer!" clapped out to a steady beat. It was quite rousing. Exiting, I noticed that another button-wearing retiree had joined the first — they were multiplying!

I had my sights set on the Boeing Tour Center at Paine Field in Everett and, as I skimmed the Tulalip Indian Reservation, I got on the horn to arrange a ticket. A pair of Tour Directors met me at the entrance counter. One had been a crew chief for CH47 Chinook helicopters, "responsible for everything until the pilot mans it," in Vietnam. The other joined the air force in '63 and played the same role, but for F-105 Thunder Chiefs or "Thuds," jack-of-all trade aircraft that provided troop support and detected SCUDS.

Our tour began in a theater with a series of films. One showed a time-sped assembly process of a 747 aircraft. A task that usually takes seven months, it flashed through in 3 1/2 minutes.

From the theater, we boarded a bus around the complex. Midway, a security officer boarded to remind us that no cellphones, cameras or other carry-around items were permitted on the tour. This measure was imposed after the events of 9/11.

We pulled up in front of an enormous factory building that had a very long access tunnel carrying pipe work. Above our heads, eight feet of concrete separated us from a fully assembled, 400,000-pound aircraft. With a full passenger weight, that number doubles, and 2,000 gallons of fuel are required to heft the plane into the air.

Employees used the tunnel as a jogging path on lunch breaks. It was the length of the Titanic and led to a large elevator. This carried us to an Observation Deck to see a 40-inch thick cross-section of a 747, 10 seats across. There, we learned the "7" that Boeing uses to designate its aircraft was chosen by company founder Bill Boeing for its lucky association.

From an overhead walkway, we looked out at nose, wing and fuselage sections, in enormous yellow vises or up on platforms being worked on. Above us, more than 30 miles of track allowed a ceiling-mounted crane to move around to all areas of the factory to transport parts.

According to the Guinness World Book of Records, this facility was the largest building in the world, encompassing 472 million cubic feet or 4.3 million feet of floor space, with 98.3 acres of space under one roof. That's 75 football fields or enough room to house Disney's entire theme park. Every 14 days, one aircraft was rolling off the line.

We re-boarded the bus to go across the compound, seeing JAL, KLM, Cathay Pacific, Alitalia and Singapore Air 777 aircraft being tuned and tested ready for customer pick-up. This included a new 242-foot model, their longest aircraft. Many other numbers and stats were thrown at us: 24 cafeterias on the complex, 2,000 bicycles provided to employees to get around, etc.

Steinbeck would have lumped the site in the same category as national parks I imagined. The sheer statistics and fantastic volume of the place couldn't be correlated with anything else in America. It was, perhaps, the Eighth Wonder of the World.

My head was spinning with information as we returned to the tour start and visited the gift shop. With several items in hand for my boys, I resumed my southward trek, holding fast to El Rucio as she was pulled about by continued strong wind gusts.

Landing in Seattle, I walked up 1st Avenue to Trattoria Mitchelli, a sunny Italian restaurant that set me up with a wood-fired tomato and mozzarella pizza, salad and Maritime Pacific Hefeweizen. I spoke about my journey with a fellow patron, an insurance salesperson in town on business from Nevada. When I noted Arizona as a state I had yet to tour, she dialed up a friend there — a Washoe Indian and accomplished journalist — who might serve as a local guide. Then I kissed the pearl goodbye and pointed myself south to new adventures.

Traffic on I-5 running down from Seattle was a congested mess. Making things a little more treacherous was a fine sun shower. We car travelers moved along gingerly and evenly spaced and got through to outer limits. I needed to be particularly ginger as I discovered my metal tailpipe support had rusted through, leaving the heavy rear section of the exhaust system freely swinging underneath. I guessed that it might even have broken given that El Rucio was rumbling a little more gruffly than usual. This would need to be rectified and sooner rather than later.

At Tukwila, the site of the Jimi Hendrix Museum, which was another destination on my day agenda, I sought out the local Ford dealer. A service manager received me and swiftly addressed the tasks at hand. Meanwhile, the parts and service director tried to track down the museum. He was unsuccessful but *did* draw up a map to Hendrix's famed grave in nearby Greenwood Memorial Cemetery. If I could at least take that in, I thought, I'd be satisfied.

I received the diagnosis on El Rucio: a leaking oil pan, leaking transmission pump/pan, rear differential seepage, exhaust leak and broken pipe hanger. In the time I had to spare, the dealership replaced the pipe strap, changed the oil and filter, and steam cleaned the engine underside so that I could monitor fluid levels. They spared me some pain on the bill and off I went looking for Hendrix.

After much circling, a couple "dunno dawg" shrugs, and many false turns and leads, I finally found the very green Greenwood Cemetery and the some 20-foot high granite memorial erected there. The 3-foot high center stone inscription: "Forever in our hearts, James M. (Marshall) "Jimi" Hendrix, 1942-1970." He was only 27 when he passed, the exact cause still in dispute. Some say he died of asphyxiation, choking on his vomit after consuming wine and sleeping pills. A more common theory is that he died of a drug overdose. Because of his drug use, Seattle had not officially recognized him. Unofficial tributes included a life-size bronze statue in the Capitol Hill area and a bust at Garfield High School, his alma mater.

Feeling my way through the dark back to I-5, I headed for Mt. St. Helen's, another detour off Steinbeck's original route, and just short of Oregon's border. I knew that, since it was already night, I wouldn't be able to appreciate the site, so there was no point in rushing there. So, at DuPont, I went and holed up in the corner of a Starbucks to write for a while. The counter girl took interest in my activities and told me she's going to school to be a traveling nurse.

Through on and off rain, I made quick time to Chahalis, "the gateway to Mt. St. Helen's," where I found a KOA for the overnight. As it was still fairly early when I stopped, I busied myself with paperwork, making a next-day plan and listening to the Yankees and rival Red Sox playing each other in Game #1 of the American League Championship. A hot shower in a clean, heat lamp-warmed bathroom later had the effect of knocking me out when I returned to El Rucio.

Day 34: Wily Helen, Soggy Portland

It was about 6 a.m., or so I thought, when I awoke feeling refreshed and, after some organizing, I broke camp for an ARCO for cooler supplies. Only then did I realize it was barely 3 a.m.! With no great urge to return to sleep and hours to go before sun-up, I read accumulated newspapers.

In Monday's edition of *The Seattle Times*, residents of the Capitol Hill area, tired of finding hypodermic needles, baggies, tourniquets and other paraphernalia in Cal Anderson Park, voiced their concerns about drug dealing and usage in their neighborhood. The Empty Space Theater Players, who drew crowds to Seattle parks in the '70s and '80s, had reunited to direct "Ming the Rude," a live performance featuring a fresh new cast of young local actors. The Dolphins beat my Giants 23-10, pushing New York's season record down to 2-2.

The most remarkable item to me, though, was about a road trip — the first by car from coast to coast in the U.S. — begun in May 1903 by Horatio Nelson Jackson, a 31-year-old Vermont man who had retired from practicing medicine due to tuberculosis. The trip, which he was joined on by 22-year-old former bicycle racer Sewall K. Crocker and their "goggled canine companion" Bud, was made after a discussion and $50 bet at San Francisco's University Club. Jackson's vehicle, made by the Winton Motor Carriage Co., was named the Vermont and was purchased for $3,000.

The story was turned into a PBS program, "Horatio's Drive: America's First Road Trip", narrated by Tom Hanks and William Least Heat-Moon, and featured stories of "bad luck, broken parts and delayed replacements." In fact, Jackson and Crocker fixed or replaced every part of the automobile en route, blacksmiths repaired the axles and, at one point, a cowboy on horseback towed the car. Heat-Moon noted, "There's nothing we can do that is more American than getting into a car and striking out across the country."

Yesterday's edition of the same paper broadcast that actor Arnold Schwarzenegger had survived accusations of impropriety and been successful in his bid to have California Gov. Gray Davis recalled from office after only 11 months. Gov.-elect Schwarzenegger was just one of 135 candidates who'd campaigned for the position in one of the state's most melodramatic, circus-like events.

Other items: Washington state was tops for seatbelt usage in the world according to a Traffic Safety Commission report and the Cubs beat the Marlins in the NL Championship opener.

Itching to get going, around 4 a.m. I started moving towards Mt. St. Helen's along Route 12, passing Lewis & Clark State Park. It had rained most of the night and continued to rain this morning. Because it was unseasonably mild, fog resulted, greatly reducing visibility ahead. As I shot by a Trout Hatchery, I was sure that Helen must be off to the right of me, though it was not at all visible. At Morton, there were also signs for 14,411-foot tall Mt. Rainier, but it, too, was masked by fog.

Finding a Shell station, I stopped in to seek insight about Mt. St. Helen's eruption, which took place back on May 18, 1980. The cashier, a blonde with piercing blue eyes whose hair was wet from the rain, lived and still lives twenty "air" miles from the site. She said that, "it was a beautiful morning" that morning and she "didn't hear anything," likely because of the Tumwater, Strawberry and Margaret Mountains between her house and St. Helen's. Only when "small pebbles" started raining down on her house did she first become aware of the event. Then came the ash. "It was two inches thick out here," a logger type in his mid-20s chimed in, "and we had to wear respirators." It hung in the air all that first day. "It was pretty bad," another patron added, choking engines and other mechanical equipment. I imagined it must have been like lower Manhattan after the Trade Center buildings were attacked and felled.

Along the road in Randle, I came to Adams St. Helen's Restaurant, low-lit at this time in the morning, and sat at the café counter seeking to know more about the eruption. As I began to speak with the proprietor, 73-year-old Harold Lowery, whom local folks have called "Grand Pap" or "Pappy" since he was six because of his resemblance to his grandfather, piped in. About that morning, he said, "A guy across the road, who lived in a house facing the mountain, came running over and said, 'The mountain blew!'" Sure enough, looking in that direction, Pappy could see a "big, boiling cloud going up."

As the volcano had been active for two months with "probably a dozen little explosions" and official warnings had been issued that indicated "it could blow like Crater Lake," Pappy took the event in stride and went for his daughter. He said that that was "a mistake as the dust and dirt was fallin' so bad." He continued, saying, "The car ahead started stirring up dust, the air was full of it. Then, little mud balls started coming down, splattering on the windshield with a sound like breaking glass. I didn't try to make it home, stopping at a friend's instead...stayed there four hours."

Officials closed Route 12 at Mossyrock and Highway 7 at Elbe as the river that comes down off St. Helen's heated to 90 degrees. Weyerhauser Paper owned much of the forestland at the time, Pappy noted, and harvested all the trees that had blown down over some 15 square miles. Eight to ten people lost their lives, including Keith Moore (the husband of a woman in Pappy's bowling league) and Harry Truman, owner of Mt. St. Helen's Lodge. "He's probably under 300 feet of dirt," Pappy said.

When Pappy left, a former timber faller and a forward observer in the infantry in the time period between the Korean and Vietnam Wars, settled in. "Make me some breakfast, mach schnell," he kiddingly said to the proprietor, then went behind the counter to help himself to coffee. We discussed the weather — lightning had knocked power out during the night — then our respective travels. When he was in the military, he went across the top part of the country twice, doing the trip in three days each time. Now he makes an annual trip to Alabama to see his son, a journey that takes him five days going and three days coming back.

We spoke about the logging industry, too, and how cargo helicopters pull trees from cutting areas and carry them to a site up the road for transport by truck. Since I'd arrived, at least a dozen logging trucks had passed on the road outside, coming from that direction.

As we chatted, a bearded fellah walked in, sporting a quilted shirt and great hunting hat that said on the brim "There'll be no quitters 'til we bag some critters." Besides the slogan, the hat was decorated with a shotgun shell, band-aid, leaf, aspirin packet, duck feather and a Lazy Hunter's Association symbol. It was the king of all head coverings.

I could have sat there all day long and listened to stories, but really wanted to see Helen. It was light by then and the rain had stopped, giving me a good chance to catch an eyeful. However, as I made my way up the road from the Big Bottom Bar & Grill, I found her cloaked in a towel of mist. In the foreground, there were stripped, broken stubs of trees, but I couldn't make out anything beyond. And then… the mist parted, like theater curtains being drawn back, and, there, laid bare was her ravaged skin, raped as if a steel claw had been dragged across her, pulling up anything and everything in its path. I'd never seen devastation of this nature and studied the scene intently, for the few brief moments I was afforded anyhow. The curtains once again drew closed and I thought that I would get just the one teasing 25-cent peek.

But the clouds parted again to reveal a cone-shaped mountain with a winding trail leading up to its tip. On foot, I set out to scale it and, for a very long time, was the only human for miles and miles around. Piercing the quiet were the chirps and squawks of creatures that inhabited this prehistoric-like valley that time seemed to have forgotten.

Walking back to El Rucio, I plucked up a few samples of cinder rock and then made the mistake of trying to remove a pinecone from a tree. Of course it was covered with sap, an impossible to remove gumminess that no amount of wiping and scrubbing would dissipate. Literally glued to the steering wheel and smelling like Pine-Sol, I slid down Helen, coasting through hail that had begun to fall, wincing as small ice pellets ricocheted off my windshield. The weather condition made me think of the falling mudballs that witnesses to the eruption had described.

A pickup with a plow attachment passed on its way to push fallen rock to the side of the road. It was a constant hazard here, like in the Beartooth. Though map checks indicated I was making progress towards a park exit and the town of Cougar, I was feeling like I'd gotten tangled up in Helen's tresses, unable to free myself. To abate my building frustration, I stopped at an eatery bearing the name Jack's Grill. Like a lodge house, with unstained fir woodwork, slate tiles on the wall around the kitchen area and miscellaneous antlers all about, it lured me with its atmosphere and a grilled chicken sandwich.

The "Jack" of Jack's Grill, who also served as head cook, told me that the restaurant had been there 50 or 60 years before he and his wife took it over, but had been neglected. "It was a real dump," he commented, coming right to the point. As I ate my fare, we spoke of my travels. He was envious and said he hoped to go cross-country in the near future.

Thumbing through a discarded newspaper from Vancouver, I read a chilling story about a couple's encounter with a bear in Anchorage. While videotaping it, the bear attacked and ultimately killed them. The video camera continued to roll, capturing not footage, but audio of their undoubtedly terrifying struggle.

Finally extracting myself from the mountain area and back in flat country headed for Portland, I visited a PRODUCE tent for post-lunch dessert. Gala apples, sweet, juicy and red, like those I'd enjoyed in Morrisville, Vermont and Hawley, Michigan, filled the order and were a continued snack source.

A simple sign, "Welcome to Oregon," met me at the border, as it once may have greeted Steinbeck. As his route through the state, he chose the "beautiful coast" finding "each evening a pleasant auto court to rest in." Unfortunately, trundling along "on a rainy Sunday, the gallant Rocinante bespoke [his] attention." As he described it, "Moving through an endless muddy puddle, a right rear tire blew out with a damp explosion." The water was eight inches deep "and the spare tire, under the cab, had been let down into the mud." To complicate matters, "the changing tools had been put away under the floor under the table, so that [his] total load had to be unpacked." It was an arduous process that resulted in "mud balls" in his beard, "cut and bleeding" hands and mud-covered clothes. He changed and, fearing that the other tire might go at any moment, "crawled along at not more than five miles an hour…to a damp little shut-up town." There, he found "one small service station" owned by "a giant with a scarred face and an evil white eye."

To Steinbeck's great surprise, the man was able to defy all odds, locate tires and got him up and running again in "a little less than four hours." For his exceptional services, Steinbeck "tipped him rather royally" and wished that the man might "live a thousand years and people the earth with his offspring."

Following City Center signs into Portland, I soon found myself on Couch Street, near Powell's City of Books. One of my targets, Powell's bills itself as the "largest independent bookstore" featuring 4,700 sections of new and used reading material. I wished to dwell and browse it, but because it was so expansive, I couldn't really devote the time it deserved. El Rucio was also moored to a meter that allowed only a limited stay.

Deciding to use the time to scout the area instead, I plodded down Couch. In a two-block space identified as Chinatown, I had to laugh and wonder about a business called Hung Far Low. A closer inspection proved that it was indeed legitimate and capitalizing on the humor of its name with t-shirts and related merchandise.

Seeking Happy Hour hangout tips, I polled people on the street. From a tall Welsh/Irish girl, I heard about Mcmenamin's, with its own brewery. A guy about my age pointed me to Old Town. Two Trinidadians suggested a Caribbean restaurant called Savannah. A beanie-wearing girl suggested Crystal Ballroom and Old Town Pizza on Davis Street.

As it was still early, the pizza joint seemed like the most appropriate stop — a good decision it turned out. In a great old brick building circa late 1800s, the place had creaky wood floors, worn Oriental rugs, period furniture and antiques, with old couches to kick back in.

I've always made it my habit to try local brews wherever available and here, I would not divert from that goal. I sampled three area brands to find a complement to a personal pie I'd ordered, settling on Mirror Pond Amber Ale, brewed by DeSchutes in Bend, Oregon.

While I enjoyed it, I leafed through a hardcover book titled "A Haunted Tour Guide to the Pacific Northwest." Among many stories about macabre events associated with local sites, it contained lore about Old Town Pizza. As the book told it, the establishment sits atop an intricate network of

"Shanghai tunnels" where illicit trades and smuggling were conducted. Apparently, a ghostly presence, perhaps the spirit of a departed slave or indentured servant, still inhabited the building.

The beer, pizza and warmth of the joint had a greatly relaxing effect on me and I was tempted to curl up for a snooze on the couch like Steinbeck had at the Ambassador East in Chicago. Overriding the urge, though, I hit the bricks again at the 5 o'clock whistle, suddenly becoming aware of transients, particularly in the Old Town area, as I moved along the street. They roosted in doorways, on the corners, at Union Station and at welfare hotels, or stood in line for a meal at the Salvation Army.

Everett Street Autoworks was the most intriguing looking auto repair place I'd ever seen. Customers' autos, as they sat atop lifts, were virtually on display behind huge nine-foot tall windows. The station was apparently established in the late '40s to provide service, repair and fill-ups then, from the late '70s to mid-'90s, to cater to Mercedes, BMWs and Audis.

Notably, cartoonist Matt Groening came from Portland and the names of several of the characters of Groening's wildly popular cartoon, "The Simpsons", were based on area street names/sites, e.g. Flanders and Burns. The balance of characters were modeled on his family.

Family Ginseng Plaza, an emporium of Oriental bric-a-brac, displayed creations made of green opal, anis and jade. It stood in the shadow of the towering, ornate gateway marking the entrance to Chinatown. Funding for the structure was provided by scores of local donors, whose surnames, among them Lee, Taipei, Khoo, Chan, Chin and Cho, were listed on one of the columns.

Jackpot Records offered funky sounds, hard-to-get oldies and passes to club acts. Nearby, Billy Galaxy's shucked collectibles, including an impressive assortment of metal lunch boxes like I used to carry to school. Sadly, my EMERGENCY and 007 versions were not among them. Across the street near N.W. 10th, OZONE U.K., promoting obscure imported music titles, was manned by a mainstream-defying vamp, with hair and New York Dolls tee both a shocking pink color.

On the street, young socialites, backpackers and business folks shuffled by. I drifted uptown, peering in the windows of Italian, Japanese and Chinese restaurants. When it began to pour, a Blockbuster awning became my shelter. Suddenly, I was feeling like one of the transients I'd seen earlier and an empty, lonely pang, the kind Steinbeck dreaded, started creeping over me. I needed to shake it before it completely enveloped me.

A red neon sign at a watering hole up the way winked and I went to investigate. Thisbar's bar had the Stones on the juke, two pool tables under low-slung CAMEL cigarettes lights, a black-and-red vinyl floor and, to my glee, the Yankees-Red Sox game on the TV. N.Y. was up 4-1 in the sixth, though I'm not sure anyone but me cared, it being a game between East Coast teams. Certainly not the old guy with the arthritic dog and OTB form in his back pocket; or the guy with the studded leather jacket speaking to the woman in the fake zebra fur; or the black woman with the bad blonde wig. Nor did the woman at the bar with the multi-colored hair, who, when I asked her about area amusements, snarled, "I like to drink. That's what I do for fun. Good luck, man." Her attack, like the horseflies that had pursued me at the graveyard near Presque Isle, Maine, drove me out the door.

Growing ever desperate for some sort of human connection, an anchor to keep me in town, I tried the Bitter End Pub next. It certainly had promise, with Whitmere Amber on tap and live band Acoustic Minds, bathed in red gel spots, offering palatable sounds. There were even a couple of young professionals with whom I likely could have bonded. But my heart wasn't it.

Some fresh air perked me up a bit as I began strolling back down to Old Town, though it was a short-lived feeling. The rain, now mixed with small ice crystals that ricocheted off me and were as cold as the town was starting to feel, came down heavy again, driving me into the doorway of a piano showroom. Images of Steinbeck on his way into northern Maine, throwing back vodka shots as rain drummed on Rocinante's steel roof, flickered through my mind.

I could get no lower in spirit when Kell's Pub appeared, almost divinely, on my radar. Irish, warm, fireplace, live guitars, friendly faces, darts, a towering bottle rack. It had all the ingredients of a good time. Expecting no less than a complete revival of my soul, I ordered up a Kell's lager and barley soup with soda bread on the side, and settled onto a long bench seat.

A bench mate of Micmac Indian, Irish and Italian stock was a pastry maker from Vancouver, Washington, and recently tried her work out at a fair in Portland. Her cookies went over well, she reported, "even better when everyone was drunk."

Another squatter, dressed in overalls with a checked red shirt, shared her thoughts about Portlanders, noting, "People here don't feel like they need to conform. You can really express yourself." I'd certainly seen its funky, individualistic side.

The place filled up and got very jolly, like St. Patrick's Day almost in terms of the level of festivity. Members of the audience, including a bearded guy rapping spoons on his knee, were even called to the stage to sit in. The place was really going. Sadly, I finally had to, as well, walking the few blocks to the lot where El Rucio was patiently parked. Finding the attendant's office, where I'd left my keys, dark and padlocked, I panicked for a moment, imagining that I'd have to spend a night. Then I spotted a small sign directing me to good old Hung Far Low, where keys are held after hours, and was reunited with the set.

As I rolled from Portland, I realized that it was mapped out much like Billings, Montana, with brow furrowing one-ways. And though armed with rough directional guidance to the interstate, I managed to pull a Louie instead of a Roger and ended up tied in a knot. As knots can be tied though, they can also be untied and soon I was flying down I-5.

A detour consideration had been the White Salmon Gorge on the banks of the Columbia River, due east, but something was pulling me south. Crater Lake, for one, in the lower half of the state, was calling, but also California, which I was excited to return to more than 22 years after my last visit.

As usual, my goal was loftier than the energy required to reach it when, at Wilsonville, after putting gas in at an Exxon, I got hit with the "tired fist." I went down hard, smacking the canvas with a thud, in a corner of the service station parking lot. What time I'd arrived there and how long I slept I'm not sure, but when I awoke, there was a family parked beside me. I was sure that, seeing me slumped in the driver's seat with my head flipped back and mouth hanging open, they thought that I'd expired, but they'd actually guessed I'd nodded off waiting for someone to emerge from the adjacent mini mart. Like me, they were headed to California and we rolled back onto the interstate together.

I guess I hadn't given myself long enough recuperation time, for I found it necessary to pull off yet *again* to rest my eyes. My stop was a weigh station and, despite the truck upon truck rumbling by, this time I really slept the sleep of the dead, atilt once again in the driver's seat.

Day 35: Crater Lake

Feeling able to consistently keep going, I rocketed to a Truck 'n Travel Plaza in Coburg. Another of these all-inclusive places I'd come to enjoy, the plaza allowed me to buy new socks, mail postcards, take care of bills, get laundry done on the cheap, shower and shave, have breakfast and relax in a TV room to read and write.

As I was readying myself to get going once again, I overheard a moving truck driver on his cellphone to his girl back home. She was seeking some item and he was looking for it at all the truck stops, but not having any luck. "D'other day, I stopped at fo' different truck stops," the compact, energetic black man, whose one leg was shorter than the other, said to her. "We stuck here, can't get a load out, Utah to Ohio." When he hung up with her, I asked him what he does to occupy himself when there's no load to carry. "I sit here, watch TV and spend money." I thought that there were worse places, to be sure, than this magnificent mecca of marvelosity.

On the way out, I snagged a slim brochure promoting Steering Wheel Ministries, "Bringing the LIGHT of the GOSPEL to the Transportation Industry, One Soul at a Time." The organization's "staff and volunteers are known as the SWIM Team because they are Swimming Against The Current of The World With The Gospel of Jesus Christ."

With a topped-off tank of gas from a Shell station, I blew along Old Route 58, a trucking path, past sheep, Lookout Point Reservoir and Dam, and Lowell Covered Bridge. Then, seeing a clearing, I swooped in to shovel in some leftover Indian food, noticing an advisory sign ahead. It featured a color wheel with an arrow that was pointed to green or "Low" chance of forest fire.

An amusing song by Greg Brown on KLCC Eugene radio 89.7 went, "I've got two little feet, to carry me 'cross the mountain, two little feet." The song that followed, by Edie Brickell, compared a pair of eyes to jeans, "faded and blue." These set a good vibe to press on to Crater Lake. At the same time, I was reminded of broadcasts I'd heard all across the country and a related article called "Signals From Nowhere." Writer Walter Kirn had said that he used to "take a long road trip every year or two" and instead of using a road atlas, he "navigated by radio," charting his course "by the accents, news and songs streaming in from the nearest AM transmitter." He said he "felt like a modern Walt Whitman on those drives" and "heard America singing." But that changed for him when, on a recent road trip, he lost his way and the radio couldn't help him find it. "I twirled the dial, but the music and the announcers all sounded alike, drained, disconnected from geography, reshuffling the same pop playlists and canned bad jokes," he wistfully complained. I had to agree that, in many cases, he was right, so finding gems like the Brickell and Brown tunes were a treat.

Going again, I followed the Middle Salmon Creek past Deception Campground, the town of Oakridge and its hard-faced residents, Willamette Pass with its snow-capped heights and jagged Diamond Peak stretching into the clouds. Everything was steaming in the sun at Willamette Summit where snow covered the ground and tops of the pines. Further on, Odell Lake was like a big, blue melted ice cube.

Approaching the mid-afternoon hour, I stepped off the road into the Winema Forest, putting a classical station on as background for a snooze. All around, stacks of fallen branches were gathered, clear evidence of undergrowth clearing to prevent forest fires. An hour later, I was traveling up pin-straight 138 through snowy Umpqua National Forest lands toward Crater Lake.

Like at Little Big Horn, the site's North Entrance tollhouse was closed but the road was open, and soon I reached a wide-open expanse known as the Pumice Desert. From there, I had an excellent view of both the knobbly Red Cone summit, standing 7,373 feet tall, and behind me, its larger brother, Mt. Thielsen, at 9,182 feet. Like Beartooth, tall sticks marked the road's path so it could be located when heavier snows fall.

At the first crater overlook, there were two inches of snow on the ground and a father and son pitched snowballs at one another. Climbing up the hillside upon which they fought their good-natured battle, to a spot framed by conifers, I peered over the crest at the 1,943-foot deep lake. It was, in a word, breathtaking. The surface was absolutely still and there was a conical formation, Wizard Island, to one side. With my eyes transfixed on the scene, I barely noticed that another visitor had steered into my spot to have a look, too. A student back in Portland, "Myra" had eyes as blue as the lake, hair the color of cornhusks and Birkenstock sandals providing a thin shield between the bottom of her feet and the snow. We agreed to prowl on together.

Following a branch road to Cleetwood Cove, we parked our cars and set off down the crater interior on a zig-zaggy trail, or "switchbacks" as Myra properly termed them. She was no newcomer to hiking and was outfitted with a professional-looking backpack called a Camelback Blowfish, in which she carried a two-liter container of water. Attached to it was a drinking tube that came over her shoulder, allowing hands-free water sampling.

Every so often, there was a log bench that afforded a rest and great view. But the most amazing thing to us was the blueness of the water, an effect produced by sunlight. According to a map guide, "The colors are absorbed as [sunlight] passes through clear water. First the reds go, then orange, yellow and green. Last to be absorbed is the blues."

During the warmer months, the guide continued, visitors can take a boat across the lake, a large aluminum thing we saw propped up vertically on its stern at the base of the trail. There, we continued to marvel at the opacity of the water, into which I dipped a hand to check its temperature. On a whim, Myra bet me 10 tacos that I wouldn't jump in. While I seriously mulled the offer, being a great fan of tacos, I did not take the challenge. Instead, we stepped across boulders looking for fish activity, seeing a ripple. I wished that I had my pole with me, to catch some dinner.

The climb back up was significantly more difficult than the descent and we set off perhaps a little too aggressively, getting winded quickly. Slowing our pace down, we took in the flora and fauna — fat chipmunks that popped up periodically, mosses all shades of green, mini pine cones and varying chunks of cinder. At the top, birds called Clark's Nutcrackers, squawked madly. It was a great hike, covering 2.2 miles round-trip and a vertical height of 724 feet.

We saddled back up and continued along the road, stopping periodically to take in other views of the lake or surrounding area. From one viewpoint, we were able to see, left to right, Garwood Butte, Bald Crater, 8,363-foot Mt. Bailey, 8,792-foot Diamond Peak (85 miles away), Red Cone, Three

Sisters, 9,182-foot Mt. Thielsen (14.5 miles off) and the Pumice Desert. It was almost like all these amazing sites had been moved here just for us to see.

Further up the road, we came to a massive inn called, naturally, Crater Lake Lodge. As the air temperature had considerably cooled, I hoped it housed a fireplace beside which we could get warm. Scouting it out, I discovered in a common area not one but two great stone fireplaces, with roaring fires in them. I summoned Myra, we moved chairs in front of the larger of the two and ordered nibblies and drinks, using an upended log as a table.

With other visitors, seemingly elite traveling folks, who had pulled up chairs alongside us, we had good chats and got a tip for a camping site at nearby Lost Creek Campground. We both needed lodging and thought we'd also collaborate on making some dinner, sharing supplies. Finding the camp just down the road, we pulled in and to a billboard with a map. Of course, it didn't indicate which sites were free and there was no attendant on duty. So we groped along until we found adjacent free spaces and, keeping our headlights on for light, set up our equipment. Myra's accommodation was a pop-up tent, which we erected together, using a tarp I'd brought along as an underlay.

On a tip from campers next door, we went and gathered firewood. For this purpose, I finally got an opportunity to use my Gerber folding saw and hand axe. These tools helped me chop and section a whole pile of wood and kindling which I hauled back to the site, picking my way along with the aid of my Gerber flashlight. Unfortunately, the wood was a little green and damp, so our attempts to get a fire going were, for the most part, unsuccessful. We focused on dinner instead, setting up my camp stove to get rice, two kinds of beans and tomato sauce going.

The temperature had dropped quite a bit so we were glad, at least, to have the warmth of the stove. "Totally glad," Myra said. Our dinner turned out well and was consumed quickly, along with Moose Drool beers and Tostito chips and salsa.

It was late by then and we called it a night, taking turns washing up at an unheated restroom a few short paces away. The temperature continued to plunge, dropping down to the 30s, and as we retired to our respective abodes, the moon, bright and beautiful, popped up into the sky.

Day 36: Pinnacles to Torrero's

Tumbling out of the van to light rain, I re-organized supplies and began cooking up apple pancakes and cocoa on my grill. Myra, meanwhile, broke down and stowed her tent. As we did with dinner, we shared breakfast — "the best camp food I've ever had," she complimented. I had to say that I'd become quite the resourceful and accomplished cook, necessity being the mother of invention.

On Myra's agenda was "The Pinnacles," just four miles from camp. As I had no particular morning plan, I took interest in seeing it, too, and tagged along. Tall, cylindrical and pointy volcanic vents that had been left standing some 100 feet or so tall after the earth around them eroded, they were a most unusual sight.

Heading back up the road, we pulled over to peer down at a stream that rushed through the same canyon, noticing much dead wood at our feet. As Myra was planning to spend another night in the park, I suggested we gather some of it up for her use later, and filled the trunk of her car.

Back along the rim of Crater Lake, we looked down at the "Pirate Ship," the remnant of a volcano that preceded Mt. Mazama, which had exploded to form Crater Lake. Here, our trails parted. Myra's company had been an unexpected bonus at this pre-historic destination.

I had tracks to make, to northern California to see the magnificent Redwood Forest, so joined Route 62 toward Medford, 76 miles away. Rain started to spritz down as I passed through forests of straight, tall conifers.

Needing to use the bathroom and grab supplies, I stopped at the Cascade Gorge convenience store, stocking up on canned goods, beer and peanuts. To the order, I added nightcrawlers after receiving a tip from the storeowner, Henry, about a local fishing hole: Lost Creek Reservoir. Henry was a unique guy, a wide-faced jolly sort and son of a Hawaiian sailor and Mexican/Puerto Rican mom who met each other in San Francisco. I told him how far I'd been across the U.S. and how far I had yet to go and he said, "Well, you better go catch those fish quick."

I did as I was told, motoring a few miles up the road to a turn-off right before a high bridge. Finding a picnic area, I put my kit together and started tromping down a thistle and stump covered slope to a cove that Henry had mentioned. Stepping out onto a striated plateau of sand jutting out into the teal green, raindrop tickled water, I placed my net and Styrofoam cup of crawlers on a gnarled stump and tossed out my line. With no luck after repeated casts, I tried down the way a little, unfortunately snagging my hook on a tree across a narrow channel.

As I let out line and started moving around towards it, my feet flew out from under me and I went down on my backside, splat in the mud. To make matters worse, my hand, as I sought to support myself, crushed the worm pot. There I was on my rump, with my boots sunk in 2-inch deep mud, and the worms making a fast break. Containment was my first thought so, spying a discarded empty beer can, I took my Gerber knife, cut its top off, crimped the rough edges and loaded in the would-be escapees with some extra wet mud. Then, placing the new container in my net, I continued moving around to the hook-gobbling tree.

My line came unsnagged as I approached so I kept pacing out of the cove toward the open water. Seeing something, perhaps a salmon or steelhead, jump, I hurriedly cast, but on the reel-in, my hook found a log and stayed there. Grumbling to myself that my excursion was not unfolding as I'd hoped it would, I cut the line, left my pole and went back to the truck for more tackle and rainwear. As I did, automatic rifle shots rang out in the hills nearby and for a moment I felt like Steinbeck as he and Charley made their way to northern Maine in the middle of hunting season. Should I tie a red Kleenex to myself as he had to Charley's tail?

It was clear that game was abundant here, as the footprints of deer, wildcats, large web-footed birds and possibly bear were quite visible in the sandy area I traversed as I returned to my spot. Now perched at the bottom of a steep hillside of loose boulders, I pulled my slicker about me as the rain turned from light to hard and other foolhardy souls steered in in a small, motorized aluminum craft. Though my fingers were starting to turn a light shade of blue, I remained steadfast in my mission. Then, suddenly, my line gave a tug. "Fish on!" It was a large-mouth bass and I towed him in to shallow water near me. But as I went to pull him out, he lunged, twisted and freed himself and returned to the reservoir bottom.

With the very next cast, however, I redeemed myself, hooking a pretty 13" steelhead trout, a catch witnessed by some two-dozen Canadian geese passing overhead. Firmly holding her sleek body, I turned the hook out where it was embedded near her left eye, and placed her in my landing net. Triumphant from battle, I returned to El Rucio, my boots muddied and bur-covered, pants sand and dirt stained, hands numb and smelling of fish and a hunger in my belly. I hoped to quell the latter with my trout and some leftover rice dinner. For now, I bid "aloha" to Henry's fishing hole and continued my trek toward the northern reaches of California.

Entering the Rogue Umpqua area, I sailed past the Obstinate J Ranch, Pat's Hand-Tied Flies, Elk Creek, Eagle's Nest Saloon in Shady Cove, and Cheyenne Steakhouse, enjoying the regional sounding flavor of these area and business names. All the while, big-wheeled pickups with gun racks in their back windows streamed towards me. This was not a place for nimble-fingered bean counters but of men of hardened spirit come to duel with the elements.

The sun struggled to make itself known as I passed the Willamette Egg Farm near Eagle Point. But by the time I'd reached the Boise Lumber Co. in White City, it had given up. Medford was a big place and put me on I-5 North for a very brief length just to access an appropriate south-going road. Somehow, I managed to get myself all turned around and even think I did an entire circle. It was my Steinbeck moment of the day.

Frustrated, I stopped at a lounge in Rogue Valley for direction guidance, staying on for a beer. The place was colorful, with rifles mounted on the walls, a buzz saw blade clock and paintings of local scenes by H.S. Cleveland. Beside a dice challenge on top of the microwave, there was a sign, "3 rolls for 25¢. Need five 6's in one roll." As the pot was up to $230.75, which would take care of a good amount of gas, I decided to try my luck. Of my 3 rolls, I got three 6's in one, pretty good I thought, but not a winner. On the TV, the Cubs were playing the Marlins in the NL Championship, and winning 6-0. It was time to move on.

At busy Grant's Pass, I picked up 199 South, known as Redwood Highway, toward Crescent City. The great redwoods themselves were just 85 miles off. Night had fallen by this time and rain, which had been intermittent, continued. There were many cute places on this push and I was tempted to stop but, at the same time, I was in a "California or bust" mood.

At quarter past seven, I reached the state border, marked with a light blue "Welcome to California" sign. Almost immediately, I was on a winding, twisting crazy wet road, flying around corners, sometimes on two wheels, narrowly missing rock walls and oncoming traffic. The signs for the Redwood National Forest came up, then the grande dames themselves. "Massive" is the only word that I could think of to describe them, and this was at night. I imagined that I would be even more impressed come daylight.

Of the great trees, Steinbeck said, they "leave a mark or create a vision that stays with you always...a feeling [that is] not transferable... ambassadors from another time." He had "known these great ones since [his] earliest childhood" and wanted to introduce Charley to these magnificent specimens of arboreta.

Crescent City, to me, was like Emerald City, an Oz at the end of my long and twisting yellow brick road. At a service station where I stopped for gas, up pulled a kid in a great beast of an automobile, a white 1964 Wildcat. He was high, I think, and looking for a party. Beside him, his pretty brunette girlfriend quietly sat. Some of their friends pulled up in a pickup and wanted beer. Somehow, I was recruited to buy it and snuck it to them around the corner. "Thanks dude!" they said, after giving me a tip on a local nightspot — a Mexican restaurant with a bar and disco in the back.

I spoke with the proprietor, learning about the woes of the area: 65% of the people were on welfare due to environmental restrictions on logging and fishing; local mills had been almost completely wiped out; there had been a big drop in tourism; and a fire the previous summer had destroyed a half million acres in the surrounding area.

It reminded me of the Great Depression, about which Steinbeck had written. During a period spanning 1929 to 1941, more than 12.8 million people were unemployed, or about 25 percent of all able-bodied workers.

Doing my part to support the local economy, I ordered a chicken burrito, Albondigas soup and Dos Equis, eating at the bar while we spoke. Then, with a vow to return for the disco format later, I went and checked in at an Econo Lodge nearby. The two Asian women at the desk were perturbed, I think, that the top of El Rucio tapped their 7 1/2-foot height limit sign, which I sent swinging back and forth, at their pull-in spot.

My room was large and clean, but a little cold. The thermostat had been turned all the way down. I remedied that, showered and promptly passed out on the bed, almost missing my return to the Mexican place. But make it there I did and it was much transformed from earlier. The bar where I'd sat alone was now two-deep with people, and the dance floor, with gel lights sweeping across it, crowded. I said hello to the owner again and took up a corner of the bar, another Dos Equis in hand, ready to survey the populace.

The crowd, a mix of Hispanics, Native Americans and out-of-town visitors, grew larger and rowdier. A DJ kept them moving with tunes made possible through a laptop computer and MP3s, eliminating the need for boxes of CDs or vinyl like I remember from my club days.

Last call was at 1:30 and evacuation was quick. "The Englishman Who Went Up the Hill and Came Down the Mountain," a drama based in Wales, was on TV back at the hotel.

Day 37: In the Company of Giants

The sounds of departing guests stirred me awake at 8 a.m. and, realizing that the hotel's free buffet would be ending soon, I quickly cleaned up and walked across the asphalt to the office. One of the two night clerks I encountered on check-in helped me pull together juice, coffee and pastries on a small plastic tray that I toted back to my room. The start to the day, weather-wise, was good. I hoped it would last.

Unfortunately, paperwork forced me to hole up in my room for several hours, a situation that made the cleaning staff very anxious I think, as they stole glances into my room every time they passed by my window. Finally, around 11:30, I emerged and got my traveling day started, driving through town on 101 South and spying the coast at Crescent Beach for the very first time. And, wow, what a sight: Swells 12 to 15 feet high, crashing along the shore. Several surfers up on a wave crest. Driftwood scattered across the sand.

Seated on a tree stump, the unusually named Jesca, a surfer who was sitting it out today, was watching her boyfriend tackle the waves. She was a classic California girl like those celebrated in song, with long silken blonde hair blowing in the breeze. We took in the scene and watched with amusement as this frazzled guy named Chuck searched amongst the dune grasses for his nameless cat, which was busy hunting.

"You should have been here last week," Jesca said, informing me that there had been a long board competition held. It starred longtime surfer

Greg Noll who, notably, was featured in promo posters for the surf movie, "Endless Summer."

Jesca gave me a couple of tips for places to go in Monterey, where she was born, as her longhaired boyfriend came up the beach from the water, his wetsuit dripping and board tucked under his arm. As I turned to leave, I heard the bark of a basking sea lion down the way.

Climbing up along the coast through the same kind of forests I'd come through last night, I craned my neck to look up at these mammoths and wished I'd chosen a campsite among them. At the same time, I was thankful for the conveniences I'd enjoyed after all the rain, muck and cold of Oregon. Emerging from the thicket, I joined a curling road that banked in alternating directions past overlooks of the swirling sea, which seemed to breathe and pulse as it flowed in and out from shore. It was all quite exhilarating.

A low point brought a black sand beach, which I stepped out onto to observe the thundering ocean. Standing there at that seaside altar, where I'd come to worship, I felt dwarfed by nature. The brine in the air filled and expanded my lungs. I drew it in hungrily, in large gulps.

Further down the road, a towering wooden figurine of lumberjack Paul Bunyan and his blue ox, Babe, appeared at the Trees of Mystery, a museum and gift shop at Klamath. According to legend, Bunyan walked from Minnesota and, when he reached this point, decided to stay, as these were the only trees large enough for him to scratch his back against.

Wanting to know more about local history, I focused on the museum and Native American exhibits. I read about the Hupa and Wiyot tribes, who were well known for their highly skilled basket weaving and, indeed, there were many incredible examples of their work on display. Made from bear grasses, willow roots and ferns, the baskets were used to collect acorns and berries, sift flour, serve food, transport water, and wash salmon. But they were also worn as ceremonial hats and used to present gifts and tote babies. The local Indians were good fishermen, too, and made nets from wild iris leaves, spear tips from black and mahogany volcanic rocks and fishing sinkers from smooth stones. They were skilled at turning animal hides into ceremonial dancewear and everyday use clothing.

A counterperson told me that Marylee Smith, of Irish and Cherokee descent, had bought and expanded the venue in 1946 and still privately owned it. Originally, the site was called Wonderland Park and featured a simple trail and gift shop. She sought to make this a repository for not only Northwestern Indian artifacts but of those from "first Americans" all over the country, to which individual areas of the museum were dedicated. The striking takeaway was how ingenious these peoples were at using their natural resources to survive.

In the gift shop, amongst all the hokey Redwoods-emblazoned paraphernalia, I was intrigued to find plastic cylinders containing 4-inch high mini-Sequoia Sempervirens that, with care, could be transplanted and nurtured in other similar coastal environments. I toyed with buying one but guessed that it would fare poorly in my travels yet to come.

Behind the building was a trail of crushed gravel winding through a several acre area of natural exhibits that included an "elephant tree," "family tree" and others soaring anywhere from 150 to 350 feet into the air. These were cedars, spruce, fibrous redwoods and Douglas firs. A highlight of the trail was the Cathedral Tree, a living memorial to Joseph B. Strauss, the builder of the Golden Gate Bridge, and site of numerous weddings every year.

At this hushed spot, I was approached by a soft-voiced woman who was on her own journey after losing her daughter to a tragic car accident earlier in the year. Judy had come from Anchorage, stopping on the way in Portland to make peace with the driver of the other vehicle involved in the crash.

I exited the site past a series of amusing rectangular and square chainsaw carvings and moved down the road through the Yurok Indian Reservation, thinking about exploring it. But like the Onondaga community back in Syracuse, New York, I thought it best to seek local opinion about it or permission to visit.

A trading company down apiece seemed like a good information source and I spoke to one of the owners. She painted a very different picture of the Yurok than the one I'd formed in my head, of hostility, environmental indifference, drunkenness and general disregard for law. A reservation visit appeared unwise.

I'd been advised earlier to go along the Newton B. Drury Scenic Parkway through the Prairie Creek Redwoods State Park, and so I did, the mid-afternoon light filtering through the giant beauties. I pulled to the side, in fact, to see them better in this less theme park style setting and amused myself with the thought of Steinbeck trying to get Charley to appreciate these memorials to universal tree-dom. The dog was not recognizing "the grandfather" specimen they had found as a tree because of its great height. As such, Steinbeck cut a small tufted branch from it, planted it at the base and summoned Charley over. "He sniffed its new-cut leaves delicately and then, after turning this way and that to get range and trajectory, he fired."

Further ahead at the "Big Tree" site, I stopped to study a map and consult with two travelers about possible campsites. They recommended a beach spot that I accessed through a hooded forest of redwoods and other naturally occurring fauna, rumbling along a slip-proof, graded dirt road that rattled El Rucio to her very chassis. The endpoint of the passage, though, was well worth the washer-like agitation: a fantastic stretch of sandy beach upon which wave-worn tree debris lay like pick-up sticks. A small, unmanned tollhouse came up, offering envelopes in which to slip the night's camping fee of $12. I obeyed the honor system and moved ahead, stopping to take a photo of the beach stretch. In doing so, I lost out on a prime waterfront campsite, snatched up by two large, German-speaking women in a white van that rushed from behind me. Of the remaining spaces, I selected site #4, deciding that maybe it was a good thing that I wasn't right on the water as I'd be more shielded from the elements. Whether that was true or not, it made me feel better.

Naturally, as I was just 100 yards from the ocean, I needed to take a look at it as the sun began its slide into the sea. On the way, I stopped to speak with a couple from Bend, Oregon, who proclaimed this "*the* spot," adding that they'd been coming here year after year. That was certainly encouraging, not that I needed any nudging. A redwood-circled California waterfront, it couldn't have been more Eden-like.

As I had the advantage of the light for a change, in terms of setting up camp, I quick-stepped across a field of sea grasses to the forest's edge, Gerber ax and saw in hand, seeking firewood. I found much dead stuff, cut it to a consistent length, bundled it in my arms and hauled it back to camp. An unexpected bonus, a cord of abandoned driftwood sat in a site two away from mine. I dragged it over and sectioned it, too, stacking everything by the metal encircled fire pit.

Looking forward to eating my trout friend then, I removed her from the foil in which I'd wrapped her and made quick work of slicing and deboning her. Her pink insides begged to be eaten and so I wasted no time in slipping the fine cutlets into my greased skillet, adding splashes of beer and olive oil and pinches of salt and pepper. To this, I then added a goulash of rice, tomato sauce and two varieties of beans. In effect, I'd created a fish, bean and rice chili. Spooned onto slices of bread and enjoyed with a Moose Drool sidecar, it was the perfect beach meal. I hungrily spoon-fed myself by candlelight, as the sun extinguished itself behind the dune.

Turning my attention to campfire building, I made all the appropriate layers, from paper and kindling on the bottom to medium-sized sticks in the middle and largest logs on top, and sparked her up. She took her time igniting but soon was gloriously roaring away. Positioning my camp chair beside it, I took beer in hand, contemplated the star-peppered sky, listened to the continual crash of the surf and thought how absolutely lucky I was to be alive.

For more than an hour I sat transfixed in this setting before remembering a social obligation I'd made to visit my camp neighbors, the Oregon couple. With flashlight and Mirror Pond Pale Ale in hand, I walked across the compound to their site. "We were just thinking about you," they said, greeting me. I sat down in a spare camp chair around their fire and we began chatting. They reiterated their fondness for the spot, one of the nicest they know along the whole coast and spoke of their sons and careers as the moon's light changed the onyx sky to midnight blue and a series of shooting stars streaked across the sky.

I read from my notes about the Mt. St. Helen's and Portland legs of my trip, which they connected to very knowingly. We visited until past 10 when I decided to make my exit and return to my own site. My fire had gone out, so I revived it and burned through the balance of my wood, all the while listening to station STAR 94 on the van radio. Suddenly, the latter started cutting out. At first, I thought the station was having technical difficulties then realized I'd worn down the battery. Sure enough, I tried to turn El Rucio over but she just clicked her tongue and hissed me away. I would deal with her in the morning.

Sleep would be my friend instead and, after visiting the restroom, I bed down. My dreams were of giant trees that nuzzled the clouds, swelling oceans, shaggy beasts and furry creatures studying me from dark places.

Day 38: Time Traveling

The moon had crossed the sky toward the ocean to hover right above it, highlighting its surface and accenting the large waves that curled in. Everything was awash in this bluish haze, made murkier by a low fog that embraced the shoreline. I wanted to see this magical place come alive, so bundled up, performed my morning ablutions, lit my table candle (to signal that the site was up) and paced to the beach. A 20-foot long section of tree, sliced in half and partly hollowed so that a bench was formed, sat at the waterfront. I roosted here, tuned to this nature channel, eagerly anticipating the next episode.

Getting restless for the show to begin, I walked the tide line, collecting tongue depressor shaped pieces of driftwood, turning over and examining oval-shaped, smooth stones, and studying a set of deep claw prints, clearly made by a cougar (of which campers are warned on signage). My pockets bulged with tide treasures as bear, then elk, tracks, came into view. The animals had all been for their own stroll while we bipeds were snug in our sleeping bags.

As I made my u-turn for camp, I noticed what looked like a length of rope curled by a log. In fact, it was some strange, aquatic plant measuring no less than 17 feet by my heel-to-toe boot measurement. Making my return by the water, which reflected the pink and light blues of the awakening morning, I hoped to encounter a crab. I knew they were present from the many carcasses I saw and wished to cook one up as an appetizer before breakfast. While I hunted, the frothy leading edge of the tide nipped at my heels, playfully trying to soak me.

There were stirrings back in camp, the heads of fellow campers moving about back behind the tall sea grasses. I could smell a campfire, too, or was that just campfire smoke that had embedded itself in my clothing?

Abandoning my crab safari, I returned to camp to make breakfast, a feast in mind: hot cocoa, scrambled eggs with ham and onion, marmalade slathered toast, sautéed potatoes and raisin bran cereal. It was still pretty cool outside — the temperature had dropped to 40 degrees during the night — so I ate quickly, reading a copy of the *Mail Tribune*, a daily paper I'd picked up in southern Oregon. One item concerned a blight that was affecting hazelnut orchards in Albany and Coburg, a serious development as the nut has become almost exclusive to Oregon in the United States. A cartoon showed caricatures of late night talk show hosts Letterman, Leno and O'Brien celebrating Arnold Schwarzenegger's gubernatorial victory, as it ensured that they would have plenty of future comedy material.

The park ranger came by as I was eating, I told him of my dead battery and he said he'd return later in the morning to help. In the meantime, I wandered over to the couple's site, where they were prepping to make a supply run, and where their black Spinner Labrador, Marley, was relaxing in the sun, one eye cast toward a small flock of quail hustling past. They agreed to give me a jump, while inspecting both the van and some of my camping equipment. "This grill's better than our stove at home!" they exclaimed, and, "You're dialed!" the latter a popular West coast phrase on par with "right on."

I had thought I would hike here, up on Miner's Ridge, but got that "gotta go" bug and pulled up my stakes, but not before walking amongst the giant stubs of trees on the beach, near where I initially joined it from the forest. Kicking off my sandals, I ventured near the water, trying to evade her majesty the ocean as I had on my earlier morning walk. But she lashed me with her long tongue this time, swallowing me to my upper thighs, wetting my shorts and sending me chasing my sandals and a striated, round knob of wood I'd found. To dry off before captaining El Rucio again, I leaned against a 40-foot long, seven-foot around fallen giant. Finally, I climbed back through the forest, past the wild elk and onto 101 South to resume my travels.

The Orick Market made a good stop, arming me with products from all over California: Steelhead Pale Ale from Blue Lake. Milk from the Humboldt Creamery in Fortuna. Orange juice from Dublin. Calico cheese from Willows. For good measure, I threw in a pound of chuck steak, the *San Francisco Chronicle*, a fifth of Bacardi Gold and split-shot sinkers and barrel swivels for fishing purposes.

At the gas station at the edge of town, I put fuel in, beginning to notice how expensive gas was in general in the state. "Taxes," the owner offered. "And they can do it. I'm paying 44¢ a gallon."

Trinidad State Beach seemed like a fitting place to eat the last scraps of my Indian food leftovers. The site had a fantastic cliffside overlook of the water and rock pitons below. A pony-tailed local came and stood beside me, pointing to a spot of land down the coast. "Me and the Mrs. have five acres on the other side of that hill," he said, "and we rent horses out." I asked him how the fishing was around here. "There's rock cod, link cod, crab if you're lucky. Further out and at the mouth of the Mad River, there's salmon, and they're awesome right now."

Five miles down the road, I took a turn-off for the latter — a long road with many elbows that wound past farms and horses carried me to a steel footbridge spanning the river. There, I pulled up beside a silver pickup and married couple who had come to fish.

With fishing gear in hand, we walked together over and down around under the footbridge, through a steel gate and along a path through a farmer's field. On the far side of the plot, we squeezed between barbed wire and navigated a pathway through some brush out onto a rocky bank of the river. It was a great spot and the sunny afternoon just enhanced it.

With a couple tips on how to fish the river, I fastened a nightcrawler on the end of my line and cast out. Only when I went to reel back in did I discover that my reel-in handle had fallen off somewhere. With a loaner pole from my new friends and an anchovy on the hook as bait, I repeatedly cast, letting my bait bounce along the river bottom to attract attention. Though we saw both salmon and baitfish jump and had all the right moves, we got not a nibble.

But the sun was warm and conversation easy. I returned to the van and, of course, found the damn pole handle in the back where the pole had rested! The sun was starting to go down at this point and I had to move if I was going to camp again tonight. Making my way back along the country road again, a flannel grey horse hung his head over a fence to eat the grass on the other side. As I stopped to take his photo, I thought about how I'd spent the day and decided that this is how Columbus Day *should* be marked.

Lumbering south with thick, rush hour traffic very obediently moving at the 50 m.p.h. posted limit, I passed the Simpson Timber Company and rolled through busy Eureka, seeing my first palm trees. They led me like breadcrumbs toward warmer southern areas and the reservation lands of the Wiyot Indians.

The Humboldt Redwoods State Park placed me amongst the giants again and, traveling the 32-mile main corridor, the Avenue of the Giants, I kept a lookout for a camp space for the night. The "Immortal Tree" came up, a redwood estimated to be 1,000 years old that survived lightning, loggers, a forest fire in 1908 and a flood in 1964. All along the road, plaques with family names on them identified specific groves of trees.

Realizing that once it got dark it would be difficult to gather campfire wood, I pulled to the side and scavenged dead branches, courtesy of a Madame Redwood. Up ahead, just past the almost dry bed of the Eel River, a sign pointed me to Burlington Campground. Though there was a small office at the entry, this was another self check-in deal. I took an envelope and quickly found an appropriate site. Near to a restroom, equipped with a supplies storage locker, picnic table and fire pit, and ringed by 200-foot high sentinels of the forest, it was an ideal evening cradle.

Making the most of the waning daylight, I piled my collected wood by the fire pit, set up my RoadTrip grill and unloaded all necessary food and cooking materials. Chili was on the menu, made with chuck steak cubes, pinto beans, diced tomatoes and, of course, beer. The cooking process was a fluid operation with a more than satisfying result, savored in front of a roaring fire. With Jiffy-Pop popcorn for dessert — which turned out perfectly, an accomplishment in itself — and a rooftop of redwoods over my head, I had achieved another lucky-to-be-alive moment.

Steinbeck "stayed two days close to the bodies of the giants," as I had, and sensed "a cathedral hush" to the environment. He observed that "the trees rose straight up to zenith: there is no horizon. The dawn comes up early and remains dawn until the sun is high." He felt that "time and ordinary divisions of the day are changed" and "there in the redwoods nearly the whole of daylight is a quiet time." And "underfoot," he noticed, as was the case within my roost, "is a mattress of needles deposited for over two thousand years." He suspected that folks lacking history with the place might "begin to have the feeling of uneasiness here, of danger, of being shut in, enclosed and overwhelmed" as "at night, the darkness is black." His sentiments concluded with the thought that these giants are "a stunning memory of what the world was like once long ago."

Day 39: Over the Bay I Go

If, as Steinbeck described it, the redwood forest was like a cathedral, then I fell asleep in Mass and should have been scolded by the minister. For I slept no less than nine solid hours, longer than I had slept any night since leaving home. There had certainly been a hush to this place, almost deafening, and absolute stillness. My neighbors and I respected the tranquility, awed by our guardians who had the power to fall on us and smash us like so many ants festering at their roots.

While performing morning tasks, the park ranger visited to collect the site fee. I shared some of my thoughts with him about the park and he said, "Yeah, I love it here," a twinkle of genuine passion in his eye for the place.

One of my first agenda items was to have a proper wash, having only "spit shined" myself sink-side at the previous night's beach spot. A new discovery in my travels, the showers here featured coin-operated meters, established purportedly for reasons of enhanced conservation, controlled consumption and reduced waiting time. I believe, however, they existed to gain some control over freeloading backpackers who just drop into camp to clean up.

The rates posted were as follows: 50¢ = 5 min., 75¢ = 7 1/2 min., $1 = 10 min., $1.25 = 12 min. and so forth up to 15 quarters worth of time. All fine, well and reasonable unless you don't have change. For my part, I had just two quarters. Hungry parking meters or laundry machines had consumed the rest. A degree of strategic planning would be required, an on-in-and-go approach.

I stripped down to just sandals, set fresh clothes and towel out and, with shampoo, soap and washcloth at the ready, went into action. CLINK, CLINK, SWOOSH and off I went running. If you had seen me, you would have thought I was being attacked by fire ants I was moving so quickly, my hands and washcloth a blur of activity as I scrubbed from one part to the next. When I finally had a chance to just stand there, CLUNK, the shower abruptly shut off.

As the room was open to the air via large wood slats, there was a cold factor here, too, and the nighttime temperature had dropped to 40. So, as in the shower, I was like the cartoon "The Flash", zipping about almost imperceptibly.

Walking back from the restroom, I really gazed on my site for the first time and the golden light finding its way to and illuminating it. I noticed, too, how notches had been cut into the remaining stumps of fallen trees so that anyone with the inclination could climb atop them.

I had an ingenious flicker of imagination when breakfast became the next order of business. Planning eggs, I took the skillet that still had grease in it from last night's chuck steak, and cooked diced onions. To that, I added ham squares and, then, over all, a mixture of eggs, milk and the calico cheese. The result was a steaming plate of morning goodness that had no rival. It, and a tall mug of instant coffee, warmed my soul.

A fat friendly tabby had come snooping at dinnertime last night and I half expected him to visit me again this morning. Collarless, though obviously well cared for, he mewed and circled my feet as I was cooking my supper, persuading me to mete out steak cubes to him. But that wasn't enough for the little bugger who mounted my picnic table, snatched up my last two slices of bread and scurried off into the woods. I saw him later skulking in the shadows at the perimeter of my site. I could only guess that he'd gone away in one of the large RVs that rolled out of here at first light.

The pages of the *Chronicle* that I'd picked up revealed that all was still not well in Iraq as a suicide attacker detonated a car bomb near a hotel where many U.S. officials were staying. No U.S. lives were lost, but six Iraqis were killed and another 32 injured. The most famous thoroughbred jockey in the world, Bill Shoemaker, better known as Willie, passed on in San Marino, age 72. The 135th Italian Heritage Parade made its way along Columbus Avenue in San Francisco Sunday. Joan Kroc, widow of the billionaire McDonald's Corp. founder, died of brain cancer at age 75 in the San Diego suburb of Rancho Santa Fe, which I recognized as the neighborhood where Briggs Swift Cunningham lived before he passed. The Browns beat L.A.'s Raiders at the same time the Patriots nipped my Giants in NFL action. In pro baseball, the Yankees and Red Sox's AL Championship Game #4 was rained out (N.Y. was holding at 2-1 for the series) while the Marlins stayed alive with a win in Game #5 against the Cubbies (Cubs lead 3-2).

I'd also picked up the *Life & Times*, a weekly paper serving Southern Humboldt and Northern Medocino, and flipped through its pages. Della Crabtree Womack, one of the last surviving Wailaki Indian elders, was marking her 90th birthday. Columnist Robert O. Vincent, casually known as "R.O.V.," was spouting about 'Why Men Are Happier People'. Some of his offerings: You can "do" your nails with a pocketknife. One wallet, one color — all seasons. The same hairstyle lasts for years, maybe decades. You are unable to see wrinkles in your clothes. The occasional well-rendered belch is practically expected.

While breakfast had warmed my soul, it had not warmed my hands and feet and, in this sun-shielded place, I was freezing. Without further ado but for some pot washing, I stowed my gear and got moving for warmer pastures.

First, though, a stop at the Visitor's Center was warranted, where a "paid volunteer" greeted me. I remarked about the stillness of the woods and he asked if I'd smelled smoke. I hadn't but should have given that two forest fires were in progress not 1 1/2 miles away.

More than a month old, the Honeydew Creek fire on the King Range near Shelter Cove had claimed 13,778 acres while the Canoe fire had consumed 11,104 acres. This explained the earlier pass-over of a helicopter, one of nine that had been committed to fighting the fires along with 2,126 volunteers, 63 hand crews, 20 bulldozers, 23 water tenders and 133 fire engines. At the moment, the local arm of the California Department of Forestry, comprising 75 to 100 men, were managing things using a strategy of setback fires, trench digging and dozering. Overall containment was 95% though recent high winds had fanned some hot spots and motorists were being warned to drive slowly with headlights on due to reduced visibility. The latest cost estimate for suppressing the fires had been pegged at $31 million and injuries totaled 64, most of them minor burns treatable as first aid cases.

The highlight of the Center, which showed many curiosities, was naturalist, woodsman, rancher and artist Charles Kellogg's "Travel-Log." The vehicle consisted of a 6-ton section of a giant redwood tree, about 4,800 years old, that Kellogg had hollowed out and shaped into a complete dwelling and mounted on a 2-ton Nash Quad truck chassis. The dwelling included a kitchenette, folding lavatory, toilet, clothespress, 12 lockers, folding double bed, stove, dining table, bookcase, dresser, electric lights, running water and even a guest room with single bed. To protect it from the elements, he rubbed 12 pounds of beeswax into the wood.

Born in the high and remote Sierras of California, Kellogg learned outdoor survival techniques from Digger Indians and lived amongst snakes and birds and wild creatures. He made it his lifelong mission to travel throughout the United States, Canada and Europe in his Travel-Log "to impart the love of the soil, show new ways by which man can achieve his rightful domain over the earth and awaken interest in the great redwood forest of California."

About this patch of forest where Kellogg had harvested his Travel-Log, the attendant said it's the largest stand of virgin growth redwoods in the world and that, within it, the temperature is a good 20 degrees lower than more exposed outside areas. As I made my exit, he armed me with a host of information, including a video shot by Huell Howser about the Avenue of the Giants, pamphlet about Kellogg's adventures and tip about author and Pasadena bookstore owner John Mitchell, who'd written a small biography about Steinbeck.

It was difficult to remove myself from this prehistoric playground, where each bend in the road brought another incredible sight: An overlook of an olive-green meandering river, which one could just imagine dinosaurs visiting. A straightaway of road lit up by shafts of divine sun. A marker on a boulder: This grove in memory of Samuel Hort Boardman, 1866-1923, "Only God can make a tree."

Having never driven through a tree, when the opportunity arose at the 5,000-year-old, 64-foot around, 275-foot tall "Drive-Through Tree," I took it. Unfortunately, El Rucio was too big to fit through the opening and I had to settle for watching a couple in an orange Dodge Charger part it instead. In the adjacent gift shop, I had the opportunity to speak with the pair, learning that they were from New York City and headed to San Francisco. This was their second day out on a 3-week journey, with plans to visit Bakersfield after San Fran. Hoping to see the couple again down the road, I continued on my way, San Francisco now just 218 miles off.

My brother had told me about an area, Sink Yone, near Garberville and the latter came up presently. Exiting at Redcrest, I followed signs to Shelter Cove, a 23-mile journey along some of the topsiest, turviest road I'd come across, first past the small community of Briceland, with its boxlike homes, then up and over a steep mountain in the King Range. The descent, which was so sharp my brakes literally smoked, brought me down to the Black Sands Beach, which I owned but for two women — one bottomless — and a couple strolling the shore. The black sand was the product of constant wave erosion of ovoid volcanic stones that lay at the base of the cliffs of the Range, atop which were palatial homes with wide sun decks. I ventured out knee-deep in the water, which had a very strong undertow that actually made a sucking, clattering sound as it retreated across the rocks.

Walking up the beach apace, I found an alcove and, feeling inspired by my surroundings, bared myself to nature, basking in the sun for a good hour. A stroll followed, to collect shells and rocks, and study starfish — some as much as eight inches across — sea sponges, crab shells, kelp, seaweed, the jaw of a small shark, and the skull and neck bone of a large-billed bird.

At just past the mid-afternoon hour, I gathered up my cup of treasures, passed the bottomless girl and a bearded backpacker making a pit stop, and, arriving back at the van, I began my ascent. Along the way up, I gave a ride to a shaggy bear of a hitchhiker, who was seeking supplies at the Shelter Cove General Store. He reeked of sweat and, once he'd hopped, I rolled down the windows to air out El Rucio.

As I slid down the other side of the mountain, a radio show called the "Coconut Wireless," hosted by a deejay calling himself Crazy Fingers, kept me entertained. A memorable song featured the line: "Puff the Magic Dragon is all I need, sit right back on this big ass couch and smoke a fat joint with me." Only in California I mused.

San Fran was nearly 200 miles away yet — a lot of ground to cover by sunset, which is when I wanted to cross the Golden Gate. I pulled out all the stops, except one for gas in Willits. El Rucio was mighty thirsty and sucked down $50 of high-priced NO CAL fuel.

On the way to my destination, I passed through the "Land of Bigfoot," Richardson State Park, hoping to catch sight of the wooly man-beast of legend. At the same time, I rolled by work crews shoring up unstable rock faces, the world's largest chainsaw sculpture, flatlands speckled with farms and barns and black beef cows and irrigators. Often, I had no radio reception at all.

This was all land that Steinbeck knew though he remembered it as even more rural, and was dismayed by how progress had altered it. Where the highway was once "a narrow, twisting mountain road where the wood teams moved, drawn by steady mules," it had become established and well-trafficked. The "little little town, a general store under a tree and a blacksmith shop" had been replaced with "little houses, each one like the next." A television relay station occupied the "woody hill with Live Oaks dark green against the parched grass where coyotes sang on moonlit nights." He "felt resentment toward the strangers swamping what [he] thought of as [his] country with noise and clutter and the inevitable rings of junk." He noted, too, the abundance of trailer homes in California, denser here than anywhere else, "lapping up the sides of hills, spilling into riverbeds," despising their owners as "they do not pay taxes" and "thus the owners of immovable property find themselves supporting swarms of guests."

The one hundred or so final miles to the city that my brother had called home for the past two years was one of mountains glowing pink in the late day sun, Indian reservations, strawberry groves and a multitude of vineyards: Fetzer, Jepson, Saracina, Jeriko, Brutocao, Milano.

I missed my sunset on the Bay but enjoyed it instead as it topped the straight, even rows of grapes of Sonoma County. The remainder of the way in became an ever-increasing mad rush as roads grew in width lane by lane through towns like Santa Rosa and Petaluma in southern Sonoma and Novato and San Rafael in Marin County.

On the far side of Sausalito, I shot through a tunnel shaped like elbow macaroni and hurtled onto the Golden Gate Bridge, its high supports stretching dramatically into the air. Then there was San Francisco, "The City", as Steinbeck described it, a place where he'd "spent [his] attic days… while others were being a lost generation in Paris." He "fledged in San Francisco, climbed its hills, slept in its parks, worked on its docks, marched and shouted in its revolts."

A $5 cover charge at Frisco's door let me in to this "acropolis rising wave on wave against the blue of the Pacific sky…a painted thing like a picture of a medieval Italian city which can never have existed." Steinbeck stopped to look at her, the green hills to the south and fog rolling in. I wished to have stopped, wanted to stop but probably couldn't have stopped. My fellow motorists, like so many salmon swimming downstream, pushed me along. At the same time, my focus, unfortunately, had to be on signs and the mental recall of directions Dave had given me by phone.

As guided, I stayed on 101 into the city, bearing right after Market Street, to 80 East over the Bay Bridge, its ribbing like an arching spine. It spilled me into dense traffic, caused by an accident up ahead, that the schools of carbon monoxide spewing spawn around me and I slipped by. Leaving their ranks at the turn-off for 880 South, I trundled along to 23rd Avenue and then patched in to Dave by cell to bring me in over the phone. Finally, there was their very charming Victorian residence across from a little park on Morton Street on the island of Alameda. Dave came out to greet me and led me in to say hello to Jill, who was pecking away at her computer, and their tubby cat, Coki.

Setting me up with pizza, which I supplemented with beer, Dave gave me an overview of the region using a laminated map as a visual aid. In his highly meticulous way, he also drew me a small map of the city of San Francisco, which I told him I wanted to explore first, labeled with key points of interest. He threw a coveted Frisco pop-out map into the mix, saying "this is just a loaner, with emphasis on loan," and then launched into a digital slide show via his laptop.

The presentation began to be more than my tired brain could process or my eyelids could stay propped open for at that point and I excused myself to sleep. I could have slept on a bed of nails, though much preferred to be on their padded futon in the angular front room of their partly subterranean apartment. Constructed of stone and painted bone white, it was decorated with carefully selected items from their many travels: Hats made of palm leaves. A grass-skirted, pink-and-red figurine of an island girl. A painting of many colorful fishing boats pulled up on the sand below a beach walkway. A puckered face painted on half a coconut shell.

These two met more than 14 years ago in North Carolina and, over that span of time, married and lived in places such as Atlanta, St. Thomas in the Virgin Islands, Glen Cove in Steinbeck's Long Island, and now the island of Alameda. They had become accomplished hikers with many miles on their walking sticks, master scuba divers, practiced sailors and thorough documenters of their adventures through books and magazine articles.

Their goals adjusted as their fortunes changed or opportunities arose, from seeking to buy a sailboat to sail the world to a more modest plan of buying a fully equipped RV to live on and write about the American road "for years." Their immediate plan was to relocate to the East Coast in just over two weeks. Already, they had begun boxing up household things to either ship or sell. They were a restless pair on a seemingly endless quest, not unlike many people I'd come across in my now nearly six-week trek.

Day 40: Exploring San Francisco

As the garbage truck came around Dave and Jill's neighborhood and the clunks and footfalls of their upstairs landlord became audible, I got myself in gear to begin the day's adventure. A shower and some organizing and I was rolling, out of the Victorian area, past kids on their way to school, through blocks of one-level homes with red-tiled roofs and over the High Street Bridge to the freeway. I was back in the logjam and at the worst time of the day.

Traffic carried me through mostly commercial Oakland where I watched massive dock cranes along the horizon already hard at work moving cargo containers onto large ships. Long freight trains snaking along the roadside brought them more cargo to load.

It was nippy and foggy though I imagined that this was probably how every morning here started. Edging ahead in now bumper-to-bumper traffic, seeking to cross the Bay Bridge, I fell behind a young woman in a Taurus with a "Cowgirl" decal in her back window and cross hanging from her rearview mirror. A country mouse with country morals, she was trying her luck in the big city.

A two-dollar toll put me on the silver steel span, from which I jumped at Fremont Street, leaping to The Embarcadero. Here, stone buildings that looked like banks but were labeled as designated piers formed the waterfront and served the shipping industry. Then came the fine luxury motor yachts, classic trolleys and congested, tourist-overrun Fisherman's Wharf. There, the road became Jefferson and took me out to a point where the Maritime Museum was located. A parking space that was free for four hours would give me plenty of time to do some exploring.

The fog was lifting as I set out on foot along a long cement pier from which several elder Chinese guys were fishing, joggers were jogging, bikers were biking and seagulls were looking on with great disinterest. And out in the bay was the fortress known as Alcatraz, where thousands of hardened criminals were incarcerated until 1963, when the prison was closed due to the expense of operating it and because of decaying cement. A bay ferry, loaded with area visitors, hovered near it.

As I walked back towards the Maritime Center, I asked a fisherman with limited command of English what kind of fish were here. "Rockfish… and Kingfish." For bait, he used bits of salmon. Had he caught any? "None yet."

A young Chinese girl in white chinos and a gray GAP sweatshirt sat on sunny steps enjoying the early morning sight of the sea, waves gently lapping a narrow beach and light breeze carrying the smell of the ocean with it. She was one of many student-aged kids milling about which made me wonder if there was a school nearby. "Yes, Galileo High School," she replied, pointing up to a crest behind her. She and her fellow classmates were enjoying some free time, the day abbreviated because of teacher meetings. About the spot in which she had chosen to sit, it was where her family used to bring her as a baby, to play in the sand, so she was reliving some of those memories. I guess I was doing the same, having been here last when I was only about her age.

Further along, a historical area housed old paddle wheels, steam engines, anchors and shops devoted to fishing lore and gifts. I wandered into a gift shop to buy a small wooden trolley car and history book about Alcatraz. In large rectangular tanks at the Alioto-Lazio Fish Company, two-pound Dungeness Crabs (Pacific crustaceans whose meat is white and sweet tasting) waited for seafood buyers.

Frank's Fisherman Supply, owned by brothers Ron and Ken Brown, held a voluminous collection of nautical and fishing-related antiques and reproductions. Ken and I got talking about old diving helmets and the difference in manufacturing and quality compared with those made today.

This launched a whole conversation about their business evolved from a commercial fishing equipment supplier to its present-day consumer focus.

Doing my part to support their enterprise, I purchased a brass anchor hanger and small brass compass key chain and continued along the waterfront on a path known at the Barbary Coast Trail. Restaurants with names like Pompei's, Grotto, Lou's, Castagnola's and Tarantino's were abundant here and had wonderful smells coming from them.

Deciding to combine both a lunch and boating experience, I bought a couple cans of Bud from Castagnola's bar and a large cup of chowder with soup crackers and bread, and boarded the 50-foot "Butchie B," with double inboards, for a bay cruise. Jessie was our captain, his 16-year-old daughter Desiree the blanket distributor, and Jeff the narrator.

A high school student near Berkeley, Desiree came and sat beside me when she learned I was writing a book, to say she likes to write poetry. "Mostly I write it when I'm angry. Or when things are good with my boyfriend," she said. Spontaneously, she dashed off a poem as we set out and started motoring in the Bay.

We passed the St. Francis Yacht Club, to which membership is a quarter of a million dollars, and made our way out to the Golden Gate, apparently a favorite suicide spot for many. In fact, the $5 toll to cross it was to be used to build a high fence to thwart jumpers. Jeff had seen the beginnings of it and said it was only six feet high, easy to climb over. "It would have been better to save the money and install diving boards instead," he only half joked.

Jessie pulled us alongside Alcatraz, "The Rock," with its crumbling guard towers and structures. We learned that only 280 prisoners would be held here at any one time and that, of 38 escape attempts, eight prisoners remain unaccounted for. Thirty-seven years ago, after the prison closed, Native Americans took control of the island in a push to demand greater civil rights. The effort deteriorated into building burning and scrap metal salvaging and an eventual clearing of the property by armed government soldiers. The group's legacy was a spray-painted message above a U.S. Penitentiary sign: "Indians Welcome."

When we docked, I quickly walked back toward the van, aware that my parking time there was expiring. Pointing myself toward Coit Tower on Telegraph Hill, to gain *the* view of the city, I noticed young lovers smooching on park benches had replaced milling students.

The Hill was so named, according to a postcard, "because of a telegraph semaphore, used to signal the citizenry of approaching ships, located on its 295-foot summit." In 1933, the current-day landmark was erected with a $100,000 bequest from Lillie Hitchcock Coit. She had been rescued from a hotel fire at the age of eight and became the self-appointed fire department's mascot. She would often wear fire gear and follow emergency crews to fires. When she died at 86, fire personnel attended her funeral.

The tower itself is made of fluted, reinforced concrete rising 180 feet above the hill, the summit accessed by an elevator. In the gift shop where the clerk was watching Game #5 of the AL Championship, in which the Yankees had rallied to a 5-4 lead, I bought a ticket to go to the top. The elevator operator was a small Chinese man who spoke broken English and was assigned to say a piece about the structure. "It have 21 floor, 500 feet from sea level, Coit honored for her name for her." It was a valiant attempt at a supporting narrative and, thankfully brief, as we were deposited up high.

Rounded, church-like windows circled the perimeter of the open-roofed viewing platform at the top of a short set of steel steps, allowing a 360-degree view. Many accents mingled in the enclosure, from Germany, France, China, Canada, Florida, Ireland and New Zealand. As wind gusts were fierce, I was glad there were glass plates covering the openings. At the same time, given the open roof, I wondered how the tower drained when it rained, as there were no significant run-offs visible.

From this prominent point, I headed to Chinatown, where parking was a challenge. Pay meters were expensive and limited as to time and most garages had height limits on vehicles. After some circling though, I found the North Beach Garage on Vallejo near Powell, in which every space had a fortune printed on it. Mine was, "You may make a name for yourself." I thought that boded well.

A woman at Chef Bowl, an importing company, gave me a heads-up on the area. Broadway, and streets branching off it, seemed like the place to go. I strolled by Tai Yick Trading Co., full of huge vases. Yut Hing Food Co. Yee Cheong's contractor supplies. The Asia Mall with little shops devoted to videos, clothing, jewelry and travel. Lien Hing's open-air fruit and vegetable market and the King's Co. with bundles of bananas hanging on wires out front. When I reached Columbus, everything turned Italian. Choosing to focus on the Asian area, I u-turned to pass Sun Kau Shing Co., with colorful packages of rice crackers and noodles, duck eggs, soft flour cake and fried crab chips.

Mee Mee Bakery smelled great, so I bought a small package of walnut cookies to walk around with and eat. Pang Kee Bargain Market displayed bean curd crackers, pineapple cake, shelled chestnuts, roasted squash seeds and rice sticks. Seeing all this food and teased by the cookies, I turned in at Hing Lung Restaurant and sat by the glass-enclosed, railroad car-sized kitchen where two chefs were hard at work over vats of boiling grease. As a starter, I ordered shrimp dumpling noodle soup and a Tsingtao, followed by chicken in special orange sauce. As the chicken was deep-fried in batter, something I usually avoid, I picked it from its cocoon, blended it with the soup noodles and happily washed everything down with beer.

Next door, Hung Ming Enterprise was full of pets and supplies. For a while, I looked at several cages of puppies, trying to decide which had the best chances of being taken home.

On Grant Avenue, the Chinese businesses were packed one on top of another and banners were strung across the street. At Bow Bow Cocktails, I caught the last out of the Boston/New York game, which the Sox managed to cap 9-6, forcing a Game 7 in New York.

At City Lights bookstore, started by Beat Generation writer Lawrence Ferlinghetti, I located a copy of the founder's "San Francisco Poems" in an upstairs Poetry Room. The city was where the Beat movement, which I had studied in school along with its proponents — Allen Ginsburg, Lafcadio Orlovsky, Jack Kerouac, Gary Snyder, Michael McClure and Diane di Prima — had started. Displayed here were photos taken in the area in 1965 of these literary experimentalists with Bob Dylan.

As night started to fall and the city lit up like a Chinese lantern, I wondered what the evening life here was like. I was pointed to the "W" Hotel near Howard but got distracted on the way by the Niebaum-Coppola café at the base of the historic, oxidized copper-roofed Sentinel Building, and learned that it was owned by director/producer Francis Ford Coppola. Besides the café, he also operated a private screening room in the building's basement and upper offices devoted to his magazine, *Zoetrope.*

The café served as a showcase for wines from Coppola's vineyard in Rutherford, which could be sampled with various, very reasonably priced pasta and pizza dishes. Also available were DVDs and VHS cassettes of his many films, greats like "The Godfather," "Apocalypse Now," "Dracula," "The Cotton Club," "Patton" and "American Graffiti." Production photos of the same decorated the walls leading to the unisex bathroom downstairs and this main level.

Settling at the bar, I ordered a cappuccino and New York style Luigino pizza, a personal recommendation of Coppola's as noted on the menu. Naturally, I was compelled to try a glass of wine, too, and scanned the room as I sipped it. Of note, there was a framed drawing scratched out on a menu by the aforementioned Ferlinghetti of a nude, voluptuous woman with a potential, rather enthusiastic suitor beside her. The manager said that Ferlinghetti had stopped in just two months ago. "He's a sweetheart of a guy," he said.

I was delighted when a "little bird" told me that Coppola was on the premises, working up in the penthouse, and that there was a good chance he might drop down for a meal. In case he didn't appear, though, I scratched out a little note on the café's stationery, expressing my gratitude for his body of work and complimenting him on the café's cuisine.

As I crafted the leave-behind, a young professional-looking couple who introduced themselves as Evan and Karen came and sat near. I related, of course, that Evan's name was the same as my son's, but was further amused to know that his middle name and my younger son's were also identical. Topping this, they had gotten married only Saturday and were honeymooning solely in San Francisco. As they were Houston residents and the city was on my planned route, we exchanged contact information, hoping to meet up.

Out of the corner of my eye, I became aware of someone looking in through the window at me from tables arranged on the sidewalk outside. It was Coppola himself, in a blue blazer and white button-down shirt, and he was just sitting down with the manager. Ready to leave, I walked out to greet and shake hands with the famed filmmaker, who listened politely while I mentioned my travels, graciously accepted and placed in his coat pocket the note I'd written him and bid me "ciao" as I departed.

Across the street, the L'Amour Nightclub and Karaoke Bar seemed interesting, though it was too early for the format. I stayed for a beer anyhow and the staff in the red-lit bar area kept me amused. From there, I drifted past flashing neon signs advertising massage parlors, theaters and a place called Mr. Bing's, to Vesuvio.

It was a must-visit and, inside, a long, brown leather bench offered a good roost and fine viewing perspective. Decorated with a mish-mash of dramatic black-and-white photography, magazine covers, charcoal drawings and a sign that warned "Beware Pickpockets and Loose Women", it was a warm little environment with lots of promise for entertainment.

Beside me sat an Indian couple from England. They were another honeymooning couple and their stops thus far had been Los Angeles and Santa Barbara, with plans still to visit the Grand Canyon, Las Vegas, Australia, Hong Kong, India, the Maldives Islands and Cape Town. Their adventure dwarfed mine in magnitude and I was truly impressed by their ambitious plan, which required all of their savings. They hoped to have a little left over at the end, though, "if we don't hit the shops," she offered.

Near the entry, a couple performed an extensive, exploratory tonsillectomy on each other before hastily paying and leaving. They were replaced with a group led by a guy who declared "This is like 'Cheers,'" referring to the Boston bar based television program. Naturally, I called out, "Norm!" to their surprise and delight. "You must be from Boston!" a woman in the group said. "Connecticut." "Close enough."

A foursome of old troopers followed, one of which was wearing Yankee pinstripes. When I commented on them, his buddy, obviously not a fan, jabbed, "That's a skin disease." Another guy, a Punjab, noticing the Indian couple beside me, wandered over when I took my seat again. I asked if he was Sikh and he said, "No, sick," pointing to his head. Ah, a comedian!

Our little group grew to include a new member, a young "bloke" who declared he was visiting from Fullham. Hearing that, the Indian couple cried, "Fair play!" a positive acknowledgement similar to the Californian "Right on!"

Yet another couple dropped in, also from England, in the filmmaking business working on a psychological thriller about drug companies and human experimentation.

Like a magnet for steak and kidney pie lovers, Vesuvio managed to attract one more Englander for the evening. Toting a vodka cocktail, she had been camping and working her way across the country.

The bar literally turned the lights off on us all and nudged us to the door. Great hugs and goodbyes were shared all around, I brailed my way back to El Rucio in her fortune cookie space and we giddy-upped back over the Bay Bridge onto Alameda and to Dave's nest. I'd taken San Francisco and squeezed it like an orange, milking it for every last golden drop. It was a glorious, triumphant visit.

Day 41: Steinbeck Stops

I woke at 8 to more landlord footfalls overhead, showered and tuned in to a news program on D&J's microscopic TV. The big morning story: Back in New York, a Staten Island ferry boat that was crossing to Manhattan hit a pier dock, resulting in the death of ten commuters and 42 injuries. The captain ran home afterwards and tried to commit suicide.

Steinbeck found San Francisco "the city [he] remembered, so confident of its greatness that it can afford to be kind…[as] it had been kind to [him] in the days of [his] poverty." But he, like I was now, was anxious to get going to Monterey and San Jose and his native Salinas. Allowing my brother and his wife to return to their own never-ceasing travel planning, I took my leave from Alameda mid-morning and was soon caught up in the mess that was 880 South. Never thinking I'd again long for the desolate logging roads I'd traveled, here I did.

Steinbeck would surely not have recognized the route to San Jose and would have been overwhelmed by traffic volume, highway width (10 lanes across in some sections) and commercial build-up on either side. It was certainly not what I had expected based on notions formed through Dionne Warwick's happy-go-lucky ditty, "Do You Know the Way to San Jose?" which I remembered from my youth. The only thing he might have connected with was the as-yet undeveloped rolling brown hills on the horizon, which looked like giant sand dunes.

My entry into San Jose was via Gish Road, which was industrial at first then yielded to small homes, neat front yards and neighborhood bodegas. Finding parking across from San Jose University, which looked indistinctive from the exterior, I went off prowling for Dr. Susan Shillinglaw, Director of the Center for Steinbeck Studies at the school, whom I had e-mailed during the summer. She'd encouraged me to stop in to see the vast collection here, including all of Steinbeck's published works, his contributions to periodicals, manuscripts, movie scripts, correspondence, articles and books about him, photographs, video collections and oral histories. It seemed to me to be *the* definitive Steinbeck repository and I was very anxious to see it.

With guidance from a couple of students, I found the room in the impressive, eight-story Martin Luther King, Jr. Library. Unfortunately, it was locked and dark and it wasn't known if the good doctor was on campus. I was steered to the English Department where she maintained an office but it was closed, too. Attempts to reach her on the phone also failed, though a home address in Los Gatos was provided.

Before heading to her house, I wanted to know more about this deceivingly pretty school and its student composition. The director of admissions at the student services building was kind enough to pull up stats on a monitor that showed that, of 28,000 enrollees, Asians, whites, Hispanics and Filipinos comprised the largest segments. Their many beautiful faces floated past me as I walked back through the Boyce Gate entrance, across which was strung a banner welcoming alumni Tommie Smith and John Carlos, athletes who participated in and won medals at the 1968 Summer Olympics in Mexico City.

Some jamming music drew me to the highly animated Marvin Banks Band performing in a pit by the Student Union, where I decided to grab a quesadilla. Since it was such a beautiful day, I sat out in the sun enjoying my lunch and the music.

After my break and a bit of unintentional touring around Los Gatos, I found Susan's house, but she wasn't home. Her neighbor, who was gardening, said she was likely down in Salinas and then helped me with directions to one of five Steinbeck homes in the area, this one in Monte Sereno, "a mucky muck area."

Finding the residence was no simple task and required the combined assistance of three individuals: An Apple computer product design manager passing in his SUV. An area resident who was gardening and had read "East of Eden" with her book club back in January to mark the Steinbeck

Centennial. And a gentleman who lived right next door to what turned out to be the Steinbeck home.

It had been expanded upon from the original photo I'd seen but still had the similar architectural features, a three-car garage and azaleas surrounding the property. Again, like Sag Harbor, it was not an ostentatious house, but comfortable. In May 1936, John and his first wife, Carol, purchased the 1.6-acre plot and designed and built the original 1,452-square-foot home that summer. It was the first home Steinbeck owned and to ensure his privacy, he built an eight-foot grape stake fence around it and placed a carved wooden plaque, "Arroyo del Ajo" (Garlic Gulch) on the gate. Here, Steinbeck completed "Of Mice and Men" and began "The Grapes of Wrath", while entertaining such guests as Burgess Meredith and Charlie Chaplin. Apparently, his measures to ensure privacy were not enough and, because of intrusions, they moved in September 1938.

Their next home was called The Biddle Ranch, and was located in the Santa Cruz Mountains above Los Gatos, less than 10 miles away. To find it required another collaborative effort, between the owner of a local restaurant, a real estate agent and a pair of mountaintop neighbors. A loop down 17 to Bear Creek Road brought me back up the mountain, along a right branch and to the great ranch, once 47 acres, now 20, and owned by a young family. They were kind enough to let me park behind the house and show me around.

John was finishing "The Grapes of Wrath" at that time, and he and Carol moved into an existing old farmhouse on the property while a new home was being built on the lot, completed in December 1938. Unfortunately, their marriage began deteriorating, they separated in late April 1941 and they sold Biddle Ranch in late August the same year.

We followed a brick pathway past a pool that was a good 50 feet long and eight-feet deep. Trees on the property included lime, almond, walnut, plum, pear, poplar and willow. Though the old farmhouse was gone, a small greenhouse and old barn that now housed a ping-pong table lived on. There were also two "Sears kit" houses, where guests or ranch hands would stay, that had been completely updated by the former owners. When I spotted a large buck sprinting past the front of the house, I was informed that there were about 30 deer on the property. Other life included goldfish and newts in a brick-lined pond on a front patio. Inside, the "Great Room" featured original beams overhead that had come from a nearby primitive oil well, while the kitchen, back room, bedroom and bathroom had been completely remodeled.

The family wished me a good trip and I rolled down the other side of the mountain, through Santa Cruz, to the coastal route toward Salinas. Desiring a beachside spot for the evening, I found Seacliff State Park at the mouth of which was a market. There, I replenished my cooler with ice and stocked up on supplies including two large bottles of beer: an Anchor Steam from San Francisco and Sea Bright India Pale Ale from Santa Cruz. The latter was a great complement to franks and beans that I cooked up in a parking slot by the beach. It was not a very private spot — El Rucio was sandwiched amongst a whole line of RVs — but near adequate restrooms and a fine-looking bit of sand.

People jogged and walked past and we exchanged pleasantries, then I curled up in the van to watch the latter half of the AL Championship Game #7 on my on-board TV. The Yankees and Red Sox had tied things up 5-5 and the game had gone into extra innings, to the 11th in fact. That's when Yankee Aaron Boone, a new recruit, socked a ball over the fence — his first post-season home run and only the 5th post-season game-winning home run — to break the logjam and give New York the pennant. "This is just stupid!" Boone exclaimed in an interview afterwards. Manager Joe Torre looked on the verge of joyous tears and pitcher Mariano Riviera, the game's MVP, kissed the ground in elation. New York had bought a ticket to the Big Dance against NL champs the Florida Marlins.

All set to bed down after a long but satisfying day, I was disturbed by a "thud thud" on one of El Rucio's windows, followed by a flashlight beam in the face. It was a ranger come to inform me, at the late hour of 11 p.m., that my vehicle did not qualify as an RV and, therefore, I could not park in this waterfront area. Per some technical mumbo jumbo, that allowed no exceptions to the rules, he was rousting all non-conformists. Spitting mad, I removed myself and hugged the coast south seeking an alternative place. I found one in Sunset Beach that, though I could barely see where I was parking, didn't seem to have any tin badges patrolling, and bed right down.

Day 42: In the Author's Birthplace

When I arose, the sun was coming up over an embankment of new pine plantings and fellow campers were stirring and making coffee. Climbing a small ridge to look about, I couldn't really see much of anything, so my get-up-and-go and I got up and went.

Back on the main, cars were parked end to end on both sides of the road and, at first, I thought there must be an event going on nearby. Then I saw them: scores of field hands, hunched over, harvesting row upon row of cabbage plants, under the watchful eye of a foreman in a white pickup. The laborers appeared to be Hispanic for the most part and kept a very fast pace. I'm sure that there were bonuses to be had if they made a certain quota. The other thing I noticed was cacti, which I first saw growing out of the stump of an old tree. These were the sights, I imagined, that Steinbeck grew up around, inspired his writing and would most certainly be welcome were he alive today.

Another field, this one containing strawberries, adjacent to another string of cars and tended by more workers, came up ahead. I wanted a closer look, so parked, walked out to where they were toiling and spoke with a Spanish man overseeing the picking. He directed me to "el padrone" in the "camione" across the field. "El padrone," or the foreman, handling the picking process of some 70 acres for a Santa Cruz-based produce company. He oversaw 60 pickers in all, the majority of whom lived in Watsonville. Every year, they start picking in May and finish in October, harvesting twice a week. At the height of the season (late September), they will fill 5,000 to 6,000 flats a day, working 9 to 10 hours a day. At this time in the year, they pull in 1,400 a day, working about six hours daily in the 70-acre field.

When I asked if I could buy a small container, the foreman *gave* me one, a whopping two-pounder, of the plumpest berries you might ever encounter. Driving on, I happily munched the red treats, thinking there could be no sweeter or more satisfying breakfast.

Field hand sightings continued as I stumbled into Monterey County, then onto Route 1 again toward Salinas. Here, produce vendors were many: Dominic's offered pumpkins and flew a banner advertising the Salinas Air Show to be held tonight. Frank Capurro & Sons offered vegetables.

Other sites included the Moss Landing Marina, a Mexican eatery called The Whole Enchilada and the Moss Landing Café, near the Salinas River State Beach, where teens boarded a North Monterey County school bus. Approaching Castroville, "The Artichoke Center of the World," signs for, not surprisingly, artichokes, oranges and Brussels sprouts were posted all along the road. The faces of the people in these parts were brown, the hair and eyes black, and the lands consistently lush with produce, bright green and fertile, smelling of manure and good earth.

With great excitement, I arrived in the town of Salinas, following signs for the National Steinbeck Center, a brick and glass building in front of which a school class was gathered. I offered them strawberries, which they readily accepted and hungrily devoured.

When I gained admittance, the museum had not yet opened and the majority of the staff was making its way up the street with steaming coffees in hand. This included Mr. Kim Greer, the Center's CEO, who promptly began leading me on a tour of the exhibits here.

At the start, there was a photo of Steinbeck as a boy, his ears, like taxicab doors thrown open, jutting from his head. Beside that, a photo of his surviving son Thomas, in a pool with his own family. Tucked in a corner, there was Steinbeck's first bed, some school photos and scenes of Salinas as he would have known it as a child. Centering the room, a Model T Ford that John would have seen as a young teen. Posters from movies based on his novels hung on a wall. Other exhibits related to the valley overall, showing common farm and horse-related equipment. Around the corner, a placard featured the quote from which the title "Of Mice and Men" was chosen: "The best-laid schemes o' mice an' men/Gang aft agley," written by Robert Burns in "To a Mouse."

Hearing Steinbeck's actual voice, which I had the opportunity to do in three places in the museum, was quite fascinating. And there was Steinbeck's old friend Ed Ricketts' safe, retrieved after Ed's marine biology lab burned down. It contained models of cheese, pie and sardines, the only items discovered in the safe apparently.

Kim was especially proud of a model of the Western Flyer, a 76-foot-long single-mast fishing boat that he had an opportunity to pilot and that Steinbeck popularized in "The Sea of Cortez."

The crowning glory for me, of course, was the beloved "Rocinante." My eyes actually welled up at the sight of her bright green skin, windowed cabin, and curtains, hand-sewn by Elaine and depicting English fox hunt scenes. The vehicle was behind tall, plexiglass panels and I thought that, standing outside the corral would be as close as I would get to her. But Kim said, "Here, grab hold," laying his hands on a plexi panel at the rear, and we removed it. "Go on in," he invited. "Inside?" I asked incredulously. For me, this was like entering a sacred temple, a literary shrine and, instantly, all of Steinbeck's references to the truck and its interior flooded to me. The small laminated table behind the driver compartment was topped with period props — a Courvoisier bottle, can of root beer, brown bottle of beer and an Underwood manual typewriter. There was the Preway 4-burner gas stove, the compact Murphy-Richards Astral refrigerator and a toilet compartment, which he apparently enjoyed visiting even after his travels were completed and Rocinante sat home in Sag Harbor. I imagined the visitors he entertained at the table and the rain hammering the aluminum roof.

When Kim said I could even climb behind the wheel if I wanted, I had the opportunity to semi-experience the difficult moment Steinbeck had in Oregon, changing his flat tire. Because of how the truck was squeezed into a corner, I had to go flat on my stomach underneath her, scooch along the dusty floor and come up by the driver's side. There was just enough room for me to squeeze in, and when I slid behind the hard, thin steering wheel, the long bench seat, upon which a cast of Charley sat, gave a little crack under my weight. It may not have felt a passenger since Kim placed the vehicle here. Holding the steering wheel and looking out over the dash with its very rudimentary levers and controls, including hand cranks for the windows, I had an amazing connection with how he felt and his frustrations, thoughts, pains and hardships on the road.

Processing everything I'd seen, I sat for a while on a bench in the open space of the Center. This was an extraordinary place and treasured highlight of my voyage. Growing hungry, I went next door to old-time Sang's Café, an apparent Steinbeck hangout. Smiling Don Sang and his quieter brother Jim welcomed me and had great stories to tell about the café and area's history. Though their family home was catty-corner to the Steinbeck home over on Central, their mom, who spoke little English, didn't know who Steinbeck was until the museum opened in 1998.

The duo's dad, Lee Sang, started the café, which included a bar many recognized as the "biggest this side of the Mississippi," in 1948. "All the big rollers used to come in here, including some of the wealthy growers," Don said. He got to meet them as a boy, working at the cafe after school "washing dishes, helping my father in the kitchen." In 1989, an earthquake damaged the place, resulting in Lee's retirement and the sons taking over.

Sitting at the lunch counter, I ordered a "Californian" burger made with Salinas lettuce, served up by a brown-eyed Mexican waitress.

Two blocks over was the Steinbeck family home where John was born on February 27, 1902. He lived in the fine Victorian until he was 17, when he left to attend Stanford University, and wrote his first short stories and the novels "The Red Pony" and "Tortilla Flat" in an upstairs room. Built by John's grandfather in 1897, the house became an official national landmark in 1995.

Ann Brown, the day manager, met me at the door and walked me through the finely furnished home, boasting 11 1/2-foot-high ceilings, wainscoting, brass doorknobs, old family photographs, lace curtains and assorted silverware. A Salinas resident since 1944, Ann was acquainted with John's sisters Esther and "Beth." Beth, in fact, was a member of the Valley Guild, organized to preserve and enhance the Steinbeck house. Ann permitted me to view the upstairs, not normally open to visitors and dedicated to office space for staff. Its outstanding feature was a wonderful glass skylight with corners stained blue. While the second story was being completed, John and his sisters roller-skated on the unfinished floors. The cellar area, now a gift shop, housed horses then the family car. As a pre-teen, John used to go down there to roll and smoke cigarettes with his friends, dubbing the room his "Opium Den."

Glenn, a reporter from the local paper, *The Californian*, intercepted me on the steps and asked me a series of questions about my travels. Together, we walked to El Rucio so he could see my chariot, then I returned to the Steinbeck Center to visit the gift shop. Seeking to get inside Steinbeck's head, I bought a book containing select personal letters he had written through the years, including several penned while he was on the road in 1960.

At the register, I met another traveler who carried a business card that showed on one side what he "was" career-wise (corporate CPA and submariner), and, on the flip side, what he "is" now (retired, and "a recreational chef and enologist available at all times for: fishing, sailing, golf, travel and parties"). He termed his card a "WAS IS." For the past five years, he had been doing what he called "drive-abouts." His current trek began in Merritt Island, Florida, and has taken him zigzagging across the country north to North Dakota, west to Washington and south to Salinas. He would ultimately travel 31,500 miles over a period of 96 days.

His choice of transportation, a pickup, made me think of a *Times* article I'd read late summer about America's love affair with it and their S.U.V. cousins. The writer pointed out that, "Not long ago you went to the country if you wanted to see pickups" but "in the past couple of years, pickups have become predominantly suburban vehicles [reflecting] essentially suburban values: the need for family space, comfort and status."

I'd certainly seen my share of pickups on the American road, being utilized for a myriad of purposes.

Browsing town, I peered into an antique mall on the main drag then popped into Rollick's Specialty Coffees for some hi-test. The guys there pointed me to a truck stop — Valley Weigh & Wash — where I could grab a hot shower and get El Rucio properly washed. She was looking pretty shabby and my brother had humorously pointed this out by writing "WASH ME" and drawing an outline of the U.S. showing my route on the van's back windows.

Both tasks went well and my girl and I were looking sharp when we rolled up to Monterey Coast Brewing, a stone's throw from the Steinbeck Center. There, the jet black-haired Mexican bartender set eight five-ounce glasses of beer in front of me, a sampling of every brand they brew, from the lightest shade to darkest, along with a plate of quesadilla triangles. While eating, I leafed through *The Californian*, the front-page focus of which was the local air show, which I had been lucky enough to view from the truck stop. F-16s flew straight up, biplanes did loop-the-loops and A-10 Thunderbolts shot across the sky.

I brought along my copy of "Travels..." too, and was intrigued by Steinbeck's notation about Salinas' population in 1960, which was 80,000, and his prediction that it would perhaps be "two hundred thousand in ten" years. His estimates were high — 42 years later, the census pegged the total at 151,060. Still, concerns about growth were on the minds of Salinas' residents. A key worry had been proposed construction of a 14-story hotel right in downtown, an area where building height had long been restricted to three stories. While a good turn for the local economy, I feared that the monstrosity would bring congestion and non-descript fast food chains bound to squeeze the small town flavor out of the place.

My beer glasses emptied, I happily floated out the door to the tune "The Girl from Ipanema", which brought with it great childhood memories, and got on the road for Pacific Grove. Taking an educated guess as to direction, I submarined along, sensing water and certainly smelling it nearby. When I surfaced, I found I'd sonar located the town. Not only that, I was just blocks from Steinbeck's homes in this area, Cannery Row and Ed Ricketts' lab. For the moment, I needed an overnight spot. After two inn tries, I found Veterans State Park and a pleasant little campsite where deer were roaming about and the barks of sea lions could be heard down by the water. It was warm enough that I didn't need to do any preheating, so right to sleep I went.

Day 43: Magnificent Monterey

Up at dawn, I followed the sound of the sea lions down into Monterey, pulling up behind a taxi. Its driver was helpful in tipping me off to area Steinbeck sights, so I stowed my van in a Safeway lot and, stepping past a stumbling drunk who reeked of booze, walked Alvarado Street, named after Governor Alvarado who served the state in the mid 1800s. Once so familiar to him, Steinbeck found the passage peopled by strangers. With the exception of the drunk and a dirty bearded bum on a bench, it would have been completely unrecognizable to him today. It was another manufactured-for-tourists thoroughfare with such places as SuperCuts, Starbucks, Walgreens and Taco Bell, and any number of gift, jewelry and souvenir shops.

Needing food if I was going to do extensive exploring, I stopped in at the Old Monterey Café, which wasn't old at all, but did serve me a tasty helping of eggs, hash and coffee. For visual interest on the walls, this clean, efficient eatery showed framed covers of "comic magazines" based on 1950s-era TV programs. The shows were classics but the teasers on the covers were even more so. One devoted to "Perry Mason" read, "A gun! A glass eye! Perry Mason must solve the case with only two clues." A "Zorro" cover offered, "Zorro attacks a pirate ship to recover Garcia's plundered gold." One for "Laramie" hissed, "A stage driver's body is found on the Sherman ranch and Slim is accused of murder!" Yet another, for "Wyatt Earp," said, "It took brains and a Buntline…to tame the Terror Town." It was a wonderful collection that brought back great remembrances of early, innocent television programming and one with which Steinbeck would have connected, particularly the Westerns.

The authentic-looking Mucky Duck English Pub, just down the block, was one that Jesca in Crescent City had mentioned. A worker was out front sweeping up the previous night's debris. Down the way was the Golden State Theatre, one of the very few structures that Steinbeck would have recognized. Built in 1926, the ornate showplace presented the first "talkies" on the Monterey Peninsula. He would certainly not have known the *new* Doc Ricketts Lab, a comedy club around the corner that served sushi and dictated a multitude of rules about its dress code: No tank tops, sports attire, punk rock attire, heavy metal attire, baggy clothes, excessive display of jewelry or hats. Another long list of rules pertained to smoking, beverages, blocking of space and glassware. These restrictions would have made Steinbeck dizzy. They certainly made *my* head swim.

The waterfront, known as the Monterey State Historic Park, was a brick plaza anchored by the Pacific House Museum and a Maritime Center, with a marina beyond. The Old Fisherman's Wharf looked a little grittier, and was, the t-shirt vendors and galleries aside. Already I saw whole Dungeness crabs, claws up, on shaved ice, smoked salmon on warmers, and bright orange cooked lobster curled and humbled. At the end of the pier, three lazy seals lay in the bow of a small rowboat warming themselves in the sun. This was not the only watercraft these slippery harbor hounds occupied. As I studied the boats moored here, those that didn't have protective netting around them had barking passengers aboard. And what a chorus!

Continuing along a pedestrian path around the harbor, I came to San Carlos Beach where some 100 scuba divers, all in small groups, were gearing up, already exploring the water or returning from dives. Apparently, this was a convenient spot for the activity, as the divers didn't have far to tote their equipment. A certified PADI diver myself, I wished I could join them.

The famed Cannery Row, which Steinbeck wrote about in his 1945 novel of the same name, housed a dozen canneries during World War I that output 1.4 million cases of sardines in 1918 alone. The E.B. Gross and San Carlos Canneries were perhaps the most influential here. Seeing a well-scrubbed woman in a red silk robe sunning on a balcony of the luxurious Monterey Plaza Hotel, it was very clear that this was no longer the place that Steinbeck had described as a collage of "weedy lots and junk heaps… honky tonks…whorehouses…laboratories and flophouses."

Seeing a Hispanic-looking woman paused on the street waiting on a friend, I asked about the location of Ed Ricketts' lab, which I guessed had to be near. An editor for a newspaper Guadalajara, Mexico newspaper, she was visiting like me and equally curious about Monterey. We crossed the street to review a long stretch of murals picturing its history. It explained that the Ohlone, who lived in brush shelters and ate acorns and shellfish, were the first to people its shores. The Spanish followed in the mid-1500s but it wasn't until the 1770s that Monterey started to take shape. From 1880 to 1906, a community of some 70 Chinese fished for and processed squid, abalone and sardines, until their village was suspiciously destroyed by fire. The canneries took hold then, becoming a $10 million a year enterprise by the '30s and '40s.

It was during the height of the cannery era, in 1930, that Ed "Doc" Ricketts opened his Pacific Biological Laboratories here, working in the tide pools collecting marine animal specimens for research. Steinbeck gravitated to him, became his close friend and was greatly saddened by his death in April 1948. Ricketts was tragically killed when a Pacific Railways train broadsided his rickety old car. My curious new friend and I ultimately discovered the marine biologist's lab, a non-distinct, two-story place where the self-taught scientist worked and stored a sea of specimen jars, at the far end of the murals. It had been right there before us all the time.

The folks at the Monterey Bay Aquarium kindly allowed me to see the small exhibit of Ricketts' equipment, the highlight of which was a three-foot high glass cylinder containing a jumbo squid. From there, I climbed up to the 400 block of very steep Eardley Avenue to the home Steinbeck moved to after his separation from Carol and where he and Ricketts recalled their memories for "The Sea of Cortez." When his divorce from Carol was finalized, he married Gwyndolyn Conger and they moved to New York City.

The home's entry was framed with an ivy-covered arbor, the main house was one-level and grey, and there were two small guesthouses at the rear. Hearing a clunk at the back, I found a tenant of one of the cottages, on her patio. She was a transplant from New Jersey who moved out here to start a "cosmic" general store. When she became ill, she sold the shop and moved to the property, unaware initially of the Steinbeck tie.

Thanking her for her hospitality, I walked along Pine and turned toward the water on Grand. Just shy of the rocky shore, I stopped briefly at the home of Tom Fordham, a Steinbeck acquaintance who had maintained an apartment on Cannery Row.

From there, I started working my way back to El Rucio along a high shoreline walk that was absolutely stunning, with the ocean crashing against rock jetties, a lone surfer riding a curl, a large white sailboat seesawing on the horizon and a couple paddling a bright red kayak through a mat of seaweed.

Quite unexpectedly, four ladies, who'd run out of steam peddling their five-person bike, offered me the captain's seat. Accepting their appointment, I commandeered the craft and we zipped off, occasionally finding ourselves in some peril from metal pillars, crossing cars and daydreaming pedestrians. In the end, though, we'd had a great time of it and I'd been able to make a quicker return than on foot.

I had not seen Johnny Garcia's bar, where Steinbeck had a "touching reunion" and drank and sang songs with his old friend Johnny, and suspected that the DoubleTree Hotel at the foot of Alvarado had long ago replaced it. Like Steinbeck, I strolled back up along Calle Principal, parallel to Alvarado, where, again, he saw only strangers, and concluded that Thomas Wolfe's book, "You Can't Go Home Again", rang true.

El Rucio was still where I left her, resting in the shade of a knotty tree that had kept her interior cool, and she bore no tickets or tire boots thankfully. I had tasted Steinbeck country, savored its essence and was now eager to explore the southern coast of the state. My last vision of Monterey was the AAA-rated Steinbeck Lodge, a dubious tribute to the author.

In my flight, I felt I needed to pass through Carmel, a community, in Steinbeck's words, "begun by starveling writers and unwanted painters… now a community of the well-to-do and the retired." He concluded that, "If Carmel's founders should return, they could not afford to live there, but it wouldn't go that far. They would be instantly picked up as suspicious characters and deported over the city line."

On Ocean Boulevard, beside a high fallutin' leather shop, I parked to observe the populace. In the street, they passed in their shiny Benz convertibles, flashy BMWs and zippy Audis. On the sidewalk, they strolled by with their French manicures, spa-tanned skin, and designer label clothing. From behind their $200 sunglasses, while clutching their shopping bags bearing high-end store names, they peered at the spectacle that was my truck. When the gents d'arme circled twice, regarding me with some alarm, I retreated to Route 1, imagining what total chaos would have erupted had I shown up in an *unbathed* El Rucio with her bug mantle and WASH ME billboard!

Later, I had an opportunity to read a copy of *The Carmel Pine Cone*, advertised as "Your source for local news, arts and opinions since 1915." The paper seemed a lot more modest than the town itself appeared and was a great source of fascinating detail. I learned that Carmel got its name courtesy of Spanish explorer Sebastian Vizcaino, its residents officially voted to form a town in 1916 and this year marked the 100th anniversary of the formation of the Carmel Development Company. The latter was established by Frank Powers and J. Franklin Devendorf who spent great sums of money on advertising to attract "brain-workers" — people like schoolteachers, professors, artists and writers, who would appreciate the picturesque scenery. Newcomers camped in tents while building their homes and the community quickly grew, from 30 families in 1903 to 400 regular permanent residents in 1911. The San Francisco earthquake and fire of 1906, which displaced creatives such as George Sterling, Jack London, Mary Austin and Sinclair Lewis, spurred some of this growth. A competitive developer named Santiago Duckworth, whom Powers and Devendorf bought out, built the Hotel Carmelo. The two renamed the hotel the Pine Inn, where Steinbeck met wife Elaine, and moved it from Junipero Street (then Broadway) down Ocean Avenue. In addition to pooling diverse folks, the development duo was praised for not leveling hills and creating roads that curved around trees.

In other stories, high levels of a toxin produced by an abundant organism called pseudo-nitzschia were affecting Monterey Bay. An official warning not to eat anchovies, sardines or bivalves had been issued but there was no protection for the chief victims of the poison, marine mammals like sea lions and squid that feed on the organisms.

An 8-year-old Greyhound racer named Blue Pelikan, abandoned after it broke its leg on the job, had found a home with a young family in Carmel-by-the-Sea. Formerly kept in a crate and only taken out to exercise or race, Blue was now enjoying her new loving environment.

Six Carmel High School students had gotten into a tussle with a 65-year-old Australian tourist while filming their own version of "Jackass: The Movie." After making fun of the man's name — he was wearing an I.D. tag — one of the students punched him in the head.

Carmel was on the verge of celebrating its incorporation, as it does annually, with a Halloween parade, barbecue, horse-drawn Wells Fargo stagecoach, costumed dogs, dignitaries, stiltwalkers, jugglers and strolling musicians. At a schoolhouse-turned-theater called the Sunset Center, a time capsule reflecting the year's events and trends would be sealed, before being secretly buried within the community.

Finally, I was amused by a real estate listing for the area that spoke to Steinbeck's complaint: "Conveniently located, with fabulous views of Pt. Lobos, Carmel Mission, and the blue Pacific, and bordered by a greenbelt, this stunning remodeled home is basically new from the ground up! Four bedrooms, three baths plus an adorable guest house, set on a meticulously maintained 4/10th acre parcel," priced to move at $3.9 million!

Though it was not part of Steinbeck's circuit, L.A. was a stop I had hoped to make during my travels. But when I learned that my wife and boys would be arriving in Houston on the 23rd, leaving just four days for me to travel to that rendezvous point, I struck the city of smog from my agenda.

The shore grew more and more dramatic as I moved south, with large, green sloping hills sliding down to a rugged base and wild, churning turquoise surf. Connecting each shoreline peak were bridges with cornerstones dating them to the 1930s, likely built under F.D.R.'s tenure. Where it was flat, cows grazed on scrubby lands, a sight I'd missed from Midwestern passes.

The flats gave way to hills again and a Visitor's Center. "I heard that Big Sur had the best beaches up here. Which one do you recommend?" I asked the ranger there. "The closest is Pfeiffer Beach," he said, passing off a map. It was practically right across the road.

It seemed that the greatest beach spots in Northern California were those hardest to get to as I started down a winding road only a car-width wide, with turnouts every so often to allow passing. This two-mile offshoot brought me to a tollhouse where five bills opened the gate to a semi-secluded wonderland. Here, some two-dozen people watched unswimmable mountainous waves wallop the kelp-strewn beach. Spreading my towel out, I went on walkabout.

There wasn't much to scavenge given the violence of the surf, but a pathway weaving up a wildflower-blanketed cliff, where a pair of couples had trod, looked inviting. As my flat, smooth-bottomed sandals were not ideal climbing shoes, I carefully stepped from boulder to boulder. Halfway up, I met a couple that had been taking photos in various spots along the way. As she posed for him, a wave snuck up from behind and drenched her. Though she'd nearly been swept from her perch, she laughed it off and pulled strands of her wet hair from her face.

Continuing up the peak, I encountered another couple sliding down from a high perch, and replaced them in their mountaintop aerie. It was a great overlook but a little precarious and the gravel underneath me was loose. Coming down was an adventure and I thought I'd go tumbling into the void, but hit sand safely, scooped up my towel and started back for the parking lot.

Nearing the couple who'd been snapping photos on the cliff, I stopped to visit with them and their Dogue de Bordeaux "Hooch" dog, which shook its head periodically sending spittle flying through the air.

We looked on as another beachgoer took a long strand of kelp in hand and snapped it like a bullwhip. On his third snap, he caught himself in the hindquarters and showed all that were looking on, his swollen left buttock. We roared in hysterics.

With no real plan for the evening, we three decided to camp and combine resources, much like I had with trail pal Myra at Crater Lake. Following them out of the beach area, we visited a gas station for fuel and both dinner and breakfast supplies. At their campground, I checked in at the gate and pulled up beside their pickup. Space was tight but not so cramped that I couldn't set up my most magnificent RoadTrip grill to facilitate our meal for the evening: Diced Louisiana Hot Links sautéed with onions, tossed over angel hair pasta with tomato sauce.

Accompanied by Steelhead beers, it was a satisfying chow and followed by mulatto S'Mores and "V" orange vodka that buried us like an avalanche. We polished off a bottle of Tequila Rose, too, which tasted like Pepto Bismol and went down fast. Firestone Double Barrel Ales from Paso Robles, CA, rounded out the bar counter.

As you might imagine, we were in good spirits and speaking loudly, so loud that we attracted the attention of a camp supervisor who came up the road to chastise us. The policy was no noise after 10 p.m. and she had come to enforce it. Being hushed to a whisper took the wind out of our sails, but by then, our sleeping bags were calling us anyway. As headlamp-wearing campers at the site adjacent to ours turned in, so did we, for a very sound night's sleep.

Day 44: The Castle on the Coast

The passing footsteps of one of the headlampers at first light was my morning knell. Dropping out the back of the van, I crossed the compound to the restroom, finding homey, tiled shower stalls. The warm water brought me around and rinsed away the film of wood smoke that had settled on my skin and in my hair from the previous night's campfire. In my vodka and tequila induced haze, I'd forgotten to carry a towel, or new set of clothes, with me, so used my shirt and walked bare-chested back to the van.

My campmates were still sacked in their six-man tent so I went about cleaning away last night's debris — empty liquor bottles, big splotches of cherry vanilla ice cream and salsa drippings. All that was soon replaced with breakfast settings as I whipped up a frothy egg mix, fried up smoked bacon strips and, in the grease of the latter, sautéed onion, mushroom and ham slivers. Hot cocoa was bubbling on the side, too, as my new friends emerged sleepy-eyed from their cocoon.

Over a meal that settled nicely in the pits of our stomachs, we decided we'd stay together to travel to William Randolph Hearst's castle by the sea at San Simeon, some 60 miles to the south. We consulted a map and brochures to make our day plan.

We shot a short way down 1 to a site that I had spotted the day before, the Henry Miller Memorial Library. Though it was not yet open, its director came out and unlocked the gate. I went in solo, immediately fascinated by what I found inside.

A plaque noted that Miller, the playwright and author of such books as "The Tropic of Cancer," lived from 1891 to 1980, spending many years in Paris in the '30s before moving to the Big Sur area in 1944. A month after his arrival, his Paris friend, painter Emil White, moved here as well and this museum site was one of his homes. A handwritten note by Miller further explained the attraction and provided a good summary of Big Sur living: "Life along the South Coast is just a bed of roses, with a few thorns and nettles interspersed."

Jumbled metal sculptures were erected nearby and a huge, human-sized cocoon hung from a tree. Across from it, 13 computer monitors had been vertically arranged into the shape of a cross. Around a courtyard, where tables had been set up to accommodate a wedding that had been held the previous night, were several terra cotta nudes. One had been textured using chicken wire and other imprinting tools and had coiled snail shells for nipples.

Invitations, song sheets and even drawings, which guests had sketched, still lay on the tables. The traditional Irish song, "Red Is the Rose," had accompanied the processional while Pete Townshend's "Let My Love Open the Door" served as the recessional, according to a program.

Feeling honored to be privy to the seeds of the start of this couple's life together, I moved toward the library itself. To the left of the entry, there was a display case containing foot-high "Wooden Wise Men" carved for Emil by Hiro Shirai. Inside the building, there were books by Nin, Burroughs, Kerouac, Salinger and, notably, Steinbeck; a collection of paintings by Emil; and photography books with erotically posed or leather and black vinyl accessorized nudes.

As remembrances of the area, I bought a volume of Miller's work and overview of Big Sur. With these, I included a postcard showing the bare bottom of a woman, beside which Emil's face was pressed. It had so offended a past visitor that she sent a letter saying so and declared that she would not be returning. The letter, with the postcard displayed beneath it, were framed and shown on one wall, a symbolic thumbing of propriety.

I had dallied and had catching up to do, so raced along the looping cliffside byway. Every bend brought another unforgettable view of sheer drop-offs, roiling ocean, exotic plant life and the occasional seal. When I caught up with my camp companions at a pullout, we really stepped on it, gunning for the Hearst home where they had tickets for a 1 p.m. tour. With a Park Aid's assistance, I was able to join them and, soon, we were aboard a bus parting the browned 123-acre ranch.

At the front steps of Hearst's Pacific palace, a guide spelled out the numerous rules about how we were to conduct ourselves on the tour, which seemed to extend even to the tempo of our breathing, then away we went. Designed for Hearst by San Francisco architect Julia Morgan, the property was spectacular. A first terrace held a deep, clear "Neptune" pool guarded by white, Acropolis-like columns and a dark statue of a shoeless Nike. In Casa del Sol, the 18-room guesthouse, we noticed how abbreviated a bed was, the porcelain and brass accents, and the intricately carved and ornate ceilings. Another terrace gave a fantastic look out at San Simeon Bay, offered fish a refuge in a small stone pool and featured a cathedral-like mountain of a home called Casa Grande. Inside, there was an enormous sitting room full of tapestries and artwork, a dining room divided lengthwise by two tables 50-feet long placed end to end, a cozy morning room that would witness a day's start and billiards room with 300-year-old Persian mosaic tiles embedded in the walls.

A movie theater that rivaled modern commercial cinemas, red and gilded and chandeliered, was a brief stop before exiting into the mid-afternoon sunlight. Below were cement tennis courts and, beyond, the Santa Lucia mountain range and gray peak of Mount Junipero Serra, named after the founder of the Mission chain. The latter was 38 miles off and marked the border of the entire Hearst land holding.

Our last stop was at an indoor pool area constructed over a three-year period with thousands of blue and real gold tiles. Actor Cary Grant, an occasional Hearst guest, once commented, "This is the most romantic spa in the world."

A short bus ride returned us to the Visitor's Center, built for a sum of $8 million, twice what it cost to build Hearst Castle back in the '20s, for a brief film shown on a floor-to-ceiling giant screen. Through the presentation, we discovered that the Hearst fortune began with 38 tons of silver that patriarch George had mined in California, the windfall from which he used to buy cattle and the land here. When William came into his own through his newspaper and publishing empire, he built his dream home from mental pictures of great castles, estate homes and artwork he'd seen as a boy traveling through Italy, Spain, Germany and England. Toward the end of his life, as his health failed, Hearst relocated on doctor's advice to a home in Beverly Hills, where he ultimately died at the age of 88. His will gave a mistress controlling interest of the Hearst Corporation, though she signed it back to the family for just $1.

At the film's conclusion, I exchanged goodbyes with my traveling companions and went to commune with elephant seals I'd seen laying in the sun just a few miles north. Hunted nearly to extinction for their oil-rich blubber, they now enjoyed the protection of marine mammal laws and come ashore just a few months out of the year to give birth, breed and molt. Studying them as they snorted and flipped sand across their smooth, black bodies, some belly up, others belly down, I thought how perfectly delightful it would be to be a seal.

Following a quick loop by the San Simeon Mission, I stopped once more at Hearst State Park, a beach across from the castle entrance. Seeing tree treasures on the ground, I snatched up a small Ziploc and set off along the sand collecting unusual specimens. I felt like Ed Ricketts for a moment and was quite proud of the trove that resulted from my efforts.

It was time again to travel on, to make my momentous turn east now, leaving a trail of vodka, Haagen Daz and seals for dry moguls, desert and dogies.

PART SIX

Banking east

The rolling brown hills with their patchy toupees of green trees were a beautiful sight from which to retreat. Steinbeck's last memorable image of California was from Fremont's Peak in his native Salinas. The crow's nest overlooked "the whole of [his] childhood and youth, the great Salinas Valley stretching south for nearly one hundred miles." He recalled his Uncle Charley, his trusty companion's namesake, and how he'd fished for trout with him, and the place where his mother shot a wildcat. In another direction was the family ranch, the dark canyon with the "clear and lovely stream" and the oak onto which his father had burned with a hot iron his name and that of the girl he loved.

Looking ahead in his travels, Steinbeck realized that he could not see everything he'd hoped to, that his mind was getting muddled with his impressions and that he could no longer keep them all straight. So he resolved to focus on just two more sections of the country: Texas and the deep South. I wanted to see these areas, too, and more.

As I came through the pass, with ranches on one side and dense vineyards on the other, the sun set and night curled around me like a blanket. In up-and-coming Paso Robles, I fueled and decided on my destination for the evening: Bakersfield. Steinbeck had pursued this very route, one he knew from the '30s, through Fresno and my target city, to the Mojave Desert.

With the inland areas came a return of the bugs. I could see them in my headlights and then they were mash in my grill and across my windshield. Collecting them at a rate of ten a minute, I imagined that I might need a spackleknife to scrape them off. They were hitting with such velocity and finality that I expected to see small indentations all across the van façade.

On this long, straight flat road, I tuned in Game #2 of the World Series, starring the Yankees and Marlins, on ESPN radio. At the end of seven, it was New York on top 6-0! I was glad to hear it, particularly after learning they'd lost Game #1.

Feeling a hunger coming on, I dropped anchor at the Village Market in Lost Hills. At this bodega that saw mostly Spanish-speaking traffic, I was a curious sight, a gringo in a crazy van with Connecticut plates. But it was the ideal purveyor of burrito fixings, Tecate and limes. I was happy to have made this fortuitous seventh inning stretch.

When I resumed listening to the game, New York pitcher Andy Pettitte was on target for his first scoreless World Series win, when an error led to a blooper that resulted in a run and Andy's removal. Soriano came in and saved the game, securing a 6-1 win. Switching over to an FM station afterwards, I heard a line in a song called "Bright Lights" that seemed very appropriate given my return journey: "Turn yourself around and come on home."

As my eastern route merged into 99 south to Bakersfield, I fell in behind a line of souped-up, customized street-racing cars whose drivers looked like they were seeking a place to drag. Suddenly, I began smelling a bad odor. Was it wet cow? Urine? I couldn't put my finger on it but was glad I wasn't having dinner by my dashboard light this evening.

Arriving in "B" town, I spotted a 7-Eleven, one of over 25,000 that now exist in the world, and stopped in to get the inside scoop on Sunday night activities. From a guy reading about the very low-riders, or "rice rockets" as he called them, that I'd seen moving south, I got a tip to go to Chester Ave. off Rosedale Highway. Lining the wide avenue were scores of Bail Bondsman outlets and I thought that, if I ever needed one, I'd know where to come. One called "Buzzy's" sounded particularly reputable!

Looking for a good watering hole on 19th Avenue, I found the venues oddly disparate and not hooking me. I faded back into the darkness headed east to Mojave, making it as far as Tehachapi before having to stop. There was a parking lot spot between a truck cab and U-Haul at a chain hotel that was just big enough for El Rucio and that became my evening campsite.

Day 45: Desert Passages

Repeated attempts to get a motor to turn over was the sound that stirred me come morning. The battery of the truck beside me had gone dead and the driver went seeking assistance from another trucker. Before the commotion that was sure to follow began, I pulled away and to a Texaco station up the block.

There, I spent the next couple of hours fueling, washing up, having a juice and apple breakfast, seeing to paperwork and writing, as the sun came up and made things sticky. My morning tasks also included a read of *The Bakersfield Californian* that led with a story about the birth of quintuplets to a Bakersfield couple. A team of more than 25 doctors and nurses assisted in delivering the five, the heaviest of which was 3 pounds, 6 ounces. The event proved the declaration the Riley's patron had made about the town being an area conducive to family making and raising.

In the course of events, I contacted Vern Alexander at Avtel Services whom I'd spoken with in the summer after reading a *Times* article about his company. It was the accompanying photograph, though, that really captured my interest, an aerial shot of hundreds of commercial passenger jets in neat rows on the tarmac at Avtel's Mojave facility.

When the major airlines don't have the customer demand to warrant having their planes docked in expensive spaces at airports, they store them with Avtel, which ensures their proper maintenance and upkeep. I was very keen to get a tour of this aircraft depository and Vern, a fan of "Travels…" was eager to host me. In fact, he related to me how, in the '60s, he bought a Volksbus camper for family travel and sought Steinbeck's permission to call it "Rocinante II." Steinbeck sent him back a handwritten note, signed by him and Elaine, granting it.

My quick eastward route was splashed with pockets of cypress trees; more brown hills topped with dozens of three-blade, energy-making, steel windmills; and jagged rock outcroppings. Quite by surprise, I spied an old cabin cruiser marked "S.S. Minnow" permanently moored in the brambles on the far side of the highway.

Mojave, a left-back oasis in flat scrubland bordered by blue mountain outlines, came up. A sign on the side of an old jet aircraft parked near the entry gate denoted its airport. Further ahead, the metal bones of various aircraft lay in jumbled, mass grave heaps. Thinking that Avtel was located at Edwards Air Force base on Mojave's far side, I rolled through, pausing near a grove of undisciplined Joshua trees to inspect the curiosities. Birds nested in their branches and dined on resident insects. Fallen limbs sheltered yucca night lizards and termites. Stilt-legged stinkbugs munched on their fibers and reared up at my approach, emitting a pungent odor.

The proud gatherer of samples of fauna and Joshua boughs, I noticed wavy markings in the tan-colored dirt as I stepped back to the van. They were likely made by a sidewinder and though I knew the snake to be nocturnal, I trod nimbly and avoided sizeable holes in the dry earth.

Sighting the base, I bobbed and weaved to the North Gate through an obstacle course of barriers and sharp spikes guarded by M-16 toting soldiers in fatigues. The lead guard didn't recognize the names I spouted, directed me to the side and had me call Vern for gate entry authorization. Avtel, it turned out, was back at Mojave Airport!

It was high noon and hot and dry when I made the u-turn, and the Joshua trees and jet graveyard were a blur as I raced back past them, to the airport entrance. A few rights and lefts and a pass through a security gate and I was in the Avtel compound. Unfortunately, Vern had gotten tied up with family business, so I was steered to a supervisor.

I learned that Avtel maintenance folks perform such tasks as tire rotation, engine start-up, system checks and venting (done April to October when the temperature inside the aircraft can reach 115 to 180 degrees). I imagined that, because of the high desert temperatures that this would be a harsh climate for aircraft storage, but the dryness and very low humidity is actually ideal.

The number of planes on the site had dramatically declined since 9/11 and Avtel's role had transitioned from heavy plane maintenance to sales and storage. Started in 1947, the airport itself was established for Marine Corps use then converted to public purposes. Bob Laidlaw started a business here called Flight Systems, building drone aircraft. It evolved into Tracor Flight Systems and Avtel, the latter established in 1990 as a FAA-licensed aviation repair station. From time to time, Hollywood film companies, including production teams for "Waterworld," "Speed" and the TV series "Pretender," have occupied the building. Most recently, an episode for the TV reality show, "Fear Factor," was filmed here.

The facility had also enjoyed celebrity clients such as "very approachable" actor John Travolta, a licensed pilot who brought his Boeing 707 here for maintenance. We recalled Travolta's New Year's Eve 2000 exploits wherein he flew from time zone to time zone to mark the new millenium over and over in different parts of the world.

Ultimately, I was guided outside into the 90-plus degree air to tour the complex. The first airplanes we looked at closely were inside a hangar. On one side was a DeHavilland Dash-7 surveillance plane, complete with infrared equipment and missile avoidance systems on board, being serviced for the air force. On the other side, a 757 was undergoing a "heavy check" and being patched in preparation to be painted a flat white. From the hangar, we made a small circle around the tarmac to see other planes being serviced, studying a CF-6 turbine engine and standing in the wheel well of a DC-10.

Hopping in a pickup, we rolled past row upon row of idled passenger jets. Looking over at them, I noticed their windows and various openings were taped over with plastic, which was done to protect these areas from sand abrasion. Down another road, I spied fighter jets, a drone, and research and development buildings.

When I spotted a hawk flying overhead looking for a target, Rich said that that was the least of the critters they have to contend with out here. Snakes, called Mojave Greens, which curl up in airplane wheels, scorpions, coyotes, owls and something called a vinegaroon, also present hazards. Weather can have adverse effects, too — high winds have actually tipped aircraft over and heavy rains have pooled around airplanes and caused some to sink into the ground.

At the back of the lot, where old, disused airplanes meet their maker, an orange, tractor-like machine referred to as a "muncher" was tearing apart a fuselage with a large metal claw, dropping scraps in a blue dumpster for recycling. Pilots, who have a special relationship with their aircraft, don't like to go back there as the sight brings them to tears.

With lizards fleeing in our path, we returned to the main building and I got rolling again. By 3, I was gunning through the desert, blistering hot like El Rucio's insides were when I rejoined her. Atop flatbed trucks traveling in both directions, tan-colored tanks were being carried to undetermined military locations.

I thought about the cowboys of the Old West and their crossings of these arid plains, imagining how dust must have gotten into all exposed cavities, the sun heating their leather saddles and boots, their parched throats and all those endless miles. I could understand their hunger for the simple things a civilized destination might offer: a stiff drink of good bourbon, a thick cut of beef, a good soak in a tub, a clean shave, and a soft mattress to throw down on.

Barstow connected me to I-15 North and marked a juncture with historic old Route 66, "The Mother Road" as Steinbeck dubbed it in the "Grapes of Wrath" — 2,448 miles long from L.A. to Chicago. Initiated by the U.S. government in 1925 and the first paved road of such length, it was largely replaced by more modern highways in the '70s.

As I continued, billboards for Vegas attractions like "Mr. Las Vegas" Wayne Newton, Little Darlings Gentleman's Club, Stardust Casino and the Sahara Hotel briefly flew at me, though the desert pearl was still a long way off. Seemingly antiquated Rock-a-Hoola Waterpark & Resort was a momentary curiosity, the sighting of which timed with the employment of my on-board air conditioner. The hills to either side rose up on their craggy haunches and let their grooved faces be seen. Broken rocks at their base were like crumbs tumbled down their stubbled chins. Sadly, trash lay strewn everywhere, tossed from car windows by thoughtless motorists. Amusement soon took disgust's place, however, at the sighting of the uniquely named Zzyzx Road.

At Baker, I'd hit the far edge of the Mojave Desert and Vegas lay 90 miles off. There was an incline here and El Rucio's horses kicked in to meet the challenge. We climbed to 2,000 feet, 3,000 feet, 4,000 feet. Finally, we reached the crest, at 4,730 feet, where whole groves of Joshua trees stretched out, looking fantastical like something from Dr. Seuss.

I had most certainly taken the high road, wanting to see Vegas at night, while Steinbeck took the lower below the desert, to Needles. He described the Mojave as "a big desert and a frightening one" with "shimmering dry heat [that] made visions of water on the flat plain." For Charley's part, he "panted asthmatically...a good eight inches of his tongue hung out flat as a leaf and dripping." Steinbeck refreshed him with water and himself with beer, at a gulley pull-off where he spied two coyotes. He took out his new .222 and was going to pick the "vermin" off, but could not and even left some dog food "as a votive."

The tops of the appropriately named Shadow Mountains glowed red and pink as the sun sat upon them. Soon the dark would engulf all and a chill would settle in, setting the stage for the dance of the night creatures. Ahead, the waystation known as Primm looked like an amusement park and, in fact, contained one: Buffalo Bill's. Its neighbor across the road, Whiskey Pete's Casino, hungered for the contents of wallets, purses and pockets. It was the portal to Nevada, the 21st state on my voyage.

Lighting up the horizon at dusk was the garish Gold Strike Hotel & Gambling Hall followed by the equally outlandish Nevada Landing, which resembled a Mississippi Riverboat. As the sky turned to pastels of blue and pink and the night crept in, I peered ahead for the eyeful that I imagined "Sin City" would be. Over a rise, the twinkling lights burst into view like shards of glass on the straight black road.

Las Vegas Boulevard, "The Strip," was like a runway waiting for the arrival of Liberace's diamond-studded plane. Thomas Edison, I mused, would have been dazzled by the extensive and creative use of lighting. When the "Welcome to Fabulous Las Vegas" sign came up, a photo stop was mandatory. More billboards and sights fast-rushed past: Wild Wild West Rooms $19, Tony Roma's at the Stardust, Tilted Kilt Bar, Jubilee at Bally's, Righteous Brothers at The Orleans, and the massive pyramid and King Tut that was the Luxor Hotel. Traffic slowed way down as we motorists tried to absorb everything.

Spying the classic Tropicana Hotel, one of the first on The Strip, I decided it was a must-stay and wheeled up into a self-park spot. Almost blinded by the spectacle that was the casino — whistling, clanking, flashing and chunking out quarters — I signed on for a room in the Paradise Tower. Dodging croupiers, fattened tourists, showgirls atop platforms, change makers and cocktail waitresses, I found the room, took a World Speed Record shower, dressed neatly and darted to the Tiffany Showroom for the world renowned Les Folies Bergere. A few minutes late, I was led to my stage-side seat for the colorful spectacular already in progress.

The platform was a blur of boas, bare buttocks and loosely secured boobs and the show a reflection on dance through the years, beginning in the mid-1850s in Paris. Fantastic period costumes, acrobatics, the skirts-up can-can, tumbling and cartwheels were ordered up. The Roaring '20s, with its shimmery flappers, sultry, predatory vamps, elegant dames, top hat and tailed men and pronounced tangos, followed. A number that opened with the girls laying on their backs waving bright pink flamingo feathers while revolving on a platform and reflected in a mirror above signaled the transition to the '30s. The Rosie the Riveter era was boogie-woogie doodle boyed in polka dots, costume pearls and sailor outfits, bright Wurlitzer jukeboxes forming a backdrop. Hep cats, daddio shades, a burlesque number done with clever neon lighting and a mag-wheeled Chevy ushered in the '50s. Then hippy beads, bellbottoms, Afros and peace signs gave way to hyper-caffeinated Wally Eastwood, an unbelievable juggler of clubs, rubber balls and ping-pong balls.

"It gets better...but not much," Wally kidded at one point, juggling hats. "I know. I've seen it. Two shows a night, six nights a week, every day of the year. I got issues. Truth is, I hate hats. If you want to applaud, go ahead. If not, that's O.K., too."

A five-foot nothing self-described "Redneck Mexican," Wally was certainly a showman, a master vaudevillian. He had us hook, line and sinker. He was Ricky Ricardo on speed. "Never swallow one," Wally cautioned about the ping-pong balls. "It hurts, twice."

One of his final acts was playing notes on a small piano with rubber balls. "Don't laugh, you paid $60 for a ticket, $100 for a hotel room, to watch some Mexican guy play the piano with his balls. Priceless."

The dancers returned to illustrate the modern era, which rocked with a flash of bulbs, hoodies, hip hop, girls on velvet-cushioned swings jettisoned over the audience, and a whole lot of attitude.

We filed back into the casino to see more show activities atop a slots-lined stage. A couple in sea blue leotards performed amazingly agile, gravity-defying acrobatics, followed by Tina Turner-esque singers and two bare-chested beefcakes swinging off a harness. Vegas didn't get the "Entertainment Capitol of the World" crown for second-rate show biz.

Looking hard for a restaurant and thinking about clubs and hot tubs and the multitude of experiences I could have in this city of lights, I stumbled across Mizuno's Japanese Steak House, and pulled up a seat at a cooking station. Miso soup and salad with ginger dressing came my way along with a Kirin Ichiban 21-ounce beer. Then a humorous chef stepped up and began juggling, tossing, flicking and rolling vegetables, meat, rice, seafood and eggs. I tackled my fare, washed it down and finished it off with green tea ice cream.

I hopped a tram to the Mandalay Bay, to check out the scene there. Folks whooped and cheered at a craps table. Another cluster of well-groomed individuals waited in a long line to pay a $30 cover for a rooftop aerie. Then I was sucked into the vortex that was Rum Jungle, a pulsating tropical environment with underdressed women of paradise gyrating in cages on high or performing aerial maneuvers on a swing above the bar. Drinks were at premium prices but the beats and eye treats made for a fair monetary trade. I sat below one of these caged beauties as she swiveled back and forth, her long curly locks flipping around wildly and her pouty mouth grinning demonically. You might say this jungle had a fever, a sweaty, restless condition from which one might not easily recover.

Prowling through the undergrowth, I realized the driving drumbeats were live, provided by two guys in sleeveless black tees mounted in towering, striped, larger-than-life bongos. Behind a large plate of glass down the side of which water flowed, a dancer's gyrating profile was silhouetted in varying gel lights. More people, eager looks on their faces, a party spirit in their hearts and mischief in their minds, flowed in. The place was way over the top and frothing down the sides. It was threatening to combust.

Before it did, I hopped out of the pot, rode the tram back to Luxor and crossed over to and made my way to my room, eyeing framed historical photos on the walls. I saw the Trop in 1957. The "Rat Pack" at the Sands in 1960. Bugsy Siegel's desert dream, "The Flamingo," opening in December 1946. The puff of an above ground atomic blast beyond Las Vegas' downtown in late 1951. And all the Trop stars: Eddie Fisher, Pearl Bailey, Ann Margaret, the Osmonds, Louis Prima, Jack Benny and Mitzi Gaynor.

To satisfy my hot tub longing, I drew a bath and sprinkled in the package of salts I'd been given at the Farmer's Market in Seattle. The steamy soak made me sleepy and soon I was enjoying slumber, a last balcony look at the Disneyland castle-like Excalibur hotel and recreated spires of the Empire State and Chrysler buildings at New York New York Hotel my lingering mental images.

Day 46: Making Tracks Through Arizona

I had sites to see outside Las Vegas, and Arizona and New Mexico to breach yet, so gradually pulled myself together, answered e-mails and made phone calls. One was to another Mike Lauterborn, the managing editor of Adventure Southwest Publishing Company right here in town. I'd found a photo of him on the Internet wearing a swamp hat and holding a very large Swing-Lock muzzle-loading rifle and learned that he evaluates products for many gun industry manufacturers and retailers. He was also an international shooting champion and I thought we might meet up at a gun range. Unfortunately, he wasn't around.

Before pushing off, I took a moment to reflect on what I knew about Vegas. I thought about the trained white tiger that, back in early October, attacked magician Roy Horn of the duo Siegfried & Roy during a performance at The Mirage. It bit his neck and dragged him off stage "like a rag doll" as an audience member described it, and sent Horn to the hospital for surgery to the neck area. I recalled the amendment of a state law back in late September lowering the legal blood alcohol limit from .10 to .08, falling in step with 44 other states. I mused about how Nevada's Governor Kenny Guinn signed into law a new 10 percent tax on brothels and a photo I'd seen of an "entertainer" known as Air Force Amy at the Bunny Ranch on the outskirts of Carson City. About the gambling industry, I'd read that nearly 135,000 slot machines and over 4,300 gaming tables were located here.

As I loaded El Rucio, tropical birds called to one another in trees near me, whirring propellers droned at nearby McCurran International Airport and a sightseeing helicopter flew by overhead. The Strip was just getting up, rubbing its sleepy eyes and looked even more Disneyesque by day. Rolling out of town, I looked at all the fantastic sites around me. There was the MGM Grand with its giant gold lion and big screen TV out front. The Statue of Liberty's twin stood tall at New York New York. The roller coaster at the Boardwalk Casino awaited passengers. A big yellow M&M character stood waving to passing traffic at GameWorks. The front of a large motorcycle protruded from the façade of the Harley Davidson Café. A very authentic reproduction of the Eiffel Tower guarded Paris Las Vegas. Bellagio and Caesars Palace projected a stately image while Gladys Knight was booked for shows at Conrad's steakhouse. Atop Harrah's, jesters trumpeted as gondolas bobbed in the canals at the Venetian. Full-size pirate ships at Treasure Island waited for tourists to board, while cranes worked to put up a new, massive Steve Wynn property. On Vegas' northern edge, older structures like the Frontier, Stardust, Silver City, Circus Circus, the Sahara and the famous Wedding Chapel held fast.

Everything about this city was big, loud and bright, demanding to be seen and heard, and all with a deal to whisper in your ear. I was deaf to it by this point and bucking to gallop out of town. "Viva Las Vegas!" I shouted, leaving colorful poker chips in my dust.

Working my way southeast, I paused on the far side of Boulder City to take in a view of sky blue Lake Mead and Spanish-style, terra cotta-roofed homes in the foreground. On a hill beside the Hacienda Hotel, a helicopter, its rotors whirling, readied itself to take area visitors for a Hoover Dam flyover.

Passing by a guarded checkpoint and clusters of substations and electrical towers, I followed a steep winding road down to the massive concrete Dam itself. It was an impressive structure, with clock towers at either end. From a brochure my brother had shared, I read that it stands 726 feet high, is 1,244 feet long at the crest and was built using 3.25 million cubic yards of concrete. Begun in 1931, it was officially dedicated by President Roosevelt on September 30, 1935. Power plant extensions were completed the following year.

Spanning the Colorado River in Black Canyon, it was also the gateway to my 22nd state, Arizona, "the Grand Canyon State." On the opposite bank, I rested El Rucio a moment to observe the scene and a memorial marker to "The Mojave County Miner" publisher Anson Smith, to whom President Herbert Hoover gave credit for smartly suggesting the dam be located here.

With this passage, I was also definitively in the Southwest, which Steinbeck described as "a great and mysterious wasteland...deserted, free of parasitic man." A place of mysteries, of "stories told and retold of secret places...where surviving clans from an older era wait to re-emerge." A place of "true secrets."

The hills above and beyond the Dam were bunched up, with "V" shapes blasted through them to make way for roads. And it was hot, no two ways about it. As I descended to Kingman to rejoin Steinbeck's route, there wasn't a shadow to be had. Fortunately, there were water purveyors and I promptly stopped to get a bottle at, of all things, a mid-desert zoo.

If boxing promoter Don King had blond hair, it would look just like the unruly tufts of grass all along the roadside. Scanning for cactus, I spotted clumps of heart-shaped specimens and stopped to slice off an ear, placing it in a Ziploc along with yellow wildflowers and varying rock samples. I was never sure if buzzards really circled or whether it was cartoon myth until I saw three of the large winged scavengers patrolling over a carcass in the distance.

Running on fumes, I coasted into Kingman and El Rucio drank like a thirsty horse until she'd bled the trough dry. Down the road, I quelled my own appetite, for bric-a-brac, at Turquoise Traders. I came away with a few items including a howling wolf on a flat metal stand that had been painted with a turquoise derivative and a postcard showing the path of the Old Route 66 through the Southwest. Its join was here in Kingman so I decided to "get some kicks," taking the loop up and over to Seligman.

All along were located the old hotels, motels and other sites that had been bypassed by the new interstate. These included the Lido Motel, Abe's, the Skyline with kitchenettes, The Hackberry General Store and Bert's Country Dancing, and they were now capitalizing on the rediscovery of the historic drive. Burros and horses appeared every so often.

The rock here was so constantly sun-baked that it had cracked and crumbled to the extent that all that was left was mountainous piles of boulders. Noticing a good photo opp, I pulled over and backed up on the shoulder. Disturbingly, El Rucio sputtered to a stall. I may have been driving her too hard in this heat, so sat a spell for her to recover. When she sparked back to life, I stroked her dash in thanks, promising I'd be gentler on her. Cruising more evenly, I entered the Hualapai Indian Reservation and rolled past their high school, called Music Mountain. All the faces that passed me now were broad and brown.

El Rucio spoke to me again, winked "CHECK ENGINE," then coughed and slowed and came to a dead stop. She did not want to get up and go this time, so I popped the hood. Suspecting she needed a shot of oil, I thumbed a ride in the back of an Indian family's pickup to the nearest gas station. Luckily, a tribal patrol truck was filling up and the officers gave me a lift back. We looked over the engine together and didn't see a problem other than the obvious oil leakage. In fact, she only seemed to need a quart. As I continued on, she remained sluggish and temperamental and, suddenly, I felt that all my plans for the days ahead were in jeopardy. Perhaps if I could make it to Flagstaff, less than 90 miles away, and pit in for service first thing tomorrow, I'd get through.

Reaching Williams, I made a Denny's stop. It wasn't my preferred choice of eateries, being part of a chain instead of a one-off, but the hostess had a friendly face and offered a pot of strong coffee and a Swiss mushroom burger and fries. While I noshed, I eyed a weekly newspaper, *Grand Canyon News*. Mule rides, I noted, had been halted for the winter on certain trails in the Canyons due to safety concerns after a woman died from exhaustion this summer. A blaze on the North Rim covered 7,898 acres. Search-and-rescue personnel evacuated from Boucher Creek two men and a woman who were suffering from dehydration. A cartoon showed how to identify a West Nile Virus-affected mosquito: the affected one was striking an ancient Egyptian pose and sporting a related hairstyle.

With a whispered prayer for luck, I nudged El Rucio and she purred back to life, her earlier troubles seemingly gone, and into the night and elk territory we rolled. Soon, Flagstaff stood up to welcome us and I steered to a Walgreen's for toiletries. Chiefly, I sought hydrocortisone as I'd managed to contract an itchy rash on my legs that was beginning to get distracting. How I'd picked it up, I couldn't fathom. Nettles? Ragweed? Some other abrasive plant? Sheri the pharmacist suspected chiggers and set me up with what I needed.

Familiar with Flagstaff from a business-oriented stay here back in the spring, I went directly to the Beaver Street bar area. There, I settled in at a place I'd remembered as cozy with good beats. Sitting at the bar, I scribbled in a notebook, spurring a guy beside me to ask if I was making out a grocery list. Nearby, two women began wrestling each other, sending a chair toppling and a bouncer running over. Karaoke performers took turns belting out songs, which I evaluated in my head. And as people played trivia challenges on a TV monitor, I guessed at the answers.

Needing a room and a meal, I signed up for a $15 shared dorm at a hostel called DuBeau, hauled my cooler into one of two kitchens and began preparing much-anticipated beef burritos. Other hostel guests came sniffing around including a warm Vietnamese girl from Australia who had been traveling the world for the past 15 months.

I reported to my room to shower and slather myself in hydrocortisone, taking care not to awaken my three other bunking roommates.

Day 47: Arizona to Texas

It was 4 a.m. when I woke, itching madly in my bunk bed. If it was chiggers that had bitten me, had they made a home in my wool blanket? It had been the only cloth item to leave the van during any camp stay, most recently at Big Sur. I swiftly went into action to nip this event in the bud, taking yet another shower, applying more cream, then collecting up into a pile in the rear of the van all worn clothing and used sheets, towels, blankets and comforters. Dropping my room key in the hostel's mailbox, I set out looking for a 24-hour laundromat. Up and then down a main drag I traveled, with no success, and I thought I'd just return to and wait for the hostel's own laundry machines to open up for the day.

On South Milton, I drifted into a turn lane looking for a back way to the hostel and, not finding one, made a left at the corner to loop back around again. WHOOP! WHOOP! A patrolman who had observed my actions pulled me to the side. I was informed that I had conducted "unsafe lane usage" — a 28-724-1 violation — though the officer issued me a warning only, as "a courtesy." I wasn't sure how courteous it was to be detaining a lost out-of-towner at 4:30 a.m., but I prudently kept my comments to myself. The real favor he did provide was to tip me to a laundromat and Ford service facility. I arrived at the former, which was open, and was assisted with my washing and drying operations by the owner. She was a Maytag and Huebsch fan with respect to her machines.

While my wash rinsed and spun dry, I sat next door at a coffee shop. It seemed like business-as-usual until four female students at the next table joined hands, closed their eyes and took turns voicing aloud their hopes and prayers for the day, beginning "Dear Heavenly Father." Much hugging followed as two of the four departed.

Locating the local Ford dealership, Jim Babbitt, I explained my particular challenges to the service advisor. He suspected my fuel pump had gone rotten on me, unfortunately didn't have the part in stock but phoned a dealer in Gallup, New Mexico that did. So, at a steady rate of speed and before the merciless barrage of sun began, I got going on 40 East. I kept the window down not only to keep alert but also to air the van out from all the Lysol I'd sprayed inside to kill possible lurking chiggers.

When I hit the area Two Guns, I just had to have a look at the famous Meteor Crater, and the pause would give El Rucio cool-down time. The highest point in an otherwise dead-flat zone, the crater was formed some 50,000 years ago by a meteor hurtling towards Earth at about 40,000 miles an hour. Its impact was so fierce — an estimated explosive force greater than 20 million tons of TNT — that it destroyed itself and created a hole 700 feet deep by 4,000 feet across and threw out some 175 million tons of limestone.

A mining engineer by the name of Daniel Moreau Barringer was convinced the meteorite had buried itself below the surface and purchased the rights to the land in 1902, with an aim to excavate it. His digging was fruitless, of course, but the land deed paid off when the Barringer family collaborated with the Bar T Ranch Company to create a tourist attraction here.

An elder woman who was viewing the site like me and had taken interest in my journey, told me about her son, a fellow adventurer who'd driven his jeep down into South America, Colombia. Though he was robbed and had run-ins with authorities over the three to four months he was there, he ended up pursuing South American studies.

Back on I-40, I passed a truck spewing out hay strands along the side of the road and realized that it was being spread to protect newly deposited grass seed. Of course, as I passed through Winslow a short while later, I thought of the Eagles' song, "Take It Easy", which referenced the town, and started singing it aloud.

Navajo County contained a big piece of the Painted Desert and both the Hopi and Navajo Indian Reservations. At the Jackrabbit Trading Post, I bought ice, water and gas, got a lead from the Mexican owner on an attraction in Holbrook and traveled another piece of the Old Route 66, running parallel to 40.

The trading post tip led me to the door of The Petrified Wood Company where the co-owner spent an hour giving me a walkabout of this highly unique Parthenon of Petrified Products. "My husband lives and breathes petrified wood. He even carries photos of it instead of his kids," she said of her partner. They offered a far-ranging assortment of items — tabletops, bookends, spheres, fossils and Indian merchandise — and also operated a small museum area onsite showing rock specimens gathered from 30 years of collecting. There was a rock cutting shop on the premises, too, which could be viewed through a window. The proprietor mentioned that the petrified wood is so hard it requires diamond blades and oil coolant to cut it. A 14-inch slice, for example, can take from two to three hours to cut. They really appeared to derive great joy from the business: "Every rock is different, like treasure," she said.

It was past the lunch hour when I left with a few samples from their Rock Yard, along with some petrified dinosaur poop. The air temp had climbed considerably and my thoughts returned to El Rucio's well being. For this reason, I decided to forego the 26-mile drive through the Petrified Forest, to keep plodding east. Billboards screamed in capital letters FREE PETRIFIED WOOD, GOLD NUGGETS, CACTUS MOCCASINS and INDIAN JEWELRY.

The buttes in the distance displayed a myriad of shades and tones from light red and pink to white and blue, as I entered Apache County and buzzed by the north entrance of the Forest and Painted Desert. Steinbeck "knew this way so well from many crossings" and noticed only that "the towns were a little larger" and "the motels bigger and more luxurious."

El Rucio had been a good girl today, though I'd also been her thoughtful liege, and I wondered if the service visit would even be necessary. One thing I did know and that was that I needed a food and rest stop, especially given my early morning rise. I couldn't have picked a more appropriate place than the Route 66 Diner in Sanders at the southeast corner of the Navajo Nation.

Highly praised by *Route 66 Magazine*, the diner was '50s style, with sheet metal walls, pink swivel stools at a front lunch counter and pink and black booths in the larger sit-down area. Both the staff and majority of patrons were Navajo, including a family of four across from whom I sat. That group included a young woman, her young son and the boy's grandparents. The child's mannerisms and way of being reminded me of my own sons and my comments to that effect were a chat opener.

Interested to know more about Navajo culture, I asked about their craft making, learning that their exports are moccasins, rugs and silver. About their customs, it was suggested I see a documentary called "Changing Seasons," about a Navajo girl's passage from puberty to womanhood. The old gentleman, a medicine man, had appeared in the film. As to language, they taught me the words "hello" (yateh, pronounced ya-tay) and "goodbye" (goonah, pronounced go-oh-nah).

As they were leaving and I was midway through a very large "66 3/4 pounder" burger, the woman came and sat across from me momentarily. In a hushed manner, she said that the Nation was busy seeking to have the name "Navajo," a white man's word meaning "thieves," stricken in favor of the tribe's true name, Dine (pronounced din-nay). Close up, I could see reflected in her face and shining black eyes the beauty and grace of her people. "Have a safe journey," she offered.

Rejoining the interstate, I rolled into my 23rd state, New Mexico, known as "The Enchanted State." Red Rock State Park was the dominant sight at the border and I snapped a photo of some of its rock structures as I rushed by, a Santa Fe express railing at me in the opposite direction. The flatlands here seemed to bear more green, more fertility and lushness. But the poverty I'd noted in rural Arizona was also here. Vehicles had been permanently rooted and built upon to form homes. Tin shacks had roofs held on only by tires. An old man scavenged for roadside debris.

Galloping by Gallup, I passed a turn-off for north-running U.S. Highway 666, more commonly known as the Devil's Highway because of its numeric designation. When the American Association of State Highway and Transportation changed the number to 491 back in June to address state complaints about the old number's negative connotations, virtually all the signs marking the route were stolen for their collectible value. Now, only the metal stubs of the markers remain.

Looking south at Ft. Wingate, I could just make out the cap of El Morro, a great rock promontory resembling a huge fortress. Spanish explorers gave the rock its name and left over 50 inscriptions, the earliest dating back to

1606. Hundreds of other writings mark visits by missionaries, soldiers and other passers-through.

The Continental Divide was located here, where Steinbeck had camped in "a little canyon out of the wind...by a mound of broken bottles... to rest and refurbish." Given his rapid pace, he felt as if he "was no longer hearing or seeing," that he had "passed his limit of taking in...helpless to assimilate what was fed in through [his] eyes. Each hill looked like the one just passed." To get rid of "the mullygrubs," he made up a plate of hotcakes with syrup and even a candle on top, inspected the broken whisky bottles, found a bit of mica and went to bed.

As for me, though itchy, I was still going strong and, near Grants, eyed a large column of smoke rising into the sky from a mountaintop fire. Then, at a pullout, I looked over at a hillside pueblo called Laguna, founded in the late 1600s and named after a nearby lake. It was a beautiful sight, with the facades of the adobe homes shining in the sun. On up the road, the Route 66 Casino on the Canoncito Indian Reservation advertised "SLOTS SO HOT THEY SIZZLE."

Albuquerque was an intimidating city, and I made a SWAT Team-like raid on it, storming a Walgreen's to seek out stronger or alternate relief for my camping-caused condition. Three layers of liberally applied hydrocortisone had not helped and my legs were on fire. I was counting on the pharmacist to be my savior. Her sell was Claritin tablets — tiny things to counteract my body's allergy reaction — and BOIL-EASE, designed to flat-out numb affected areas. I evacuated east and, soon, night had descended like a heavy velvet curtain.

To make the Houston reunion with my family, I planned to make as much headway into Texas as I could physically manage. El Rucio had been performing like a thoroughbred with not a whinny or uneasy shift, tearing up the road that had become our racetrack. The oval led us to Moriarty and the Rip Griffin Travel Center where I organized a shower, fetched some gas and stuffed down a burrito made with leftover fixings from the hostel feast.

Just northeast was New Mexico's own Las Vegas, where John Fassel, son of the New York Giants head coach, had taken over coaching the New Mexico Highlands College team, the Cowboys. He faced an uphill climb as the team had gone 0-10 in 2002 in NCAA Division II play.

I was not connecting with New Mexico at all like I'd wanted, but it was not because of saturation, as in Steinbeck's case. I was sure I had capacity for more. It was a combination of the mad itch, anticipated reunion and eagerness to get on with my return that drove me.

For company, I checked in on Game #4 of the World Series. New York was now ahead in the Series two games to one and Roger "The Rocket" Clemens, in his last career start, was the lead pitcher. In this game, Florida led 3-1 going into the 9th then gave up a hit deep into the right outfield corner that brought two Yankee base runners home to tie, sending the match into extra innings. As I listened, it was finally decided in the 12th when Florida's Alex Gonzalez spanked one just inches over the left field wall to give the Marlins the win, tying the Series at two games apiece.

My first Texas-oriented sign was a mileage posting for Amarillo: 239. I could hit that for sure, beyond would be a question given the now mid-evening hour. Looping under Santa Fe to Santa Rosa, all of which appeared to be under renovation, I dropped in for a beer at a local cantina. A table of Spanish men in ball caps and Stetsons, their table heaped with empty beer bottles, looked hopefully at the door for senoritas. But only heavy-set, masculine-acting women in polo shirts rolled in. The DJ, in his booth designed like a Wurlitzer, spun tunes for no one.

Further along the road, the one-horse town of Cuervo, all shut up and asleep, drew me in for a nap. The brilliantly clear sky was truly beautiful as I regarded it. When I resumed my push, it was the trucks and me again and friendly radio station KOAY out of Tecumcari providing background music. Then, out of the dark, "Welcome to Texas — Drive Friendly The Texas Way" greeted me at the border of State #24, The Lone Star State. I'd told Marlene that I would meet up with her on the 23rd and aimed to keep my promise, practically the whole of Texas the space between me and our meeting point. The ride would take extraordinary effort, this much was clear.

Day 48: Beat the Clock

As I barreled on into the night, Texas started to reveal herself. There was the cattle pen near Potter County, an exotic reptiles wholesaler around

Bushland, and the twinkling lights of Amarillo stretched out across the horizon.

My cell rang at 3 a.m. — Marlene was on the other end. She was at LaGuardia Airport anticipating flight boarding and eventual takeoff at 6 a.m. EST. We figured that she and the boys would touch down in Houston in about eight hours. I would try and join them as soon as I could.

Amarillo was a long, loping stretch of car lots, hotels and fast food chains, like many highway-side cities I had experienced. I peered through the dark for the Cadillac Ranch, which I knew to be somewhere along here, but never saw it. Conceived by Stanley Marsh III, a millionaire who had made his fortune in the helium trade, the "ranch" is actually ten graffiti-covered old Cadillacs half-buried, nose-in, in a row by the roadside. The late architect and artist Doug Michels, who fell to his death this past June while climbing in Australia, assembled the production in 1974.

Banking a hard right to pick up I-27 toward Lubbock, I scooted past a digital display, at a very brightly lit car dealership, that read, "4:09 a.m., 57 degrees." It reminded me that I'd crossed another time zone as I pulled this mad all-nighter.

I was looking for food and gas and, while the town of Happy seemed happy enough, it offered neither. Then up came Tulia and another Rip Griffin's Travel Center. As soon as I stepped from the van, I smelled cow, an odor emanating from a cattle trailer, in which the beasts stomped and bellowed. While filling up, I slapped on more BOIL-EASE and got a line on a breakfast place down the road a spell in Plainview. As the town was where 75-year-old sausage king Jimmy Dean was raised, I hoped it might offer tasty links.

The Nu-Griddle Café turned out to be a gem of a diner. Suspended by strings all around the top edges of each wall were old 45s. Photos and clippings of Elvis, Marilyn Monroe, James Dean and '50s style roadsters were glued right to the cinder block walls. Chrome-trimmed mini jukeboxes affixed near each table offered classic tunes. Seated in a booth, I loaded quarters in for songs appropriate to my journey: "Waltz Across Texas" by Ernest Tubb, Aaron Neville's "The Grand Tour," "Drive" by Alan Jackson and Montgomery Gentry's "Speed."

The waitress, a woman not more than four-and-a-half feet tall — "call her Shorty," a patron said — promptly brought me coffee followed by a neatly arranged breakfast of scrambled eggs, hash browns, toast and, joyfully, sausage patties. She was very attentive to my coffee, never letting it get more than an inch down from the rim, and had a decent, friendly way about her. As I ate, I overheard another patron, wearing a Stetson, boots and a red button-down, say to an elder gentleman near me, "Let's go pour concrete. I need a finisher." The reply, "I tried that once. I didn't like it."

My plate cleaned, I paid and followed the main road southeast a short way to a well-lit Burger King parking lot for a nap. The grueling drive and filling breakfast had done me in. And though the nap helped, I moved to the top of a small rise across from the Hale Center Gin Mill for extra Z's. By then, the sun was up and hovering over the flat, flat farmlands, my first good view of Texas. I'd seen her before as a kid, but the Laredo and San Antonio areas, not this swath of the state, and certainly not in this investigative manner.

Pointed at Lubbock still, more sites revealed themselves: A second cotton boll gin factory, fields of thorny cotton, a John Deere Equipment Center, an irrigation machinery vendor, grain processing companies and the Lubbock International Airport. On the matter of airports, my family had arrived at the one in Dallas — Dallas-Fort Worth — and was waiting to board a connecting flight to take them the rest of the way to Houston. Historically, DFW, formerly Dallas Love Field, was where President John F. Kennedy flew to the morning he was assassinated in downtown Dallas, almost 40 years ago to the day.

South of Lubbock, snowy cotton fields, some already being harvested by farmers atop their John Deeres, dominated the land, and cotton bolls that had separated from their stalks drifted along the roadside. Ahead, a large truck, open at the back, hauled a huge block of the crop, fly-aways landing in the road behind. Elsewhere, farmers plowed new channels in the reddish, brown earth or stacked bales beside their barns. In another patch, pumps bobbed up and down and a single-engine plane swooped low to crop dust.

At 10 a.m. Mountain Time, Marlene called again to say she had arrived safely in Houston. As my rash was stinging and burning again, I asked her to locate a walk-in clinic I might visit. But then, coming through Big Spring, I spied a billboard for Scenic Mountain Medical Center. Figuring that I'd be half out of my nut if I put off treatment any longer,

I climbed the mountain to the large, well staffed, modern facility. Much processing and interviewing ensued as I was passed by a candy striper to an ER check-in person to a nurse in a triage room to a nurse practitioner and finally to the good Dr. K. He guessed I'd been bitten by flies or ants, suspected the spots were infected and prescribed antibiotics and a shot. The shot-giver was the next to file in, with two threatening looking needles, one for each "cheek." I didn't feel the first at all and barely felt the second, which was supposed to be the more painful of the two. She was surprised, saying, "Most men cry out or scream." I felt pretty good about my heartiness.

Some paperwork and financial transactions followed and I was on my way to the local Wal-Mart for prescription filling. It was well past noon at this point and a searing 88 degrees outside. After shoveling another burrito into my gullet van-side, I crossed town to shower and apply cream at a Rip Griffin's.

Though I seemed to be on the way to healing, El Rucio started ailing again, stalling at a light in Sterling City. The local sheriff and a guy with a pickup helped me push her to a side street where, in the shade of the State Dining Room, I let her cool. Sitting on a step, I noticed a plaque on the building: "On May 8, 1768, this was declared the first condemned building in North America." Only I could pick such a spot.

After a half hour or so and a few false starts, we burst ahead through an intersection and limped along through the merciless heat toward San Angelo, playing the CHECK ENGINE game again. To prevent stalling, I kept the cruise control on and went gangbusters, until just short of San Angelo where she stalled yet again at a Chevron. A guy who helped me push her said to add some fuel to fool the on-board computer. Borrowing a gas container, I tried his suggestion and, realizing success, got underway again, holding my breath at subsequent red lights.

In this way, I made it to Eden, the main attraction of which was a restaurant called The Garden. Unfortunately, there was a snake lurking there, an officer who pulled me over for allegedly traveling 58 miles an hour in a 45 m.p.h. zone. He determinedly went ahead and wrote me a ticket — the only one I'd received in 24 states and four provinces of Canada — which came with an absolutely outrageous $130 dollar price tag. To add insult to injury, as he delivered it to me, El Rucio stalled out again. If there was any upside, by sitting for a longer while this time, I was able to push off first try.

It seemed that I was not meant to get to Houston or, if I was, I really had to earn it. Texas had been a difficult state for Steinbeck, too, his chief challenges, like mine, automotive- and health-oriented. Auto-wise, "a passing car on a gravel road had thrown up pebbles and broken out the large front window of Rocinante" and it had to be replaced. While the part was shipped down from the Wolverine Camper Co., he spent three days in a "beautiful motor hotel" in Amarillo.

Health-wise, "Charley had been taken with his old ailment and...was in bad trouble and great pain." A young male doctor, also in Amarillo, with "trained and knowing hands," saw the dog. Charley responded positively to him, sighing "a great sigh and [wagging his tail] slowly up from the floor and down again." The doctor treated him at his facility over four days and, when he was returned, he was "completely well."

As Marlene and the boys had, Elaine flew to Texas, and, with John, went to a friend's ranch to celebrate Thanksgiving. The gathering was a "Texas orgy, showing men of great wealth squandering their millions on tasteless and impassioned exhibitionism." As to the property, it was "beautiful," nestled in "a grove of cottonwoods on a little eminence over a pool made by a dammed-up spring," stocked with trout. All around were "well-grassed flats, [where] the blooded Herefords grazed." The house itself was "a one-story brick structure" with three bedrooms, each with a bath, and a living room "paneled in stained pine" that doubled as a dining room.

Upon arrival, the Steinbecks were given scotch and soda and a tour of the property: "The barn...the kennels in which there were three pointers... then the corral, where the daughter of the house was training a quarter horse named Specklebottom." They also "inspected two new dams" and "communed with a small herd of recently purchased cattle."

After a short nap, neighboring friends, toting a large pot of chili con carne — "the best [Steinbeck] had ever tasted" — arrived, and drinks and "gay conversation having to do with hunting, riding and cattle-breeding" ensued. From a window seat, Steinbeck regarded "the subtlety of their ostentation" as well as "wild turkeys come in to roost," noting that "the smell of money was everywhere." John and Elaine took a walk "around the trout pool and over against the hill," feeling the chill air and wind that hinted at winter. They "heard a coyote howl and cow bawling" and, at the barn, smelled "the sweetness of alfalfa and the bready odor of rolled barley." The cold air made them sleepy and they retired.

Thanksgiving Day, John awakened first, to go trout fish. He "brought in a ten-inch rainbow" then four more, which the "cook dipped in corn meal and fried crisp in bacon fat and served under a coverlet of bacon." Mid-morning, he went on a quail hunting excursion with his "old and shiny 12-bore with the dented barrel," a trek that was unproductive, but a good lead-up to the holiday meal. The latter, notably, consisted of "two brown and glazed turkeys" accented by "two good drinks of whisky."

There would be no dining with filthy rich Texans for me I thought to myself, passing, first, a column of military Humvees pulled to the side of the road, then a herd of antelope in a field of cactus near Brady. El Rucio was running fine again and we gratefully welcomed a sign for Austin, 126 miles along Texas Route 71.

Sites on this very scenic, pleasant route were classic Texas: Grazing longhorns and Black Angus. Red flowering cactus clumps. A bleached-white bull's skull marking the entrance to a ranch. Wild deer looking out from tall green grasses. A turtle that would most certainly have been soup had I not plucked him out of the middle of the road and placed him in the grass.

Llano, "Land of Legend and Lure," was very authentic Old West with low-rise, movie western building facades, BBQ joints and a spur company. It seemed like a good place to linger, but then I noticed Poodie's Hilltop Bar & Grill. Owned by country singer Willie Nelson's stage manager, the place had a big screen TV showing the Series. Though the Yanks had a 1-0 lead when I walked in, the Marlins quickly adjusted the score with three runs. The blonde bartenderette, sporting an abbreviated fire engine red tank top that allowed for a generous presentation of middle, dished me up a Coke and basket of hot wings.

My seatmates were a couple from Michigan, who had met and lived in Greenwich Village back in the '60s. They were also headed to the Houston area but to participate in a Renaissance Festival, the largest in the country. He played an instrument called the chitarra batente, and would be performing with his band. In fact, as I exited, he fetched me a CD of his group so I'd have some road music. I'd never been one to delay the unveiling of gifts, so immediately popped the CD right in my player. It was an elegant, spiritual, finely produced collection providing a marked contrast to the sagebrush and ranch entries I flew past. I was re-energized by the meal, music and making of a new friendship.

El Rucio shared my uplifted spirit, now that her skin was cool to the touch, and trotted us hard past Austin, a jumble of curling concrete spans, barricades, taco purveyors and carnival amusements. I'm sure there was much more to the city that I wasn't seeing and felt badly writing it off like this. I also remembered that it was where the President's twin daughters, Jenna and Barbara, had attended high school and where Jenna was enrolled as a senior at the University of Texas. Not 100 miles north, on Prairie Chapel Road in Crawford, the family maintained a ranch, where dad George typically retreats for R&R.

I could smell pine trees, though only see their dark outlines around me. Columbus came and went, then, at last, Houston appeared, big and wide and bright. Car dealerships, restaurants, hotels and nightclubs all clamored for motorist attention. Leaping at Highway 6, I circled around to the 20-story Holiday Inn where my family was staying. It was midnight and, at the door of the 10th Floor room she'd been assigned, my sleepy-eyed wife met me and, with a tight embrace, let me know I was home, if only for a while.

Day 49: Family Time

The boys were up first, as was their norm at home, and when I said, "Hi guys," they looked over from the other double bed in the room and, with surprise in their voices, said, "Oh, hi dad! You made it!" We hugged hello and I noticed they both looked bigger and they showed me their new toys and we spoke about the excitement of their plane ride here. Like Carolina, this was a wonderful reunion.

Waiting for me in a Fed Ex package was a second installment of CDs from my Burbank friend, Tim. These were much more road pertinent than the first batch, with selections like "Road Trippin,'" "I Can't Drive 55" and "On the Road Again." He enclosed a note wishing me "clear skies" and reminded me of a Steinbeck message: "A journey is like marriage. The certain way to be wrong is to think you control it."

My family went ahead to the hotel restaurant where I joined them for a feast of breakfast foods. Our waitress was of Navajo and Spanish descent, a combination that made her a "half-breed" in the eyes of the tribe. As such, she was not permitted on the Reservation.

Our day began with a drive along the Sam Houston Tollway to the Lyndon B. Johnson Space Center at which a marketing manager had arranged passes for exhibits in the five-story tall Visitor's Center. Space travel, I realized, was just in its infant stage when Steinbeck passed through and this facility still a far-off dream. We'd come a long way in four decades.

The displays went beyond space-oriented attractions to include a "Dino Dig," an oversized sandbox in which plastic bones were hidden that the boys had to find with archaeology tools. Evan buckled into the MMU Trainer, a chair outfitted with air jets and an overhead control panel to which he had to respond. I sat in a simulated space shuttle pilot's environment where, via a monitor and joystick, I landed a craft by aligning a "diamond" and "bug" in center screen crosshairs. Similarly, we docked the shuttle, planned and conducted a Mars mission, and stood in the cockpit, lower deck and wheel well of a shuttle.

In another area, we built and launched computer rockets and were treated to a live demonstration of "Living in Space." The boys flew through the place, excitedly pushing buttons, sliding levers and listening to pre-recorded monologues.

At the rear of the facility, we boarded a tram for a tour of the complex, first passing through a metal detector and having our photo taken, measures put into place after 9/11. The tour took us past a full-size rocket, which shared lawn space with longhorns, an antenna shop and a space food research lab (likely inspired by Apollo astronaut "Buzz" Aldrin who hated the early food so much that he smuggled a corned beef sandwich aboard a flight).

We stopped to explore the Apollo-era Mission Control Center, active from 1965 to 1996. Astronaut Neil Armstrong radioed in to this very room from the surface of the moon when he took his first steps on July 20, 1969. Not quite five years old at the time, I struggled to stay up to see the historic event on our black-and-white General Electric TV set.

Exiting the Center to join the tram again, we made a final stop at a large hangar that contained mock-ups of modules used for astronaut training. These included an airlock, living quarters, operations, cockpit, cargo bay and partial gravity simulator.

Our day agenda included another aviation-oriented stop: the Lone Star Flight Museum. As it was in Galveston, a half-hour to the south, we really had to step on it to make it there by its 5 p.m. closing time. Luckily, I'd made an inside contact who held the door open for our visit. We rocketed down I-45 at break-neck speed, over a series of bridges traversing Gulf of Mexico inlets, to the facility.

The place was a kid's dream, full of vintage aircraft, the majority of which were in flying condition. Larry started our tour with the thick-bodied PB4Y-2 Privateer, nicknamed the "Flying Boxcar." It was a Navy flier used mainly in the Pacific and was being restored to working order with full military armaments.

A sleek and flat P-38, known to the Germans as a "fork-tailed devil" and one of only six in flyable condition in the U.S., was our next stop. A B-17, the craft an active flier logging over 100 hours a year traveling to 20 to 30 aviation events, followed. We gazed on a Blue Hellcat marked with 19 Red Suns representing Japanese planes downed and a P-47D Thunderbolt labeled "Tarheel Hal's," referring to the pilot's NC birthplace.

We admired an F4U Corsair with fold-up wings, a twin-prop H118 BeechCraft Larry referred to as the "company pickup truck" and a Douglas Skyrider curiously named "Marlene," known as "Uncle Ho's Nightmare," that saw fighting action in Vietnam and could carry more armaments than the B-17. Further on, there was Jimmy Doolittle's B-25 Mitchell, that launched the first surprise attack on the Japanese mainland, and a TB-58 Hustler, which could reach a speed of Mach 2.3 and was a nuclear threat to Russia before land-launched nuclear missiles. A bright black, red and yellow TBM Avenger, the type that former president George Bush Sr. flew, dropped torpedoes in its active days while a Mitsubishi G4M "Betty," essentially a bomb with wings, was the type of plane Japanese suicide bombers flew.

As we concluded our tour, we learned that the facility houses the Texas Aviation Hall of Fame featuring "everything from barnstormers to moonwalkers." It was the dinner hour by this time and the sun, red like those on the Hellcat, was plummeting into the Gulf beyond Galveston's oceanfront seawall. The return north on I-45 was quick, with little traffic, and gave us a few moments to talk. Marlene wondered what I was going to be like when I got back home a month from now. I told her I'd probably prowl around the house at night, make backyard campfires and hunt squirrels. I'm not sure she could tell I was joking.

A free paper that I'd picked up, *The Beach Sun,* advertised as "A Guide to the Greater Galveston & West Bay Resort Communities," promoted an appearance by native Texan Michael Martin Murphey at the Grand 1894 Opera House. Recognized as the "Cosmic Cowboy of the '70s," the singer, songwriter, producer, actor, Western historian, cowboy and rancher was planning to perform his country-rock hits "Wildfire" and "Geronimo's Cadillac."

The annual Oktoberfest celebration, centered around the First Lutheran Evangelical Church on Winnie Avenue, that had hosted the tradition since 1847, promised "German food, Wurst, libations and Oompaa music."

R.T. McCauley described fall on the Gulf Coast as "the start of the flounder run, dove hunting, and clear breezy months that briskly move sailboats over the water with a feeling of purpose and determination." He continued, "The weekend drudgery of cutting our lawns and trimming our hedges past, and a shortened 'honey-do' list," afforded more time on the water. Overall, tourists were "for the most part gone, bait is plentiful, and marinas less crowded due to the reduction in transients" who had migrated to "places where sweaters may not be required."

The redfish, described as "garbage guts [that] eat anything from crabs to hard heads," were migrating south to Mexico, providing fishing fun for those with "patience and a wait-and-see-attitude." Mullet was the recommended bait because of its "toughness and availability," though shad might also be used.

Becky Smith discovered that crustacean shells are good for battling garden pests, so started burying shrimp in furroughs. While great for her plants, the scent of the scraps attracted seagulls (their "digestive tract never ceases to amaze me"), a great blue heron, wild cats, snakes and land terrapins from a nearby pond.

We'd arranged to have dinner with the couple I'd met in San Francisco, at a restaurant near their apartment in downtown. On the approach, we came to a fork in the road, managed to follow the wrong tyne and found ourselves on the beltway circling. Hopping before we got too far astray, we lucked out and stumbled onto North Main, where the eatery was located.

Spring Flowers Mexican Restaurant was the latter's name and it was bright, colorful, inviting and loud. It was the perfect family environment and the prices were very easy to swallow. Enchiladas and tacos were the orders all around, followed by a pumpkin flan and coffee.

The young couple's marriage, now two weeks old, was going swimmingly. We spoke of my adventures since San Francisco and, somewhat off-topic, I showed them a sample of my infected sores, which looked terrible — pink, blotchy, scabbed and swollen. I wasn't sure whether my affliction was getting better or worse — the itching hadn't abated and I kept a tube of hydrocortisone in my pocket for emergency's sake.

It felt strange for me to have other people in the van and El Rucio lumbered a bit under my family's weight. Was she jealous that my attention was diverted? We convoyed to an upscale area called River Oaks and one of two Starbucks on the block. To complement coffees, we had a spot of ice cream from Marble Slab Creamery. As it was a clear, mild night, we sat outside to watch the Hummers and Beamers and Benzes go by and talked about Halloween plans and costumes. Then we hugged goodbye and returned to the hotel.

Itching madly again, I dropped into a hot bath to scrub away with a washcloth. That felt good but made the affected spots swell. Afterwards, I took my prescribed pills and decided to try a little experiment, and that was to forego the hydrocortisone. That seemed to make a world of difference. The reddened blotches changed to pink and then almost skin color, and the itching subsided enough so I could drop to sleep.

Day 50: Floodwaters & Peanut Shells

This day marked seven weeks that I'd been on the road and, in that time, I'd driven over 10,000 miles. I still had many miles to go and states to see but I was not feeling as intimidated given that I was in a return mode.

It was 3 a.m. when I snapped awake and I felt like writing, but didn't want to disturb my family. So I dropped down to the lobby and, with the sound of a gurgling fountain in the background, settled into an oversized, comfortable chair. No sooner had I done that than a wild tempest of a woman blew in from the warm night. She had a broad, beautiful Mayan face and blue eyes and walked like a sleek cat. She'd been clubbing, had had a blow-up with a girlfriend and was now hurling curses at her via a flip-phone pressed to her ear. Awash in perfume, she settled in a chair near me and had a sad story to tell of cross-country migration from Virginia and failed marriage, the upside of which produced two beautiful children. As we spoke, she got a series of calls, intensifying the wildcat in her and drawing the attention of a security guard, who tried to contain her. Finally, a cab came and, as she continued to spit fire into the cellphone that had become affixed to the side of her head, took her away.

Another person wandered onto the scene, a light-skinned black woman with a Portugese accent who was having no luck making a phone call to her mom back in her native Angola. We listened to the fountain and chatted and tried together to put her call through again, without luck. She returned to her room once more to attempt to get some shuteye.

I did the same around 7 a.m., finding only Evan up. A little newspaper reading made me tired enough to lie back down again to sleep, which I did while my family rose and went to breakfast. When they returned, we hatched a plan to attend the Texas Renaissance Festival where my Poodie's friends would be.

Motoring north, we were concerned that it was spritzing out, but didn't think it would amount to much. We turned out to be very wrong, as, at Magnolia, not more than a few miles from the festival grounds, we found ourselves in a torrential downpour that stopped traffic in its tracks. We watched a poor policeman wearing an orange slicker and holding onto the Stetson on his head, direct traffic. He was being blown sideways by strong gusts of wind and lashed by rain that whipped horizontally. We decided to retreat back to Houston and adopt a Plan B. As we went, severe storm and flooding warnings were issued during a TV program the boys were watching in the back.

I'd been in such a rush to get to Houston the other day that I hadn't stopped to read rash care instructions the Medical Center supplied. I realized that I'd been doing the opposite of what I should have. They advised staying away from hot water (I'd been taking hot baths). They suggested I not use soap (I'd been rubbing soap into the areas). They said to avoid exposing the areas to sun (I'd purposely worn shorts and let the sun fall in my lap as I drove). They directed me to pat the skin dry (I'd been rubbing it). For relief, moist compresses were called for and cream usage not advised (I'd slathered on hydrocortisone). I had brought misery on myself it would appear and I'd need to immediately get with the program if I wanted any significant easing of discomfort and healing to begin.

Upon arrival back at the hotel, the boys were anxious to go swimming in the pool. Marlene escorted them and while they were all out, I caught up on paperwork, including sending the $130 check to satisfy the speeding ticket I'd received back in Eden. Thank you again for taking advantage of an out-of-towner. These tasks kept my mind off my condition, which was holding at swelling, redness and throbbing — no worse but no better either.

Since the day had been a wash, literally, with rain that continued through the afternoon, we felt we needed to at least have an authentic Texas-style dinner. A hotel clerk referred us to Logan's Roadhouse on Highway 6, a rootin' tootin' country place that served up a bucket of roasted peanuts at every table. The added plus was that you could throw the peanut shells on the floor!

Another fun attraction was being able to see into the kitchen area to watch the chefs cooking up various meats. On a return from the bathroom, Phil and I inspected the latter, seeing three-foot high flames shoot up as a cook brushed sauce on a rack of ribs. Music, ranging from Motown to honky tonk, enhanced the experience. Our meals (mesquite grilled chicken with pineapple over rice for me) were stars, too, and kept us going through the final game of the World Series. Both the Yankees and Marlins played hard but, to our disappointment, it was Florida that ultimately came out on top.

Despite the loss, the night ended well. At a drug store on the way home, I'd bought a box of Aveeno bath salts designed for skin affected by various conditions. Running a room temperature bath, I added one packet and soaked for a half-hour. Almost immediately, any itching stopped, swelling subsided and the color of the affected areas lightened from red to light pink. It seemed I'd found the elusive magic elixir that would save the day!

Day 51: Wine, Women & Song

It was Daylight Savings Time, so when I stirred at 4 a.m., it was actually 3 a.m. My family was flying back home this morning so I made myself first bathroom shift. Another Aveeno bath got me started on the right foot and inspired me to type for a while as my significant others got ready and packed. We set out at 4:30 headed north on the Sam Houston Tollway and, in a half hour, had pulled up to the American Airlines curbside check-in area at George Bush Intercontinental Airport. Phil got a little upset that I wasn't coming with them but was O.K. when it was explained to him that I couldn't take the van on the plane and would have to drive it home. Still, he looked back over his shoulder at me, a little unsure, as Marlene led him into the terminal.

I was back on my own again, to see my journey through to its finish. Upon return to the hotel, I reported directly to the restaurant for their tasty buffet helpings and observed folks as I ate. Business travelers were the majority of my companions. The married men on their own here all seemed to have a little bit of a lost look on their faces and ate quietly. Those folks in company groups, so different from each other but thrown together for some conference or meeting, made awkward, polite conversation. All seemed to focus or steal glances at one young family in the room, envious of their being together. The one solo woman — and I've found this true of most traveling professional women — seemed to be the only person completely comfortable in this environment. She strode confidently from the buffet with her organized breakfast to sit at her organized table with her organized, color-coordinated luggage and work portfolio. This was a breed that had been empowered in the workplace and would mow you down if you got in her way or tried to shake her off the corporate ladder she was determinedly climbing. She did not exist in Steinbeck's male-dominated era and I wondered what he would have thought had he encountered her.

I did interact with one group, four Trinidadian men here for a British Petroleum meeting. Two of the men wore concert t-shirts bearing the name "Renegades," a calypso group. They seemed too young to be fans of the genre, a style of music born more than 40 years ago, but they enjoyed it nonetheless. We spoke of island traditions and food and funny expressions before I excused myself to snooze and then write for the rest of the morning in the room.

At noon, I broke out of my comfortable incubator and powered north to try and attend the Renaissance Fest again. Unlike yesterday, conditions, for the most part, were dry, though still overcast. Reaching the Fest grounds, I followed a dirt road to a field parking spot, collected my ticket and made my way to a Media Center office above the King's Feast Hall. There, I met up with the marketing director, who made a grand entrance anon dressed in a slashed doublet — a black leather vest through which a red wine-colored linen shirt peeked. We set off walking and talking, passing several of the 300 contracted performers, whom he greeted as "M'Lord" or "M'Lady."

It was George Coulam, my host explained, who founded the Fest 29 years ago, inspired by similar events in California. Starting small with simple, temporary structures, lean-to's and volunteers, the site has grown into a re-created 16th Century village with over 300 shops designed, built and owned by the vendors within them. There were also 20 stages on the premises and a large, open-air arena with low stone bleachers wherein jousts are held.

My guide had started as a full-time actor here, playing the part of Sir Berit of Miller, the Knight of Lite — "the only corporate shill of the festival." He became a vendor coordinator, then took the marketing slot when the former head moved on. Now he's responsible for all the print, TV, radio and mail promotion for the seven weekends a year the show runs. It's become a big success spurring a great number of attendees to dress the part, a la "Rocky Horror Picture Show."

The grounds were still muddy where we walked, showing horseshoe and boot tracks. We stepped to the Leek & Daffodil Royal Beer Tasting Hall, one of numerous properties owned by Charles Prince, a 3rd generation Texan. Here, we joined 15 others divided between four tables, with small glasses set out at each place. Wenches "Jenny O'Manion" and "Heidi Ho", their bodices overflowing, kept things lively with bawdy humor and off-color song. Jenny guided us through each of six beer brands we were charged with sampling, and soon glasses were clinking and toasts were being made.

Next door was the Prince of Wales tavern. Its focal bar was a 150-year-old teller's bank from Lloyd's of London, accessorized with a brass foot rail. A finely carved hutch on the far side of the room was 200 years old. Beams supported the ceiling; gold-like gravel was the footing.

Seeking to blot some imbibed brew, I sauntered to an onsite eatery called The Battered Pig, to wolf down some barbecued dragon (a shredded beef sandwich). Then it was on to a wine tasting, hosted by "Marsala D. Vino", who set the rule that spillage = spanking. Naturally, a guy in this crowd of about 20, arranged around a horseshoe of long tables, committed the offense and was stood up on a chair to be given the business. His wallet was also picked and its fake contents announced: a condom, Viagra, a photo that was not of his wife, etc. When there was no more tasting to be done, Marsala offered her own self up for spankings, choosing the men to administer the abuse and straddling two tables to expose purple bloomers that said, "SPANK ME."

I'd had uproarious fun here but it was quite dark and time to go. I hopped in El Rucio and meandered back to the hotel. My room, which my family had filled with noise and activity, was silent, and already I began to miss them.

Day 52: The Calm before the Catfish

I had a solid slumber, even oversleeping, which caused a great flurry of action once I *did* get up. The urgency was over van servicing that I'd planned for the day at Champion Ford on I-10 West. The service adviser there said that they could accommodate me, though I knew I'd need to be swift about bringing El Rucio to him. Sparing no time, I dropped into an Aveeno bath —now a twice-daily routine — checked e-mail and got myself over to Ford's facility, pronto. The crew would take care of the basics and advise me on the status of any other concerns.

Via a courtesy shuttle, I was whisked back to the Holiday Inn just in time to catch the hotel's excellent buffet breakfast. In the nearly empty dining room, my server was a Mexico City-born girl who mentioned that she had competed in a recent Nationals Inc. beauty pageant last month, one of 400 girls from all over Texas to do so.

Back in the room, I sent Evan's teacher a latest update on my journey, to share with the class. I also got an initial report on El Rucio: My differential and transmission fluid leaks, as well as exhaust rupture, remained minimal concerns, but my oil leak was "severe." However, the adviser was confident that if I kept checking my oil status upon fill-ups as I continued on, that I'd probably be O.K. The other item being investigated, thought to be related to a jammed butterfly valve, was the stall-out problem.

Concluding my room stay with another Aveeno bath, I checked out and set up camp in the lobby, my cellphone at the ready to receive the Ford call. My background this time was a player piano that tinkled away for a half-hour every other half-hour. For more than a couple of hours I sat there, starting to feel like Steinbeck in the lobby of Chicago's Ambassador East.

Finally, late afternoon, Ford took me off the Holiday Inn's hands, sending their shuttle to collect me. The crew had gotten El Rucio "real hot" but could not reproduce a stalling condition, so they were satisfied I'd be alright from here on home. With a bill that was easy to swallow, I was rolling again, working my way east on I-10. The roads were clogged with cars belonging to the working folks in the region who had just finished up the week. They inched along in building fumes, just trying to get home to a cooked meal and the sanity and safety of their family environments.

It felt good to be in the chase again and New Orleans was now the target in my crosshairs. Since I had never attended a Mardi Gras celebration there, much less visited the state of Louisiana, I hoped to be front and center for Halloween activities. I'd be arriving about three days early, however, and wondered if I could afford to lose those days in a waiting mode or whether another city on my route might be equally kooky. I would play things by ear.

Steinbeck had a very different feeling approaching the South, an area he "dreaded to see and yet knew [he] must see and hear." It was a place, for him, of "pain and confusion and all the manic results of bewilderment and fear." For here, "an original sin of the fathers was being visited on the children of succeeding generations," that of discrimination based on race. Steinbeck felt that he was "basically unfitted to take sides in the racial conflict," though any "cruelty and force exerted against weakness" made him angry. Certainly, he found the accusations that blacks were inferior, dirty, lazy and dishonest perplexing and misinformed, based on his personal experience growing up in Salinas with the Coopers, a black family that he knew intimately to be just the opposite.

In late 1960, New Orleans, in particular, was a focus of national attention in the conflict — "violence set loose by the desegregation movements." The newspapers and television broadcasts hopped on the story of a group of stout middle-aged women, known as the "Cheerleaders," who, with a crowd in tow, "gathered every day to scream invectives" at black children being escorted into school. "This strange drama seemed so improbable," Steinbeck remarked, "that [he] felt [he] had to see it."

Winter caught up with Steinbeck, striking "with a black norther" that "brought ice and freezing sleet and sheeted the highways with dark ice." Though cold, his spirit was warmed by Charley, with whom he'd been reunited and who "looked half his age and felt wonderful." They "stopped dawdling and laid [their] wheels to the road," shooting by Sweetwater, Balinger and Austin, bypassing Houston and on into Louisiana.

Gunning east as he had, I took in the spectacle that was an enormous Budweiser plant, its neon sign a very large version of one you might find in a bar, glowing red against a pink horizon. The Pabst Distributing Company, with its own family of glowing signs, immediately followed it. Slot machine repair shops, fireworks warehouses and Chevron's oil refineries, which belched out a distinct fuel smell, lay further on down this cement corridor. Industrial scenery was soon replaced by rivers and swamps and signs for bayou this and shrimp that. I knew the state line couldn't be far off.

Beaumont introduced itself with the Goodyear Chemical Plant and its busy smokestacks, and the highway there ballooned to four lanes in each direction. Predictably along such a stretch, the hotel chains and fast food joints, like Waffle House, Howard Johnson, La Quinta and Stuckey's, popped up like stubborn weeds.

At 7 p.m., I crossed over the Sabine River Bridge into Louisiana, state #25. The sign there: "Bienvenue a Louisiane." Right off, I saw the Delta Downs Casino and adjacent Lucky Peacock, advertised with all the bells, lights and horns their owners could find. Up ahead, I saw what looked like the bright lights of a city, but it was the facilities for Arch Chemicals and Biolab.

Cajun music played on the radio as I flew past Harrah's Casino and Steamboat Bill's in Lake Charles, and it was after eight when I hit the town of Welsh, to visit Cajun Tales Seafood Restaurant, a place that claimed "Cajun Food At Its Best." This family eatery offered such dishes as fried frog legs, catfish any way you cared to try it, crawfish etoufee, seafood gumbo, alligator, a bayou lily (a colossal onion specially cut to blossom when floured and fried) and Cajun fries.

My waitress highly endorsed the Broiled Catfish stuffed with crabmeat and shrimp, with a baked potato and salad on the side. Near us, a little girl with glasses, part of a group of 12 sitting at a table together, circled a fluorescent-lit glass case in which desserts with plastic wrap over them were displayed. One of her brothers, about 14 I guessed, with a white cowboy hat on his head and jeans secured by a large belt buckle, toyed with his mom, putting her in a half Nelson hold. Their accents were as thick as the shrimp and crabmeat gumbo being dished out.

As the catfish was going to take time to prepare, I busied myself with a book on display titled, "Cajun Humor," featuring the witticisms of Louisiana-born humorists Dave Petitjean, Murray Conque and Ralph Begnaud. Their surnames reminded me of those I'd noticed in Madawaska, Maine and I guessed that there were likely family ties between the two areas.

The large group departed and Mitzi started sweeping under their table. All the crumbs and food debris that she'd collected amazed her and she remarked, "They must've been from the swamp. I heard the name Cletus and I ain't heard that in a long time."

The meal was well worth the wait and disappeared into my pie hole. Once again back on 10, two lanes went to one and slowed down measurably. It was not so much because of road construction but because of a tractor-trailer that had gone off into a ditch and bent at different angles.

At Lafayette, approaching the midnight hour, I started looking into hotels, wanting a place where I could squeeze in a couple more Aveeno baths. However, there was an oilman's conference in town and all the accommodations were booked solid. If I wanted to find something, I'd have to go rural.

Route 90 going south from Lafayette, a scenic road running close to the coast, seemed a good branch to follow. It took me past New Iberia, which I remembered to be home of Marion and Sue Blair, the parents of the Opera House Café owner back in Bar Harbor, Maine. If my pass-through had been earlier in the day, or even earlier in the evening, I may have called on them.

Jeanerette followed, then St. Mary's Parish, Franklin and Morgan City. By the time I'd reached Terrebonne County, on the eastern side of the Atchafalaya River (where scenes for made-for-TV movie "Red Water" starring Lou Diamond Phillips had just been filmed), I was done for the night. Seeing a "CAMPING" sign beside the road in Bayou Blue, I turned off the main, rolled quietly past many permanent trailer homes and pulled into an RV area with hook-ups. As it was 1:30 a.m., I wasted no time with formalities, simply tilting back and arranging myself comfortably in the passenger seat directly behind the driver's seat, pulling a blanket over myself and sacking out.

Day 53: Laissez les Bon Temps Roullez

Steinbeck had "dogged it on through Lafayette and Morgan City, too, to Houma, in the vicinity of my stopping place and, to him, "one of the pleasantest places in the world." There resided his old friend "Doctor St. Martin, a gentle, learned man, a Cajun who has lifted babies and cured colic among the shell-heap Cajuns for miles around." Most notably, he recalled him making "the best and most subtle martini in the world by a process approximating magic" and a dinner of black duck they'd enjoyed, memories that "filled [his] frosty windshield." He wanted to stop to pay his respects but knew that if he did, his "will and determination would drift away." Thus, he "only bowed in the direction of [his] friend, scudded on toward New Orleans" and parked, at dawn, in a parking lot "well on the edge of town." When the attendant there saw Charley, he remarked, "Man, oh man, I though you had a nigger in there." The comment sent a chill through Steinbeck that was to stay with him throughout his visit.

Skedaddling from the camping area around 6:30 a.m., I passed school kids in navy and violet uniforms waiting on a bus at the corner of the camp road. As New Orleans lay just 50 miles to the east, more Cajun music was called for, served up by a French-only station that greeted its listeners, "Bonjour, mes amies." It was a good morning wake-up call.

Some roadside signage: "Your mama called...She said bring home oranges...Oranges $2.00 a pound." Other signs on the approach offered airboat and swamp tours, BAIT, Bloody Mary's and boiled crabs. On the political front, a good southern gentleman named Laque was running for Parish President. And Bridge City called itself the Gumbo Capital of the World.

Traffic got swampy again, which wasn't a bad thing this morning as it gave me a chance to look about. Remarkably, I saw a large, prehistoric looking crane-like white bird lift itself into the air and flap away across some treetops. Then I passed over the Huey P. Long Bridge spanning the Mississippi River, a waterway I'd crossed many, many states ago in Iowa when I was making my westward push.

At New Orleans' door, I saw a trolley car being boarded by students, in uniforms like the group I'd seen earlier, their colors blue or dark red plaids and solids. By the Superdome, where the New Orleans Saints pro football team plays, I hung a right onto Martin Luther King Blvd., then a left on St. Charles, to head to the popular French Quarter.

Eager to set out on foot, I stowed El Rucio in a U-Park lot at St. Joseph and Magazine where, to pay to park, one must fold up the appropriate number of bills and insert them in a multi-slotted machine with the aid of a metal tab. It was a much less interactive experience than Steinbeck's, wherein he "locked Charley in Rocinante's house after giving the attendant a tour of the premises, a drink of whisky and a dollar" and caught a cab to the Cheerleader gathering site. He donned his sailor disguise once again, guessing that no one would give a sailor a second look in a seaport and even lied to the cab driver that he was from Liverpool. His alleged British orientation was a relief to the cabbie, who said he was glad Steinbeck wasn't a "goddamn New York Jew" come to "stir the niggers up."

The streets in the direction of the Quarter were cobbled and shuttered residences done in pastels with ornate iron railings fencing in balconies. On Camp Street, there was a small park in which a bronze statue of Ben Franklin stood. Around his neck, a beaded necklace had been draped. He looked across at the U.S. Court of Appeals and the Hale Boggs Federal Buildings.

Poydras Street was a wide thoroughfare along which banking institutions and major hotels — the large buildings that defined the downtown area — were located. Very broad Canal Street signaled the start of the Quarter, immediately recognizable by its classic two- and three-story buildings with their Old World facades. Entering via Chartres Street, I stepped into a business to use a bathroom, realizing it was a bar. Obviously, the liquor laws that would allow a drinking establishment to be open at eight in the morning must be highly relaxed.

Pierre Maspero's restaurant housed a slave exchange back in the late 1700s and was where Andrew Jackson and the Lafitte brothers planned the defense of New Orleans against the British. On the opposite corner was Girod's Bisto, named for Nicholas Girod, mayor of the city from 1812 to 1815. At Wilkinson, a tiled placard noted that New Orleans was the capital of the Spanish Province of Louisiana from 1762-1803 and that Chartres bore the name Calle d'Chartres at that time. La Place Jean-Paul Deux, beside the Cathedral de St. Louis, was a hangout for painters, the homeless and a group of leather-clad, spiky-haired, nose-ringed punk rockers. Iron-gated Jackson Square, laid out in 1721, was where the ceremonies symbolizing the transfer of Louisiana from Spain to France and from France to the United States took place in 1803. It featured a large statue of Andrew Jackson on horseback at its center.

Seeking a breakfast nook, I found La Madeleine, at the corner of the square, bumping into a Filipina woman visiting from Vallejo, CA, as I entered. Since we were both on our own at that moment, we decided to share a table and have breakfast together. For me, this was Ham Florentine, a creamy ham concoction wrapped in a crepe and topped with a mushroom sauce. We ended up taking in some local sights, together, too, including an adjacent museum, the Cabildo, at Jackson Square. The sturdy looking structure was built as an armory in 1799 and housed a large collection of historic artifacts and information. Native American tribes like the Atakapa, Tunica and Mugulasha were the area's first residents. They were hunters, fishermen, pot makers and basket weavers who wore fine robes and skirts fashioned from feathers, bark and animal hides. From a European standpoint, the Spaniards were the first to venture here, in 1519, from Florida. They found the area very hostile and largely ignored it. It was the French who first established a permanent and lasting settlement in 1699, and held the region until 1803. Jean-Babtiste Le Moyne, Sieur de Bienville, founded New Orleans in 1718 on a crescent-shaped section of the Mississippi's left bank, naming it after the ruling regent, the Duc d'Orleans. Today, residents are an ethnic gumbo of cultures, from Spanish and African to German and French —reflected in the foods served in the many restaurants here.

We admired one of four bronze death masks of Napolean Bonaparte, this one presented to the city by Doctor Francesco Antommarchi who attended the dying French leader. A second floor held paintings of the many French dignitaries that made their homes here. The third floor spoke to agriculture, the major economic activity in Louisiana in the nineteenth century, and the state's chief crops, cotton and sugar. This tier also focused on the Civil War, New Orleans being a key port on a major waterway that both the Union and Confederate forces sought to control. It fell to the Union in May 1862 after a six-day battle involving sea and ground forces, despite Confederate defensive actions at both Fort Jackson and Fort St. Philip. A subdivision of the 2nd floor, labeled the "Arsenal," contained riverboat history and miniatures of steam yachts, tugs, paddle wheelers, sailing ships and clippers.

This had been a good introduction to area history for me. I thanked my new friend, who was off to plantation hop, for her company. By now, it was early afternoon and I had worked up an appetite, so dipped back into the Quarter, this time via Carondelet Street, leading to famed Bourbon. The business folk, who had spilled out of the law offices and oil companies on this path, remarked on the pleasant weather.

The landscape changed at Canal, downshifting into pizza joints, lingerie shops, oyster bars, blues clubs and go-go palaces. Seeking lunch tips, I spoke with a Jersey-bred cocktail waitress, who suggested Mike Anderson's. Anderson was a former LSU football player who went pro for a year but was benched due to injuries. Though reportedly crowded on weekends, the café was quiet today.

Another passerby mentioned Hell's Kitchen, for red beans and rice, or Déjà Vu, for ribs, gumbo and po' boys (meat or seafood pressed between two slices of French bread). Déjà Vu, sadly, was also empty so I ambled to Cajun Cabin, a block or so east. The place was open air with a great view of the street and passersby. Like Steinbeck, I liked to observe, to peep at the populace, as it were, and this setting would allow me to do that.

My waitress brought me bread, salad and three ice cream scoop-sized pods of spicy jambalaya — a rice dish into which andouille sausage, tomatoes, peppers and bits of chicken had been mixed. Syrupy bread pudding, the meal capper, was an added plus. It was a tasty chow, a bon repas, if ever there was one.

Down the street, a place called the Old Opera House was throwing out some jamming tunes courtesy of a five-piece group of good old boys. I listened for a bit then tumbled along to another music club called The Rock. The group there was a no-mess-around blues quartet known as SRB, New Orleans natives. They were fronted by the high-styling Sherry, a molasses voiced, hip-swivelin' songstress.

Maison Bourbon, "dedicated to the preservation of jazz," sucked me in with the sounds of Dwight Burns. The man himself was a maison all by himself, tipping the scales at a good 350 that a black suit somehow managed to cover. "Blueberry Hill" was one of their song selections, which Dwight tooted along to on his shiny brass trumpet.

Moving off Bourbon to perpendicular backstreets, I glanced at voodoo shops, the former site of a celestial observatory, witchcraft dispensers, potion purveyors and, finally, to the French Market beside which a golden statue of a horseback-mounted Joan d'Arc stood. The live jazz there put a sashay in my step and the Mississippi waterfront beyond wowed the orbs. The Latgale, a southbound oil tanker, passed beside a northbound riverboat, as a couple at a makeshift music stand crooned light-hearted, kick-along folk music, strumming away on guitars with nary a care in the world. In a short while, the Daviken, from Sweden, and the two-stack paddle wheeler, Natchez, blasting its deep bellowing horn, chugged by.

Along Jackson Park, a painter had set up shop and was doing some touch-up to one of several paintings he had on display there, but mostly eyeing the pretty girls and maintaining his shit-eating grin.

In several locations, living statues posed absolutely still, intriguing passersby. Somewhere else, a sad sax cried "Somewhere Over the Rainbow." A film crew wrapped up equipment from a commercial shoot. Tarot card interpreters sought out willing subjects at tables upon which sticks of incense burned in little pots. A Dixieland brass band led by "Tuba Fats", that had taken up residence on and around a street bench, strummed out a happy melody. The people that lived in the dark alleys and cool, shaded rooms were creeping out into the open, their beady eyes blinking away the dying day.

Seeking coffee to boost my body batteries, I started working my way back into the heart of the Quarter. Wild paintings that glowed off their canvases caught my eye as I passed the Horizon Gallery on Royal. The woman minding the shop informed me that the pieces were the work of a local artist, Robert Cook.

I shuffled back to Déjà Vu where both patrons and staff were watching a "Simpsons" Halloween special. I thumbed a copy of *The Times Picayune* instead, reading about wildfires, fanned by Santa Ana winds, burning out of control in Southern California. Already, 15 people had died, 900 homes had been destroyed and 450,000 acres burned. Perhaps it had been wise for me to avoid that area of the state.

Bourbon Street was now alive with people out on the town and I waded through them to the Blues Bar, where 66-year-old Rooster and his Chicken Hawks were entertaining tables of out-of-towners. On the bar counter, a jack-o-lantern glowed brightly.

Things had really begun to erupt at the Bourbon Vieux where, from a balcony, two-dozen men lined up at a railing called down to passing women, "Show us your tits!" This was the New Orleans that I'd heard about but had imagined that this activity was restricted to Mardi Gras week. Apparently not, and as I looked on, ladies that answered the cries were showered with beaded necklaces.

In front of The Steak Pit, a large black fellow waved a sign advertising "HUGE ASS BEERS." At Pat O's Courtyard, the same beads-for-a-flash deal was happening though the tossers weren't getting the traffic for which they hoped. In fact, the only flashing going on was from other guys, which was met with booing and catcalls. One guy even shoved a glowing blue wand down the front of his pants, turning himself toward the balcony, inviting a ring toss. Mounted troopers trotted by quietly, followed by a black drag queen in a blonde wig, sporting an enormous false chest. The hoots reached a crescendo, merging with the sounds of live music acts up and down Bourbon — a cacophony of sound pounding the airwaves.

Like Steinbeck had claimed to be from Liverpool, a guy standing beside me gave the city as his homeplace. But it was the New York town of Liverpool near Syracuse, of which he was referring, where my dad grew up.

They were peers, in fact, and he had similar memories of Lakeshore Drive and the drive-in, sites I had visited with my folks. A painting contractor, he was in N.O. for a convention and, in fact, some of the guys in his group were among those up in the balcony.

Club 735, down the block, offered unique fare: Evil Dr. Cameron's Disturbed Movie Lab, a Tuesdays-only film series with themed selections. Tonight's lineup included "The Invisible Man", made in 1935 and starring Claude Rains. The host, wearing Mickey Mouse ears and a red plaid bathrobe (pajamas were an optional dress code requirement), greeted me at the door and hustled up a bag of popcorn. I settled into an oversized, worn, antique chair to enjoy the black-and-white classic.

Back at The Old Opera House, Dwayne Dopsie and the Zydeco Hellraisers were driving a Cajun locomotive, power jamming with machine gun intensity on a range of musical equipment including a chest-worn washboard and a squeezebox. When they broke for tequila shots and Dwayne came by me, I noticed the irises of his eyes were white, leaving only his pupils as the distinctive part. It gave him a wild, almost demonic look. The guy next to me said, "He's the voodoo man, been like that since birth."

In the street, pedestrians streamed by in an unceasing flow, drunk, half-drunk and getting there — smiling, slurring and stumbling. I joined the rushing river of humanity to find another hot spot, Razzoo. There, folks were packed in like sardines, shaking their booties and moving as a collective mass to the disco sounds The Connection Band was laying down.

At Fat Catz, across the way, a longhaired rock band belted out RUSH's "Tom Sawyer" to an appreciative jeans-and-leather audience. Shot girls kept them soused with test tubes containing a mysterious, berry-colored elixir. A corner spot, Howl At The Moon, featured two pianists at back-to-back Steinways taking audience requests, simulating rap beats and hurling humor at a cigar chomping, spirits swilling, mostly out-of-town group.

I was chomping, too, chomping to get going. I'd spent the day with this city, waking up by her side, dining with her, walking her streets and alleys, and putting her to bed. I'd forego a Halloween stay, let her sleep and slip out the back door quietly. The road waited impatiently for El Rucio's tires to burn along it.

Steinbeck made a quick exit from the city, too, though for a different reason. He was repulsed by the Cheerleader face-off he'd witnessed, which he described as a "frightening witches' Sabbath." Using "bestial, filthy and degenerate" words, the women had jeered and shrieked at "the littlest Negro girl you ever saw," the whites of whose eyes "showed like those of a frightened fawn." Meanwhile, the crowd they played to just howled and roared and whistled in delight. The scene filled him "with a shocked and sickened sorrow" that drove him to a retreat on the outskirts of the city where he could digest and contemplate what he had seen, and where he entertained with coffee and conversation a neatly dressed elder man who was passing. They spoke of the event and wondered how the situation would resolve itself.

Local station WTIX serenaded me with oldies as I made my own exit, climbing up and out of the city by way of a cement skyway. Suddenly, I was back in darkness and barreling along into another place and new day. At 1 a.m., I crossed a high bridge into my 26th state, Mississippi, and streaked to a midpoint on its southern coast, Gulfport. A state I'd never visited, it deserved a fair look in the daytime. As such, I dropped anchor at a Holiday Inn, gathered up some brochures from a display rack and soaked in a tub before bedding down at about 3.

Steinbeck was also fatigued but decided to press on, stopping to "offer a ride to an old Negro who trudged with heavy heels in the grass-grown verge beside the concrete road." The man became restless when Steinbeck asked him about the schools and sit-ins and excused himself from the vehicle though he had not yet reached his stop. This perturbed Steinbeck whose sleep was restless when weariness finally steered him to a motel.

Day 54: The Biloxi Three

The sound of low-flying aircraft was my nudge awake. Coast Guard helicopters, commercial choppers, air force transport planes, observation aircraft and business jets were amongst the winged and rotored flying machines that passed overhead every five minutes, coming in for landings at Gulfport-Biloxi International Airport. I really didn't mind their presence actually and, since it was about nine by this time, I felt well rested and refreshed and non-intruded upon. Standing outside my room, I even watched them arc over the parking lot and was able to see the pilots' faces.

Clean up and organizing, mandatory tasks at stops like these that afford that luxury, followed. Crawling out of the room at noon and craving food, I tumbled into the adjacent Pelican's restaurant and was seated in a booth near four officers from the Mississippi Highway Patrol. Eggs Benedict was my breakfast pick, enjoyed along with copies of *USA Today*.

The California fires, ten separate spots in all raging between the Mexican border/San Diego area to L.A.'s suburbs, continued to be the lead story, further convincing me that I'd been wise to pass on dipping south from Paso Robles to see friends in Burbank. Already, over 560,000 acres had been devoured by fires, at least three of which were intentionally set, six were under investigation and another started accidentally by a hunter. Dozens of neighborhoods of medium-priced to million-dollar homes had been transformed into "ashen moonscapes" according to reports, some 80,000 people were without electricity, sporting events were relocated, flights cancelled and highways closed. The director of the State Office of Emergency Services expected that it would be "the most expensive fire in California history." With the unfolding news came the stories of dashed hopes, tragic loss, heart-breaking destruction and miraculous survival. One couple that had tried to evacuate was turned back and cheated death by jumping into and hunkering down in their swimming pool as fire rushed like a speeding car across their property.

Back in Chicago, an alarming cluster of meningococcal disease cases forced thousands of emergency inoculations. Minnesota experienced its first significant snowfall of the season, causing several cars to slide off roads. Solar eruptions, which had been happening in steady spurts since October 19th, reached a crescendo yesterday when a solar storm caused a blackout in Sweden, damaged two Japanese satellites and upset radio communications and navigation systems for jets and on ships. Airliners traversing northern latitudes purposely flew lower to protect passengers from extra salvos of radiation. The report made me feel so small in the realm of the universe.

My path and Steinbeck's were now divided. He headed due north, when he awoke at the motel, "toward Jackson and Montgomery," giving a lift to a young man in a light gray suit he'd met at a hamburger stand.

They breached the topic of the Cheerleaders and the man made it known that he supported their position — "somebody got to keep the goddamn niggers out of our schools." The stance pushed Steinbeck's buttons and he pulled over and ejected the man, absorbing shrill cries of "nigger lover, nigger lover" as he sped off.

Having experienced no similar events and still buoyed by a spirit of adventure, I wanted to continue east, to the Atlantic coast and Florida *then* up to rejoin Steinbeck's path, thereby truly traveling the perimeter of the United States. I believe it was his intention to do the same, but the disturbing things he'd seen in New Orleans and the increasing grind of the road had worn him down. As such, I sprinted the quick four miles down Highway 49 to the oceanfront, joined Route 90 near the Marine Life Oceanarium and took the intersecting shore route east.

Forming the waterfront here was a wide open, sandy but inexplicably empty beach and a departure point for a ferry to Ship Island, the site of a strategic fort during the Civil War. The history of the latter dates back to 1699, when French explorers named it for the deep-water anchorage it afforded ships, and it became a "Plymouth Rock" or arrival point for many French settlers. In 1812, it was also a rendezvous site for British ships when they made their unsuccessful attack on New Orleans. The beach was sugary white, like those I'd known in Sarasota, Florida, and clean from all appearances. Whole flocks of pelicans bobbed or stood around in the gentle ripples that nuzzled the shore.

Very quickly, I was in Biloxi and didn't feel like doing anything more than admiring this coastal view. However, Beauvoir, the stunning home of Jefferson Davis, the only president of the Confederate States of America, appeared and demanded a look. On 51 acres fronting the Gulf of Mexico and shaded by oaks and Spanish moss, the property also contained antebellum outbuildings, a Civil War museum, cemetery, Tomb of the Unknown Soldier and nature trails.

My timing was perfect as an orientation film was just beginning. It divulged a litany of facts of which I'd been unaware such as Davis' efforts to modernize the United States Army, expand the Capitol building in Washington, D.C. with its present-day dome, and build up the railroads. He sacrificed much in service to his country and was celebrated as a beloved Southern son. Not a particularly good student as a cadet at West

Point, he graduated in the bottom third of his class. As to his family, he lost his first wife, Sarah, to malaria, first child, Samuel, at age two to measles and two other sons in the war.

The film room exited into a small exhibit area where I fell in with three women touring the complex together: Tarrah, named after the plantation from "Gone With The Wind" and part Cherokee; Jaime, a Mississippi native married to an architect; and black-haired Olivia, another Mississippi girl, and part Apache. Continuing on together, we headed outside onto the grounds, to a cottage/office with large rocking chairs on the porch facing the Gulf. Then, it was on to Beauvoir, the house Davis initially visited, boarded at and eventually came to own when its keeper, novelist Sara Ann Dorsey, passed on. This main house was built with cypress, and featured 14-foot high ceilings and wonderful, original period furnishings.

In a magnolia-shaded cemetery, 771 war veterans and their family members were buried. Amongst the stones, one was dedicated to Sarah Peebles, who "having finished life's duty…now sweetly rests." Another was marked William Conway Summers, who died 74 years ago to the day before New York's Trade Towers fell. Davis' father Samuel's grave denoted him as a major in the Revolutionary War from Lincoln County.

Our tour concluded in the gift shop where the girls donned straw hats for a photo opp and collapsed in laughter. Though there was little chance that I would forget the trio, Jaime shared an acronym that would cement them in my memory: G.R.I.T.S. = Girls Raised In The South.

Scooting on down the coast past casinos and amusement parks that lit up in blinking neon at day's last light, I crossed over the island-dotted Back Bay of Biloxi, a scene through which a Navy transport plane, highlighted against the rosy sunset, flew. Enjoying the tomato soup-colored sky reflected in my rearview mirror, I sped through towns like Vancleave, Fountainebleau and Gautier.

A long, low, cement bridge rolled me across the Pescagoula River to Escatawpa, Moss Point and Franklin Creek. Then, whammy, I was in Alabammy, my 27th state, dubbed on the entry sign as, simply, "The Beautiful."

Mobile Historic Highway sounded intriguing but dropped me into a mess of gas stations and waffle houses. I imagined there were sites of historic significance to be seen further along, but it was night now and

I wouldn't be able to appreciate them. Taking a bead on downtown at the mouth of the Mobile River, I connected with Water Street near the financial and restaurant area, took a loop around, and pulled into a slip space beside Heroes. An independently owned sports bar that offered sports entertainment on 11 TVs around its spacious brick interior, the place, to my joy, was featuring a Knicks/Orlando basketball game broadcast. The bartender served me up a Coke while fulfilling a food-to-go order for another patron, with whom I chitchatted.

A long-time ad sales rep for the local paper and area native, she said of Mobile there was a lot of "lovingness" between people but that it was "run by old money" and "clique-ish." The key to getting ahead, she believed, was "not what you know, but who you know." Mobile was not without its problems, she continued — "Race is an issue still, people pretend with each other," there was a "major serious crunch" with the schools and the economy had "taken a slump."

When she exited, I ordered up one of Heroes' classic burgers and tapped the bartender for his knowledge on Alabama-born celebrities. Off the top of his head, he reeled off: Jimmy Buffett, Hank Aaron, "Forrest Gump" author Winston Groom and Jeremiah Denton, former senator and author of "When Hell Was In Session." At the far end of the bar counter, the owner shared more tidbits of information, noting that Heroes had once been the Catholic Maritime Club.

I moved along to Veets, once a whorehouse apparently, where I looked through an "Old Mobile Photograph Album" showing turn-of-the-century photos of the town. Back then, the main drag was busy with theaters, independent retail shops like Pearson's Ladieswear and Kenny Company Teas, Coffees and Sugars. The schooners at the dock would take on cargoes of lumber from railcars and unload bananas from the Caribbean. Sternwheelers plied the Alabama, Tombigbee and Mobile Rivers, carrying cotton from plantations upriver. Small fishing boats worked the oyster beds.

Hurricanes have been a hard fact of life here, smashing ships against the wharves and causing wide damage down through the years. In the early 1900s, a fire also wiped out several blocks on the South Side. I imagined Mobilians would commiserate well with Fargoans, given the host of disasters the two towns have endured.

"Over the Bay", an expression I'd heard several times during the evening already was and has always been where Mobilians have summered. Monroe Park on Mobile Bay was also a favorite destination, offering outdoor movies, a roller coaster, merry-go-round, baseball park and concession stands. For a quieter time, Mobilians strolled along a bayside walk, to watch boats and other pedestrians, or lounged in Bienville Square.

Theater was big, with vaudeville acts at the Lyric and 10¢ movies at the Queen, Crown, Strand and Dauphine. Movers and shakers of the day were Admiral Raphael Semmes of the Confederate Navy, Father Abram Ryan of St. Mary's Church, *Register* editor Frank Craighead, and Augusta Evans Wilson, the first American woman to earn in excess of $100,000 as a writer.

A guitar trio, "Captain" Jerry Smith, longhaired Mark Willis and clean-cut Bobby Butchka, got pickin' and a-grinnin,' lit up in a red glow from overhead gels. I shifted over to listen, the local paper in hand, noting a lead story about California Governor-Elect Arnold Schwarzenneger, who was at the Mandalay Bay Hotel in Vegas presenting a medal to the winner of the 39th annual Mr. Olympia competition.

A song choice that I offered, America's "Horse With No Name", inspired a couple to get up and dance beside a pumpkin-topped jukebox. It turned out that Jersey-born Bobby had appeared in one of America's videos about six years ago. White-haired Jerry was the senior member of the three and hacked his way through a couple chords remarking, "Have I got CRS Syndrome? Can't remember shit?" The band played songs by Phil Collins, Dan Fogelberg, Led Zeppelin, Bob Denver, Arlo Guthrie, The Beatles and more, sending a warm vibe floating through this railroad car-shaped tavern. These were the tunes that filled my youth and brought all the years and associated memories tumbling back for a few intimate moments.

Drifting back along Dauphin, I came to Banana Joe's, a big place with an island theme — nets, floats, sea murals — punchy radio beats and a live act, the Coattails. Their repertoire ranged from reggae to rock and made for many happy feet. The drummer, wearing a black tee with the slogan, "Got crabs?" across the front, wailed on his skins.

I got chatting with a Mobilian whose great-grandfather was a lighthouse keeper on Dauphin Island. Her great-grandmother's seven sisters married her great-grandfather's seven brothers, not only unique but mathematically complicated!

At last call, I located the van, steamed across the architecturally impressive Bay Bridge and followed the Cochrane Causeway through a web of industrial complexes to a well-lit lot behind a hotel, in eyesight of the U.S.S. Alabama Battleship Memorial. This seemed as good a place as any to camp and so I did.

Day 55: Steel Britches & White Sands

My day began aboard the mighty U.S.S. Alabama, permanently stationed at the mouth of the Mobile River in Battleship Park, a property that also contained the submarine U.S.S. Drum, an Aircraft Pavilion and several tanks. Stepping into the Main Deck Wardroom of the 680-foot long, 108-foot wide, 35,000-ton ship, I immediately knew her inside and out, having slept, eaten and seen films on her sister ship, the U.S.S. Massachusetts in Battleship Cove, MA. The two, along with the South Dakota and Indiana were South Dakota Class battleships, so followed the same design. The "Mass" had been an overnight destination three years running for my son Evan and me and our scouting program.

Fully laden with 127 officers, her crew and all her munitions, the Alabama's weight would be 10,000 tons greater, but she was agile in the water and earned nine Battle Stars for shooting down 22 enemy aircraft during World War II. Commissioned in August 1942, her tour of duty took her from Norfolk, VA to her ultimate field of action in the South Pacific: the Gilbert and Marshall Islands, Truk, Hollandia, Guam, Leyte, Saipan, Hawaii, Okinawa and Japan. From Japan, in August 1945, she cruised to the western U.S. coast from where she was towed to Mobile in 1964. Her class was an improvement on the preceding North Carolina class, as she was outfitted with 16-inch (versus 14-inch) guns and armor to withstand fire from the same.

A middle-aged mustachioed former Coast Guard serviceman was busy mixing up paint in an adjoining room and gave me more recent detail about the ship, as an Andrew Sisters tune crackled from an overhead speaker. Working aboard her almost nine years, he'd known of two hurricanes that had hit here and caused damage. The first was Freddie in 1979 with "winds so strong it pushed the Alabama over three degrees" to port as it rested in 25 feet of mud. Its caretakers wanted to straighten her but were worried they'd "rip the top of the ship off its bottom half" if they tried, so left her atilt. In 1997, Hurricane George struck, producing surf that flooded the grounds of the complex and left "snakes and fish inside the pavilion, enough treated wood to build ten decks" caught between the ship and bank, and other objects like "a refrigerator still full of beer."

Descending to the Third Deck, I toured the crew's quarters — steel-framed bunks strung with canvas mats — and some of the many service areas for crewmen. Indeed, these were floating cities with all the accoutrements that one would find on land: a laundry, tool maker, bakery, kitchen, tailor, barber, cobbler, soda fountain, blacksmith, church and butcher. A notable crewman was "Bullet Bob" Feller, whom I'd learned about back in Cleveland at Jacobs Field. A pitcher with the Indians in the 1940s and 1950s, he was inducted into the Baseball Hall of Fame.

An on-board film showed what life was like during the active years, when you had to eat in synch with the rocking of the ship and steel yourself for the adrenaline-pumping challenge of dive bombing Japanese planes, the "akk akk" chop of the 20mm. machine guns and roar and bone-jarring blasts of the massive 16-inch 45 caliber. The latter used 2,700-pound armor piercing projectiles taller and bigger around than I was, that traveled 2,300 feet per second and a maximum distance of 36,900 yards to penetrate 16 inches of steel. The ship was a beauty and her crew obviously loved her and brought her to life.

The sun was climbing to its highest point of the day and the beach was calling so, with a quick stop at Argiro's Store and Deli for smoked turkey and bacon on a po' boy roll, I sped along 10 East into state #28, Florida, "The Sunshine State." The state was well known to me, having vacationed here numerous times and attended my freshman year of college at Rollins in Winter Park, near Orlando. I knew its flatness and pines and roadside drainage ditches frequented by alligators, and its small, single-level homes. It had tolerated my mischievous New York attitude, bronzed my skin, offered me its native lasses and shown me its magical sea life.

Skipping south on Blue Angel Parkway, named after the world-class aerial acrobats that make their home at the air base here, I felt my way to Perdido Key. A brochure about the site promised, "A natural paradise lined with miles of unspoiled beaches, bays, estuaries, wetlands and abundant native sea life and wildlife." American artist George Catlin, upon his visit in 1834, described it as "deep and bottomless," a land of a "thousand charms."

The claims were true and the sand white as snow, crystalline and soft, a private thrill to set foot in. Dunes of light green grasses leaning with a constant breeze lined the ridge. Sandpipers piped along, hammering the sand at intervals with their needlenose bills. Black, angel hair-like ropes of seaweed added a sharp contrast. Delicate scallop and clamshells lay beside their sturdier oyster cousins. Bleached sand dollars were the infrequent treasure. Waves crosscut each other to race up the beach.

I hoped the healing properties of the salt water would buff the now dried and scabbed areas on my legs where rash rings had been. My ankles, particularly my left, had swelled inexplicably, to the extent that just walking around had to be conducted gingerly.

Staking out waterside real estate, I waded in up to my waist and wrestled with the waves. When that got tiring, I sat on my backside in the shallows or picked along the sand for bright shells. The sandwich went down easy and the sun's rays warmed me. In this way, I idled away the afternoon.

When a little chill set in, I gathered my gear, rinsed off under an outdoor shower and went west on the shore road looking for drinks and eats. Flora-Bama, a lounge and package store on the Florida/Alabama border waved me in with its "Do It With Us On The Line" banner. Settling into a front barroom, I ordered O.J. and butterflied fried shrimp and listened to the tongue-in-cheek hilarity of guitarist/songwriter Jay Hawkins. His themes ranged from golf to being down on your luck to unfounded lawsuits. As the sun set, the lights went down rather suddenly, leaving him in a red spot. "Must be daylight savings time again," he remarked. Above him in the rafters, hung bras of various colors and proportions, which had been abandoned by their owners. A customer near Jay, a tall guy with a long, grey beard and hair, tapped out a beat with his cowboy boots. His t-shirt bore the name of a tattoo business and he had the artwork on both arms to support it.

To satisfy a sweet tooth, I bought chocolate chip ice cream in a sugar cone from a place called Cakes & Cones. Though I tried to be careful with it, naturally, it dripped down the front of my sweater as I continued east. Not sure *where* I wanted to be for the night, I just kept going, through spread-out Pensacola, and its shore area, Fort Walton Beach and Santa Rosa Beach. My passage alternated between oases of neon, fast food and clubs and dark stretches of seashore.

Destin was a bright patch and brought AJ's Club Bimini, an oversized bamboo and palm hut sheltering an oceanfront bar. In one corner, a band served up Bob Marley's "Jammin'" to the tanned and casually dressed crowd, while a large white sailboat with a bright green light on its bow slowly drifted past.

When a drop-dead beautiful Asian girl strolled up all tan and halter-topped, one of the bartenders towed her in and slid free drinks her way. His investment, he hoped, would keep the woman there and draw other customers to make the cash registers ring. It was a simple matter of supply and demand.

Back on the trail, I shot past Grayton Beach, Carillon Beach, Sunnyside and Santa Monica before arriving in Panama City, a good overnight destination I thought. For accommodations, Sugar Sands Beach Resort served up a 425-square foot room with a full kitchen, dining area and balcony with a Gulf front view. It was a lot more than I needed but the price couldn't be beat, so I gladly piled in. A soak and some TV and I was fast asleep, the sound of the surf my lullaby.

Day 56: Seashells by the Seashore

Stepping out onto my balcony at the Sugar Sands, I believed that I'd found paradise. A light gust kept the air temperature at a perfect 75 degrees. The sands, like Perdido, were fine and, I would find, cool underfoot even at the hottest point in the day. The water by the shore was shallow and only gently deepened, with no jagged rocks, glass or other underwater hazards to worry about. The waves lazily rolled in, crested and fell more in exhaustion than in fierceness.

The only food I'd brought to the room — really the only food I had other than Tecate, summer sausage and a few sun-softened chocolate chip cookies — was cereal, so I had a bowl rail-side, looking to see if other resort neighbors had stirred. I was surprised to find a few adults and several children in the pool area below. Not wanting to waste a moment of the day, I shoved myself into overdrive, pulled my things together, checked out and set up shop on a wooden lounge chair on the beach.

The water looked so inviting that I went to drop in it. A crab, claws up like a surgeon who had just scrubbed his hands, ushered me into the shallows. As shell collecting had always been a favorite pastime, I stepped out and along the high tide line where many fine examples, and the broken homes of large snails, lay at intervals. To ensure a varied take-home crop, I made careful selections and placed them on the lounge next to mine. They made a neat display against the blue vinyl cushion topping the recliner.

My greatest pleasure, however, was taking the occasional dip and letting the jade green ocean current carry and rock me as I was suspended in it. Its effects were truly rejuvenating and, soon, sore skin and swelling was a memory, replaced by a bronze and golden pallet and great feeling of being alive. Early afternoon, I staged my reluctant retreat, showered poolside and began my advance on the central part of the state. The digital readout at the A.G. Edwards office back on Route 98 said 82 degrees.

Schlotzky's Deli in commercially choked and congested Panama City's downtown took care of my appetite with slabs of turkey and bacon piled between thick slices of sourdough bread. The cashier at the drive-through window was dressed as a sumo wrestler, reminding me that it was Halloween. In fact, I started seeing its signs everywhere: A local church holding a Pumpkin Patch Party to "mobilize God's Army" and a gas station using black and orange letters on its signage.

Turning east onto 20, I skirted a roadside stand selling Indian River Citrus and Sweet Taters. Diana's Open-Air Market displayed bright green watermelons and "Boiled P'nuts." To say that this section of Florida was rural would be an understatement. Just ask the prairie dogs whose holes were everywhere along the side of the road. Or the cows chewing their cuds at the Thistle Dew Farm. Or the old man spreading seed by throwing it from the back of a four-wheel motorcycle. Or Connie, whipping up possum stew at Connie's Country Kitchen Home Cookin.'

Shelled Peas, Turnips and Collards were the vegetable names spray-painted on a series of boards at the backside of Blountstown, just before the Apalachicola River crossover. Curious to know what's been capturing the attention of Blountstonians, I stopped at a convenience store and shelled out 50¢ for *The County Record*, serving Blountstown and Calhoun since 1907. A lead story was about the Calhoun Correctional Institution tracking team, which won top honors in a regional competition wherein they had to hunt down fictitious fugitives. The paper also celebrated the life of Bessie Davis Wynn, who had resided in the same house in Blountstown for most of her 95 years. As a child, she went to school at a Methodist church, since there were no schools for black children to attend. There she discovered poetry and learned to make jewelry before marrying, raising children and working as a family's maid for 35 years, outliving her employers.

My curiosity satisfied, I moved along to Hosford, which delivered me into the hands of the Pat Thomas Parkway. "Pat" led me to Interstate 10.

I'd wished to spend some time down in Ocala (where El Rucio was customized), would be passing through there, but preferred to make my stop Winter Park if I could arrive at a decent hour. It was twenty years prior that I first arrived in the community, to report to Rollins College, or "Jolly Rolly Collie", as I knew it, for my first year of higher education. It was an exciting, distracting, eye-opening year, and reconnecting to the place all these years later, and on Halloween, seemed fitting.

There were whole parts of the country where I'd felt out of place, because of the clothes I was wearing, the vehicle I was driving or the way I spoke. But now I was connecting with familiar things and expected I'd recognize most items on a menu.

Still, I was not quite home as upcoming sightings would prove. At a rest stop east of Tallahassee, a large pickup and its trailer were piled high with bright green watermelons. A burgundy minivan I'd been following bore the plate JCLUVSU (Jesus Christ Loves You). The Suwannee River was definitely not the Connecticut River.

Soon I was riding 75 South, "The 100+ mile short-cut to Disney World," the last south-going route I would take on this American Tour. And as I passed through Gainesville, hunger crept up on me. A convenient café with stools along a counter served me a plate-sized mushroom and Swiss burger and side order of chips. My waitress was a tall Mexican woman with straight black hair that trailed all the way down to her hips. In the spirit of the holiday, she was decked in thigh-high black boots and a black outfit, a "biker chick" getup she explained. Other servers had adopted outfits like Dorothy from the Wizard of Oz, Zorro and a French maid.

The Mark III facility, where El Rucio was accessorized, was visible from the highway as we breezed through Ocala. As if she sensed it, she pulled slightly in that direction. I steered her left, though, and onto the Ronald Reagan Turnpike for the stretch to Winter Park. The East-West Parkway picked me up from there and delivered me to I-4 for the skate by beautiful Orlando, defined by big business like Wachovia, Trusco Capital, CNL, SouthTrust Bank, Bank of American, Travelers and the Radisson.

Fairbanks Avenue was my exit, one I knew so well, but a route that was hard to recognize once I was on it. Where was the dance club, the used records shop? The corner store was still there, where I'd get a 12-pack of Old Milwaukee for four bucks, but it faced these elaborate, illuminated arches framing what used to be a simple main entrance to the campus.

Campus itself looked the same and I was glad to see a few rowdy students with drink cups in hand standing in the middle of the street. They were glad to see me, too — a throwback to a freer, rowdier time — a time they wished they knew.

Circling back to the arches, I started down Park Avenue. Was I lost? What were all these upscale shops and wine bars doing here? Where did these BMWs, Audis and Lexus (Lexi?) come from? Where were the bars and discos and pizza joints that we all used to frequent? Where were the crowds of students? The noise? The commotion? Who were all these elder folks in their pleated trousers, buffed shoes and polos? These spa-maintained ladies of society? I was in Carmel, California all over again!

Starbucks, and an empty pizza shop that would have been jammed in the old days but struggled to keep afloat now, was all to which I could relate. To two off-duty waitresses from 310 Park South, where the staff had dressed in army fatigues as characters from the old TV program "MASH," I mourned the loss of Winter Park's gritty character.

I-4 carried me fast through more places I didn't recognize and ultimately over the Port Orange Bridge to the well-lit hotel and beach stretch known as A1A or Atlantic Blvd. There were still beach ramps I was pleased to see, assuming that that meant one could still drive along the beach like the old days but, like so many other things, I couldn't be sure now.

As it was two in the morning, I found an oceanfront hotel lot from which I thought I was least likely to be rousted and crawled into the back bed, the first time I'd slept there since the "itchies" started. Keeping one sliding window ajar, to enjoy the rush of the surf, I dropped to sleep.

Day 57: Sand, Surf & Sweets

Just before first light, I rolled out of the van, walked through the lobby of this hotel in the lot of which I'd camped, and down back steps to the famed Daytona Beach. Soon, the sun came up over the horizon, seagulls began their scavenging and the beach patrol appeared, to pull 10 m.p.h. signs out onto the sand, signaling that the auto parade was, indeed, not dead.

In the hotel's oceanview breakfast room, I nabbed a danish, juice and Cheerios, settling at a table to eat and read the local daily, *The Daytona Beach News-Journal*. A special insert further confirmed the existence of the car path on the beach, which enjoyed bicycles and horse-and-buggies even before cars were invented. A $5 fee allowed beachdriving sunrise to sunset, except during turtle nesting season, May through October, when cars were allowed only from 8 a.m. to 7 p.m. daily. Autos were also prohibited in Conservation Zones, to protect marine and plant life.

Fetching my laptop from the van, I made a more permanent home for myself, on the pool deck, fighting a bit with a crosswind as I typed. When the pool man needed to hose the deck down, I moved back into the breakfast room, now full of folks and their families. A large black fellow, who reminded me of Eddie Murphy's Buddy Love character in "The Nutty Professor," was telling a fellow guest about a rampant drug problem in his home city of Baltimore. "We got fitty thousand drug addicts up there, high on crack cocaine, throwin' their lives away. I wanta get out of there... You goin' to the parade?" The event of which he spoke was related to a homecoming weekend at Methune-Cookman, the local college. Many of the diners here appeared to be in town for the occasion.

The beach was calling and I answered, plopping down in the sand. It was very, very fine and not as white as the Gulf sand, with not a shell to be seen. The surf, as in Big Sur, California, was too intense for crustaceans to inhabit and pounded them to smithereens if they tried to take up residence. To me, though, the surf was a playground and I stood waist-deep angled to it, letting wave after wave crash into me. On occasion, a single engine plane, towing an advertising banner, would pass. I strolled along through the waves and then back onto the sand past vehicles that had pulled in down the way.

Hungry again, I walked down the road to a chain eatery for a foot-long tuna sandwich to which I added nearly all their toppings, from pickles to peppers. It and some chips made a filling beach lunch. The balance of daylight hours was spent lounging by the pool where I met a couple from Orlando, who had escaped from their five kids for the weekend.

As I watched the ripples move along the length of the pool, reach the opposite end, and coil and snake, the sun started to fall behind the hotel, outlining the pointed leaves of palms across the road. Seagulls, planning their evening fishing strategy, conferenced on the beach. The surf continued its endless cycle, tumbling forward, falling back.

Quite suddenly, the sun was extinguished as an ominous grey cloud moved in front of it, instantly chilling the air and producing goose bumps across my skin. More threatening cloud clusters that took hold of the sky followed the grey mass. It was as if they were purposely trying to drive me inside, telling me to find shelter in this inn that had unknowingly hosted me for much of the day. I obeyed, securing an oceanfront room with a balcony, where I hung my towel and swim trunks to dry. Night had fallen fast and, though dark, the white ridges of waves, reflecting the moon, could be seen as they rolled in.

After a brief shower, which I couldn't seem to make warm enough, and brush of my teeth, during which I managed to snap my toothbrush in half, I got motivated for dinner. Though I'd read about several eateries, I didn't have a specific place in mind, and so chugged along Atlantic. An Italian place a short piece down the road seemed inviting, but would have been too easy a stop. I wanted to work harder for my dinner and see all my options. There was a Hawaiian place, with a luau-style dinner and hula dancing show, further on the right, but it seemed tacky. I let a diner or two slip by me, then noticed Shells.

A seafood place, it seemed an appropriate choice given my locale. Just inside, I passed beneath a sign that threatened, "Unattended children will be used as bait," and followed my diminutive waitress to a back table with a birds-eye view of other patrons.

The heat of the day and saltiness of the ocean had left me parched and so I guzzled the tall glass of water brought to me, which the busboy couldn't refill fast enough to keep up. A bowl of thick, creamy clam chowder, into which I dunked rolls, came next. When my seafood Siciliano arrived, I devoured the linguine that served as a base and picked like a sandpiper at the morsels of clams, mussels, shrimp and scallops.

My eyes were definitely bigger than my stomach and I was TKO'd after only the second round. Conceding the fight, I removed my gloves and left the arena seeking caffeine, like smelling salts, to keep me going. No purveyor met my standards for quality, however, and so I had to settle for the next best thing: a small cup of coffee ice cream.

With no other visible evening attractions, a beach walk behind my hotel was in order. Again, the whoosh of the surf was a constant and I amused myself deciphering messages scrawled with sticks or fingers in the sand. It seemed too early to be down, but I was flagging from the day by then and heeded the hints. Lying in my king-size bed, I listened to the sounds of the ocean, filling my room.

PART SEVEN

Homeward Bound

Day 58: To the island of Herons

I woke as I had fallen asleep, to the ocean, and another glorious day. Sitting in a big chair, I caught a television weather report, indicating clear skies with a slight chance of an afternoon shower. Not wanting to waste another second, I cleaned up, removed my gear to the van and visited the breakfast room, this time as a legitimate guest. My visit timed with the appearance of the Orlando couple and we gabbed while I nibbled on a hard-boiled egg and bran muffin. They were not beach-attired at all, explaining, “We’re going to go home and clean before the doggone kids come back.”

While there were activities — a flea market, the Cape Canaveral Space Center, Daytona Speedway — for me to do in the area, I was interested in the beach only, knowing that I’d soon be in cooler environs where I wouldn’t have this luxury. With a plastic bag containing appropriate necessities, I threw down in the sand again, alternating between snoozing, enjoying the water and noshing on grapes, cheese and crackers that I’d secured for the occasion.

I’d also bought the Sunday edition of the *News-Journal* from a vending machine in the hotel lobby and leafed through it as I soaked up the sun. Though not a local story, I took note of an item about a 13-year-old surfer girl in Kauai who’d had her left arm bitten off by a shark as she paddled out into the waves on her board. Her friend’s father saved her from bleeding to death by using a surfboard leash as a tourniquet. An accompanying photo showed a fireman holding the board, out of which a 16-inch wide, 8-inch deep bite had been taken, pegging the shark at 12 to 15 feet long.

Back in Mississippi, a woman who snapped from stress rammed her car with three children inside into the DeSoto Civic Center in Southhaven, where President Bush was speaking. The President was never in danger and continued his tour schedule.

The paper, incidentally, was marking its 75th anniversary under the control of the Davidson family, who took over in 1928. Then, editor, and later publisher, Herbert Davidson promised that the daily would be "not just five cents worth of reading matter, but a daily informant, counselor and entertainer."

My dad rang to check on my position and was surprised to learn I'd made it to Florida. He spoke of the Halloween holiday in Chapel Hill, mentioning that 78,000 people and 300 police had participated in the parade down Franklin, the main drag through the university town.

It wasn't until 3, and after a last refreshing dip in the pool, that I climbed back aboard El Rucio to make my big turn north, the last stretch to home. Guessing that A1A would be a much more interesting and scenic route than I-95, I began along it. If the Drive-In Christian Church, a lot where you could tune in a recorded sermon, was any indication, I would be entertained.

Businesses on the route reflected life here: Side 'o Sea, Water's Edge, Beach Comer, Buccaneer, Grand Seas, La Playa, Oceanside and Tropix. Any which way you could spin a sea or beach theme. Atlantic Avenue stretched far, through Ormond Beach, more residential cactus-lined Ormond By-The-Sea, the North Peninsula Recreation Area, and the grand condos and long pier at Flagler Beach.

Stopping for a moment at the latter, I strolled its long, narrow shoreline. It was a reddish color and, scooping up a handful of sand, comprised of tiny, shattered shell bits. Clumps of brown seaweed lay everywhere. Sandpipers played with the tide while gulls hung in place on the breeze overhead. Whole shells were few, in fact, and those I found were of only one or two varieties. It was a pleasant stop.

As I picked up to go again, a live performer on the upper deck of Finnegan's Beachside Pub started in, "Well, they call me the breeze, I keep blowin' down the road." "God wants spiritual fruit, not religious nuts" was the message a small Baptist church in Palm Coast wanted to project. Its neighbors were folks in gated communities like the Sea Colony and Matanzas Villages, who were definitely in their right minds when they bought land parcels here.

Marineland, across from a University of Florida research laboratory, seemed like one of your typical Sunshine State tourist traps featuring a pool and bleacher set-up with performing seals and other aquatic creatures whose names I'd be safe to bet were Flipper, Nemo, Sammy or Namoo.

Summer Haven was anything but summery as the clouds let loose with a cool, saturating downpour. First Federal Bank reported that it was 77 degrees at 4:35 p.m. when I breached St. Augustine, a place I remembered visiting when I was not more than eight. At that time, it filled my imagination with thoughts of pirates and lost treasure and great sailing ships flying the Jolly Roger. For old time's sake, I crossed the Bridge of Lions and stopped to walk the bright green crabgrass-covered grounds of the Castillo de San Marcos. Built between 1672 and 1695, the Spanish fort, with its domed, arrow-slit lookout towers and black cannons pointed at the bay, stood for decades against English attacks. During the American Revolution, it was a British stronghold. Later, it served as a key battery for U.S. coastal defense.

From an Exxon up the road, an Old Town Trolley was taking visitors on a tour that included historic St. George Street and the Old Jail, built in 1891 by railroad magnate Henry Flagler to resemble a fine hotel. As I fled the now completely commercial area that attracted poorly attired, corndog-stuffed tourists, I sighted the Fountain of Youth, purported to be the site where explorer Ponce de Leon found the secret of eternal youth.

To make up some yardage, I reluctantly joined the interstate south of Jacksonville. Some 20 exits north, at the very tip-top of Florida, an exit for Fernandina Beach came up. I'd heard that open fires and alcohol consumption was permitted there, which encouraged me to go explore it as a rest stop for the evening. Needing dinner and breakfast supplies, I stopped at an airy Winn-Dixie and made the aisle-to-aisle rounds.

All camping related signs steered me to Fort Clinch but when I got there, the entry gates were closed. Seeking alternate suggestions, I was tipped to Talbot State Park.

On the way to the area, I streamed by some posh spots and unique oceanfront homes and found myself near Amelia Island. Crossing over a long land bridge, I came to a boat ramp near a public bathroom. That area was one possibility, though I'd noticed another, designated as Amelia Island State Park, back on the other side. There was a large lot there that appeared to be for the use of fishermen, but would suit my purposes, too.

Before long, my grill was set up, a sauce was going in my skillet, pasta was bubbling in another and the Tecate was going down easy. Across the way, an SUV pulled in, but remained dark and still for a long while. Then, when a man and woman did emerge, they climbed in the back and it was dark again. A little while later, after food had happily found its way to my belly, a pickup carrying another couple came in and circled down around a dune onto the sand. It appeared I'd found make-out point. Folks arrived and departed at intervals as I found my way to my van bed and finally dropped, a ceiling of sharply defined stars overhead.

Day 59: A Bite of the Peach

The sound of maintenance workers piling out of a Chevy pickup stirred me this particular morning. They set off with their garbage bins and mops and spray bottles for the restroom/bait shop on the other side of the long bridge from me. Several cars, belonging to fishermen, had pulled in and parked for the day by this time. They continued to arrive, with handcarts to tote their multiple poles and extensive gear. A couple of herons soared in like big aircraft and landed in a marsh in front of the van. Things were getting crowded. It was moving on time.

A Chevron, back along A1A North in this community that threw together hardcore men of the sea and the golf-and-tennis set, served as a great stop for freshening up and changing. Soon, I was climbing back over the high bridge that had carried me across the Amelia River to the island and zipping through rush hour traffic to the interstate. En route, I saw a lot with a sign that shouted "CAMPING", and wondered how they could call it that. "PARKING" would have been more appropriate given that one's great outdoor adventure there would consist of pulling one's hulking RV up window-to-window alongside someone else's hulking RV to sit and watch TV and eat pre-packaged food and maybe walk the dog on the tarmac. Where had all the adventuresome outdoorsmen gone? Had they all been reduced to propane-sustained aluminum cocooners?

Rain stayed with me, and headlights were in use, as I approached state #29, the great state of Georgia. "We're glad Georgia's on your mind" the border sign exclaimed while also trumpeting its role as 1995 World Series champs and host of the 1996 Summer Olympics. My brother Dave had lived in the state then, in the Atlanta suburb of Alpharetta, where he and his wife hosted a Nigerian athlete for two weeks. Atlanta, itself, had just marked 40 years since its hometown son, the Rev. Martin Luther King Jr., gave his memorable "I Have A Dream" speech.

I had no past experience with Georgia's coastal area, though had shot past it many times on the big highway. Despite poor weather conditions, it deserved a look. Exiting at Jekyll Island, I followed a route northeast through wide patches of sea grasses that waved in the strong breeze and through which twisting canals ran. Up and over an attractive bridge and past tropical palms and flora and the "Marshes of Glynn" I continued.

Crossing the Frederica River into St. Simon's Island and taking a passage called Kingsway, I could see there was money and breeding here. I looped through the Sea Island Golf Club, a handsomely manicured place with mosses hanging from trees and maintenance vehicles buzzing about.

Near here was an uninhabited island known as Cumberland, off the southernmost Georgia coast. A 17-mile stretch half occupied by salt marshes, mud flats and tidal creeks, it hosts a variety of wildlife from sea turtles to bobcats. Reportedly, it is the largest patch of undeveloped coast on the whole Atlantic seaboard: No resorts. No t-shirt shops. Not even telephones, and only reachable by boat. Journalist John McPhee had said about it: "It was Earth in something close to its original state."

Remarkably, descendants of the Carnegie family can be thanked for the island's preservation. They bought Cumberland in the 1880s as a family getaway destination and built several large homes there. When Hilton Head developer Charles Fraser tried to swoop in and buy it, the National Park Service stepped in and secured it as Federally protected land. Camping spots and only one hotel was ever established, a former Carnegie home built in 1900. Besides the Carnegie connection, the inn's other claim to fame is that John F. Kennedy Jr.'s wedding reception was held there after he and Carolyn Bessette married in a small church on the island's north end.

I made at stop at the Book Mark book store, whose owner, coincidentally, was writing a book about Cumberland. He spoke of its past tenants, including the Olsens, who founded Coca-Cola, plantation owner Robert Stafford and General Nathaniel Greene, second in command under George Washington during the Revolutionary War who built the first home, called "Dungeness," on the island. The latter, which was ultimately purchased by the Carnegies, burned and was rebuilt several times, but today stands in ruins.

I pressed on, through tunnels of trees along the coast and back to I-95. Now well past the noon hour, I wanted to make up some time — the upside to taking interstates as Steinbeck had pointed out — and get to Savannah to see it in the daylight.

Approaching "Georgia's First City", I was reminded of a regionally relevant *New York Times* article about the discovery and salvage operation under way, of The Republic. In late October 1865, a week after the steamship left New York bound for New Orleans, it got caught in a hurricane off the coast 100 miles south of Savannah. For two days, the crew and 59 passengers battled the storm, scuttling cargo to try and keep her afloat as the engine, paddlewheels and pumps failed. Forty-two escaped with their lives when the ship went down, carrying with it its most important stowage: 20,000 gold coins worth up to $150 million. Odyssey Marine Explorations of Tampa, Florida found the wreck and began recovering artifacts in September. The trove promised to be the richest salvage of a ship to date.

It was good to see license plates from northeastern states again — Pennsylvania, New Jersey, Massachusetts — and I was sure to see more on this well-traveled Atlantic seaboard corridor. It was still raining, though the sun was trying to break through. The result of the struggle was a rainbow that arched over the roadway, like a heavenly portal to the historic southern city. I jumped at I-16, a slick route as the unlucky driver of a green pickup discovered, sliding nose first into the depression between the east- and westbound lanes.

Arriving at the Visitors Center in the historic district, I connected up with Old Town Trolley, for a city tour. It was not how I preferred to explore an area and I knew things would be fast rushing past, but I thought if might help me decide if I wanted to spend more time here.

The trolley set off from a depot area where cotton shipments had rolled in from the regional plantations in the late 1800s and were stored in nearby brick warehouses. City Market, a long-time trading place for produce, had been converted to a modern shopping plaza. Trucking along Bay Street, parallel to the Savannah River, we reached Johnson Square, dedicated to our friend Nathaniel Greene, who was also awarded Mulberry Plantation here in Savannah for his military service. Greene died here, in fact, from heat stroke. Notably, one of his daughters met and married Eli Whitney, who developed the cotton gin.

A house on Oglethorpe (named after James Edward Oglethorpe, the founder of the colony of Savannah) was the birthplace of Juliette Gordon Low, who founded the Girl Scouts of America in 1912. Madison Park served as the setting of the "life is like a box of chocolates" park bench scene from the movie, "Forrest Gump." Savannah was also the original setting of the 1960 Robert Mitchum version of "Cape Fear."

Nearing twenty-acre Forsyth Park, with a white, cascading fountain at its center, Live Oaks (the state tree) and crisscrossing footpaths, our guide gave us the background on the phrase "sleep tight, don't let the bedbugs bite." Allegedly, particular mattresses could be tightly closed with a drawstring and were stuffed with Spanish moss, often home to chiggers — of which I now had rudimentary knowledge.

Schoolgirls, in their white socks, green plaid skirts and blue tops, strolled past the Colonial Park cemetery, where the first burial occurred more than 250 years ago. In 1970, former New York Jets quarterback Joe Namath bought nearby Kehoe House, seeking to turn it into a gentleman's club. The city forbade him and he sold the house two years later. The Owens-Thomas House featured a unique wrought-iron "open arm" staircase, with separate steps for men and women, as it was not proper for men to look upon ladies' ankles. The "Old Pirates House" was a reference in Robert Louis Stevenson's classic tale "Treasure Island."

A series of homes known as "Rainbow Row" was painted in pastel colors so that slaves, who were forbidden to read, could easily identify them when errand running was requested. Near the golden-domed City Hall was Moon River Brewing Co., home of a microbrew of the same name.

The trolley almost shook itself apart on cobbled River Street, where the Cotton Exchange was located and Georgia Queen and Savannah River Queen paddle wheelers were moored. The thoroughfare, unfortunately, was jammed with tourists carrying bundles of souvenirs from the overabundant knick-knack shops. Back along Bay Street, the guide shared that Savannah hosts the second largest St. Patrick's Day Parade and that all the fountains and beer are died green in accordance.

Back at our starting point, I decided I had gotten enough of a feel for the city's spirit, and so made a run for Charleston. The rain, thankfully, had stayed away for the duration of the hour-plus long tour but showed itself again as I excused myself from this theme park of history.

"Smiling Faces Beautiful Places" was the promise at my 30th state, South Carolina, which I reached in a flash. Hilton Head, Charles Fraser's playground for club-and-racquet fans, was one of the first exit opportunities. An area called Coosawhatchie on up ahead seemed more enticing, given its name, but I kept on going to the "lowcountry."

At an old plantation house that had been converted to an information center and was framed by live oaks and hanging moss, I got bearings to Charleston. Soon, along a route absent of advertisements shucking gifts and souvenirs, I was passing signs for Black Bing Cherry Cider, the Huspah Baptist Church and Peach Jam and seeing double-wide trailer homes tucked back in the swampland. The trees were tall and spindly with tufts of growth at the top, like underfed cousins of the California redwoods. There was a very noticeable up-tick in humidity levels, too, as my windshield fogged over inside. El Rucio was getting a good bath, the salty film that had collected on her in Florida rinsing off. The passage gave me my first true sense of being in the real South.

Charleston's city limits were dotted with FIREWORKS shops. Being from north of the Mason-Dixon line, I was not familiar with the concept of explosives being available 365 days a year.

Landing in Charleston proper, I pulled a Steinbeck, getting myself lost in a sketchy area, where people just materialized out of the dark or were hanging on the corners, then straightened out to fly right down Meeting Street. At the intersection of Broad, known as the "Four Corners of Law", I parked El Rucio and set out on foot for nearby Queen Street. A woman at the plantation house had told me about a couple of good "insider" restaurants there. While looking for these, I happened upon a woman emerging from the shadows of her apartment and asked for guidance. She was headed to Griffon Pub, and invited me to tag along.

The unpretentious, regular person's bar was decorated with one-dollar bills stapled to almost every available wall and ceiling space and served a good local brew called Palmetto Pale Ale. We ordered up a round and assumed a table. A potpourri of ancestry, great-granddaughter of a Boston whaling boat builder and granddaughter of a shoe copper that heeled the military, she had great history and adventure tales to share.

At the wrap of our meet, it seemed appropriate to add a dollar bill to the collection here, so I pulled one from my wallet and upon it wrote, "30 states traveled, 5 to go, Charleston's been a jewel in a field of coal. Still Chasing Charley."

A bed and shower was in order. A Days Inn on Meeting Street fit the bill. As it was too early to retire, though, I wandered a couple blocks up to North Market Street and Kaminsky's "Most Excellent Café." The coffee/dessert stop was aglow and alive with activity and had a perfect little table where I could plug in my laptop and play writer for a while, tipping back mochas in the process. As folks circulated in and out, I banged away at my keyboard, bopping along to a mellow soundtrack as Casablanca fans spun around overhead.

Further along, the Bull & Finch, a four-story brick and iron establishment with British accents like distinctive red phone booths and signs for Newcastle Brown Ale and Bass, was showing a New England Patriots - Denver Broncos game. With just a few minutes left, it was as tight as a match could get, with Denver up a point 24-23.

The day finally caught up to me and I retired, with excitement to tour the city by day.

Day 60: Charleston to Chapel Hill

Rain had been in the forecast and I expected to wake to it, but rose instead to glorious blue skies and bright light that streamed into my cozy second floor hotel room. To begin my Charleston prowl, I needed a good meal, something I found at Diana's, adjacent to the hotel property. It offered "American and Lowcountry Favorites." I went for the Cajun

Eye-Opener: shrimp and crawfish etouffe served with creamy Carolina stone ground grits and topped with fried green tomatoes. It was the perfect choice for the late morning hour and went down in a very satisfying way, chased with homemade buttermilk biscuits, orange juice and cappuccino. Sitting beside a sunny window, I watched Charlestonians, the tourist set and the occasional horse-and-buggy stream by. Like the horse, I was chomping at the bit to explore.

Across the street, the Circular Congregational Church, a Presbyterian concern established in the late 1600s, offered a cemetery. A lichen-covered and cracked marble stone, erected by the "afflicted husband and children" of Mrs. Eliza Catherine Bryan, led me to other markers bearing surnames like Lehre, Dart, Peronneau, Flagg and Theus. Inscriptions on them told of premature deaths of adults and children alike and fatal bouts of yellow fever. A large brick tomb marked the burial site of Richard Hutson, who was a delegate to the Continental Congress, signer of the articles of confederation, lieutenant governor and first mayor of Charleston (in 1783).

Passing the many antique stores and fine art galleries on Queen Street, I discovered another cemetery, at St. Philip's Episcopal Church. There, Charles Pinckney, a signer of the U.S. Constitution, and Edward Rutledge, a signer of the Declaration of Independence, were interred.

At the Charles II Art Gallery, I admired the wild, fish-eye lens depictions of Charleston by Corning, New York-born artist Kevin Harrison.

At the Waterfront Park, where along a cement pier couples lazed in hanging swings, I learned that it was England's King Charles II that gave the city, at the juncture of the Ashley and Cooper Rivers, its original name, Charlestown, in 1670. Exports of lumber, naval stores, salted beef and deerskins were the basis of its first fortunes. In the early 1700s, Spaniards, French, Indians and pirates repeatedly attacked the city, though it continued to grow rich from exports of rice and indigo. During both the Revolutionary and Civil Wars, with Fort Sumter shelled and then besieged and the area driven into economic ruin, it was a critical port. She was down, too, but not out and military build-up, historic preservation and a cultural renaissance all through the 1900s brought her back to prosperity.

Like the Days Inn, workers here were busy pulling up and changing over plant life to heartier stock like snapdragons that would fare better through the winter. Moving on, I circumvented the massive, columned

U.S. Custom House, a building like many I'd seen in D.C., and walked through the open-air, fan-cooled Old Charleston Market, filled with scores of vendors. On one table, gloves and scarves made from the fur of Peruvian alpacas were laid out. Several tables over, turtle- and fish-shaped pendants made from carnelian were shown. In another corner, a woman was weaving a basket out of sweet grass and pine needles — it was a craft her mother had taught her and she had been doing it since she was a little girl. Saltwater taffy, pralines, pecan rolls and malted almonds decorated another table. Adjacent, pecan tea cookies, benne wafers ("the sweet chip of the South") and lemon coolers were displayed.

Nearby Moose Mountain had an iced coffee waiting to refresh me for my walk along East Bay Street. When I turned toward the Maritime Center, a Union Pacific freight train lumbered by. I'd wished to take a boat from the Center over to the island-based fort but had just missed the last one. Still, the view of the Cooper River and bridge beyond was pleasant and a good pause. Making my turnaround, I passed through "The Borough," a former African-American community of low-income homes that were demolished in 1993 to make way for an auditorium, public library and school board offices. The inhabitants here spoke an almost extinguished patois known as Gullah Geechee. A project had been launched to preserve some of the history lost through the destruction, though just two original, rundown homes remained standing.

On Market Street, the College of Charleston girls' tennis team was sweating it out on courts behind the tall brick walls of the school's gymnasium. A block east, Sea Grant College was the home of the Washington Light Infantry, which saw action during the War of 1812, Seminole War, Mexican War, Civil War and modern conflicts right up through the Persian Gulf.

What looked like living statues at the E.S. Lawrence Gallery turned out to be body casts of models, their realistic look achieved through the creative use of polyester resin, oil paints and prosthetic eyes. The statue that greeted me was a security guard modeled on the artist's dad.

The City Market, like the Old Charleston Market, housed modern items such as sea and area-related artworks but had originally been used for the trading of beef, vegetables, fruit, fish and other provisions. It was the last stop on my self-guided walking tour and brought me full circle back to the Days Inn. There, I boarded El Rucio for a Charleston withdrawal and sprint northeast to Chapel Hill, calling my Dad to alert him while barreling back out to the interstate.

Thinking about the state in general, my mind drifted to Strom Thurmond who, at age 100, was laid to rest behind a Baptist church in Edgefield, in the northwestern part of South Carolina. A former segregationist, he was the longest serving senator in history, a reign that he began as a Democrat when Franklin D. Roosevelt was in office and ended as a Republican this past January. Notably, he ran for president in the late '40s as leader of the defunct Dixiecrat Party. While his early views were often controversial and harmful, he was known equally for progressive actions, like being the first senator from the South to hire blacks to his staff and pushing for better education for minority students. If one so rooted could change his ways, it seemed there was hope for improved relations between people of all races.

Rain visited me again as I reached Santee on the banks of Lake Marion in Clarendon County. There, the come-ons started early: Mouse Roller Coaster. You've never had it so good. If you can't come — write. Fireworks Capital of the U.S.A. Talk of the town! The references, for those unfamiliar with the phenomenon, were to Alan Schafer's South of the Border and Pedro's Pleasure Palace complex at the South Carolina/ North Carolina line. It first becomes visible as a glowing red and green sombrero atop a high tower, a Mexican space needle if you will. Below are multiple facilities, all with the word "Pedro's" adjoined to them: Pedro's Campground, Pedro's Pantry, Pedro's Tacos and Foot Long Hot Dogs, Pedro's Leather Shop, and so on. You honestly don't know what to make of it and the looks on the faces of the brave of heart that venture here are also incredulous, disbelieving and curious. And while the confused peer in, the counter people peer out, wondering if you're coming in. In this way, I tumbled into North Carolina, my 31st state.

By the time I reached Lumberton, it was well past the dinner hour, so I bailed off 95 looking for a pizza purveyor. Uncle George's registered on the radar screen and promised, inside of fifteen minutes, to have a small cheese pie for me to take. I figured I had time to sit for a soda and small tossed salad and did, near a table of truckers smoking, drinking and feasting on similar edibles. Right off the highway, and bordered by three gas stations, it wasn't the kind of place you'd take a date to and, yet, here were two guys in their best NASCAR t-shirts treating their tattooed lady friends to George's finest cuisine.

Fayetteville, mid-state, was the site of Fort Bragg and Pope Air Force Base. Originally called Camp Bragg after native North Carolinian General Braxton Bragg, the fort was designated a military reservation during WWI by Chief of Field Artillery, General William J. Snow.

I-40 turned me west toward "American Idol" Clay Aiken's hometown, Raleigh, the state capital, which allowed access to itself and its hospitals, schools and arenas via no less than nine interchanges. I came right on up through the University of North Carolina's Chapel Hill campus, past the big medical center and to my folks' house. Leaves were scattered across the deck where Dad rushed out to greet me. In order of priorities, we hoisted a beer, took in van gear and spoke with my Mom. She was in Flagstaff with my brother and his wife, en route from California. They had pulled up their stakes in Alameda to seek better prospects on the East Coast.

Half past midnight, I laid my weary head to rest in one of several semi-subterranean guest rooms, looking forward to a couple of days of rest and recuperation.

Day 61: Playing Catch Up

Some clunks emanating from the upstairs area of my folks' glass, woods-rooted chalet got me going this overcast yet mild and moist Carolina morning. It was my Dad preparing to head to a morning appointment at the school. Looking out of the large picture window beside the bed upon which I was lying, I watched brown, crinkled oak leaves — the specters of winter — blow past.

With a land base again, I got myself up to address e-mail, answering voluminous "where are you?" messages I'd encouraged. Rewarding my productivity at midday, I cut slices from the log of Usinger's beef salami I still had from Milwaukee and arranged them on multi-grain bread with squares of pepper cheese. With my favorite tortilla chips on the side, it was a splendid delicacy savored while reading back copies of *USA Today.*

Monday's edition was chock full of news, some good, some bad, but all noteworthy: Our troops trying to stabilize Iraq continued to have a hard time of it, when two missiles fired from a palm grove in Baghdad brought down a Chinook helicopter, killing 16 U.S. soldiers and injuring 20. The chopper was in the process of shuttling the troops to the international airport there to connect with flights back to the states where the soldiers had planned two weeks of leave with their families. It was the single deadliest attack on U.S. forces in Iraq since our operations to unseat Saddam Hussein began earlier in the year.

In Southern California, ground crews reported almost 100% containment of two-week old wild fires. Nearly 3,500 homes had been destroyed and 20 people killed across six counties. U.S. Forest Service leaders noted that such devastation will surely happen again given that hundreds of thousands of people have pushed into and established homes in areas naturally prone to fire. A parallel item polled readers about what they were likely to take should a fire threaten their home.

In Seattle, a man suspected of being the "Green River Killer," responsible for the killings of 49 women whose bodies turned up near ravines, rivers, airports and freeways in the 1980s, was facing multiple charges of murder. Expected to admit to the crimes, Gary Ridgway would be the country's deadliest killer in history.

In sports, former New York Mets manager Bobby Valentine signed a three-year contract with a Japanese baseball team. Kenyans won the top men's and women's spots in the annual New York City Marathon, in which 30,000 people competed. Competitors included rap mogul Sean "P. Diddy" Combs who raised money for New York's public school system and two kids' charities. My Giants held the line against their intra-city football rivals, the Jets, to take a 31-28 win on Sunday, bringing their record to 4-4 for the season to date.

The day, at that mid-afternoon point, had brightened and calmed somewhat and birds flitted from tree to tree or visited Morgan Creek, which trickled in the valley below. Near the woodpile in the back garden, a doe ambled with her two fawns.

Though I'd made the one visit to Carolina back in late September, it was family focused and hadn't given me a great opportunity to capture the state's essence. As such, I planned activities over the three days that I would be here on this back-end to achieve that. Certainly, sports events were a necessary, being such a strong focus; nightspots, where people's guard would be down; and sites unique to the region.

To fill the first bill, Dad and I ventured out to Cary to see the first round of the ACC (Atlantic Coast Conference) Women's Soccer Championship. It pitted the undefeated UNC Tar Heels against the North Carolina State University Wolfpack at the SAS (Statistical Analysis Software) stadium. We were racing the clock to see this highlight game and with directional help from the gate guard at the SAS headquarters, we found the open-air stadium and the match, already in progress, with NCSU up 1-0 fifteen minutes into the first half. State scored again as we took our seats, which surprised the UNC crowd given that UNC was the 2002 titleholder, their 38-0-1 tournament record, 15 ACC titles and goalkeeper Aly Winget's strong on-field record.

UNC didn't stay down for long as its star forward, Heather O'Reilly, led an assault that finally put the Heels on the board. UNC midfielder Lori Chalupney added a goal just before intermission to tie the sides. The break time was filled with trips to the concession stand and accented with songs like "Wolly Bully," "Low Rider" and "Respect."

Well into the second half, UNC's Lindsay Tarpley had scoring honors, followed by sophomore Kacey White, who snuck one past State's goalie for insurance. Mary McDowell stuck a fifth goal in, while Anne Felts made it an even half-dozen, giving the Heels a 6-2 win.

As we made our way back toward "home" territory, I happened to see a youth sprint out of a fast food joint into the woods and guessed I'd witnessed a robbery. Reaching a stoplight, my guess was confirmed when we saw two patrol cars pull out in his direction, activate their sirens and race past us.

It was mid-evening and only popcorn and peanuts had kept us going. The time had come for greater sustenance and Brixx wood-fired pizza in Meadowmont called us to action. The community, like many in this part of Carolina, had sprung up almost overnight in the last four years, with 2,500 units where a field had been. Rumor had it that one of the units had been snapped up by Paul Newman, after wife Joanne was awarded an honorary chair at Duke University's drama department.

Brixx was one of the first businesses to break ground in the fledgling community and was part of a chain begun by a team of six partners. The business idea was hatched in Aspen after one of the owners dined at a similar place and noticed its popularity. Plans were in the works to open two more outlets by year's end.

Part of the secret to Brixx's success, we imagined, was its wide range of draught choices — 27 on the list, including 11 international brands. Matt had us try several, starting with Blue Moons and moving to Denver micro Flying Dog Pale Ale. These were ideal sidecars to our crispy, thin pies, in my case a Bronx Bomber: spicy Italian sausage, prosciutto, Gorgonzola, tomato sauce and fresh oregano.

We progressed (digressed?) to trying brands like Rogue Dead Guy Ale from Newport, Oregon, one I'd missed on tour. Naturally, as the beer went in, the entertainment level went up and relationships were forged at the bar counter.

Back at the house, TV news noted that the day's high, 85 degrees, beat an old record for this date in the Raleigh-Durham area, by three degrees. At the same time, the humidity was 100%. Mom checked in by phone, reporting that she, Dave and Jill had reached Albuquerque, after standing on the corner in Winslow, Arizona and visiting the meteor crater. It was amusing to all of us that they were following in my wake, just two weeks behind me.

Day 62: A Mess of Martinis

A large bowl of cereal and a read of *The Herald-Sun* began the day as Dad hurried off to teach classes at the University. The paper carried a wrap-up of the soccer match we'd seen and noted that UNC would play the Duke Blue Devils, which beat Virginia in the evening game that followed, in the semifinals tomorrow night. High school point guard Shaun Livingston of Peoria, Illinois, considered the top men's basketball prospect in the nation, made Duke his college choice. Meanwhile, the Tar Heels' men's basketball team lost a man, sophomore David Noel, for the next six to eight weeks due to torn ligaments in his thumb.

I also noticed that the New York Rangers pro hockey team was scheduled to face the Carolina Hurricanes at the local RBC Center tonight, a match that would feature 42-year-old Rangers captain Mark "The Mess" Messier. He had scored two goals the other night to surpass

Gordie Howe's career points total with 1,851, putting him in 2nd place behind Wayne Gretzky on the all-time goal list. With interest in attending, I rang the marketing folks at the center and they kindly arranged a pair of tickets for me.

The day wore on in self-imposed solitude, spent alternating between working at my laptop, nibbling more salami, listening to the mad buzz of a fly trapped inside this glass menagerie, and poking through *The New York Times*, National Edition. In the latter, I noted a story about Wal-Mart, which I'd visited several times on the road, and its cleaning crews, allegedly comprised of illegal aliens paid off the books and forced to work under harsh conditions. Meanwhile, the good people of Mississippi had appointed Republican Haley Barbour to the office of governor, joining other Republicans in that seat in Alabama, Georgia and South Carolina, an apparent indication of the South's "rightward march."

Mid-afternoon, I spoke with my long-lost high school friend at Longworth Industries, one of my travel sponsors. When I last saw her, she was a cheerleader, math class seatmate and neighbor. Now she was a married mom of three and marketing director for one of the company's brands. We planned a meet-up.

With a nap, gas and stop at Amante Gourmet Pizza on 54 East, I was good to go to the RBC Center for ice festivities. The weather wasn't going to make it easy on me though — torrents of rain and whipping wind combined with high humidity that fogged up El Rucio's windows, made it difficult to maintain a straight line. I was glad to see the white, domed façade of the RBC Center, locate parking and collect my tickets.

In I went solo to the modern, red-seated arena to the match already in progress, finding myself outnumbered as a Rangers fan except for a family to my right. Their cheers paled in comparison to the thunderous roar, rock music and belch of a baritone boat horn that erupted when the Canes tied the score. The same loud celebration was repeated only moments later when Eric Staal gave the home team a 2-1 lead.

It was good to see Messier out there and I watched him through my binoculars expertly navigate the ice, chase down the puck and play the veteran role. After New York tied the score once again, I took a moment to look around the stadium, home to the NCSU Wolfpack basketball team.

Their many ACC Champion banners down through the years waved from the ceiling.

With the score holding at 2-2 at the end of the 1st period, two Zambonis, each with a fan aboard, came out to smooth the ice. Then a promotional team slingshot a fan from one end of the rink to the other, targeting giant inflatable bowling pins beside which shapely Hurricanettes stood. The halls and concession counters were jammed with folks, of course, a sea of red swirling around islands of blue.

When play resumed, the Canes served puck after puck up at Rangers goalie Markkanen. When they squeaked another goal past him, the crowd blew its top again and a digital projection of white-haired former WWF wrestler Rick Flair came on the big screen barking, "Hurricanes goal, woo, woo…woo, woo!"

During the second intermission, the "Storm Squad" propelled bundled t-shirts into the audience and a fan played "Let's Make A Squeal" wherein he was given opportunities to trade-up for better merchandise. Some of the latter turned out to be oversized "tighty whiteys."

In the 3rd period, the Canes scored yet again, leaving the storied Rangers with frosty countenances. An unpopular penalty shot opportunity awarded to New York allowed the blue-and-red to catch up by a goal, but the Canes' Chris Adams abruptly capped the celebration with the team's fifth goal. With just a minute left to play, I made a retreat for the exit hearing the place explode as the Canes finalized the score at 6-3.

Chapel Hill demanded I report in to visit its many nightspots, which I'd sporadically tromped during the years since my folks had moved to the area. These included Bub O'Malley's on a back street; and HELL, the former Troll's, a place now illuminated in red as you might expect. At the latter, a trivia contest was underway and I pitched in for a bit to support a team that had adopted the name "Insane in the Membrane."

A very busy corner spot, the East End Martini Bar, boasted 101 martinis with such names as Almond Joy, Bikini Tini, Ebony and Ivory, Hairy Monk, Nuclear Kamikaze, Pink Panty Pull Down and Velvet Kiss. Also available were a smattering of wines, champagne and their signature drink, pineapple-infused vodka, which was served in a funky angled glass. It was sweet and smooth and had character like the crowd, who milled about enjoying conversation in the light of a glowing "EE" logo on the mirror at the bar back.

Players was my next station stop. Brick-walled, low-lit and vibrating with a deep thump, it served up a healthy helping of funk, groove and rhythm. Bodies snaked and writhed and contorted into all sorts of creative positions as the young crowd got way down to the beats.

A café above the martini bar, called Hectors, was the spot to go for a late-night bite. People filed in there like hungry soldiers in a mess hall to the lunch counter style set-up, which served easy-to-prepare, quick-to-gobble foods like BLTs, hamburgers and hot dogs. I ordered a BLT on a pita that I didn't really need or want at that hour I decided. As it was delivered in tin foil, I simply took it to go. I'd enjoyed Carolina's night shift and looked forward now to seeing some of its day crew.

Day 63: Factory Facts & Pottery Palaces

My awakening was abrupt and late (9:30 a.m.), especially as I'd promised to meet my old classmate mid-morning. I fast showered and was out the door chowing on the BLT that had sat on my bedroom floor overnight.

My route was 15-501 south down to Cameron then over to Candor. It was one of the most pleasant routes I could have taken — initially single lane, rural, past small country homes and tall, straight pines. Many of the homes, particularly those closest to the road, seemed to quake in the face of a widening project, signaled by striped orange traffic cones all along the way.

Churches near Pittsboro and Sanford carried billboards declaring "The Bible, Nothing but the truth" and "Pray for our nation" or "Praise God for Whom All Blessings Flow". This was the Bible Belt for sure and these were God-fearing folk here.

Linking to 24/27 headed west, I saw autos rotting, pickups parked in front yards, trailer homes, cows scratching themselves on trees, home-based pottery shops, tractor trailer cabs and RVs. It seemed Northern impressions of Southern life were all confirmed here.

The trek down was a lot more time-consuming than I'd expected and the fact that I'd gotten a delayed jump didn't help. Finally, the Candor exit and the long, white brick headquarters of Longworth came up. My friend's trademark laugh, twinkling blue eyes and broad smile were instantly familiar and the years melted away. We launched right into a tour.

On the factory floor, there were 65 sewing stations and 44 female operators, the majority of whom were Mexican, come for better benefits and working environments than they might realize in their home country. Together, they were outputting 2,000 dozen completed garments per week. Their workload depended on orders — the crew was currently working on men and women's pants. A denim-clad maintenance guy, with a screwdriver jutting out of his back pocket, circled them, on patrol to address technical problems.

The materials the operators work with start as millions of pounds of yarn that are knitted down into fabrics that arrive in large rolls. An employee who introduced himself as "Fonz" cuts them down into smaller lengths with a machine called a cradle feeder. The smaller sheets go to a patterning area, then a cutting area, where an operator wearing a chain mail glove on one hand, trims out the garment pieces. After the garments are completed, they go to several ladies who inspect them for imperfections. One, Inspector Number 12, was moving quickly, looking forward to leaving at the noon hour. "Praise the Lord," she exclaimed about the company's half-day Fridays. Beyond her sat a new computer-programmable embroidery machine, used to stitch logos onto clothing.

At noon, my friend and I rolled out to lunch, motoring along Route 211 past sod farms, a Purdue chicken plant, a vineyard, a logging business, cotton fields and peach trees, to Mac's Breakfast Anytime Restaurant.

Over a sandwich and salad, we caught up on each other's news, then zipped to her company's distribution center. A customer service person there, on hearing of my countrywide travels, related her own: a trip from her childhood home in Michigan to California and back. She saw sites like Mount Rushmore, the Grand Canyon and even had close calls with nature, having to take shelter in a motel basement when a tornado hit. Her dad worked for Chrysler and during the trip, they broke three manifolds. He saved the parts and brought them back to his engineers.

Ultimately, I motored back toward Chapel Hill, taking the quicker route up 73/74 through the Cape Fear River Basin. It would take me by Seagrove, an area I'd dubbed "pottery row", where I paid a visit to Phil

Morgan Pottery. Dawn, the brown-eyed Japanese-American counterperson, her mother-in-law Julia and their basset hound Baby "Bubba" Duke warmly welcomed me.

Julia took me outside to see their 25-foot long, 8-year-old wood-fired kiln, where half of their end products are baked. The kiln is fired up four times a year, an event that brings many area potters calling and turns into a big party. It takes a whole mountain of wood to accomplish the feat and seeing the woodpile beside the kiln, I imagined that they were ready for the next firing, just a week away.

While showing me the inside of the kiln, detailing the firing process and explaining why certain pieces didn't materialize properly, Julia added that she doesn't often do pottery these days — "I'm the electrician, the plumber, the bookkeeper, and the whip cracker."

As she showed me a gas-powered kiln that her nephew, also a potter, used, she noted that this region breeds potters: "When you're raised in this area, you've got a potter hiding in your family." In fact, she grew up digging clay and gathering wood. "If you touch that clay and you like it, you stick with it." In summary, she joked, "We have a tough life. We can take something from the earth and make something beautiful from it."

She noticed my van as we started back into the shop and mentioned a 1962 blue Chevy van nicknamed "Nellie" that she and her husband had driven to the end of the earth and back. "We rode her hard, and put her up wet," she exclaimed in her colorful way.

Inside the shop, amidst all the vases, mugs and candleholders, I noticed an area where Dawn, an artist, had some of her work displayed — photographs and graphic designs. One piece in particular caught my eye: a three-frame depiction of a heron at rest and in flight that she'd scanned and to which she applied a blur technique. It reminded me of my early morning view at Amelia Island and would be a great remembrance of my visit here.

With the print under my arm and a couple of pottery samples in a bag, I bid them good luck with the kiln firing, followed the "Pottery Highway" back to 73/74 and zoomed north, first to Asheboro then toward Graham. The latter was the hometown of another old friend who had once been a fellow tenant in a house in Port Chester, New York. I had approximate directions to her place but no phone number, and aimed to locate her on a whim.

Signs for BBQ, gun & pawn, crickets, carports, ribs, and biscuits abounded en route to Ramseur. From there, it was saw logs and pulpwood, saddles, deer corn and Orange Crush into Graham. I stopped at Rod's Bar, "Where real friends meet", for guidance — no luck. El Carbonero, a Salvadoran restaurant, was strike two but had an appetizing menu, so I stayed for supper: a beefsteak (bisteca encellado) with onions and salad.

Jim's Hamburgers & Hot Dogs was busy with dinner customers, though one employee from Graham got on the horn to someone and reported that the address was in Eli Whitney (a small town south of Graham), and served up guidance. This had become a mission, now, that had to be played out.

Miracle of miracles, I managed to find her cozy home, staked on a big patch of land, and rang the bell. She opened the door, registered quite a surprised look and ushered me in, a small baby in her arms and her husband soon joining us.

It was a pleasant reunion and, as it turned out, I was just a stone's throw from Chapel Hill. There were still places to be explored in the sprawling collegiate town.

Stop One was Caribou Coffee, where I enjoyed the upbeat stylings of Sleeping with the Enemy. They played beneath a long brown canoe, aligned with the Alaskan theme the establishment had effected.

There was a red glow and great bass emanating from a place called The Library that drew me in like a moth to a bug light. A while later, I reported to Top of the Hill, which was absolutely jammed with upscale socialites, kicking back with drinks with names like "Monkey Gone Nutz" and "007," and fine spirits and cigars. I opted for a Kenan Summer Lager named after William R. Kenan Jr., a generous benefactor of UNC.

"Top" had a stormy beginning, opening the night Hurricane Fran hit Chapel Hill, September 5, 1996. Since, the establishment has been bestowed with multiple honors including 18 medals in the World Beer Championships. Six brewing tanks each contain the equivalent of 4,700 pints of beer. Just the thought had me salivating.

It was a cool night but not so cool that one couldn't assume a spot along the stone rail of Top's outdoor patio for a fisheye view of the Columbia/

Franklin intersection and all the clubgoers and cars traveling and traversing the thoroughfares below.

Pantana Bob's, on Rosemary, offered both indoor and outdoor spaces to entertain oneself, too, and was six deep at the bar with both parent types and well-scrubbed co-eds with names like Brooke and Buffy.

A pizza place back on Franklin heated me up a slice that I curled within a paper plate to munch on and walk. At the "last call" hour, I drifted back to El Rucio and Dad's.

Day 64: Two for Two for Carolina Blue

Dad appeared with juice and announced that he had made "P & S's" (Lauterborn code for pancakes and sausages), and reminded me that a reporter from *The Chapel Hill Herald* would be visiting. I slapped myself awake and joined him in the kitchen, wolfing food down while reading the morning headlines.

A missile had taken down another U.S. chopper, this one in Tikrit, Iraq, killing all six soldiers aboard. We compared these sniper-like attacks to how Colonialists fought the British during Revolutionary times and the tunnel rats fought U.S. forces in the jungles of Vietnam. If we turned tail now, we would be lost and dash the hopes of those Iraqis who desperately wanted the U.S. there. At the same time, one's heart bled for the families whose sons and daughters would not be coming home from their tours of duty. To date, the Defense Department said that 1,994 U.S. soldiers had been wounded in action, 342 more injured, and 399 killed, with 272 from hostile action. The wounded include at least 58 amputees — 47 single-limb removals, 11 multiple-limb amputations. The Homeland Security Department, meanwhile, worried that terrorist organization al-Qaeda may be planning to fly cargo planes into U.S. targets like nuclear plants, bridges or dams.

The reporter dropped in mid-morning, along with a photographer, to capture details on my voyage.

Dad and I had planned a big sports day and, after their departure, we organized to make a pilgrimage to UNC's Kenan Stadium where the Tar Heel football team was set to play Wake Forest's Demon Deacons.

Light blue was the dominant color of the attire streaming in, with UNC stamped on visors, baseball caps, seat cushions, sweatshirts, jackets and backpacks. Carolina fans are serious about their sports, devoted as they are to church and country. The merchandising powers that be had responded to this devotion with all the paraphernalia the fans required to honor their heroes. I was sure, though, there was a wish that the team had a better record this year. The embattled Heels were 1-8 for the season.

When Dad appeared, we took our seats up in aluminum bleachers, catching introductory ceremonies. Whether they won or lost, the game was going to be a full-blown event with a comprehensive dog and pony show.

WF had a first score attempt, for a field goal, that UNC managed to block and recover. The rejection was inspiring and one side of the stadium yelled "TAR!" to the opposite side's "HEELS!" It was an overcast day, sweater weather, with a steady light breeze flapping the ACC school flags around the top lip of the outdoor stadium.

WF got yet a second shot at a field goal with less than three minutes in the 1st and, again, UNC blocked. Unfortunately, on the very next play, one of UNC's linemen, tailback Chad Scott, got injured, was placed on a backboard and carted to an awaiting ambulance. Another Carolina tailback went out limping shortly thereafter as the battle intensified.

In the 2nd, UNC started to show fatigue, making costly mistakes that led to a WF touchdown. My attention wandered to UNC's mascot, a ram named Ramses, lying by a hedge on the opposite side of the field. The blue-horned beast hadn't moved an inch the whole game. I suspected he'd been out on Franklin drinking last night. Perhaps he was trying to lay low given that his predecessor, who lived on an area farm, was killed and partially eaten by a drunk on his way home.

Amazingly, Carolina's QB Darian Durant connected with TB Jacque Lewis for UNC's first score, tying the sides. Though the Deacons quickly lobbed one to go ahead again, UNC popped in two points when a ball got loose. As the half neared, freshman Ronnie McGill scored for UNC, to make it 16-13 for the blue-and-white pigskin handlers.

In the 3rd quarter, the Heels struck again, with a field goal, capitalized on a turnover, but then blew a two-point conversion try. I ducked down to concession for popcorn and peanuts, missing another Heels' score, a field goal.

Close to the end of the third, the Heels slam-dunked another, thanks to McGill, but were not in the clear. The 4th quarter brought back-to-back Deacons' TDs, a little dose of reality for the Heels, putting us on the edge of our seats. For insurance, Carolina added seven, relieving some of the pressure, and inspiring the cheerleaders to hoist a male in their ranks up onto a platform to do a pushup for every one of their 42 points. The home crowd counted them off.

It looked like the game was in the bag but, to be sure, Dad yelled, "Nothing stupid!" The Heels must not have been listening as their lazy pass led to a WF TD, suddenly making it an 8-point game with five minutes yet to play. We were on the edge of the bleachers again. However, a few prayers and a Hail Mary or two and the Heels held on to win, 42-34. McGill's 244 yards was a top record for a Carolina freshman.

We walked across campus to the Carolina Club, where my folks' anniversary had been held, and went to the restaurant, the O'Hare Grill, to celebrate.

Part Two of our sports day featured a men's basketball exhibition game: UNC Tar Heels vs. North Carolina Central University (NCCU) Eagles, in the Smith Center. UNC got out to an early lead and kept a fast tempo rushing down court, lead by Sean May, Jawad Williams, Rashon McCants and Raymond Felton.

At the end of the 1st period, the Heels led 51-27 and a clamor arose as both the band and the cheerleader squads entertained. I looked about the arena, noticing UNC-grad-turned-legend Michael Jordan's jersey, with his retired #23 on it. Surrounding it were the many NCAA, ACC and NIT Champion banners the team had won.

UNC was like a locomotive mowing NCCU down as if the opponent were a wayward cow caught on the tracks. In the last two minutes, UNC's second string went in and, with the team's points total at 97, the focus became breaking 100. The crowd "ohhed" and "awwhed" at each missed opportunity or shot. They never did hit the magic number and the final was 97-59.

Locating my Dad's "ark" at the parking lot, connected by aerial breezeways to UNC's Medical Center, we drove to Caribou for coffees. Reading a copy of *The News & Observer* that was laying about, we realized there was a celestial show under way — a lunar eclipse wherein the moon drifts through Earth's shadow. It hung in the night sky like a dark, reddish-orange coal. "In ancient times," according to the paper, "the phenomenon was believed caused by some unseen monster bloodying the moon — an omen of disaster." We took that into consideration but didn't let it cloud our viewing.

Mom radioed in from Nashville, Tennessee, when we arrived home, then I organized my gear, ready for my next-day departure. I'd enjoyed my stay here but had become increasingly anxious to return to Connecticut. Still, I had a few more stops to make before reaching my finish line.

Day 65: Blue Ridge Beauty, Staunton Surprises

Dad had scrambled eggs and English muffins for us first thing, which we topped with my blueberry-lime jelly from New Hampshire. As the temperatures had plunged into the 40s overnight, I had to run El Rucio for a while afterwards to get her warm. Mom checked in again from Nashville as she, Dave and Jill prepared to make their last dash, with a goal of arriving in Chapel Hill late in the evening. Unfortunately, I expected to be in Maryland by then, on the way home myself. All loaded up and with a family trademark "toot-toot-toot-toot-toot…toot-toot," I was off, choosing 501 North as my route out of the state. The parking lot and sides of the road by St. Thomas More church were piled up with the cars of the faithful, and dead leaves blew across my path as I left Chapel Hill behind.

Even though Thanksgiving was still around the corner, tree farms in Durham were already advertising their stock. Beyond, cows and ducks lounging in the fields and alongside ponds watched me pass.

Nearing Roxboro, I watched a hawk float and circle on a wind current. Tobacco warehouses held a recent crop. Two ladies strolled out of the Cornerstone Community Church, walking to the Exxon next door for biscuits and coffee.

On the flip side of Bethel Hill, I hit the Virginia line, my 32nd U.S. state crossing, and flipped my road atlas page. This western part of "The Mother of Presidents" (so dubbed as the state was the birthplace of eight of our leaders) was unfamiliar to me, my typical corridor through being interstates 85 and 95. It was at first indiscernible from Carolina, then I came across Sheetz, a phenomenon I'd not seen elsewhere. A gas, sub, salad and "coffeez" stop, it was a clean, well-run destination. Even the restroom was accommodating, to the handicapped, blind and parents all.

Halifax offered gas and I pulled up beside a bright orange '46 Chevy pickup street rod piloted by a middle-aged couple on their way to church. The driver was a polite country gentleman who bid me hello as I looked over his ride and good day as he motored off. Ahead, the Bannister River, which featured a turn-of-the-century Sportsmen's Club with a boat landing beside it, was the brownest body of water I'd ever seen, no doubt muddied from the rich, clay soils here.

A local Pentacostal radio preacher chanted on the radio, "If we're going to take the world for Jesus Christ, we need to get some discipline in this war against Satan. Can I get an amen?" As I continued to listen, I noticed words like 'pretty' and 'pulpit' pronounced "purdy" and "pool pit," in step with the area vernacular. Part of his sermon was devoted to the error of judging a person and his credibility by his or her face and presence, citing comments he'd heard from radio audience members. "They thought I was over six feet tall and 280, but I'm just a little bitty man." I noted other unique pronunciations as I went through the area where Patrick Henry was buried. 'Pattern,' 'you,' 'dragged' and 'murderous' were 'patterin,' 'yew,' 'drug' and 'murdous' respectively.

He started getting heated up, speaking on his service in Vietnam but saying, "I no longer war on the flesh." He punched up his speech by adding an 'a' at the end of words — 'threw' became 'threw-a', for example — and tossed in the odd 'hallelujah.' It was a stirring oration for a sunny Fall Sunday.

"Three little words and a little diamond ring can open up the heavens and make the angels sing, it's a powerful thing" was a lyric that caught my attention on a sister country station. The DJ was gearing up to bring the listening audience "pole to flag" live coverage of the second-to-last NASCAR race of the season, being run back in Rockingham ("The Rock"), North Carolina. Driver Matt Kenseth was seeking to take the last Winston Cup title there.

Lynchburg, where Thomas Jefferson had planted a poplar forest, pointed me northwest toward the Blue Ridge Mountains and Parkway through them. Excitedly, I climbed up on the latter at its intersection with the James River. I'd traveled the southern half of this remarkable route in the past, but not its northern end, a single-lane road that wound through forests and beside creeks. Stopped next to Upper Otter Creek, I climbed down its bank and stepped out on a rock to look upstream, listen to its babble and watch fallen oak leaves float by. These leaves created a brown floor in a forest full of gray, mostly bare trees but for stubborn pale green and faded gold patches.

Stopping again, I looked out at 3,600-foot tall House Mountain, with clusters of rhododendrons the flora in my foreground, then moved down through Licklog Springs Gap. As the twisting road climbed again, Yankee Horse Ridge showed a section of an old logging railroad track. Narrow gauge and built around 1920, it was part of a 50-mile length that carried some 100 million board feet of logs out of the mountains to the mill. It seemed like a good lunch stop, so I perched on a rail where the track spanned a cascading waterfall that trundled down through a tunnel beneath the parkway. A couple wearing ski hats, gloves and quilted vests stopped to hike a trail that curled up past me along the waterway.

In Montebello, I decided to make a detour west to loop up to Staunton (pronounced "Stan-ton") for both film and to see this historic frontier town that was the birthplace of President Woodrow Wilson. On the way, I went by a country inn or two, Gertie's Country Store, and many small brick homes that relied on outhouses for their bathroom needs.

A town of 24,000, nestled in the Shenandoah Valley, Staunton was founded in 1747 by immigrants from Germany and Northern Ireland and Brits who had relocated from eastern Virginia. Its peak years were 1870 to 1920 when the railroad put it on the map. Besides its historic significance and mix of log cabin, Italianate and Colonial Revival architecture, it was home to the country group, the Statler Brothers.

Pulling up across from the Historic Staunton Building, I walked to the Welcome Center and, there, received a very warm greeting from a well-informed attendant. He equipped me with a walking map, circled noted attractions and sent me touring. Just a few steps away, I found the ticket office of the Blackfriars Playhouse, a recreated Shakespearean theater devoted to providing greater access to that fare and similar works. It so happened that there was a performance, "The Changeling" — described as "a vortex of lust, corruption, murder, sex and death" — scheduled for early evening that seemed worth staying on to see. Best of all, it was free, with a suggested donation.

I was glad that I needed film, and that it was a mile's walk to the Rite-Aid that sold it, as it gave me a chance to really see the area. Like my stop in Herbert Hoover's Iowa hometown, the smell of burning coal, an aroma that never failed to remind me of South Wales, reached my nose. However, Staunton had the steep hills and cold air to add authenticity. Trodding along Coalter Street past Wilson's birthplace and the green grounds of Mary Baldwin College, I found my film, a bathroom and bank and circled to Coffee on the Corner.

With my usual mocha and a few tips on dinner spots, I fell onto a worn, teal-colored couch to read *The News Leader*, the local mouthpiece. A local Veterans Day parade held over the weekend featured Civil War re-enactors and a Wilson look-alike riding in a Model T presidential limo. In another section, FBI analyst Linda Franklin, who had survived a double mastectomy only to be brought down last October in northern Virginia by a sniper's bullet, was profiled.

I'd brought some clippings from yesterday's *Sun* that had caught my eye, too. One in particular was about Madalyn Murray O'Hair. She was the Baltimore housewife who inspired a lawsuit that resulted in the 1963 ruling by the U.S. Supreme Court outlawing prayer in public schools. Four years after the landmark decision, she was featured as a guest on, then unknown, Phil Donahue's debut talk show. To the shock of crew, staff and the audience, she literally tore a page from a Bible. This incited an initial uproar but also elicited a flurry of questions, comments and criticisms from the housewives attending the live show. Donahue secured a hand microphone from his floor crew and began running from person to person to capture all their viewpoints, a tactic that ultimately became a standard element of his show and set a talk format precedent.

From the coffee shop, I also tapped into e-mail, learning that a traveling campadre in spirit had hit a mule deer in Dodge City, Kansas, which totaled her companion's car. Fortunately, they were not hurt but they had to hole up in nearby Boot Hill until an insurance adjuster could pay a visit. They guessed that they would catch a bus or hitchhike home at that point, but ended up buying a car for the ride home to New Hampshire, the end point of a 59-day trip.

As the old clock tower bell tolled five o'clock, I quickly looped through the Co-Art gallery, which featured many local artists' works. The Trinity Episcopalian Church, founded in 1746, was an elegant brick place where the town's founders and early settlers were buried: John Sowers, "an enterprising and successful merchant"; John Howe Peyton, an "eminent lawyer"; and General Samuel Blackburn, "a distinguished patriot." In June 1781, the Virginia General Assembly met here to avoid capture by British raiders.

The Mill Street Grill was all me and its large brick home was steeped in history. Built in 1890, it housed White Star Mills, established for the processing, manufacture and warehousing of flour branded Melrose that was "a staple in southern kitchens for the entire life of the mill." Told that the steak here "falls off the bone," I ordered a 10-ounce Center Cut Top Sirloin sautéed with roasted garlic, beefstock, onions and mushrooms and served in port wine and sundried tomato sauce. Garlic mashed potatoes, steaming hot fresh bread with apple pie butter and a Star Hill Amber Ale rounded out the feast. It was a wonderful melt-in-your-mouth meal in a warm, cozy atmosphere with service people that went the distance to be accommodating. Though I had no room for dessert, I couldn't resist having a small, complimentary silver dish of peppermint sorbet that my waitress placed before me.

It was nearly showtime so I relocated myself to Blackfriars where the house manager received me. The playhouse space was fantastic: overhead, nine spoked chandeliers with simulated candles hung; velvet cushions were provided to make wooden bench seating more comfortable; throne-like chairs accommodated cast members; and six species of Virginia white oak comprised the trim. The facility was built as authentically as possible from personal descriptions of the original Blackfriars Playhouse, established inside a monastery's banquet hall in 1599 by eight members of Shakespeare's acting company. Seeking to destroy anything related to Catholicism, the Queen of England ordered it torn down in 1642. The Great Fire of 1666 destroyed any remaining vestiges.

The players, numbering a dozen, were casually attired and provided their own props, and their style was often improvisational. The plot twisted and turned as one might expect from Shakespeare contemporaries, in this case, Thomas Middleton and William Rowley.

We were spelled briefly for coffee and baked goods, and joined by the cast, before returning for the program's conclusion. Chris Patrick, who donned a gray curly wig for his role as a jealous and somewhat touched doctor; Jim Byrnes, who played the certifiably disturbed changeling; and Bree Luck as a mad bride were particularly clever, though all were commendable.

The always-clamorous road was calling again and El Rucio was cold. I got her fluids circulating and launched her into the night, opting for the highway, with the D.C. area my goal for the night. Drafting a tractor-trailer all the way up 81 to the northeast part of the state, I followed an elbow onto 66 East. The farther along I moved, the wider the roads and the brighter the lights got until I was almost on top of D.C. Tuned into a metro radio station, I heard it was just 26 degrees at Dulles Airport near Fairfax. At Falls Church, I stopped to use a gas station restroom, brushing my teeth in prep for a side-of-road overnight stay. There was no real opportunity for that, though, so I just kept going, right over the Theodore Roosevelt Memorial Bridge into D.C. proper.

Our U.S. Capital has always been an impressive sight but never more so than tonight, wherein I was one of only a couple dozen cars snaking through this monument checkerboard. There was the Jefferson Memorial. The tall, skyward reaching Washington Monument. The White House. National Archives. Capitol building. All spectacularly lit up. I pressed along Constitution Avenue which, in a few short hours, would be jammed with Monday rush hour traffic and, like before, decided to keep on truckin.' Reaching the far side of D.C., near Good Luck Road, I saw a shooting star streak across the clear sky. It was, perhaps, a sign that my journey was over and, as Baltimore and even New York mileage postings came up, I could think only of home. No plans or other visit ideas I'd had were going to keep me. My physical capacity to keep on driving would be my sole inhibitor.

Reaching Virginia — Abingdon, in the dogleg of Virginia, to be specific — Steinbeck, as I had, experienced the same, sudden urgency to conclude his voyage. The feeling came "without warning or good-by" and, though he "tried to call it back," his journey "was definitely and permanently over and finished. The road became an endless stone ribbon, the hills obstructions, the trees green blurs, the people simply moving figures with heads but no faces." He "bulldozed blindly through West

Virginia, plunged into Pennsylvania and grooved Rocinante to the great wide turnpike. There was no night, no day, no distance...The way was a gray, timeless, eventless tunnel, but at the end of it was the one shining reality — my own wife, my own house in my own street, my own bed." Rocinante "leaped under [his] heavy relentless foot."

The Maryland Welcome Center was the gateway to my 33rd state. I hoped there would be abundant food options there, but found only vending machines and bathrooms. Soon, I was passing through the port of Baltimore where, on the backside, a Travel Center was located. Unfortunately, at 2 a.m., besides the Greyhounds and Amtrak trains, the only thing going was a KFC. I buckled in for a two-piece meal with biscuit. An orange juice along with it made me feel a little better about the choice. As I ate, I half-looked at a bulky Sunday copy of *The Sun*, Baltimore's paper, but could get no further than the front page.

Though it was now 3 a.m., I still had energy so nudged El Rucio back out onto the interstate to give me some more. She was up for it and we went at it, clawing north, flying by the Ripken Museum and Susquehana State Park and River. Finally, when the Chesapeake House Service Area came up, that was our finish line for the night. I did the recline in the front seat, pulling my wool blanket over my head to keep the parking lot lights out of my eyes and myself warm.

Day 66: Through the Apple to Home

It was only five when I stirred, and the outside air temperature had fallen into the 20s. Actually, the temperature inside El Rucio had dropped likewise, as any warm air that had built up, had seeped out. Unfortunately, it was too early yet for the Starbucks in this plaza to be open, so I had nothing to warm my insides and no caffeination.

Despite my condition, I zoomed into Delaware, my 34th state and gunned it for the Delaware Memorial Bridge. Up and over we went into state #35, New Jersey. I was happy to be able to use my EZ Pass for tolls again and as I rolled through the tollgate, noticed police cars parked nearby were frost covered. That was my last image before pulling over again to snooze. As ever, my desire to move ahead was greater than my physical ability to accommodate the urge.

It was nearly 7 when I had my Second Coming, waking to a Philadelphia morning show on the wireless, a white frosty wonderland and the gleaming chrome grill of a Freightliner in my rear view mirror. I realized that, with the body willing, I would be home in a few hours and called Marlene to give her the alert. She was surprised, of course, and we looked forward to one final, lasting reunion.

New York City was just 90 miles away, the Beatles' "Roll Over Beethoven" was jangling from Philly's WGMK station and the sun was thawing the Jersey farmland around me. There had apparently been a "beaver moon" last night according to the DJ, the mention of which activated an oft-repeated "nice beaver" sound effect.

Just past Cherry Hill, I saw a "V" of Canadian geese over the highway and clouds of steam rising off Rancoran Creek, a branch of the Delaware River. The Philly DJ admitted to having a difficult time making a television viewing selection last night. It was a choice between seeing an NBC made-for-TV drama about Iraq war hero Jessica Lynch or Britney Spears' "Unzipped" performance. As he put it, "I had to decide if I was going to be an American…or an American."

South of Trenton, I pulled into the Woodrow Wilson rest stop where I found another Starbucks, this one open. I picked up my mocha order and sat with my cup at a small table to engage in people watching. The standout here was a private in a desert camo uniform. He'd been stationed in Al Fallujah, 40 miles west of Baghdad on the Euphrates River, "one of the worst areas you could be in" he claimed. More commonly, he called the area "Baath East," referring to the Saddam-allegiant Iraqi political party that had been a thorn in the allies' side. The soldier's dad and a friend had driven down to New York this morning to pick him up in Baltimore, where he'd flown into from an air force base in Germany.

I overheard him describing an interaction he had with the enemy. Monitoring a civilian protest, his unit started taking fire. Because they'd been told to exercise restraint, the private radioed a commander to get permission to return fire. "Is the firing direct?" Bremen was asked. A bullet came by his face. "Yep." "Bust caps," was the order. They opened up with everything they had.

Asked how the morale was, he said it was poor. "It seems like no one supports us over here." I reassured him that the majority of us do though the press liked to slant it otherwise. He needed to hear that, I think. "Go get 'em and come home safe," I told him, we shook hands, and the three of them got in a car to head home for his two weeks on leave.

My encounter reminded me of an article Will Ross had written about his time spent with troops traveling home from Iraq through Baltimore's airport. Awaiting an available flight to L.A., Ross noticed young soldiers standing around, their own connecting flights delayed. Two airline customer service reps, who had been focused on seeing that the soldiers move through quickly so they could enjoy the most of their leaves, made a public, passionate appeal to the entire terminal of travelers to give up their seats. The travel-weary responded in droves and all the soldiers went out on the next flight.

Back on the trek, in Elizabeth, I rolled between big white Citgo and Mobil fuel storage tanks like a bowling ball leaving a split. The song on the pop station I had tuned in was "Waiting for Tonight", which summed up my feelings pretty well.

As I passed Newark International Airport, a major hub for FedEx as illustrated by their cargo planes sitting out on the tarmac, and watched a string of passenger jets descend from the sky to make their runway approach, my heart quickened. It was not so much because of the sight, though I'd always loved to watch the great metal flying machines take off and land and been excited by airport environments in general, but because Manhattan lay ahead.

For me, The Big Apple has represented many things. It was a far-off, wondrous curiosity when I was a boy growing up in upstate New York. It was where my Dad was employed for many years and a place to enjoy festivals, theater, restaurants and major sporting events when I was a teen living in the suburbs. It became a work destination for me, too, and playground when I was an energetic, young man in my late teens and early 20s. It was a sad site to go and see in the days and months following the World Trade Center attacks. Lately, it had become a place to visit on occasion with my family and nightlife target when the opportunity presented itself.

In his 1966 novel, "America and the Americans," Steinbeck pointed out the many paradoxes of America. I believe that New York is the epitome of paradox. It is at once beautiful and gritty, huge and intimate, concrete and grassy, friend and foe, fast and slow, your oyster or ruination.

I've dined, loved, laughed, cried, toiled, sailed, gotten drunk, slept, wandered, motored, been robbed, cheered, danced, gotten engaged, celebrated birthdays and anniversaries, and almost died here. I've consumed the big apple in every sense and still I hunger for it. It's truly like no other place in the world. It tests you, knocks you down, and pushes you aside and, if you put your tail between your legs and run, it's beaten you. But if you hold fast and come back for more, it rewards you for your perseverance. Better put, "If you can make it here, you can make it anywhere."

New Yorkers had certainly been put to the test, most recently back in mid-August, just three weeks before I set off around the U.S. That's when nine million city residents were affected by the multi-state power outage I'd recalled when passing near Cleveland. All the major TV stations covered the event, of course, and their stories were illuminating. On Manhattan streets, only the red taillights of cars were visible amidst the black silhouettes of buildings. Uptown, major league baseball events and Broadway shows were cancelled. Droves of sweaty subway commuters emerged from underground access points, blinking in the light after slogging from stopped trains through pitch-black tunnels. Thousands of people waited on the few ferryboat shuttles running between the Lower West Side and New Jersey. Hundreds more, guests of the Marriott Marquis, camped on the sidewalk in front of the hotel, unable to use their electronic keys to get into their rooms. A man, perhaps one of many, walked from Brooklyn to his home in Fordham in the Bronx, and mentioned seeing bottled water priced at $7. Other New Yorkers tried to make the best of things, trading stories in bars about past blackouts and holding spontaneous sidewalk parties.

This was the third major blackout, in fact, that New Yorkers had experienced, the first in November 1965 and the second in mid-July 1977. When the latter happened, caused by lightning, I was just 12 and standing with my family near the *Daily News* building, redubbed *The Daily Planet*, on the set of the first "Superman" movie. It was evening so the crew was using large searchlights run by gas-powered generators to provide extra illumination. When the power blinked out, we were in the only spot in the city with light and barely aware of the chaos that had begun to erupt in every borough and continued over the next 33-and-a-half hours. When the lights came back on, five people had been murdered, 191 injured and over 3,500 arrested. New York City Mayor Abe Beam referred to it as a "night of terror."

There had been no more trying event for New Yorkers, however, than September 11, 2001. From our living room in Fairfield that morning, with toddler Phillip rolling on the carpet, Marlene and I watched our TV set in horror and incredulity as the majestic World Trade Towers that we had intimately known, crashed to the ground. In total disbelief, I had to convince my brain that what my eyes had seen was real and traveled down to the city's southernmost point just 28 hours later.

The images that I captured in my head that sunny, surreal Wednesday afternoon will stay with me forever. Houston Street trafficked only by an army Humvee with roof-mounted gunner passing a screaming hook-and-ladder truck headed downtown, a large American flag flapping in the breeze behind it. A sign on a school door: "Closed due to City Emergency." A line of blue barriers cutting the city in half, with police officers stationed along them checking identification cards. F-16 fighter jets patrolling the skies overhead. DEP boats and Coast Guard cutters monitoring the empty waterways. A completely vacant F.D.R. Drive. Exhausted police personnel taking a breather on benches by the East River. Police cars flattened by falling debris dragged from and lined up along the street near the on-ramp to the Brooklyn Bridge. Abandoned bagel carts, their contents filled with dust, and high-heeled shoes laying in the street, kicked off by women who desperately fled the toxic clouds that were produced by the towers collapsing and that came rushing through the streets. Six inches of concrete debris like powdery snow, covering streets and steps. A message scrawled with a finger in dust on the windshield of a car: "Bomb bin Laden." A darkened Stock Exchange building, normally a beehive of activity on a Wednesday afternoon. Con Ed workers, EMTs and firemen, all wearing dust masks or breathing apparatus, streaming toward me with glassy, dazed, tired eyes. A tank stationed in Battery Park. Truck after truck carting twisted steel to awaiting barges on the East Side. Papers and shipping forms bearing 1 and 2 World Trade addresses or Port Authority logos all over the streets. A souvenir hunter shoveling concrete dust into an empty Snapple bottle. Streets torn open with steam pouring out of broken pipes. A man preparing food in a small hibachi on a sidewalk. A family vacating their apartment, suitcases in tow. City buses put into service to carry workers to and from the site. Soldiers at the foot of West Street, barring passage. The sad, jagged stub of the South Tower barely visible through billowing clouds of dust and smoke rising into the sky from Ground Zero.

New York had been brought to her knees and was down for the count — but not out as we soon saw in days to follow. An incredible energy took hold. A spirit that could not be quelled. A unifying force that brought New York's citizenry out on the streets to cheer its civil service workers and the uncountable volunteers that rushed to the site to help in any way they could, even if their efforts were fruitless. It was an altogether proud yet frightening moment to be a part of that also signaled the transition of our existence as Americans from one of innocence to one of measured caution.

Catching glimpses of its familiar skyline, I saw the Empire State Building at 34th Street, standing like a lone sentinel guarding the city as the Trade Towers once had. I thought I'd take the Holland Tunnel in, accessing it by 78 East. Steinbeck had come up the New Jersey turnpike as I had but when he reached the same crossing, a policeman waved him out of traffic and flagged him to a stop, saying, "You can't go through the tunnel with that butane." Though Steinbeck explained that it was turned off, the officer said he still couldn't take it through.

The reply was a crushing blow to Steinbeck. He "fell apart, collapsed into a jelly of weariness." I absolutely knew how he must have felt, to have come so far and gotten so close to home, only to encounter a stumbling block in the last stretch. The policeman sympathized and suggested that he make the crossing via the George Washington Bridge or take a ferry.

Steinbeck described the next moment: "It was rush hour, but the gentle-hearted policeman must have seen a potential maniac in me. He held back the savage traffic and got me through and directed me with great care. I think he was strongly tempted to drive me home." Steinbeck opted for the Hoboken ferry, which delivered him far downtown amidst "the daily panic rush of commuters leaping and running and dodging in front, obeying no signals."

The temperature was a degree above freezing when I turned onto 78, spying first the hazy outline of the city, then the wide Hudson. I already knew that the pass-through would cost me fifteen minutes according to a traffic report and was soon in a bumper-to-bumper backup. I never thought I'd be happy about traffic but, here, with a drive-by view of the skyline, I had to make an exception.

On the Jersey City side, landmarks included STATCO Pick and Pack, A-1 Self-Storage and the Lackawanna Railroad building. Banners on the light poles promoted the tunnel's 75th anniversary. I slipped through the white-tiled loop and cruised along Canal to Chinatown, turning north. The fruit stands were busy with morning traffic as I zigged west on Broome over to the West Side Highway. Pier 40 was quiet as no cruise ships were in port, while, in contrast, the waterside walkway through Hudson River Park was trafficked by joggers, walkers and cyclists getting in their morning workouts. It was too early for Chelsea Piers, a sports and entertainment complex, to be kicking.

From downtown, Steinbeck "made a turn and then another, entered a one-way street the wrong way and had to back out, got boxed in the middle of a crossing by a swirling rapids of turning people." He suddenly "pulled to the curb in a no-parking area, cut [his] motor, and leaned back in the seat and laughed, and couldn't stop. [His] hands and arms and shoulders were shaking with road jitters." As had happened to him so many times on the road, Steinbeck had gotten lost, but this time in getting to his Upper East Side apartment in a place that he knew like the back of his hand.

"An old-fashioned cop with a fine red face and a frosty blue eye" approached him, thought he was drunk then, realizing his unusual dilemma, guided him to his final destination. And "that's how the traveler came home again."

I still had a handful of miles to go before my final destination and decided my journey would not be complete without a pass through Times Square. Swinging wide onto 42nd Street, the Empire State off to my right, I passed Holy Cross Church, Chevy's, Loews, AMC Theater, Coldstone Creamery, McDonalds lit in neon and Amsterdam Theatre. I read the digital news wraparound, skirted Bryant Park and passed busy Grand Central. Passersby were bundled and had coffee cops in hand. The Helmsley, Tudor City and the U.N. marked the East Side, where I jumped on the F.D.R. Drive. A DEP boat was coming south underneath the Queensboro Bridge as Robin Quivers, Howard Stern's sidekick on his KROK radio show, was doing the news. They focused on a report about new parents and how they had named their babies after products like Skyy, Courvoisier and Special K, or materials, such as rayon and cotton.

On the AM dial, my main area news source, 1010 WINS, was giving a sports wrap-up. My Giants (4-4) had literally dropped the ball against the 1-8 Atlanta Falcons, losing their Sunday game 27-7. The home crowd had called for head coach Jim Fassel's head with chants of "Fire Fassel!" It was Big Blue's fourth loss out of five home games.

The radio also reported the death of actor Art Carney, who was 85 when he passed at his home in Chester, Connecticut, outside Hartford. The world would best remember him for his role as Ed Norton, Jackie Gleason's upstairs neighbor in "The Honeymooners."

Hanging from the top rim of Yankee Stadium, in the Bronx, was the sign, "3 MILLION THANKS," a tribute to fans' support of the team. Co-Op City, old stomping ground New Rochelle and my one-time residences Mamaroneck, Port Chester and Byram were all blurs.

Marlene was at the local grocery buying supplies for her famous stew dinner when I buzzed her from Cos Cob, just over the Connecticut border. I caught her off guard — she'd been expecting me around 2 and it wasn't even 11. We agreed to meet at the house.

I barely noticed Stamford, my old workplace, as I shot past it, but saw that the road there and north of the city was still under construction, the bane of many a commuter's existence. When I hit Westport, my eyes were slits and I was thoroughly exhausted, sure that the only thing powering me now was the vision of home and family. Then I was in Fairfield. There was our beautiful main street, a neighbor I recognized hurrying along the sidewalk, the windows of Victoria's Secret displaying snowflake-patterned terry cloth robes, and leaf-covered Sherman Green.

The house, with Indian corn on the front door as a seasonal accent, was like a dream realized. As I pulled up our gravel drive and gave the trademark toot, Phillip came tearing out to greet me, then Marlene. Almost wordlessly and misty-eyed, we had a group hug there in our sunny backyard. Evan was equally surprised to see me when I collected him later from school, crying out, "Dad!" with a big smile when he emerged from his classroom. Reflecting on all the receptions I'd received on the road, I had experienced none warmer than this one.

And like a soldier returned from the war, I was anxious to reconnect with my family and resume some semblance of normalcy, even if that came with a to-do list as long as my arm: Fix the leaky faucet. Paint the bathroom ceiling. Cement the hole in the front steps that had become home to a mouse ("I put a rock in there, Dad," Evan reported). Trim the monster hedge.

My tour of duty had taken me 66 days, through 35 states and four provinces of Canada, and along 15,550 miles of American road. I snapped 665 photographs contained in 29 rolls of film, one of the largest orders our local store had ever processed, aside from one placed by a new bride who'd outfitted all her guests with disposable cameras. I'd filled 23 pocket-sized notebooks with my impressions of deserts, mountains, plains, valleys, beaches, lakes, rivers, farms, towns and cities, and the people all over this land that I'd met. This included simple folks who'd spent their whole lives in one place and the wealthiest of people who knew the world intimately. I heard tales of tragedy, hardship and horror but also hopes, joys and aspirations. The stories were riveting and I felt honored for their having been shared with me.

My takeaways and lessons were many. The most important is that there's nowhere sweeter than home. It's not the place that's special so much as the people there that care for you: The ones that get concerned when you don't call. The ones who wonder where you are and what you're doing. The ones you think about as you fall asleep at night in a strange place, in a dark field, in a noisy truck stop, under a different roof. The ones who ask if you are okay and if you've been eating enough. The young ones who miss you but are being brave in your absence and trying to smile and be happy. The spouse that says she's managing but could really use an extra hand and lays at night in an empty bed looking for the familiar body to snuggle up against and keep her feet warm.

I gained an appreciation for simple things: A hot shower, home cooked meal, comfortable chair, an accessible toilet, dental floss, dry socks, a child's hug.

Small Town America is alive and well and if you stay off the interstate, you'll discover that, too. While every town I traveled to had its own character, the people had many things in common: A hometown pride even though that hometown might be so small that the welcome and farewell signs share the same post, back-to-back. An acceptance that Hardee's is the main hangout and candlepin bowling, bingo or a warm stool at the local gin mill is the big draw on a Saturday night.

While we've given John Steinbeck godlike status as an author, he was also very human, subject to all the things that affect us as men. During the period he traveled the country to pen "Travels with Charley", he was in the later years of his life, ailing and feeling mortal, which was much to his distaste. His youngest son was floundering in school, a fact that greatly troubled him, though he himself and step-mom Elaine may have been part of the problem. He admitted to going "through the motions of being a husband, father, man, householder like a sleepwalker" and commended Elaine for being patient with him. At the same time, he suspected "that perhaps the failure of my first two marriages might have been caused by the fact that most women can't live with a Zombie." Traveling in his RV was rough on his aging body and he missed the familiarity and comforts of home. He was desperate for companionship but an introvert who struggled to make social connections. This was his last look at America and I think he knew it as he gazed out over Salinas and the surrounding area from Fremont's Peak. He rushed through areas that deserved more of his time and didn't make the most of it in many of those that he visited. He was less upset by the state of race relations in America and more exhausted with the trip and eager to just get home — the New Orleans incident was partly the excuse.

Americans are indeed a people on the go and always have been, since the days of our earliest ancestors. There was Lewis & Clark, about whom I learned more when I visited Montana, who mapped much of America as they worked their way west with horse-pulled wagons. And Horatio Nelson Jackson, who motored from San Francisco to New York in 63 days 100 years ago. Dr. Peter Kesling, an orthodontist from Indiana, imitated Jackson's journey this past summer in the same model car, completing the 3,720-mile trip in 40 days doing a top speed of 30 m.p.h.

America is singly the most diverse country — and I've experienced many intimately — of which I personally know: Coastal areas that range from sandy beaches to wave-worn rocks with water temperatures that are unbearably icy or blood warm. High, lush or snow-covered mountains or deep valleys in which clouds constantly sit like cotton balls in a basket.

Wide-open, neatly tended farmland or closely pushed together tenements with postage stamp-sized lots and slivers of grass. Houses with snowmobiles in front of them and houses with jet skis in front of them. Houses framed by big leafy maples that rustle in a biting northern gust or houses with palm trees that bend and sway in a warm southern breeze. Tractors that rumble down the side of the road pulling a trailer of hay or a fast, new convertible with its occupants sporting deep tans and flashy sunglasses. One's maple syrup is another's pina colada. A homemade apple pie is a bean burrito with an extra helping of guacamole. A Starbucks coffee is a piping cup of homebrewed tea.

You can take the same road and have a different journey every time, for it's the people you meet — the former pilot, the dairy farmer, the pancake house owner, the railroad man, the bartender, the camp proprietor, the rancher — that make the experience unique. I listened to their tales of hardship, of personal loss, of rejuvenated spirit and of personal triumph and can tell you that the American spirit is also alive and well, even more especially since the world-changing events of September 11. While politics may put us on opposite sides of the table, we are united in our determination to protect our way of life and freedoms that we enjoy.

Understanding all this changes you as a person. You develop an insight about people and their lives that you carry with you always and apply in social encounters, subconsciously tempering your attitudes and opinions because of the special knowledge you own.

The best-laid plans do often go astray. So many times did I have lofty intentions of accomplishing a certain agenda during the span of a day or have particular goals and objectives that I wanted to achieve in this trip, and they were not realized. As long as they are only intentions and not plans that must be fulfilled without exception, then you are okay. You don't own the journey, it owns you and the road will take you where it wants. You must learn to put yourself on autopilot and enjoy the ride. Stop to smell those roses. Appreciate life for it is short. Go for that dream that you've always wanted to achieve. Hold your nose and jump. Let "Carpe Diem" be the rule by which you live your life and I think you will find wonderful new journeys awaiting you.

AUTHOR ACKNOWLEDGMENTS

I'd like to thank the following individuals and companies whose generous support eased my passage along the road: Mike Robson of TK Auto Wholesalers; Coleman's Ann Walden and Sommer Sweeney; Scott MacNamara at CompUSA; Exxon-Mobil's Ken Bulls; Allison MacDowell at Longworth Industries; T-Mobile's Chuck Kalander; Mike Gast at KOA; Frito-Lay's Peter Robinson; Mark Schindel at Gerber Legendary Blades; DVC Worldwide's Glenn Garcia for connecting me with Rolling Rock; Wolcott Tire & Auto; Planet Hi-Fi; and Stop & Shop. Additional thanks to members of the press nationwide who took interest in my tale and to the many individuals who extended their hospitality and friendship.

ABOUT THE AUTHOR

Mike Lauterborn, a longtime resident of Fairfield, CT, has been the Editor, Writer and Photographer for Fairfield HamletHub online news service since 2011, serving Fairfield County, CT. He also serves as a freelance photographer and writer on a contract basis. As a lad, Mike was an inveterate journal writer and graduated from college with a BA in English Literature. Following graduation, for over 20 years, Mike worked in corporate America in various marketing, promotion and advertising leadership roles. In 2010, Mike transitioned to journalism and served as a feature writer, columnist and photographer for a number of regional magazines, newspapers and online news services before fully dedicating himself to his current Editor role.

Mike has documented over four decades of American culture, including all of his past travels. This passion for writing runs in his blood — Lauterborn's father and brother are both published authors.

During his 66 days on the road, Lauterborn traveled some 16,000 miles through 35 states, filling 23 notebooks with his observations and snapping more than 650 photographs to document the journey. While on the road he was interviewed by more than a dozen newspapers, two national magazines and an NBC-TV affiliate in Raleigh, N.C. This is his first book.

Contact Mike via e-mail at bornies@optonline.net.

Printed in the United States
By Bookmasters